THE MIDDLE PALEOLITHIC: ADAPTATION, BEHAVIOR, AND VARIABILITY

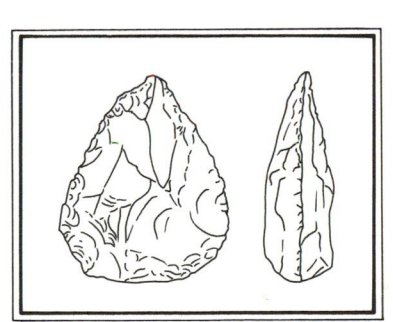

Roc de Jayac

Sketches in Dordogne N° 1

University Museum Monograph 72

UNIVERSITY MUSEUM SYMPOSIUM SERIES
VOLUME IV

THE MIDDLE PALEOLITHIC: ADAPTATION, BEHAVIOR, AND VARIABILITY

Harold L. Dibble
Paul Mellars

Editors

Published by
The University Museum
University of Pennsylvania
1992

Editing
Publications Department
The University Museum

Design and Production
Garret Schenck

Printing
Science Press
Ephrata, Pennsylvania

Library of Congress Cataloging-in-Publication Data

The Middle Paleolithic: adaptation, behavior, and variability /
Harold L. Dibble, Paul Mellars, editors,
    p.   cm.—(University Museum monograph: 72) (University
Museum symposium series: v. 2)
  Includes bibliographical references.
  ISBN 0-924171-07-3
  1. Paleolithic period—Europe.   2. Paleolithic period—Middle
East.   3. Anthropology. Prehistoric.   4. Europe—Antiquities.
5. Middle East—Antiquities.   I. Dibble, Harold Lewis.
II. Mellars, Paul.   III. Series.   IV. Series: University Museum
symposium series; v. 2.
GN772.2.A1M53   1992
936—dc20   92-6361
                                                                   CIP

Copyright © 1992
THE UNIVERSITY MUSEUM
of Archaeology and Anthropology
University of Pennsylvania
Philadelphia
All rights reserved
Printed in the United States of America

Printed on acid free paper

+
GN
772.2
.A1
M53
1992

TABLE OF CONTENTS

EDITORS' PREFACE

The evolution of the human line has been the subject of debate since the mid-nineteenth century. Recently, the later phases of our evolution, and specifically the emergence of modern *Homo sapiens*, have been receiving increasing attention, due largely to new kinds of genetic data implying a large-scale movement of modern humans from Africa into other parts of the Old World and their replacement of the indigenous hominid forms. Such a scenario has, of course, important implications for major questions that have long been of interest to anthropologists in general, and Paleolithic archaeologists in particular. Among the most important of the Paleolithic problems related to this notion is the explanation of the transition from the Middle to Upper Paleolithic and whether it was somehow related to a change or replacement of archaic hominid forms.

Fundamental to these questions, however, is an accurate understanding of the nature of hominid behavior and adaptation *before* these changes began to occur, that is, during the Middle Paleolithic. In other words, we have to know how different was Middle Paleolithic behavior from that which followed before we can attempt to explain the change. A reconstruction of Middle Paleolithic behavior in turn depends on identifying the factors, behavioral and other, that affect the variability that we see in the Middle Paleolithic archaeological record. This is the central problem for all archaeological research, of course. But it is especially acute for the Middle Paleolithic, which represents a period for which there is considerable controversy concerning even the basic nature of hominid behavior and culture.

This volume is a collection of papers originally presented in a symposium on the Middle Paleolithic of Europe and the Near East organized as part of the annual meeting of the Society for American Archaeology in the spring of 1989. Europe and the Near East are two regions that continue to provide important new data on the emergence of modern humans. These new data are, of course, partly the result of new excavations in these areas and the recovery of new material. But they are also the result of the new insights and approaches being applied to this material, as reflected by several of the papers presented here. Some of these approaches have led to completely new interpretations of Middle Paleolithic behavior and adaptation, which have important implications for our understanding of the nature of later developments in both biology and culture.

Paleolithic archaeology, especially Middle Paleolithic archaeology, has entered a period in which new interpretations and even new research paradigms are competing with traditional ones. This is clearly seen in these papers. The lack of consensus is not bad, however. In fact, it is a sign of a healthy, growing discipline. But it underlines the need for continued dialogue among Paleolithic scholars, exemplified by the discussions that took place at the symposium and further reflected in these papers.

We would like to thank all of the individuals and institutions that made the symposium and its publication possible. This includes the Society for American Archaeology, and particularly Ken Kvamme, who served as Program Chairman and who somehow put up with numerous last-minute changes and alterations. We also thank The University Museum of the University of Pennsylvania for funding this publication and Karen Vellucci of the Museum's Publications department for overseeing its production. We are grateful to Steve Kluskens and Gilliane Monnier for their translation of some of the papers. We thank Katharine Moreau for her contribution to the preparation of the publication and Georgianna Grentzenberg for redrawing some of the figures. Garret Schenck of Design To Go was responsible for the design and layout of the publication. A special thanks goes to Helen Schenck for her careful editing and final preparation of the manuscripts.

Harold L. Dibble
Paul Mellars

January 1992

ABBREVIATIONS

AA	*American Anthropologist*
AAASH	*Acta Archaeologica Academiae Scientarum Hungaricae*
AAC	*Acta Archaeologica Carpathica*
AFEQ	Association Française pour l'Etude du Quaternaire
AGSO	Association des Géologues du Sud-Ouest
AIPH	Archives de l'Institut de Paléontologie Humaine
AK	*Archäologisches Korrespondenzblatt*
AmAnt	*American Antiquity*
ARA	*Annual Review of Anthropology*
ASPR	American School of Prehistoric Research
ASU	Arizona State University
AV	Archaeologica Venatoria
BAFEQ	*Bulletin de l'Association Française pour l'Etude du Quaternaire*
BAR	British Archaeological Reports
BIGBA	*Bulletin de l'Institut Géologique du Bassin de l'Aquitaine*
BJ	*Bonner Jahrbücher*
BPH	Bibliotheca Praehistorica Hispana
BSAHC	*Bulletin de la Société Archéologique et Historique de la Charente*
BSB	*Bulletin de la Société de Borda*
BSPA	*Bulletin de la Société Préhistorique de l'Ariège*
BSPF	*Bulletin de la Société Préhistorique Française*
CA	*Current Anthropology*
CERP	Centre d'Etudes et Recherches Préhistoriques
CIMA	Centro de Investigación y Museo de Altamira
CMM	*Casopis Moravského Muzea*
CNRS	Centre National de la Recherche Scientifique
CNSS	Congrès National des Sociétés Savantes
CQ	Cahiers du Quaternaire
CRASP	*Comptes rendus de l'Académie des Sciences de Paris*
CSAV	Ceskoslovenské Akademie Ved
EP	*Etudes préhistoriques*
EQ	Etudes quaternaires
ERAUL	Etudes et Recherches Archéologiques de l'Université de Liège
FNRS	Fonds National de la Recherche Scientifique
GP	*Gallia préhistoire*

INQUA	International Union for Quaternary Research
IPH	Institut de Paléontologie Humaine
IPI	Institute for Prehistoric Investigations (Chicago and Santander)
IPUB	Institut Préhistorique de l'Université de Bordeaux
JAA	*Journal of Anthropological Archaeology*
JAR	*Journal of Anthropological Research*
JAS	*Journal of Archaeological Science*
JFA	*Journal of Field Archaeology*
JHE	*Journal of Human Evolution*
JRGZM	*Jahrbuch des Römisch-Germanischen Zentralmuseums Mainz*
LPHP	Laboratoire de Paléontologie Humaine et de Préhistoire (Université de Provence)
LT	*Lithic Technology*
MIPUB	Mémoires de l'Institut Préhistorique de l'Université de Bordeaux
MSPF	Mémoires de la Société Préhistorique Française
NATO	North Atlantic Treaty Organization
NSF	National Science Foundation
OJA	*Oxford Journal of Archaeology*
PPS	*Proceedings of the Prehistoric Society*
QR	*Quaternary Research*
QRA	*Quarterly Review of Archaeology*
RA	*Revue anthropologique*
RAST	*Réunion de l'Association des Sciences de la Terre*
RSP	*Rivista di scienze preistoriche*
SAA	Society for American Archaeology
SAAB	*South African Archaeological Bulletin*
SciAm	*Scientific American*
SJA	*Southwestern Journal of Anthropology*
SMU	Southern Methodist University
SPB	Studia Praehistorica Belgica
SPF	Société Préhistorique Française
UCLA	University of California at Los Angeles
UISPP	Union International des Sciences Préhistoriques et Protohistoriques
UM	Urgeschichtliche Materialhefte
UNESCO	United Nations Educational, Scientific, and Cultural Organization
WA	*World Archaeology*

I

On Assemblage Variability in the Middle Paleolithic of Western Europe

History, Perspectives, and a New Synthesis

Harold L. Dibble

Nicolas Rolland

INTRODUCTION

Variability in Middle Paleolithic assemblages of the Western Old World is measured primarily on the basis of relative frequencies of various uni- and bifacially worked stone tools as defined in the typology of Bordes (1961a). Interpretations of this variability focus almost exclusively on two factors that underlie general lithic variability, namely style and function. Depending on which of these factors is seen to be the most important, assemblage variability in Western Eurasia is linked either to discrete, co-existing phyla of Middle Paleolithic culture groups, or to different activities carried out by one (or more) groups.

This debate, which is often referred to as the Bordes-Binford debate, has continued for over two decades and it does not appear that we are any closer to its resolution. Admittedly, this failure is due in part to limitations of our data and methods. We believe, however, that a more significant problem lies in our general perspective of these assemblages and of the underlying nature of their variability. One problem is that the current research paradigm actually encompasses only two possible interpretations of variability—style and function. Recent studies have demonstrated many significant constraints on lithic variability imposed by aspects of raw material, technology, and post-depositional factors. But because such factors, especially the first two, do not have any logical place in explanations within the current paradigm, arguments over archaeological assemblages keep coming back to function and style instead of moving forward and successfully incorporating these other factors in a new synthesis of Middle Paleolithic variability. A second problem concerns the assumption that Middle Paleolithic assemblage groups, and the lithic types on which they are defined, represent discrete units instead of continuous distributions of typological and technological characteristics.

Our purpose in this paper is to propose a new synthesis of Middle Paleolithic variability, especially that seen in Western Europe. We begin by outlining some of the characteristics that seem to represent Middle Paleolithic assemblages in order to define our database explicitly. This is followed by a brief review of the history of Middle Paleolithic research emphasizing its theoretical underpinnings and the state of some of the current arguments concerning assemblage variability. Next we critically examine the assumptions that the defined lithic types and assemblage groups represent discrete, behaviorally real, units. This leads to the main discussion and integration of those factors seen by us to underlie a significant portion of currently observed aspects of Middle Paleolithic variability.

GENERAL INDUSTRIAL AND TEMPORAL CHARACTERISTICS OF THE MIDDLE PALEOLITHIC

Clearly, the term Middle Paleolithic encompasses a great deal of industrial variablity and is represented by several named complexes throughout the Old World. In addition to the Mousterian complex of Western Europe that is the focus of this article (Bordes and Bourgon 1951; Bordes 1961b), other Late Middle Pleistocene and Early Upper Pleistocene archaeological industries that are generally considered Middle Paleolithic include some examples of "Tayacian," Premousterian, Pontinian, Taubachian, "Micoquian," "Altmühlian" from Western, Central, and Eastern Europe (Ulrix-Clossett 1975; Gábori 1976; Klein 1969), the Zagros Mousterian and the Levantine Yabrudian and Upper Acheulian of Western Asia (Dibble 1984b; Dibble and Holdaway, in press; Hours et al. 1973; Jelinek 1982a; Skinner 1965), the Middle Stone Age (MSA) of Africa (Sampson 1974; Clark 1970), and probably various "Mousteroid" industries of parts of Asia, including India, China, and Southeast Asia (Chard 1969; Ranov and Davis 1979; Movius 1949). Most of these industries share one or more of a number of characteristics, including the use of prepared-core flaking techniques and a limited range of major tool classes (principally *racloirs* [i.e., "scrapers"], denticulates/notches, and bifaces).

Recent work has radically altered our notions regarding the chronology of the Middle Paleolithic. Traditionally, the Mousterian was thought to date from only the early part of the last glacial, with some occurrences of earlier last Interglacial industries termed "Premousterian" (Bordes 1947, 1952; Laville et al. 1980). The revised chronology, based on correlations of marine and terrestrial sequences (Laville et al. 1983; Laville 1988; Wolliard 1978), now suggests that the date of the onset of the *Würm ancien* (oxygen-isotope stage 5d) is 115 kyr, extending the duration of the Würmian industries by as much as fifty percent. Moreover, assemblages absolutely characteristic of the Middle Paleolithic are now known to date to oxygen-isotope stage 8, or about 250 kyr (Tuffreau 1982; Tuffreau and Sommé 1988; Laville 1982; Roebroeks 1986; Schwarcz and Blackwell 1983), which eliminates the need for any separation between Mousterian and "Premousterian." Altogether, this greatly expands the duration of the Middle Paleolithic from what was formerly believed and undoubtedly has some implications regarding the distinction between the Lower and Middle Paleolithic in terms of rates of change.

In fact, the extent to which the Middle Paleolithic represents a economic and behavioral complex distinct from the stages that precede and follow it is far from settled. Many researchers see more continuities between the Lower and Middle Paleolithic than between the latter and the Upper Paleolithic (Combier 1962; Breuil and Lantier 1959; see also Müller-Beck 1988 and various papers in Ronen 1982). The significance of the transition to the Upper Paleolithic is the subject of considerable controversy (see, for example, Mellars 1973, 1989a, b; White 1982; Chase and Dibble 1987), as is the relationship between these stages and hominid taxa (Bar-Yosef 1988, 1989; Bar-Yosef and Goldberg 1988; Stringer 1988; Hublin 1988; Rightmire 1984; Valladas, Joron, et al. 1987; Valladas, Chadelle, et al. 1987; Valladas et al. 1988).

HISTORY AND THEORY OF MIDDLE PALEOLITHIC ASSEMBLAGE VARIABILITY

Although the first scientific excavations of European Mousterian sites were undertaken in France by Lartet, Christy, and Tournal, and in Belgium by Schmerling, it is Gabriel de Mortillet (1883) who is most often credited with a comprehensive theoretical treatment of this period. It was he who placed the "Epoch of le Moustier" between the Acheulian and Solutrean, characterizing it as an industry composed of points, *racloirs*, Levallois flakes, and triangular bifaces. Some years later, Commont (1913) suggested a chronological development within the Mousterian, from a last interglacial "Warm" Mousterian, followed by a "Lower" Mousterian characterized by a high frequency of Levallois flakes, triangular handaxes, *racloirs*, points, and notches; the Middle Mousterian with numerous *racloirs*; and an "Evolved" Mousterian with *racloirs* (especially Quina types) and no handaxes.

Later, both Breuil and Peyrony began to recognize variability in the Paleolithic assemblages that was not temporally linked. Peyrony (1921) developed a model of parallel traditions within the Mousterian: a Mousterian of Acheulian Tradition (MTA), with bifaces, *racloirs*, notches, and denticulates; and a Typical Mousterian composed of many *racloirs* and points. In effect, this model mirrored his later model for the Aurignacian and Perigordian (Peyrony 1933, 1934, 1936), as well as Breuil's (1932) parallel phyla model for the Lower Paleolithic industries of the flake based (Clactonian) and handaxe based (Acheulian) phyla. The latter, in Breuil's view, ultimately gave rise to the Middle Paleolithic Levalloisian (with several chronological subdivisions) and the "Cave Mousterian" (with or without handaxes). Thus, by the early part of this century, de Mortillet's notion of purely diachronic evolution of the industries of the Paleolithic had been modified by the recognition of synchronic variability as well.[1]

As is well documented in Sackett's (1982a) historical review (see also Audouze and Leroi-Gourhan 1981), much of the work during this early period of French Paleolithic research was based on the notion of *fossiles directeurs*. Like their analogs in paleontology, these diagnostic artifact types were linked to specific cultural traditions bounded in both space and time. Thus, they could be used to document the presence or absence of specific industrial traditions at any point in time, and interstratification of them was evidence of industrial contemporaneity. But as Sackett notes, the analogy with paleontology did not stop there:

> The key notion at work here was that fundamental patterning in the artifactual and fossil records is essentially the same and that, as a consequence, culture history can be regarded and accounted for in essential organic terms. This notion more specifically entailed two unspoken assumptions. The first was that a direct parallelism exists between the cultural and organic worlds of such a kind that we can expect to find a one-to-one correlation between archaeological and natural stratigraphy. The second was that any given cultural complex, like any given paleontological complex, should be more or less invariant in the manner in which it expresses itself. This last means that the cultural entities recognized in archaeological systematics are to be regarded as natural categories, which—in the manner, say, of organic species—are inherently discontinuous and do not modify their form from one context to the next (Sackett 1982a:90).

It follows from this view that a specific tradition should give rise to but one characteristic type of industry in any specific block of time and space in the archaeological record. This in turn led to a disregard of other elements of the lithic assemblages that were not thought to be diagnostic, resulting in turn in a kind of empirical tautology—what was saved and studied from a particular industry was that which was diagnostic by virtue of its displaying little variability. As a result, artifact assemblages looked more homogeneous and stereotypic than they really were, which in turn supported the original distinctions made between the major industries.

The major revolution in Paleolithic method and theory was brought about by François Bordes, who introduced two important elements. The first was a comprehensive type list, which enabled the incorporation of all aspects of the lithic assemblage in the analytical framework (Bordes 1961a). The second was a separation of typology from the ordering of assemblages into major groups or phyla (Bordes 1961b; Bordes and Bourgon 1951; Bordes 1950, 1953; Bourgon 1957). This latter element completely dismissed the notion and use of *fossiles directeurs*, since the simple presence of one or another type was not a consideration for assignment of an entire assemblage into one or another group. Rather, it was the relative frequency of a number of types, along with particular technological attributes, that formed the basis for the classification of different assemblages. On this basis, Bordes defined six major groups of Mousterian assemblages in France.[2] These groups comprised the classic "Mousterian Complex" and were thought to be synchronic based on their interstratification at sites such as Le Moustier, Combe-Grenal, Pech de l'Azé, and others.

It is important to note, however, that while Bordes eliminated the use of one aspect of the paleontological analogy—the *fossiles directeurs*—he still retained a paleontological analogy, both in his views on the lithic types that he defined and in terms of the interpretations of synchronic assemblage variability. First, Bordes continued to assume the prehistoric "cognitive" or behavioral reality of the types he defined, that is, that each type represented an intentional end-product, analogous to paleontological species that reflect real, biologically meaningful units (see especially Bordes 1967). This concept is still essentially retained in the French notion of a *chaîne opératoire*, which models the decision-making processes involved in lithic reduction sequences, from the initial choice of a nodule to the production of the intended finished tool

(Geneste 1985). There is still an assumption that stone tool morphology is, to a large extent, premeditated, and that each type reflects discrete units or designs conceptualized by their makers. Variations from the ideal type forms do occur in the final end-product (as intratype variability), but these are either errors or ad hoc accommodations to specific circumstances or materials. Intertype variability, on the other hand, relates to differences in style (different peoples or cultures with different desired end-products, or diachronic variation in the same group) or to different activities that required specific tools.

Second, Bordes assumed that any Middle Paleolithic assemblage represents the sum of hominid behaviors that took place at that site and at that time, reminiscent of the notion that fossil assemblages reflect the distribution of fauna present at the time of their deposition. If the tool types that make up an archaeological assemblage are behaviorally or cognitively real categories, it follows that the assemblages themselves are reflections of intentional behaviors, assuming minimal post-deposional disturbances. The interpretation of assemblage variability then directly follows from the interpretation of the lithic typological variability. If the tool types reflect primarily differences in style, then differences among the assemblage groups would reflect the presence of different stylistic groups or traditions (analogous to various paleontological phyla) that made their tools according to the norms of their respective cultural traditions. If the tool types reflect different functional categories, then inter-assemblage differences must reflect different activities that were carried out during the deposition of those assemblages (as different paleontological facies are associated with different environments). Thus, paralleling the model used in paleontology, function (facies) and style (phyla) represent the two logical possibilities for explaining Middle Paleolithic assemblage variability (see also Dunnell 1978; Isaac 1972; Sackett 1982b). Of course, given that there is a complex interplay between these two factors reflected in the comprehensive typology (Bordes 1967; Semenov 1964), assemblage variability is relatively complex as well. Nonetheless, the argument is easily reduced to these two factors.

In interpreting his six assemblage groups, Bordes himself argued that they represented separate cultural phyla. His reasoning was based on two lines of evi-

dence. The first, negative, was the lack of clear temporal ordering among the assemblage groups and a lack of one-to-one association with specific environmental indicators or faunal remains. The second, more positive, line of evidence was based on what appeared to be a multi-modal pattern in the distribution of the Racloir Index, or the proportion of *racloir* types to all retouched tools. It was on the basis of the Racloir Index that the assemblage groups were defined, and so this multi-modality, coupled with the lack of environmental patterning, led Bordes to conclude that these six groups appeared to be distinct logical units (rather than arbitrary groups along a continuum). In his hypothesis of *"Evolution Buissonante"* (Bordes 1954), he suggested that the roots of these various phyla could ultimately be found extending back into distinct industries apparent in the Lower Paleolithic. Thus, the tracing of evolutionary developments within the major phyla continued to be an important research focus in French Paleolithic research (see, for example, Bourgon 1957; Le Tensorer 1978), although these roots were difficult to trace in practice (Bordes 1954).

The alternative hypothesis, that functional or activity differences explained Middle Paleolithic assemblage variability, was put forward principally by L. and S. Binford (1966, 1969), and also by Freeman (1966). It was based on multivariate statistical analyses (Factor Analysis) of several European and Near Eastern assemblages, focusing primarily on the retouched component classified according to Bordes' typology. In their study, the Binfords (1966:245) isolated five factors which "define clusters of artifacts that exhibit internally consistent patterns of mutual covariation," which they interpreted as different tool kits with different functions, including manufacture of non-lithic tools, killing and butchering, cutting and incising, and cutting and shredding of plant materials. They argued not that the various Mousterian assemblage groups represented one or the other of these tasks, but rather that they were differentially composed of these clusters of related types. In other words, these factors cross-cut the various assemblage groups and each assemblage group could have several different activities represented in varying proportions. But an important point of their work was that the different assemblages represented "facies" of a single, though heterogeneous, Mousterian entity.

THE DISCRETENESS OF MOUSTERIAN
LITHIC TYPES AND ASSEMBLAGE GROUPS

Thus, the paleontological model provided the first major method and theory paradigm for Paleolithic research and set up the logical possibilities that ultimately led to the Bordes-Binford debate. However, the controversy that ensued had at its heart an assumption on the part of both parties that the analytical units under investigation, i.e., the lithic types, were discrete units and behaviorally real and that they gave rise to assemblages that reflected discrete behaviors. In fact, recent evidence strongly suggests that such an assumption is not warranted. Our attention will be focused first on the behavioral and/or cognitive reality of the lithic types.

It is beyond question that Middle Paleolithic lithic artifacts were deliberately manufactured by hominids and thus are of behavioral significance. But it is not so clear that the types recognized and defined by Bordes truly represent desired end-products that only reflect either cultural norms or discrete functions. There are at least two lines of evidence that suggest, in fact, that this is not the case.

The first line of evidence comes from the recognition that lithic artifact forms are not always stable once they have been first manufactured. It is clear, for example, that a particular flake blank, useful for certain tasks even in its unretouched state, can potentially be modified into any number of different forms suitable for many different kinds of tasks. However, even after it has been modified for one task, at the completion of that task it can still be remodified for others. This is what Jelinek (1976) calls the "Frison Effect," after Frison's (1968) initial clear demonstration of these processes. In effect, lithic materials, as raw nodules, as unretouched blanks, or even as already shaped tools—in all of these forms—represent a resource that can be continuously and repeatedly remodified and reused.

Demonstrations of such remodifications have been made for Middle Paleolithic material. One of us (Dibble 1984a, 1987a, 1987b) has shown that much of the typological variability among 17 of Bordes' racloir types could be explained on the basis of resharpening and subsequent reduction of the tools. Specifically, single racloirs (types 9-11 in Bordes' typology) appear to represent an initial phase of reduction of the flake blank, with other types (double [types 12-17], convergent [types 8 and 18-21], and transverse forms [types 22-

24]), reflecting further reduction. In other words, as resharpening continues the shape of the tool changes, and therefore the type (which is defined on morphology) changes as well. The final type that an artifact represents is thus dependent on where it was in this reduction continuum at the time it was last discarded. In a similar manner, notches (types 42 and 54) can be transformed into denticulates (type 43) with just the addition of one or two notches on the same edge. Such reduction may or may not take place at one time, since an already retouched blank may be picked up and remodified at any time.[3]

An important implication of the Frison effect for Middle Paleolithic assemblages is that the forms of stone tools found in the archaeological record do not necessarily represent desired end-products. Indeed, certain forms, such as the heavily reduced racloirs, may be pieces that were discarded because they lost all of their potential usefulness. This immediately calls into question the prehistoric cognitive reality of the lithic types (see also Leroi-Gourhan 1966:105; Dibble 1989), though of course they still retain a certain behavioral reality because they were deliberately retouched. Moreover, the assumption that the different Bordian tool types reflect different functions has been challenged by microwear analysis (Anderson-Gerfaud, in press, and see note 3) which shows virtually no correlation of specific uses with the major Middle Paleolithic types.

The second line of evidence against the notion of these types representing cognitively real or functionally discrete forms comes from taphonomy, which is another factor that can affect the morphology of stone tools but with little or no behavioral ramifications. It is generally accepted that post-depositional movement of sediments will produce pseudo-tools, especially the marginally retouched types (for example, Bordes' type 46-49), but also some notches and denticulates (Verjux 1988). Moreover, given the definitional constraints of the typology, breakage of complete tools will also affect the typological composition among the racloirs (Dibble and Holdaway, in press).

For all of these reasons, then, the assumption that all of the retouched tools found in Middle Paleolithic assemblages reflect normative forms, or complete tools manufactured for discrete functions, can be called into question. This poses a major problem for interpreting

Middle Paleolithic assemblages as reflecting only functional or stylistic variation. It would appear, instead, that several factors may be operating at a more fundamental level to produce variability in assemblage typological composition.

The second question to be asked is how real are the defined assemblage groups? In other words, do the six groups named by Bordes actually represent six discrete entities and not simply arbitrarily defined segments along a line of continuous variation? As we will show, it appears that the evidence that has been presented to date for the discreteness of these groups is not conclusive and that the second alternative may be a more accurate interpretation.

Before turning to the evidence, it should be noted that a pattern of continuous variation among these assemblages should not be surprising. Already it has been shown that the morphological variability in the tool types is more continuous than discrete and this fact alone should affect assemblage variability in the same manner. Perhaps even more fundamental, however, are the numerous taphonomic effects involved in the formation of Middle Paleolithic assemblages.

As is generally acknowledged, our resolution of Middle Paleolithic prehistoric behavior is extremely coarse, much more so than is true for later periods. Middle Paleolithic stratigraphic horizons, defined geologically, are typically quite thick and can represent several hundred, thousand, or even tens of thousands of years. An excavated assemblage, in effect, collapses all of this time and treats it more or less as a single temporal event. But, given the immensity of time that is reflected in these assemblages, we must ask ourselves how realistic it is to assume that the behaviors that led to their formation were constant. This is not an argument for either side of the style/activity debate: whether the tools were left by different culture groups or if they were left in the course of different activities, the problem is that our units can only be taken as a sum of several events. In the course of the formation of a geological couche, there is a clear and inevitable potential for considerable variation in both the kinds and intensity of those events. This alone would produce a considerable amount of "noise" within a single assemblage and blur distinctions among assemblages. Added to this are the randomizing effects of taphonomy, raw material constraints, manufacturing errors, sampling errors, and so on. When all of these factors are considered together, one would expect variability among these assemblages to be more or less continuously distributed, in spite of whatever patterns of behavior may have contributed to their formation.

But whatever our logical expectations may be, it is clearly reasonable to investigate whether or not the numeric parameters that define Middle Paleolithic assemblages distribute themselves into statistically significant groups or clusters. In his original formulation, Bordes relied on an observation of multi-modality of the Racloir Index to make three major separations of his groups. But in fact, such multi-modality, while clearly suggested in the data available to Bordes, is not statistically demonstrable. For example, Figure 1.1a shows the distribution of 88 Middle Paleolithic assemblages along the Racloir Index, on the basis of which Bordes and de Sonneville-Bordes (1970) inferred that there was evidence of multi-modality. In fact, when this distribution is compared with an even distribution (using Chi-square and applying Yate's correction for continuity, given the small expected cell frequencies), the difference is not statistically significant ($X^2 = 20.232$, df = 16, P > .1).[4] This in itself weakens the interpretation that the assemblages fall into discrete modes along this measure. Moreover, independent data based on other assemblages (Fig. 1.1b) show a unimodal distribution of this index (Rolland 1981).

It is true, however, that Bordes' groups are based not just on the Racloir Index but on relative frequencies of several classes of types. However, with 63 types in the standard typology plus handaxes, it is much harder to demonstrate statistically either continuous variation or discrete clusters among several assemblages. Some attempts to confirm the assemblage patterns have been made using multivariate techniques (Callow and Webb 1977, 1981; Doran and Hodson 1966; Geneste 1985). One major problem in these kinds of studies, however, is that the variables used to define the groups are the same ones used to assess the significance of those groups, which is a statistical tautology. The multivariate analyses of Mousterian assemblages just cited suffer from this problem because the same lithic types used to define the assemblage groups are those used to assess their differences in the statistical procedure. The result is that any patterning found is only an artifact of the way in which they were grouped. Another problem is that there are numerous methodological questions that can be raised about interpreting the significance of clusters produced by statistical algorithms. The principal problem is that these algorithms can clearly show similarities among groups of assemblages, but verifying that they form discrete clusters rather than continuous variability in multidimensional space is more difficult.

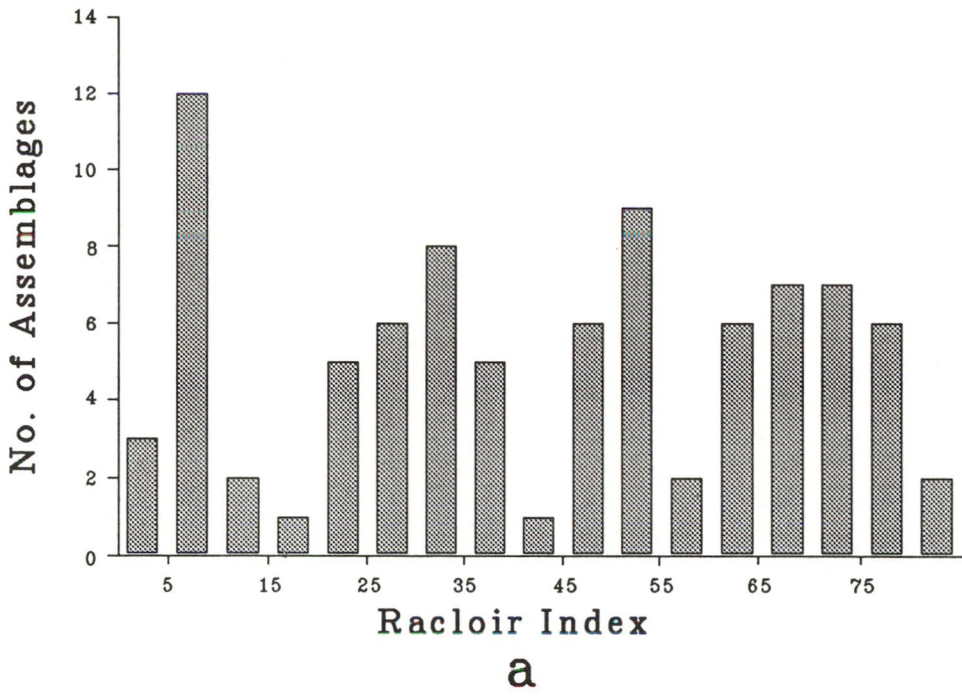

a

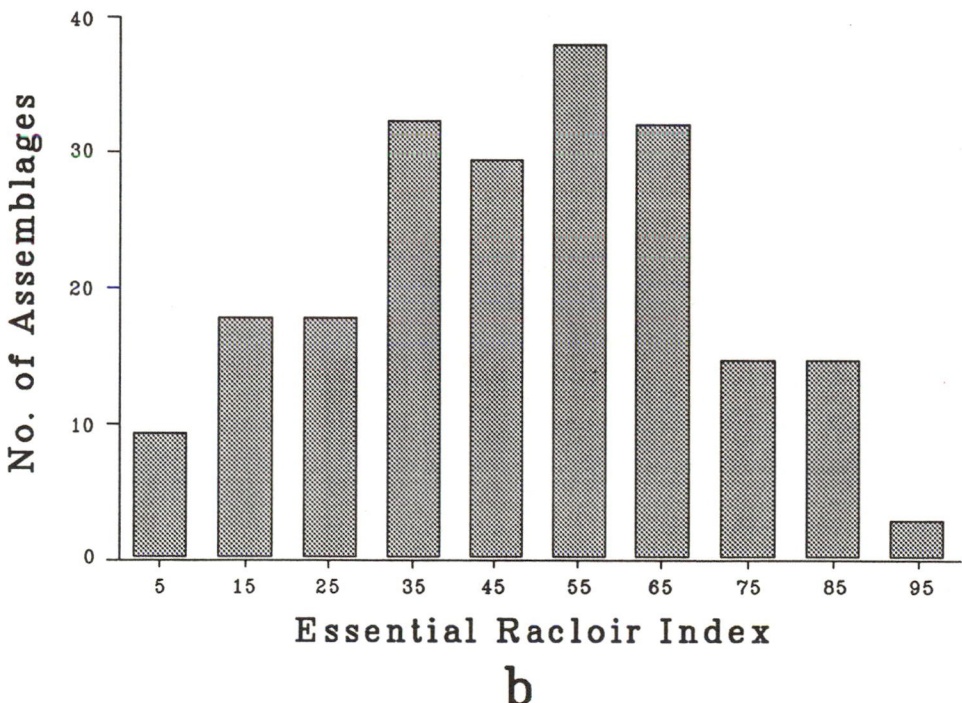

b

Figure 1.1   *(a) Distribution of 88 Mousterian assemblages from Western Europe according to Racloir Index (redrawn from Bordes and de Sonneville-Bordes 1970:fig. 15, bottom), suggesting multi-modality. (b) Distribution of 77 Mousterian assemblages from Mediterranean France (after Rolland 1981:fig. 3) which shows a clear uni-modal distribution according to essential Racloir Index.*

These problems can be illustrated, for example, with the study presented by Geneste (1985). His dendrogram of 43 Middle Paleolithic assemblages, reproduced here in Figure 1.2a, is based on computed similarities among assemblages in terms of their proportions of four of Bordes' type classes: the Racloir Index, the Biface Index, and the percentages of denticulates and of Upper Paleolithic elements (Bordes types 30-40). Although no Charentian assemblage groups or MTA type B are represented, the separation of the other named groups is excellent and could easily be taken as demonstrating the distinctiveness or discreteness of the assemblage groups being analyzed. But because of the statistical tautology just mentioned, these results do not demonstrate that variability is discrete rather than continuous. In fact, even continuous random variability can produce such clustering similar to that found by Geneste, which can be demonstrated by a simple computer simulation.

In this example, we will attempt to cluster 50 assemblages generated with random percentages of four variables simulating the four indexes used by Geneste. In computing these percentages, two constraints were followed. First, each variable was defined to have maximum percentages that grossly mirror the maximum percentages observed in Mousterian groups. Thus, our variable of "*racloirs*" varied randomly from 0 to .9, "denticulates/notches" from 0 to .9, "bifaces" from 0 to .25, and "Upper Paleolithic elements" from 0 to .15. Second, the sum of these percentages must be close to 1 (specifically, between .85 and 1.0). This second constraint mirrors the effect that happens in analyzing real assemblages when dealing with relative proportions. Because the total of all of the proportions of tools must sum to 1, an elevation in one major group (e.g., *racloirs*) necessarily forces a decrease in another group (e.g., denticulates). This fact explains why these two major typological groups are not truly independent of one another in a statistical sense and are thus always inversely correlated with each other (see Dibble 1989). In this computer simulation, the "*racloir*" or "denticulate" variable was randomly chosen to be the first variable assigned a random percentage. Given the assignment of the first percentage, the other variables were allowed to be vary randomly within their assigned maximum limits and within the remaining proportion up to 100%.

For this simulation, industrial assignments were automatically made on the basis of two of the randomly generated variables. If the value of the "biface" variable was greater than 10%, the generated assemblage was assigned to MTA: type A if the "*racloirs*" were more than 15% and type B if the "*racloirs*" were less than 15%. In the cases with a low handaxe value, the "*racloirs*" were used exclusively for assemblage group assignment: Quina for those with "*racloirs*" greater than 55%, Denticulate for those with "*racloirs*" less than 15%, and Typical for the rest. The clustering was performed with Systat 3.0, using the Complete Linkage clustering algorithm.

One might expect that with randomly generated percentages as input variables, a completely haphazard assortment of the simulated assemblages would be obtained in a cluster analysis. However, as can be seen in Figure 1.2b, the random assemblages cluster in a fashion quite similar to that reported by Geneste, in that similarly named groups tend to fall together. What the statistical method is showing is that certain assemblages along the multivariate continuum are more similar to each other than they are to others. The correspondence of these clusters to our named groups reflects the fact that the input variables are the same ones used to define the groups. But a demonstration of the discreteness of these groups has not been made since we know that the "assemblage" characteristics of these simulated cases are randomly distributed.

The same problem applies to the analysis of actual Middle Paleolithic assemblages. Among them variability in the indices is undoubtedly not random but reflects real behavioral or other factors, as will be shown below. However, since the variables used in the analyses of authors cited above are the same ones used for assemblage classification, one would expect that named groups would be statistically similar to each other. This is a result of the statistical tautology discussed above. Therefore, no demonstration of the discreteness of the named assemblage groups has been made.

To summarize, we know that the individual lithic artifacts reflect individual behavioral events. It is not clear, however, that formal tool types, i.e., the abstract categories, used to describe and analyze these objects, reflect desired end-products manufactured for specific activities. Likewise, while it is clear that assemblages reflect behaviors that occurred at these sites, it is unlikely that those behaviors were constant for the entire span of time necessary to produce any given assemblage. Moreover, it is doubtful that we can isolate the several independent behaviors that undoubtedly occurred during the formation of these assemblages. This is probably the reason why there has been no clear demonstration of distinct and separate Middle Paleolithic assemblage groups and, indeed, why such a

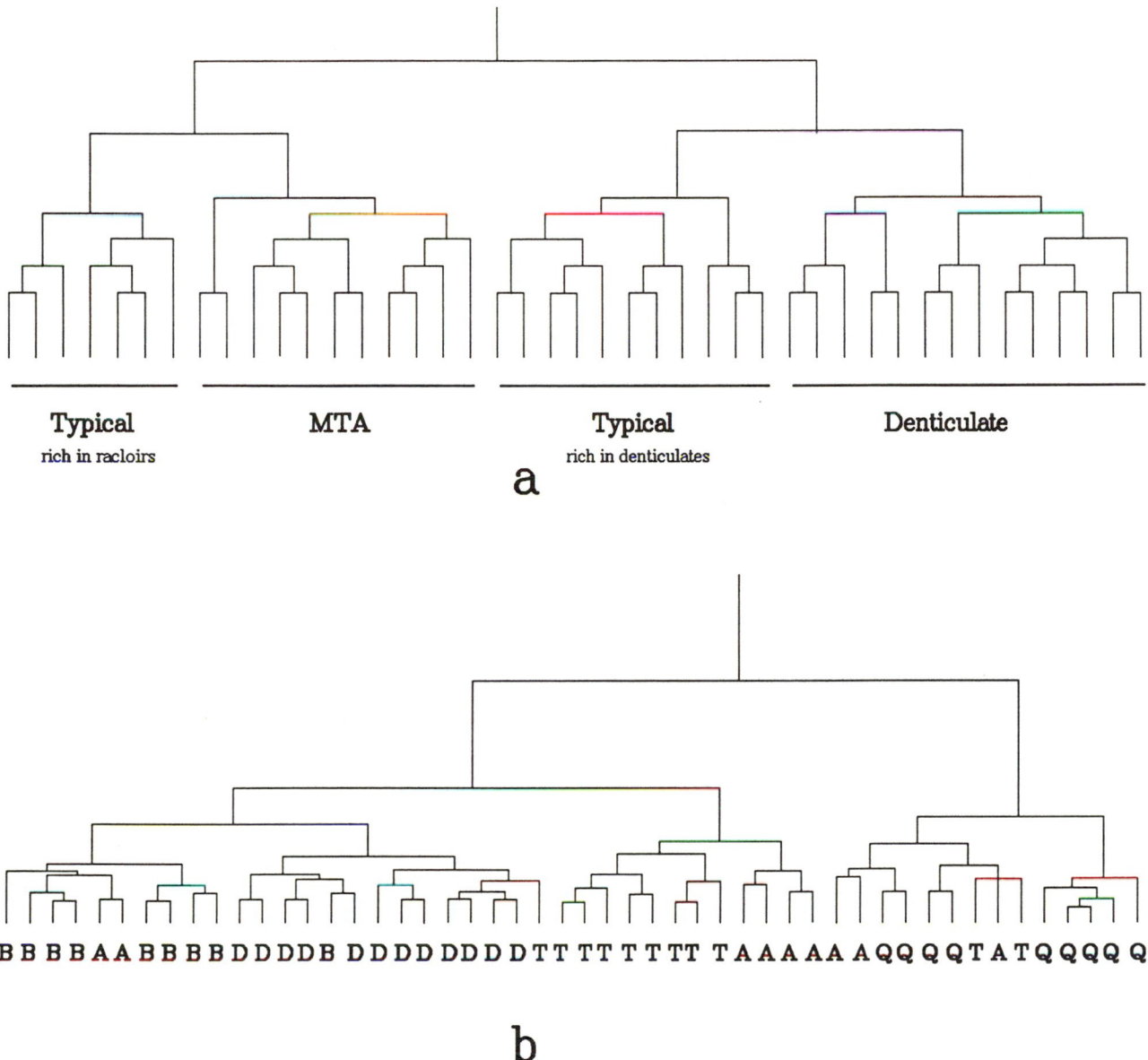

Figure 1.2   *(a) Dendrogram of 43 Mousterian assemblages from Southern France, computed on the basis of relative frequencies of racloirs, denticulates, bifaces, and Upper Paleolithic types (redrawn from Geneste 1985:fig. 26). (b) Dendrogram of 50 "simulated" assemblages, created with randomly varying percentages of four input variables representing proportions which sum to 1 (see text).*

demonstration is probably not possible. Like the lithic tool types on which they are based, the named Middle Paleolithic assemblage groups in France are probably best seen as partitions along a continuum of variability.

Thus, the principal assumption of the paleontological analogy—the cognitive or behavioral reality of discrete lithic types and assemblages—has been shown to be questionable. It would be more appropriate,

therefore, to search for other factors responsible for the continuous variation that we do see—factors other than style or function and which are, perhaps, much more fundamental than either of these. The focus for research on the Middle Paleolithic should thus be on the isolation of those factors rather than on the explanation of how or why these assemblage groups maintained their discreteness.

PRIMARY FACTORS OF MIDDLE PALEOLITHIC VARIABILITY

Even though Middle Paleolithic assemblages may be continuous in nature, it is still necessary to explain underlying causes of that variability. Two factors seem to be most important and will be discussed in turn.

RAW MATERIALS

Recently, increasing attention has been paid to several aspects of raw material and its relationship to typology and technology. Based on this work it is becoming clear that raw material variability has a considerable effect on Middle Paleolithic assemblage composition, much more in fact than just requiring minor ad hoc accomodations in the course of lithic manufacture. Unfortunately, research into this factor is just beginning and we are still far from understanding the more subtle qualities of materials that should be better quantified. At this point, it seems that several basic aspects of raw materials are important, including quantity, availability, size and shape of the nodules, and texture of the flint itself.

There have been some attempts to understand general distributions of assemblage features relating to raw material. In a review of both Southwest French and Levantine Near Eastern Middle Paleolithic industries, Fish (1981) suggested that the emphasis on Levallois technique is a direct function of nodule size, assuming that this technique is uneconomical and (p. 379) "therefore may have been practiced more sparingly where small nodules predominated." Besides a lower frequency of Levallois, sites in this situation also yielded more naturally backed flakes than sites with large nodules. Small nodule size may also have an important typological effect, as Jelinek (1976) has suggested for the Buda industry from Vertesszöllös (Vertes 1965), in which there are no handaxes but only small chopper tools. Given the small nodule size in that area, this factor alone may have constrained the production of handaxes. Similar sorts of Lower Paleolithic industries from Czechoslovakia and other parts of Central Europe are undoubtedly a result of the same effect (Valoch 1982). In addition, small nodule size, when combined with shapes such as round pebbles, seem to lead to specialized "citrus slices" techniques. These occur, for instance, in the Erd Mousterian industry or the Pontinian in Italy, also characterized by a high coefficient of unused or unusable flakes (Gábori-Csánk 1968:117-124; Taschini and Bietti 1979; Rolland 1975).

A number of studies have suggested relationships between flake and core dimensions and raw material sources. Dibble (1985) has shown an intersite patterning among Levallois flake dimensions that may reflect differences in raw material, though no studies were made of the specific raw materials used for those flakes. It is also interesting to note similarities in hand-axe forms between the Northern French MTA and those open-air stations in the Bergeracois where raw material was equally abundant and large (Mellars 1969:148). Although outside of the principal geographic focus of this paper, it is worth drawing attention to the work of Munday (1976) who, using data from the Negev (Israel), was able to show strong relationships between both debitage size and core weight on the one hand and distance to raw material on the other. As suggested by both him and Marks (see Marks 1988), there appears to have been a more intense utilization of material as this distance increased, so that cores were discarded at a later stage in their reduction and were therefore smaller.

It is becomingly increasingly clear that a great deal of movement of flint resources took place during the Middle Paleolithic. Besides its implications for the behavior of the hominids at that time (see Roebrooks et al. 1988; Marks 1988), the mixture of imported and local raw material at the same site affords an excellent opportunity to compare directly the differential utilization of one material versus another. In several examples from France, such as Tournal (Tavoso 1984), Fonseigner, Vaufrey (Geneste 1985), and Marillac (Meignen 1988), it has been shown that the poorer quality local material, represented by many more cores and cortical flakes, was differentially selected for denticulates/notches. The imported material, of better quality and often brought as blanks (and often many of those being Levallois), was more often retouched into *racloirs*. Moreover, many of the *racloir* types in the imported material are of the more complex types, including double, convergent, and transverse forms. If these types are the result of more resharpening, then they suggest a more intense use of the better raw material because it was more scarce (see also Roebrooks et al. 1988). Geneste (1985) also suggests that certain types of tools (bifaces and *racloirs* in particular) are more mobile and thus were brought into various sites more frequently. The more difficult flaking stones, such as quartz and some quartzites, impede the practice of Levallois technique and are associated with higher frequences of ad hoc tools (see also Veyrier et al. 1951:70-78).

In general, the use of flint results in assemblages with greater typological diversity and intensive reduction of tools due to economization (often reflected in Charentian and some Typical Mousterian assemblage groups), while coarser materials are associated with assemblages exhibiting more typological uniformity and the discarding of artifacts in an earlier stage of reduction (reflected in Denticulate Mousterian and other Typical Mousterian assemblage groups). The coarser grained component of certain Quina occurrences with mixed raw material composition, such as La Chapelle-aux-Saints or Mas-Viel, also present high unused blank coefficients (Rolland 1975:figs. 7-21, 7-22).

Related to the association between raw material types and typology—indeed, probably underlying it—is the repeated demonstration of the selection on the basis of size alone of certain blanks for retouching. For example, in the production of *racloirs* the larger blanks are the ones that are consistently selected, leaving an unretouched flake population that is somewhat biased toward smaller sized pieces. While this is often apparent on the basis of comparisons of overall length of retouched to unretouched pieces (Rolland 1981:25; Geneste 1985), the difference is even more striking if one considers that the finished retouched pieces have been reduced. Therefore a more accurate comparison can be obtained by comparing platform sizes, which are not affected by retouching (see Dibble 1987a). Interestingly, however, this relationship does not hold for denticulates and notches, as Rolland (1981:27) and others consistently find that these types are not bigger, on average, than unretouched flakes. Size, then, is a factor underlying the production of these two type classes. It appears that under conditions where the local raw material is small, most of the tools made on that material will be notches and denticulates. If *racloirs* are needed, they will tend to be made on larger, imported Levallois blanks, as if anticipating the need for further reduction due to resharpening. Only if better raw material is not available for importation will the *racloirs* be consistently made on the smaller material. These patterns occur at Roc en Pail, Ranc-Pointu, Le Figuier, and in the Pontinian and Tata industries (Combier 1967:133, 192; Piperno 1972; Vertes 1964).

Thus, as suggested by Rolland (1981), Tavoso (1984), and Geneste (1985), it follows that there is variability in assemblage composition related to the proximity to raw material sources and topography. For example, Geneste (1985:513) notes the relationship between topography (including access to sites) and raw material utilization: open sites are the only ones with emphasis on the primary exploitation of raw material, often very rich in cores and debris yet with few tools, and often exhibiting specialized blank production; semi-open sites, with production of blanks after transport of raw blocks of material; and caves, typically characterized by the importation of already prepared blanks and tools. Whether these site types should be seen as discrete categories, as seems to be suggested by Geneste (1985), or as representing a continuous function of distance to raw material sources and the quality of locally-available materials, could be debated. But the relationship to raw materials is clear and could, as pointed out by Rolland (1981:22), explain why "open-air sites tend to be more homogeneous, with low implement frequencies and one dominant industry (MTA), whereas enclosed sites have variable implement frequencies and are polytypic."[5]

Thus, while the overall effect of raw material availability on the classic Mousterian assemblage variability problem must be studied in more depth, the work to date suggests that raw material variability alone can account for a significant portion of observed aspects of Middle Paleolithic assemblage variability.

INTENSITY OF OCCUPATION

The second major factor affecting Middle Paleolithic assemblage variability is that of intensity of occupation and intensity of utilization of lithic resources. In effect, this factor reflects the amount of reuse or recycling of the lithic materials during their time of usefulness. It can have considerable effects on archaeological assemblages of all types (Shott 1989) and can be reflected in many ways. This factor joins that of raw material in constraining the expression of desired forms in lithic assemblages.

Mention has already been made of the demonstration that most of Bordes' defined types of *racloirs* can be interpreted as stages in a continuum of reduction through resharpening. One of the implications of this work, discussed above, is that the types themselves probably do not have any cognitive reality. The other, more positive, implication is that if tools change their form as they are repeatedly resharpened and reused, then the morphology of a discarded lithic artifact reflects, at least in part, the amount of reuse it underwent. If patterns of resharpening account for the morphological distinctions made in the typology, then the typology itself is probably reflecting this factor. And, since an assemblage is composed of those types, it follows that at least some portion of assemblage variability is related to reduction in terms of the degree to which the tools are resharpened and remodified during the course of assemblage formation.

At least a portion of the typological variability among the named Middle Paleolithic assemblage groups of France can be interpreted as due to such factors of reduction. Dibble (1989), for example, using a sample of 72 assemblages, has shown a patterning based strictly on typological reduction in *racloirs* and notches that closely mirrors the segregation of the named groups. A similar argument and findings were presented by Jelinek (1988), who relied on slightly different groupings of types, though still organized by overall reduction. Both found that Quina, Ferrassie, and certain Typical assemblages were characterized by the more "reduced" types of tools (principally *racloirs*) while the other Typical, MTA-A, Denticulate, and MTA-B assemblages had less "reduced" types in general, and showed a progression toward more reduction of notches into denticulates. Thus, although the named assemblage groups probably represent partitions along a continuum of variation, they, like the typology itself, reflect aspects of reduction and can be interpreted as such.

Moreover, different typological classes may have differential use-lifes, or periods of recycling, that can seriously distort an interpretation based solely on relative percentages (Shott 1989). In fact, *racloirs* and denticulates do appear to have different attrition rates and this fact alone can have an effect that mirrors the classic extremes of Mousterian assemblage variability.

Several lines of evidence suggest that *racloirs* are functionally distinct from denticulates and notches, with the most commonly cited (though perhaps overstated) function for the latter being woodworking (Clark 1958a, b; Bordes 1962; Leroi-Gourhan 1956; Kantman 1970). Two reasons for this distinction are: (1) differences in raw material and blank size selection for the two classes of tools (see above) and (2) numerous instances of spatial segregation on living floors (e.g., at Cueva Morín, Cantabria: see Freeman, this volume). Moreover, a body of experimental, analytical, and ethnographic observations (Gould 1968; White 1969; Crabtree 1977; Siegel 1985; Wilmsen 1968) suggests that differences in use relate to differences in working edge angles between *racloirs* and denticulates/notches. The former, along with unretouched or utilized flakes, possess generally lower angles and are more suitable for longitudinal kinetic

actions such as cutting, sawing, and whittling of softer materials, whereas denticulates and notches, possessing often steeper angles, are best used transversely for scraping, spokeshaving, and processing harder materials (Leroi-Gourhan 1966; Rolland 1981:27-28).

However, the lower edge angle of *racloirs* means that they dull more quickly than denticulates and notches, which in turn leads to more successive resharpening and a more rapid blank turnover and faster rates of tool discard. If this is true, then an equal proportion of time extended to both kinds of activities (those involving *racloirs* and those involving denticulates) will result in differential proportions of the two tool classes due to differences in their life cycles, even though the time spent on each activity is the same. This can easily be shown. Figure 1.3 is a simple simulation of an accumulation of tools with different life cycles. The left chart (a), represents the accumulating totals for *racloirs* and denticulates. For each unit of time, one additional denticulate is produced versus four *racloirs*. Although the proportion of denticulates in this example starts as being nine times that of *racloirs*, the relative proportions are reversed after a very short time because the number of *racloirs* increases faster than the number of notches and denticulates. This is made even more clear in Figure 1.3b, which plots the ratio of *racloirs* to denticulates in Figure 1.3a as a function of the total number of tools. This relationship has already been noted in actual Middle Paleolithic assemblages, that when the percentage of tools relative to unretouched components increases, those additional tools are usually *racloirs* (Rolland 1977). The important point is that a change in relative frequencies of these two classes occurs even though the total amount of time spent on both activities is the same.

Differential attrition rates for denticulates/notches and *racloirs* can account not only for variation in the proportions of retouched tool classes, but also for the accelerated blank transformation (i.e., selection of unretouched blanks) and the reduction intensification observed among *racloir*-dominated assemblage types toward the more heavily reduced convergent and transverse types. Thus, again, *racloir*-dominated industries do not necessarily demonstrate a higher proportion of time spent on activities involving those particular tools, but rather more expenditure of time on both activities; that is, a more intense occupation overall.

If the intensity of use and reduction operates at the level of the types, it follows that it should also be reflected in predictable ways in the reuse and intensity of utilization of all the lithic resources in the assemblage, not just the major tool forms. In fact, this occurs. In assemblage groups associated with more reduced types, one finds a higher ratio of tools to flakes, of tools and flakes to cores (Rolland 1977, 1981), and of retouched pieces to all other pieces (Jelinek 1988:fig. 11.5 and Jelinek 1982b). In other words, a higher proportion of retouched pieces relative to unretouched blanks reflects a more intense, or parsimonious, utilization of the lithic resources, and is not necessarily related to different activities reflecting stages of knapping (see Turq, this volume).

Putting these facts together, the transformation from a less utilized assemblage to a more intensely utilized one can be illustrated with two series from Combe-Grenal: layer 13, Denticulate, and layer 24, Quina (see Fig. 1.4). Although these two assemblages are quite dissimilar when compared on the basis of only their "Essential" counts (primarily the retouched component), they are much more similar when their entire assemblages are compared on the basis of "cutting tools" (including unretouched Levallois and non-Levallois flakes and blades, points, *racloirs*, and *limaces*)

versus other sorts of retouched implements (principally denticulates, notches, and Tayac points). The inclusion of the complete unretouched component is certainly justified, given the repeated demonstration based on experiments, ethnographic observation, and microwear studies, that they are used as cutting tools (Gould 1968; Leroi-Gourhan 1966:98; Mulvaney 1969:70; Rolland 1988:170-171; Wilmsen 1968:160). Moreover, the transformation from one industry to the other is easily seen to involve only the increased production of *racloirs*. These *racloirs* are mostly made on previously unretouched blanks (which increases the ratio of retouched pieces), though previously made denticulates can also be transformed into *racloirs*, especially classic Quina-type *racloirs* (Lenoir 1986). Thus, the principal typological differences between even these two examples, which represent extremes in the continuum of French Mousterian variability, can be explained largely on the basis of differential utilization of their lithic resources.

If assemblages reflect intensity of utilization, then what are the factors that produce variability in intensi-

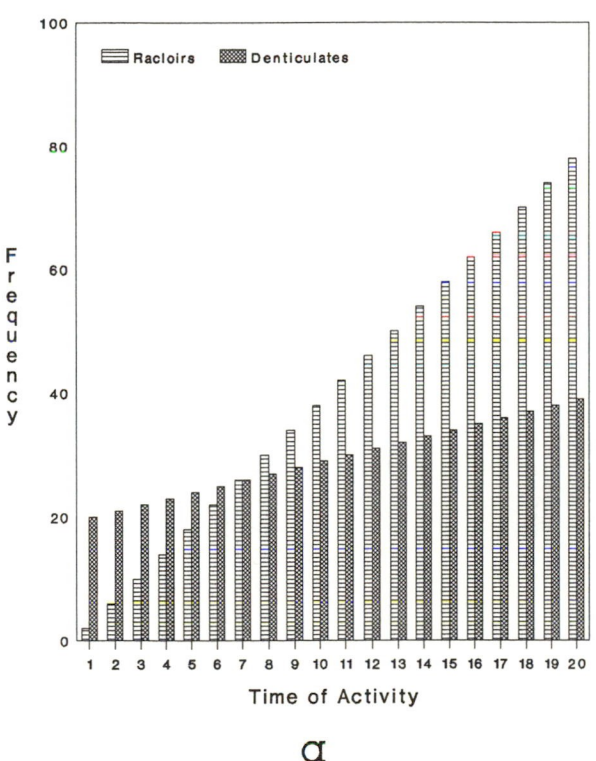

a

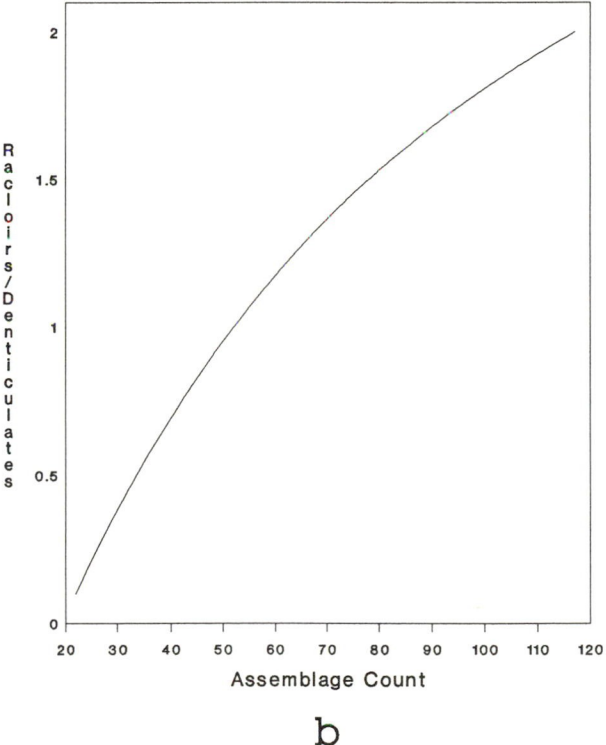

b

Figure 1.3   *(a) Cumulative frequency distributions of* racloirs *and denticulates as a function of time. For each unit of time, one denticulate is added to four racloirs. (b) The same data as in (a) but displayed as the ratio of* racloirs *to denticulates as a function of total implement count.*

ty? One expected factor would be raw material and, indeed, the relationship between intensity of utilization and raw material can be illustrated with many examples.

For instance, quarry sites in the loess regions of northern France, which exploited an abundant and high quality flint, contain a high proportion of waste material, cores, unused blanks, and few retouched tools. These inventories contrast with those of sites situated in crystalline regions of Brittany or Alsace, where flint is scarce. In southern France, a similar contrast is apparent. There the Perigord rock shelter and cave sites, with sequences marked by a variety of the Mousterian groups, often exhibit carefully reduced nodules and many intensively trimmed implements,

particularly *racloirs*. On the other hand, in the nearby Bergeracois open-air plateau sites, which have greater access to abundant raw material, assemblages tend to be homogeneous, usually exhibiting many more hand-axes and fewer retouched flake tools (Rolland 1981). Although beyond our principal focus here, some aspects of the Southwest Asian material illustrate comparable situations: the intensively retouched industries from the high-altitude Zagros caves, where good quality material is generally scarce and in small sizes, contrast with the Levantine Mousterian sites where flint is ubiquitous and the unretouched Levallois component is extremely well represented (Dibble and Holdaway, in press).

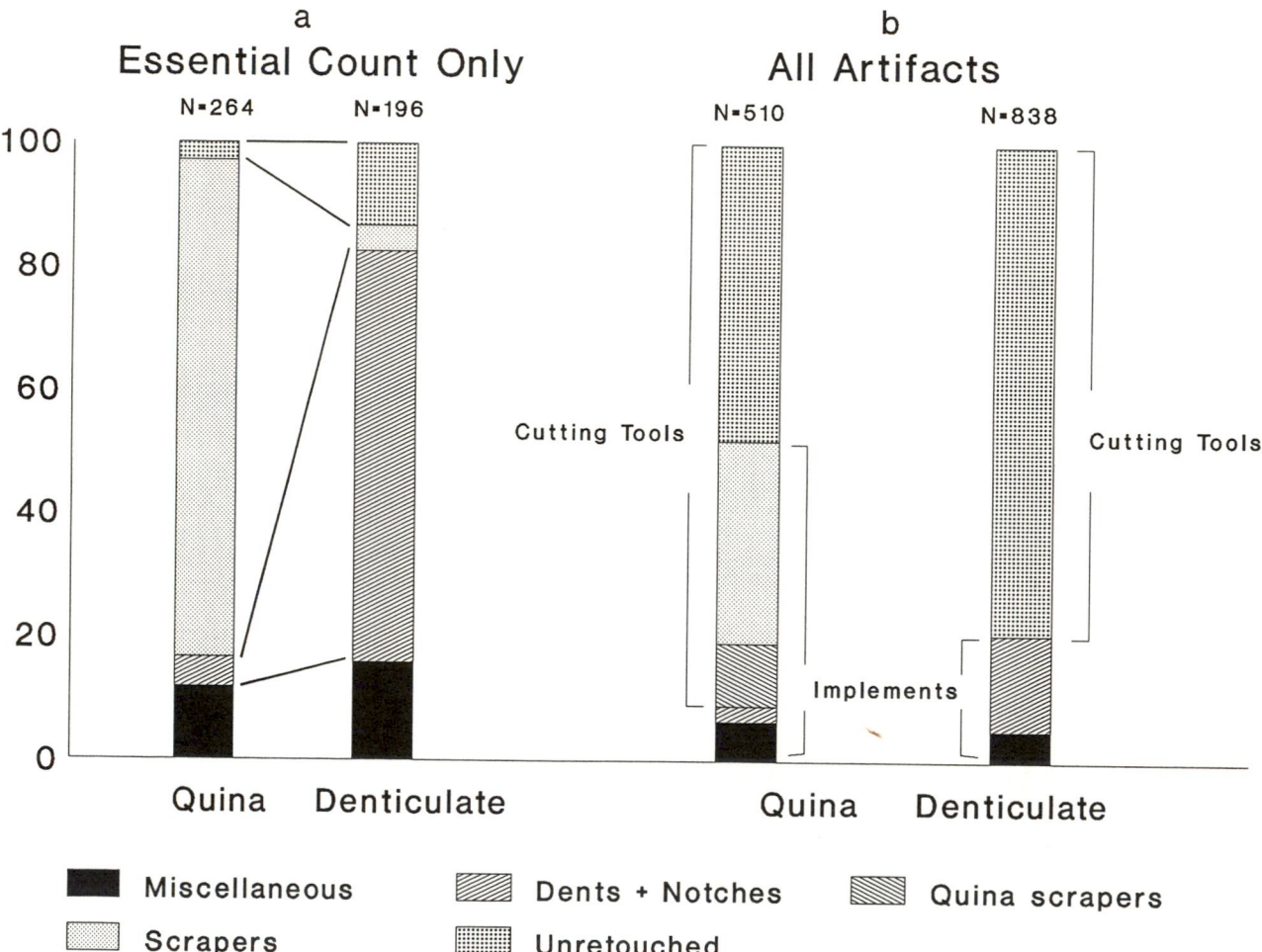

Figure 1.4   *Comparisons of differences between Quina and Denticulate Mousterian assemblages from Combe-Grenal (layers 24 and 13, respectively). (a) Essential typological counts, excluding types 1-3 and 46-50, but including unretouched types 5 and 38. (b) Comprehensive artifact counts, including all flakes, blades, and retouched tools, including those not normally classified in real count.*

The fact has already been discussed that if locally available raw material is not suitable for the manufacture of *racloirs*, then better quality flint is imported and differentially selected for this purpose. Further, the *racloir* forms represented on the imported blanks are often those types that would be interpreted as being more reduced according to Dibble's models, e.g., convergent and transverse forms (see Geneste 1985; Meignen 1988; Roebroeks et al. 1988). A further effect may be seen as local raw material sources are continuously exploited and therefore become both less abundant and of poorer quality (as the better nodules are presumably chosen first). In this vein, Dibble and Holdaway (in press) suggest a typological change through time in the Zagros Mousterian industry of the Warwasi Rockshelter (Iran) that seems to be related to increasing reduction. In another example, Pleistocene sea level oscillations created episodic difficulties of access to, and scarcity and depletion of, exotic flint beach pebbles at La Cotte de St. Brelade (Jersey). This was also reflected in variations in reduction intensity and typological diversification through the sequence (Callow 1988:203-211). In all of these examples, it appears that as good raw material is scarcer, there will be a corresponding increase in the parsimonious use (and reuse) of that material. That parsimony will be reflected in the typology of the assemblage (see Dibble, in press a).[6]

A second major factor underlying differential intensity of lithic utilization, as suggested earlier by one of us (Rolland 1977, 1981, 1988), is climate and its effect on group mobility. Variations in regional climate during the Pleistocene would have had tremendous effects on settlement patterns and mobility, with concomitant variations in lithic reduction intensity. For example, the loess regions of northern France, occupied during mild or moderately cold phases, were abandoned during full stadial/loess deposition periods (Bordes 1954; Tuffreau 1987). This was accompanied by movement into either the sheltered Dordogne valleys (Movius 1953:127-129; Bordes 1950:418) or, as seems more likely, into the equally sheltered limestone valleys of the Maas region (de Heinzelin 1984:197). It is notable that during the Early Weichsel cold episodes, cave settlements further removed from flint sources became more densely occupied and consisted mostly of heavily retouched Quina assemblages (Ulrix-Closset 1975:94). In southwestern France there is a strong association between the named Mousterian assemblage groups and paleoclimatic assessments based on sedimentology and palynology, with most of the

Quina and Ferrassie industries, i.e., those industries that are more typologically reduced, being associated with colder conditions, while most of the Denticulate groups and some of the denticulate-rich Typical Mousterian assemblages are associated with more temperate or mild conditions (see Fig. 1.5).[7]

Variation in faunal exploitation strategies could have had indirect repercussions on lithic reduction variations. Some of these effects may be related to local topographic factors favoring a combination of killing and continued residence activities (possibly such as at La Quina [Jelinek et al. 1989]), while others may be due to the influence of distinct behavioral ecological characteristics of dominant ungulate species. There are, however, many problems associated with the use of faunal evidence of Middle Paleolithic behaviors. The two most significant of these are variability in preservation—a severe problem in open-air sites, for example—and variability in recovery. Until recently, the main objectives of Middle Paleolithic research relating to fauna focused on their value for biostratigraphy and paleoclimatic reconstruction. Consequently there was a bias in the recovery of identifiable bones and teeth and a general lack of precise provenience information for these remains. Further compounding the problem is the often inadequate means of publishing faunal data. Usually only species lists are reported, without quantitative breakdowns by species, anatomical parts, or relative frequencies of minimum numbers of individuals. Nonetheless, patterns of association between the faunal remains and the typological assemblage groups do emerge.

First, it has been noted elsewhere (Rolland, in press:fig. 3) that in southwestern France, higher average bone frequencies correlate with those assemblage types containing higher implement frequencies and more heavily reduced lithic types. Along with the bioclimatic data presented on Figure 1.5, these observations suggest that animal biomass increases under colder steppic landscape conditions and decreases when milder, woodland or steppic woodland prevail. It is during these times that the less intensely reduced assemblages (mostly Denticulate and some Typical) are more common. These observations, if confirmed by additional faunal data, could also mean that plant collecting becomes more significant during milder phases, although little information concerning use of edible wild plants is available (Freeman 1981).

The most common ungulate groups found in the archaeological record of the *Würm ancien* of Western Europe include large bovids (wild cattle, bison), large cervids (red deer, reindeer), equids (horse, steppe ass), as well as ibex and mammoth. Their availability and relative abundance generally followed a mosaic, rather than zonation, pattern, but also varied according to topography, vegetation, time, latitude, and climate (Drury 1975:189-90; Guthrie 1986). Red deer, reindeer, horse, and bison represent the major animal resources in virtually all European Middle Paleolithic assemblages, suggesting a proximity between diverse biotopes.

The rather consistent dominance of reindeer with Quina assemblages seems to coincide with colder pleniglacial conditions (Mellars 1969). Based on studies of antlers and tooth eruption patterns, Bouchud (1953, 1966) originally suggested a year-round local exploitation of this resource. Bahn (1977) later argued that reliance on this species requires a constant following of the herds. More recently, Spiess (1979) and Mellars (1985) both suggest that reindeer procurement was only one aspect of the exploitation of a diverse regional herbivore community and that it did not require high mobility. Instead, the broken landscape of southwestern France, combined with reduced migratory requirements, probably favored prolonged occupation of restricted areas. In this same vein, Weniger (1987) and Albrecht (1979) observe that late glacial reindeer hunter settlements in southwest Germany tended to cluster in fixed locational contexts, such as

lower slopes and valley bottoms, in order to intercept herds during their migratory movements.

Bordes (1978; see also de Lumley 1972) considered the recurrence of horse remains with Denticulate assemblages in the Perigord, Mediterranean, and Central France, as evidence of traditional preferences. *Equus germanicus* (or *remagen*) was the dominant equid species, and probably represented a forest ecotype (Zeuner 1963:311; Cornwall 1968:160). However, bison was also a common element, and actually becomes the almost exclusive quarry in open-air Denticulate sites such as Mauran, Le Roc, and Sandougne (Girard-Farizy and Leclerc 1981; Geneste 1985). Its frequent association with a humid and, at times, mild arboreal context also suggests a forest ecotype with limited migratory habits, perhaps living in regions where woodlands formed perennial, though, variable, parts of the habitat (Spiess 1979:258), thus indicating milder climatic conditions.

These observations suggest that paleoclimatic fluctuations and variations in biomass composition resulted in phases when aggregated versus dispersed resource patterns prevailed, with concomitant effects on the intensity of occupation and utilization of lithic resources (see also Conaty 1987). Aggregated resource patterns would coincide with colder pleniglacial conditions (oxygen-isotope stage 4 [Guiot

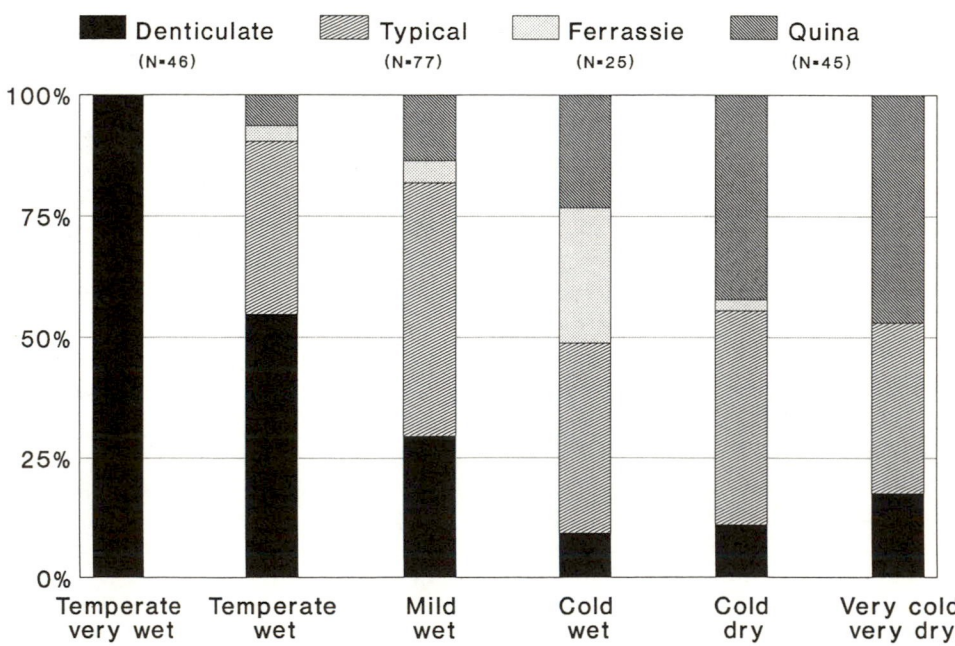

Figure 1.5   *Frequencies of different Mousterian assemblage groups associated with different paleoclimate types (after Laville 1973).*

et al. 1989:figs. 2, 3]) when reindeer formed a significant portion of the available fauna. Their comparatively larger herd sizes and more extensive, and predictable, migrations between the Massif Central and the Bay of Biscaye, would have favored migratory hunting and seasonal exploitation. A majority of Western European Middle Paleolithic enclosed sites are situated in the valleys that formed these migratory paths and provided abundant winter browse. The combination of seasonal concentrations and the tendency toward longer winter residence and less frequent lithic quarrying journeys, could account for the increased amounts of bone and the more heavily reduced stone tools that are both characteristics of assemblage groups such as Quina and Ferrassie.

Dispersed resource patterns, by contrast, would be more common under milder interstadial or early glacial conditions due to the expansion of woodlands or mixed steppe and woodland. During these times, horse, bison, and red deer would form the most important components of the faunal communities. These less migratory but locally more mobile ungulates, especially *Equus germanicus* and bison, which represent forest or mixed steppe/woodland ecotypes (Zeuner 1963:63-64, 72; Spiess 1979:258), would be dispersed along adjacent plateaus, thus requiring a change in exploitation strategies in order to survey game movements. This, in combination with shorter and more frequently interrupted winter residences,

would account for the reduced occupation intensities, with lower bone remains and less reduced retouched tools, seen in most Denticulate and some Typical Mousterian assemblages.[8]

In France, therefore, a number of lines of evidence thus come together to suggest that the more intensely utilized assemblages (reflected in the Charentian and some Typical groups) are formed during colder phases, with more reliance on the hunting of migratory game herds, and with increased parsimony of lithic resources as a means to minimize quarrying journeys. The less intensely utilized assemblages (reflected in Denticulate and some Typical groups) are formed during milder phases and reflect more mobility and reliance on plant resources.

It thus appears that there are several factors underlying the relative intensity of lithic reduction, including raw material variability and its exploitation, settlement type, bioclimatic changes in animal food biomass, and patterns of human occupation and mobility. Given the models of the relationship of lithic reduction to typological categories, including increased selection of unretouched blanks for implement manufacture, continuous reduction of certain types and the concomitant changes in their morphology, and differential rates of attrition, these factors alone account for many, if not most, aspects of assemblage composition variability seen in the Middle Paleolithic of Western Europe.[9]

CONCLUSIONS

Middle Paleolithic assemblage groups and the stone tool types on which they are defined represent our basic analytical units for organizing and interpreting the archaeological material from this time. Much of the theoretical development of the discipline has been based on a paleontology analogy that assumes that these units represented natural, i.e., cognitively and behaviorally real, categories that reflect only style (traditions or phyla) or function (facies). Given the nature of the lithic artifacts and the circumstances of their deposition, however, it is becoming clear that such an assumption is not tenable and so our focus should be on other factors that are demonstrably responsible for significant aspects of Middle Paleolithic assemblage variability.

Primary among these other factors are various aspects of raw material and intensity of reduction and utilization of those lithic resources. As we have shown, the combined effects of these account for

much of the variability that is traditionally measured in Middle Paleolithic assemblages.

Although perhaps premature, a tentative model of Middle Paleolithic assemblage variability could be proposed that utilizes only these two factors. To describe the two extreme positions there are, first, those sites where the local raw material is plentiful, of good quality, and large in size. In this situation there seems to be a tendency for assemblages to be composed of large numbers of blanks, cores, and bifaces, and few tools. In addition, absolute implement size tends to be large and specialized blank technologies, such as Levallois, predominate. Represented tool types are generally those that reflect little reduction, that is single-edged and some double-edged *racloirs* and many notches and denticulates.

At the other extreme, in sites far from good raw material and to which access is more difficult, two components are often evidenced: those tools that are made from the local raw material, which are generally notches and denticulates; and those tools, usually *racloirs*, that are made on imported materials. Therefore, the typological composition at the assemblage level is, to some extent, a function of the materials present in the site and the extent to which exotic materials were imported.

Further, the intensity with which those resources are utilized seems to vary directly with the scarcity of material and with the overall duration of occupation and extent of group mobility, which are a function of the environment. With more mobility, associated with temperate climates, there will be less reduction since the local materials will not be exploited to a high degree. The opposite will be true with low mobility brought on by more severe climatic conditions.

One of the arguments in favor of intensity of utilization being fundamental in influencing assemblage composition is the fact that its effects can reflect behavior taking place over geological time, which, of course, represents the temporal context of our archaeological couches. In the reduction of *racloirs*, for example, the retouching of a second edge of the tool can take place immediately or that same artifact can be picked up and remodified by another visitor to the same site a thousand years later. It is both the total cumulative effect of those visits and the intensity to which the previously abandoned material is exploited that ultimately determines the nature of the assemblage, not necessarily a constant level of intensity throughout the formation of the assemblage. Likewise, exposure of raw material sources will vary over vast periods of time and under different cycles of erosion, deposition, and overall intensity of exploitation. These can vary during the course of occupation of a single, deeply stratified site, such as Combe-Grenal. But the constraints imposed by raw material will be felt during the formation of an entire geological couche and thus be reflected in the technology and typology of the entire lithic assemblage.

Clearly we are not to the point where we can explain all aspects of Middle Paleolithic variability and behavior, and much remains to be done, even at a descriptive level. Furthermore, the classificatory framework established by Bordes is still sound, although the assumptions underlying that framework may not be correct. Our primary point has been that most of the available information pertaining to virtually all aspects of Middle Paleolithic variability relies on a classification of assemblage groups that is often assumed to reflect discrete units. It is becoming clear,

however, that certain technological, typological, and morphological factors transcend the named assemblage groups and link them continuously. These measures produce a dynamic continuity among several Dordogne sites from Typical Mousterian through Ferrassie and Quina to Denticulate. This continuity extends even to other regions of the Western Old World.

Our focus has been on two of the major analytical units at the heart of current research, typology and assemblage variation. We have suggested that much of the variability in these units can be understood without any reference to either function or style. We are not arguing that function and style did not contribute to lithic artifact and assemblage variability. Undoubtedly they did, but it is a question of whether or not we can recognize their effects given the coarseness of our methodology and the very nature of our data. Our argument has been that, at least in the Middle and Lower Paleolithic, the relative contributions of these factors are greatly overridden by the other factors of raw material and intensity of utilization. This does not mean that the classification system is flawed, since it still operates effectively at the descriptive level for which it was intended. But if the effects of function and style are being masked, then a continued emphasis on these two factors in attempts to explain Middle Paleolithic variability cannot be fruitful. Nor has it been fruitful for the past two decades. This alone suggests that we must abandon the paleontological analogy so that we can better deal with these other factors—factors which are much more comprehensible and amenable to objective analysis and which better reflect the processes of assemblage formation during this time. We hope that this paper is a positive step in that direction.

NOTES

1. In spite of the recent recognition of the increased time-span of the Middle Paleolithic, there is no conclusive evidence for diachronic change within this period, which may be due in part, of course, to the lack of suitable temporal controls (see Laville 1988; Mellars 1989b; Texier, in press). A suggestion of temporal change has been made for the Central European "Micoquian" (Bosinski 1967). In southwest Asia, based on stratified samples from the Tabun cave in Israel, Jelinek (1982a) has suggested a chronological change during the Mugharan Tradition (which encompasses the Yabrudian, Late Levantine Acheulian, and Amudian industries) and Levantine Mousterian in terms of flake thickness relative to width. Attempts to correlate this trend to other sites has not been successful, however (Bar-Yosef and Goldberg 1988; Marks 1983). Mellars (1965, 1969, this volume) has presented stratigraphic evidence for

technological and typological changes among Western European Mousterian assemblage groups, though it has been suggested (Dibble, in press a) that some of these technological changes may be due to changes in the availability of local flint resources at specific sites.

2. Following Bordes (1953:460-463), there are three principal assemblage groups defined primarily on the basis of the Racloir Index (IR), each of which has two subgroups, for a total of six assemblage groups. The Charentian group has an essential IR of greater than 55%. Its two subgroups are the Quina Mousterian, which has a low Blade Index (Ilam), low restricted Faceting Index (IFs), and low Levallois Index (IL), but a very high Charentian Index (IC) (reflecting a high frequency of transverse scrapers), and a high Quina Index (IQ) (reflecting the usually large number of scrapers which exhibit Quina retouch); and the Ferrassie Mousterian, which has a much higher IL, IFs and Ilam, and much lower IC than the Quina subtype. The second principal assemblage group exhibits two subgroups with essential IRs of between 22 and 37% and variable amounts of Levallois, faceting, and blades. In this case, the major difference between the two subgroups is the percentage of bifaces: the Typical Mousterian, which has few or no bifaces, and the Mousterian of Acheulian Tradition, Type B (MTA-B), which has some bifaces, though fewer and usually smaller and less well-made than is true for the MTA-A, and which has relatively more backed knives and sometimes an elevated Ilam; and the Denticulate Mousterian, with a large number of denticulates and rare scrapers, bifaces, and backed knives. Other Mousterian groups have been defined since this original formulation, mostly in regions outside of France (see Bordes 1981).

3. That lithic materials are reworked is clearly demonstrated by examples of tools with double patina (Semonov 1970:10) and this effect is clearly not limited to the Middle Paleolithic. Similar patterns of typological changes that appear to reflect reduction have been observed in Middle Paleolithic assemblages from France and the Near East (Dibble 1989; Dibble and Holdaway, in press), Spain (Barton 1988), and southern Africa (Kuman 1989). It should also be mentioned that studies of bone retouchers uncovered during the recent excavations at La Quina show patterns that are consistent with the scraper reduction model (Chase, in press). However, conflicting interpretations have also been reported, although many of these are due largely to misapplication of measurement technique or a misunderstanding of the predicted morphology (see, for example, Close, in press; Dibble, in press b; Goren-Inbar 1989; Panabières 1989). Microwear studies have also produced results that are consistent with the scraper reduction model, in that specific scraper types do not seem to be associated with different functions (Beyries 1984, 1988; Anderson-Gerfaud, in press).

4. The raw counts for this test were obtained by calculating the relative heights of the bars in the histogram showing the total counts in figure 15 of Bordes and de Sonneville-Bordes (1970). However, there is a discrepancy in the frequencies reflected by the relative heights of the histogram bars in this figure (representing the total) with the frequencies obtained by summing the distributions of the individual assemblage groups in their figure.

5. This situation is paralleled in the Levantine Near East (Israel and Lebanon), where the so-called Late Acheulian (with high proportions of handaxes) in open-air contexts appears to have much higher Levallois proportions than in cave contexts; and where the heavily reduced, scraper dominated Yabrudian industries, with a significantly higher percentage of retouched pieces (Jelinek 1982b), occur only in shelter situations (Bar-Yosef 1980:110).

6. Increasing typological complexity has also correlated with distance to raw material sources in the Negev (Marks 1988, and comment following Dibble 1989:195), but a more detailed look at typological patterning among Levantine Mousterian assemblages (Marks, this volume), finds that these patterns do not hold up. It is possible that the uniform abundance of raw material in the Levant (and Northern France, as well) may be imposing far fewer constraints on lithic use, resulting in less intra-regional variability than is apparent in, for example, the Perigord, where raw material sources are more localized. It is also possible that in the Levant, fundamentally different behavioral patterns may be affecting these later assemblages and, in fact, they do appear to be quite distinct from earlier industries (Bar-Yosef 1987).

7. In the Levant, it may be that the most important climatic variable is aridity. Here, there is evidence that the heavily reduced, *racloir*-oriented Yabrudian is associated with "extreme interpluvial/interglacial" conditions; the Acheulian with more moderate conditions; and the Amudian and Early Levantine Mousterian with "more markedly pluvial/glacial conditions" (Jelinek 1982a:72). Dry phases would generate tendencies for settlements to contract around better watered coastal Mediterranean habitants. Wetter refugia would become attractive, especially in a region that has experienced episodic encroachments from surrounding arid steppe and desert belts. In these regions, then, it is precipitation, more than temperature, that would be the controlling variable (see Higgs 1968:149-153) in affecting the extent of human population mobility. But again, less mobility is associated with more intensive use of lithic material. Bordes (1953:233) also pointed out that water availability would influence relative sedentariness in the Maghreb, with similar consequences on Middle Paleolithic assemblages. These patterns follow what has been observed about seasonal factors affecting !Kung San settlements in the Kalahari, with dry season aggregations around permanent waterholes (Lee 1972).

8. The late glacial Magdalenian of Southwest Germany provides an analogous case of differential site location among penecontemporanous and seasonally complementary occurrences, also tied with ungulate behavioral differences (Weniger 1987:298-299).

9. Beyond Western Europe, there does seem to be a certain degree of regional patterning (see Rolland and Dibble 1990) and it is likely that some of it may be stylistic in nature, at least in the sense called isochrestic by Sackett (1982b, 1986). That these, or other intra-regional variants, represent distinct cultural traditions seems unlikely, however. First, so much of the typological and technological variability can be accounted for by the factors discussed above, specifically, raw material and lithic

reduction intensity. In fact, some other industrial patterns are almost identical to those seen in Western Europe (Dibble, in press c), which suggests that factors more fundamental than arbitrary cultural choices are responsible. Second, the level of local group fluidity, home-range flexibility, and mobility requirements, suggested by the low density of sites, deposits, and living floor sizes and patterns (Mellars 1973; Simek 1987), probably indicates that these populations had not attained the socio-demographic density and structure threshold that would allow the coexistence of several "nucleated," identity-conscious communities and the formation of mating networks (Wobst 1976; see also Whallon 1989). Further, there is virtually no evidence of the regular use of iconological stylistic markers that could symbolize those identities (Chase and Dibble 1987). Thus, being theoretically improbable and difficult to confirm independently, such cultural interpretations should be considered only after other, more fundamental, alternatives have been completely ruled out.

REFERENCES CITED

Albrecht, G.
    1979   *Magdalenien-Inventare von Petersfels*. AV 6. Tübingen: Institut für Urgeschichte, Universität zu Tübingen.

Anderson-Gerfaud, P.
    in press   Aspects of Behaviour in the Middle Paleolithic: Functional Analysis of Stone Tools from Southwest France. In *The Emergence of Modern Humans: An Archaeological Perspective*, ed. P. Mellars. Edinburgh: Edinburgh University Press.

Audouze, F., and Leroi-Gourhan, A.
    1981   France: A Continental Insularity. *WA* 1:170-189.

Bahn, P.
    1977   Seasonal Migrations in Southwestern France during the Late Glacial Period. *JAS* 4:245-257.

Barton, C.
    1988   *Lithic Variability and Middle Paleolithic Behavior*. BAR International Series 408. Oxford: BAR.

Bar-Yosef, O.
    1980   Prehistory of the Levant. *ARA* 9:101-133.
    1987   Pleistocene Connexions between Africa and Southwest Asia: An Archaeological Perspective. *The African Archaeological Review* 5:29-38.
    1988   The Date of South-West Asian Neandertals. Pp. 31-38 in *L'homme de Néandertal*, ed. M. Otte. Vol. 3: *L'anatomie*, ed. E. Trinkaus. ERAUL 30. Liège: Université de Liège.
    1989   Geochronology of the Levantine Middle Palaeolithic. Pp. 589-610 in *The Human Revolution: Behavioural and Biological Perspectives on the Origins of Modern Humans*, eds. P. Mellars and C. Stringer. Edinburgh: Edinburgh University Press.

Bar-Yosef, O., and Goldberg, P.
    1988   An Outline of the Chronology of the Middle Palaeolithic in the Levant. Pp. 13-21 in *L'homme de Néandertal*, ed. M. Otte. Vol. 2: *L'environnement*, ed. H. Laville. ERAUL 29. Liège: Université de Liège.

Beyries, S.
    1984   Approche fonctionelle de la variabilité des faciès du Moustérien. Thesis, Université de Paris.
    1988   Functional Variability of Lithic Sets in the Middle Palaeolithic. Pp. 213-224 in *Upper Pleistocene Prehistory of Western Eurasia*, eds. H. Dibble and A. Montet-White. Philadelphia: University Museum, University of Pennsylvania.

Binford, L. R., and Binford, S.
    1966   A Preliminary Analysis of Functional Variability in the Mousterian and Upper Paleolithic. *AA* 68:236-295.

Binford, S., and Binford, L. R.
    1969   Stone Tools and Human Behavior. *SciAm* 220(4):70-72, 77-82, 84.

Bordes, F.
    1947   Etude comparative des différentes techniques de taille du silex et des roches dures. *L'Anthropologie* 51:1-29.
    1950   Principes d'une méthode d'étude des techniques de débitage et de la typologie du Paléolithique ancien et moyen. *L'Anthropologie* 54:19-34.
    1952   Stratigraphie du loess et évolution des industries paléolithiques dans l'ouest du bassin de Paris, II: Évolution des indus-

tries paléolithiques. *L'Anthropologie* 56:405-452.

1953   Essai de classification des industries "moustériennes." *BSPF* 50:457-466.

1954   L'Evolution buissonnante des industries en Europe occidentale. Considerations théoriques sur le Paléolithique ancien et moyen. *L'Anthropologie* 54:393-420.

1961a   *Typologie du Paléolithique ancien et moyen.* Paris: CNRS.

1961b   Mousterian Cultures in France. *Science* 134:803-810.

1962   Le Moustérien à denticulés. *Ameolōski Vestnik* 13:43-49.

1967   Considérations sur la typologie et les techniques dans le Paléolithique. *Quartär* 18:25-55.

1978   Typological Variability in the Mousterian Layers at Pech de l'Azé I, II and IV. *JAR* 34:181-193.

1981   Vingt-cinq ans après: le complexe mousterién revisité. *BSPF* 78:77-87.

Bordes, F., and Bourgon, M.

1951   Le complexe moustérien: Moustérien, Levalloisien et Tayacien. *L'Anthropologie* 55:1-23.

Bordes, F., and Sonneville-Bordes, D. de

1970   The Significance of Variability in Paleolithic Assemblages. *WA* 2:61-73.

Bosinski, G.

1967   *Die Mittelpaläolithischen Funde im Westlichen Mitteleuropa.* Fundamenta A4. Cologne: Hermann Böhlau.

1982   The Transition Lower/Middle Palaeolithic in Northwestern Germany. Pp. 165-175 in *The Transition From Lower to Middle Palaeolithic and the Origin of Modern Man*, ed. A. Ronen. BAR International Series 151. Oxford: BAR.

Bouchud, J.

1953   Le mandibule du renne. *Mammalia* 18:27-49.

1966   *Essai sur le renne et la climatologie du Paléolithique moyen et supérieur.* Perigueux: Magne.

Bourgon, M.

1957   *Les industries moustériennes et prémoustériennes du Périgord.* AIPH Mémoire 27. Paris: Masson.

Breuil, H.

1932   Les industries à éclats du Paléolithique ancien, I: Le Clactonien. *Préhistoire* 1:125-190.

Breuil, H., and Lantier, R.

1959   *The Men of the Old Stone Age.* New York: St. Martin's Press.

Callow, P.

1988   Chronostratigraphy and Ecology of Two Middle and Upper Pleistocene Sites (Jersey, C.I.). Pp. 17-24 in *Cultures et industries lithiques en milieu loessique*, ed. A. Tuffreau. Revue Archéologique de Picardie 1-2.

Callow, P., and Webb, R. E.

1977   Structure in the S. W. French Mousterian. Pp. 69-76 in *Computer Applications in Archaeology 1977.* Proceedings of the Annual Conference at the Computer Centre, University of Birmingham.

1981   The Application of Multivariate Statistical Techniques to Middle Palaeolithic Assemblages from Southwestern France. *Revue d'Archéometrie* 5:129-138.

Chard, C.

1969   Archaeology in the Soviet Union. *Science* 163:774-779.

Chase, P. G.

in press   "Tool-making Tools": Their Implications for Middle Paleolithic Technology, Cognition and Motor Patterns. *CA*.

Chase, P. G., and Dibble, H.

1987   Middle Paleolithic Symbolism: A Review of Current Evidence and Interpretations. *JAA* 6:263-296.

Clark, J. D.

1958a   Certain Industries of Notched and Strangulated Scrapers in Rhodesia, Their Time Range and Possible Use. *SAAB* 13:56-66.

1958b   Some Stone Working Tools in Southern Africa. *SAAB* 13:144-151.

1970   *The Prehistory of Africa.* Praeger: New York.

Close, A.

in press   On the Validity of Middle Paleolithic Tool Types: A Test Case from the Eastern Sahara. *JFA*.

Combier, J.

1962 Chronologie et systématique du Moustérien occidental: données et conceptions nouvelles. *Atti del VI Congresso Internazionale delle Scienze Preistoriche e Protostoriche* (Rome) 1:77-96.

1967 *Le Paléolithique de l'Ardèche dans son cadre paléoclimatique.* MIPUB 4. Bordeaux: Delmas.

Commont, V.

1913 Le Moustérien ancien à Saint-Acheul et Montières. *Congrès Préhistorique de France. Compte Rendu de la Huitième Session—Angoulême.* Paris: Bureaux de la Société Préhistorique Française.

Conaty, G.

1987 Comment on Hayden's Resource Models of Inter-Assemblage Variability. *Lithic Technology* 16(2-3):59-61.

Cornwall, J.

1968 Milankovitch and After: Some Reflections on Pleistocene Dating. Pp. 129-132 in *La préhistoire, problèmes et tendences*, ed. D. de Sonneville-Bordes. Paris: CNRS.

Crabtree, D.

1977 The Obtuse Angle as a Functional Edge. Pp. 38-51 in *Experimental Archaeology*, ed. D. Ingersoll. New York: Columbia University Press.

Dibble, H.

1984a Interpreting Typological Variation of Middle Paleolithic Scrapers: Function, Style, or Sequence of Reduction? *JFA* 11:431-436.

1984b The Mousterian Industry from Bisitun Cave (Iran). *Paléorient* 10:23-34.

1985 Raw Material Variability in Levallois Flake Manufacture. *CA* 26:391-393.

1987a Comparaisons des séquences de réduction des outils moustériens de la France et du Proche-Orient. *L'Anthropologie* 19:189-196.

1987b The Interpretation of Middle Paleolithic Scraper Morphology. *AmAnt* 52:109-117.

1989 The Implications of Stone Tool Types for the Presence of Language during the Middle Paleolithic. Pp. 415-432 in *The Human Revolution: Behavioural and Biological Perspectives on the Origins of Modern Humans*, eds. P. Mellars and C. Stringer. Edinburgh: Edinburgh University Press.

in press a Local Raw Material Exploitation and its Effects on Lower and Middle Paleolithic Assemblage Variability. In *Raw Material Exploitation among Prehistoric Hunter-Gathers*, eds. A. Montet-White and S. Holen. Lawrence: University of Kansas Press.

in press b Reply to Close. *JFA*.

in press c Les industries de type Charentien du Proche-Orient: leurs relations avec les Moustériens de type Quina et Ferrassie en France. *Les Moustériens Charentiens.* Actes du Colloque de Brive.

Dibble, H., and Holdaway, S.

in press The Middle Paleolithic of Warwasi Rockshelter and its Relationship to the Zagros and Levantine Mousterian. *L'Anthropologie.*

Doran, J., and Hodson, F.

1966 A Digital Computer Analysis of Palaeolithic Flint Assemblages. *Nature* 210:688-689.

Drury, W.

1975 The Ecology of the Human Occupation at the Abri Pataud. Pp. 187-190 in *Excavation of the Abri Pataud, Les Eyzies (Dordogne)*, ed. H. Movius. ASPR Bulletin 30. Cambridge, MA: Peabody Museum Press.

Dunnell, R.

1978 Style and Function: A Fundamental Dichotomy. *AmAnt* 43:192-202.

Fish, P.

1981 Beyond Tools: Middle Paleolithic Debitage Analysis and Cultural Inference. *JAR* 38:374-386.

Freeman, L.

1966 The Nature of Mousterian Facies in Cantabrian Spain. *AA* 68:230-237.

1981 The Fat of the Land: Notes on Paleolithic Diet in Iberia. Pp. 104-165 in *Omnivorous Primates*, eds. R. Harding and G. Teleki. New York: Columbia University Press.

Frison, G.
1968   A Functional Analysis of Certain Chipped Stone Tools. *AmAnt* 33:149-155.

Gábori, M.
1976   *Les civilisations du Paléolithiqe moyen entre les Alpes et l'Oural.* Budapest: Akadémiai Kiadó.

Gábori-Csánk, V.
1968   *La station du Paléolithique moyen d'Erd-Hongrie.* Budapest: Akadémiai Kiadó.

Geneste, J.-M.
1985   Analyse lithique des industries moustériennes du Périgord: une approche technologique du comportement des groupes humains au Paléolithique moyen. Thesis, Université de Bordeaux.

Girard-Farizy, C., and Leclerc, J.
1981   Les grandes chasses de Mauran. *La Recherche* 27:1294-1295.

Goren-Inbar, N.
1989   Typological Characteristics of the Mousterian Assemblage from Biq'at Quneitra. Pp. 125-146 in *Investigations in South Levantine Prehistory*, eds. O. Bar-Yosef and B. Vandermeersch. BAR International Series 497. Oxford: BAR.

Gould, R.
1968   Living Archaeology: The Ngatatjara of Western Australia. *SJA* 24:101-22.

Guiot, J.; Pons, A.; de Beaulieu, J.; and Reille, M.
1989   A 140,000-Year-Continental Climate Reconstruction from Two European Pollen Records. *Nature* 338:309-313.

Guthrie, D.
1986   Mosaics, Allelochemics and Nutrients. Pp. 259-298 in *Quaternary Extinctions: A Prehistoric Revolution*, eds. P. A. Martin and R. G. Klein. Tucson: University of Arizona Press.

Heinzelin, J. de
1984   Essai sur archéologie et régions naturelles. Pp. 101-106 in *Peuples Chasseurs de La Belgique Préhistorique dans leur cadre naturel*, eds. D. Cahen and P. Haesaerts. Brussels: Patrimoine de l'Institut Royal des Sciences Naturelles de Belgique.

Higgs, E.
1968   The Stone Industries of Greece. Pp. 215-222 in *La préhistoire, problèmes et tendances*, ed. D. de Sonneville-Bordes. Paris: CNRS.

Hours, F.; Copeland, L.; and Aurenche, O.
1973   Les industries paléolithiques du Proche-Orient, essai de correlation. *L'Anthropologie* 77:229-280, 437-496.

Hublin, J.
1988   Les présapiens européens. Pp. 75-80 in *L'homme de Néandertal*, ed. M. Otte. Vol. 3: *L'anatomie*, ed. E. Trinkaus. ERAUL 30. Liège: Université de Liège.

Isaac, G.
1972   Early Phases of Human Behaviour: Models in Lower Palaeolithic Archaeology. Pp. 167-200 in *Models in Archaeology*, ed. D. Clarke. London: Methuen.

Jelinek, A.
1976   Form, Function and Style in Lithic Analysis. Pp. 19-33 in *Cultural Change and Continuity: Essays in Honor of James Bennett Griffin*, ed. C. E. Cleland. New York: Academic Press.

1982a   Tabun Cave and Paleolithic Man in the Levant. *Science* 216:1369-1375.

1982b   The Middle Paleolithic in the Southern Levant, with Comments on the Appearance of Modern *Homo sapiens*. Pp. 57-101 in *The Transition from the Lower to Middle Paleolithic and the Origin of Modern Man*, ed. A. Ronen. BAR International Series 151. Oxford: BAR.

1988   Technology, Typology, and Culture in the Middle Paleolithic. Pp. 199-212 in *Upper Pleistocene Prehistory of Western Eurasia*, ed. H. Dibble and A. Montet-White. Philadelphia: University Museum, University of Pennsylvania.

Jelinck, A. J.; Debénath, A.; and Dibble, H.
1989   A Preliminary Report on Evidence Related to the Interpretation of Economic and Social Activities of Neandertals at the site of La Quina (Charente), France. Pp. 99-106 in *L'homme de Néandertal*, ed. M. Otte. Vol. 6: *La subsistance*. ERAUL 33. Liège: Université de Liège.

Kantman, S.
1970   Essai d'une méthode d'étude des "den-
        ticulés" moustériens par descrimination
        des variables morpho-fonctionnelles.
        Quaternaria 13:281-294.

Klein, R.
1969   The Mousterian of European Russia.
        PPS 35:77-111.

Kuman, K.
1989   Florisbad and =GI: The Contribution of
        Open-air Sites to Study of the Middle
        Stone Age in Southern Africa. Ph.D.
        dissertation, University of Pennsylvania.

Laville, H.
1973   The Relative Position of Mousterian
        Industries in the Climatic Chronology
        of the Early Würm in the Perigord. *WA*
        4:323-329.
1982   On the Transition from 'Lower' to 'Mid-
        dle' Palaeolithic in South-West France.
        Pp. 131-135 in *The Transition from Lower
        to Middle Palaeolithic and the Origin of Mod-
        ern Man*, ed. A. Ronen. BAR Interna-
        tional Series 151. Oxford: BAR.
1988   Recent Developments on the Chrono-
        stratigraphy of the Paleolithic in the
        Perigord. Pp. 147-160 in *Upper Pleis-
        tocene Prehistory of Western Eurasia*, eds.
        H. Dibble and A. Montet-White.
        Philadelphia: University Museum, Uni-
        versity of Pennsylvania.

Laville, H.; Rigaud, J.-P.; and Sackett, J.
1980   *Rock Shelters of the Perigord: Geological
        Stratigraphy and Archaeological Succession.*
        New York: Academic Press.

Laville, H.; Turon, J.-L.; Texier, J.-P.; Raynal, J.-P.;
        Delpech, F.; Paquereau, M.-M.; Prat, F.; and
        Debénath, A.
1983   Histoire paléoclimatique de l'Aquitaine
        et du Golfe de Gascogne au Pléistocène
        supérieur depuis le dernier interglaciaire.
        Pp. 151-161 in *Paléoclimats: actes du Col-
        loque de l'AGSO* (Bordeaux, May). CQ
        no. hors série; BIGBA 34. Paris: CNRS.

Le Tensorer, J.-M.
1978   Le Moustérien type Quina et son évo-
        lution dans le sud de la France. *BSPF*
        75:141-149.

Lee, R.
1972   The !Kung Bushmen of Botswana. Pp.
        327-368 in *Hunters and Gatherers Today*,
        ed. M. Biecchieri. New York: Holt,
        Rinehart and Winston.

Lenoir, M.
1986   Un mode d'obtention de la retouche
        "Quina" dans le Moustérien de
        Combe-Grenal (Domme, Dordogne).
        *Bulletin de la Société Anthropologique du
        Sud-Ouest* 21:153-160.

Leroi-Gourhan, A.
1956   La galerie moustérienne de la Grotte du
        Renne (Arcy-sur-Cure, Yonne). *Con-
        grès Préhistorique de France*:1-16.
1966   *La préhistoire*. Paris: Presses Universi-
        taires de France.

Lumley, H. de
1972   *La grotte moustérienne de l'Hortus (Val
        Flaunès, Herault).* EQ 1. Marseilles: LPHP.

Marks, A.
1983   The Middle to Upper Paleolithic Tran-
        sition in the Levant. Pp. 51-98 in
        Advances in World Archaeology, Vol 2,
        eds. F. Wendorf and A. Close. New
        York: Academic Press.
1988   The Curation of Stone Tools during the
        Upper Pleistocene: A View from the
        Central Negev, Israel. Pp. 275-286 in
        *Upper Pleistocene Prehistory of Western
        Eurasia*, eds. H. Dibble and A. Montet-
        White. Philadelphia: University Muse-
        um, University of Pennsylvania.

Meignen, L.
1988   Un exemple de comportement tech-
        nologique différentiel selon les matières
        premières: Marillac, couches 9 et 10.
        Pp. 71-80 in *L'homme de Néandertal*, ed.
        M. Otte. Vol. 4: *La technique*, eds. L.
        Binford and J.-P. Rigaud. ERAUL 31.
        Liège: Université de Liège.

Mellars, P.
1965   Sequence and Development of the
        Mousterian Traditions in Southwestern
        France. *Nature* 205:626-627.
1969   The Chronology of Mousterian Indus-
        tries in the Perigord Region. *PPS*
        35:134-171.

1973   The Character of the Middle-Upper Palaeolithic Transition in South-West France. Pp. 255-276 in *The Explanation of Culture Change*, ed. C. Renfrew. London: Duckworth.

1985   The Ecological Basis of Social Complexity in the Upper Paleolithic of Southwestern France. Pp. 271-297 in *Prehistoric Hunter-Gatherers: The Emergence of Cultural Complexity*, eds. T. D. Price and J. Brown. Orlando: Academic Press.

1989a   Technological Changes at the Middle-Upper Palaeolithic Transition: Economic, Social and Cognitive Perspectives. Pp. 338-365 in *The Human Revolution: Behavioural and Biological Perspectives on the Origins of Modern Humans*, eds. P. Mellars and C. Stringer. Edinburgh: Edinburgh University Press.

1989b   Major Issues in the Emergence of Modern Humans. *CA* 30:349-385.

Mortillet, G. de
1883   *Le préhistorique: antiquité de l'homme.* Paris: C. Reinwald.

Movius, H.
1949   *The Lower Palaeolithic Cultures of Southern and Eastern Asia*. Transactions of the American Philosophical Society. Philadelphia: American Philosophical Society.

1953   *The Mousterian Cave of Teshik-Tash, Southeastern Uzbekistan, Central Asia.* ASPR Bulletin 17. Cambridge, MA: Peabody Museum Press.

Müller-Beck, H.
1988   The Ecosystem of the "Middle Paleolithic" (Late Lower Paleolithic) in the Upper Danube Region: A Stepping-Stone to the Upper Paleolithic. Pp. 233-254 in *Upper Pleistocene Prehistory of Western Eurasia*, eds. H. Dibble and A. Montet-White. Philadelphia: University Museum, University of Pennsylvania.

Mulvaney, D.
1969   *The Prehistory of Australia*. London: Thames and Hudson.

Munday, F.
1976   The Avdat/Aqev Area: Its Habitat and Geographic Setting. Pp. 9-24 in *Prehistory and Paleoenvironments in the Central Negev, Israel*, Vol. 1, ed. A. E. Marks. Dallas: Southern Methodist University Press.

Panabières, F.
1989   Etude techno-typologique des racloirs de la couche 35 de Combe-Grenal. Thesis, Université de Bordeaux.

Peyrony, D.
1921   Le Moustérien—ses faciès. Pp. 497-497 in *Association Française pour l'Avancement des Sciences, 44e session.* (Strasbourg, 1920).

1933   Les industries aurignaciennes dans le bassin de la Vézère. Aurignacien et Périgordien. *BSPF* 3:543-559.

1934   La Ferrassie: Moustérien, Périgordien, Aurignacian. *Préhistoire* 3:1-92.

1936   Le Périgordien et l'Aurignacien (nouvelles observations). *BSPF* 33:616-619.

Piperno, M.
1972   The Monte Peglia Lithic Industry. *Quaternaria* 16:53-65.

Ranov, V., and Davis, R.
1979   Toward a New Outline of the Soviet Central Asian Palaeolithic. *CA* 20:249-262.

Rightmire, G.
1984   *Homo sapiens* in Sub-Saharan Africa. Pp. 295-325 in *The Origins of Modern Humans: A World Survey of the Fossil Evidence*, eds. F. H. Smith and F. Spencer. New York: Alan R. Liss.

Roebroeks, W.
1986   Archaeology and Middle Pleistocene Stratigraphy: The Case of Maastricht-Belvédère (The Netherlands). Pp. 81-88 in *Chronostratigraphie et faciès culturels du Paléolithique inférieur et moyen dans l'Europe du nord-ouest*, eds. A. Tuffreau and J. Sommé. *BAFEQ* Supplément 26. Dijon: AFEQ.

Roebroeks, W.; Kolen, J.; and Rensink, E.
1988   Planning Depth, Anticipation and the Organization of Middle Paleolithic Technology: The "Archaic Natives" meet Eve's Descendants. *Helinium* 28:17-34.

Rolland, N.

1975   The Antecedents and Emergence of the Middle Paleolithic Industrial Complex in Western Europe. Thesis, Cambridge University.

1977   New Aspects of Middle Palaeolithic Variability in Western Europe. *Nature* 266:251-252.

1981   The Interpretation of Middle Paleolithic Variability. *Man* 16:15-42.

1988   Observations on Some Middle Paleolithic Time Series in Southern France. Pp. 161-180 in *Upper Pleistocene Prehistory of Western Eurasia*, eds. H. Dibble and A. Montet-White. Philadelphia: University Museum, University of Pennsylvania.

in press   Middle Paleolithic Socio-Economic Formations in Western Eurasia: An Exploratory Survey. In *The Emergence of Modern Humans: An Archaeological Perspective*, ed. P. Mellars. Edinburgh: Edinburgh University Press.

Rolland, N., and Dibble, H.

1990   A New Synthesis of Middle Paleolithic Assemblage Variability. *AmAnt* 55:480-499.

Ronen, A., ed.

1982   *The Transition from Lower to Middle Palaeolithic and the Origin of Modern Man: A Symposium*. BAR International Series 151. Oxford: BAR.

Sackett, J.

1982a   From de Mortillet to Bordes. A Century of French Paleolithic Research. Pp. 85-89 in *Towards a History of Archaeology*, ed. G. Daniel. London: Thames & Hudson.

1982b   Approaches to Style in Lithic Archaeology. *JAA* 1:59-112.

1986   Isochrestism and Style: A Clarification. *JAA* 5:266-277.

Sampson, C. G.

1974   *The Stone Age Archaeology of Southern Africa*. New York: Academic Press.

Schwarcz, H., and Blackwell, B.

1983 ^{230}Th/^{234}U Age of a Mousterian Site in France. *Nature* 301:236-237.

Semenov, S. A.

1964   *Prehistoric Technology*. London: Cory, Adams and Mackay.

1970   The Forms and Functions of the Oldest Tools. *Quartär* 21:1-20.

Shott, M.

1989   On Tool-Class Use Lives and the Formation of Archaeological Assemblages. *AmAnt* 54:9-30.

Siegel, P.

1985   Edge Angle as a Functional Indicator: A Test. *Lithic Technology* 14:90-94.

Simek, J.

1987   Spatial Order and Behavioural Change in the French Palaeolithic. *Antiquity* 61:25-40.

Skinner, J.

1965   The Flake Industries of Southwest Asia: A Typological Study. Ph.D dissertation, Columbia University. Ann Arbor, MI: University Microfilms.

Spiess, A. E.

1979   *Reindeer and Caribou Hunters: An Archaeological Study*. New York: Academic Press.

Stringer, C.

1988   The Dates of Eden. *Nature* 331:565-566.

Taschini, M., and Bietti, A.

1979   L'industrie lithique de Grota Guattari au Mont Circe (Latium): definition culturelle, typologique et chronologique du Pontinien. *Quaternaria* 21:179-247.

Tavoso, A.

1984   Réflexions sur l'économie des matières premières au Moustérien. *BSPF* 81:79-82.

Texier, J.-P.

in press   Bilan sur les Paleoenvironments des Moustériens d'Europe Occidentale d'apres les données de la géologie. In *Les Moustériens Charentiens*. Actes du Colloque de Brive.

Tuffreau, A.

1982   The Transition Lower/Middle Palaeolithic in Northern France. Pp. 137-149 in *The Transition from Lower to Mid-*

dle Palaeolithic and the Origin of Modern Man, ed. A. Ronen. BAR International Series 151. Oxford: BAR.

1987   Le Paléolithique inférieur et moyen du Nord de la France (Nord Pas-de-Calais, Picardie) dans son cadre stratigraphie. Thesis, University of Lille.

Tuffreau, A.; Antoine, P.; Cordy, J.-M.; Fagnart, J.-P.; Moigne, A.-M.; Sommé, J.; and Van Vliet-Lanoe, B.
1989   *Livret-Guide de l'excursion dans la vallée de la Somme*. Colloquium: l'Acheuléen dans l'ouest de l'europe (Rome). CNRS.

Tuffreau, A., and Sommé, J.
1988   *Le gisement paléolithique moyen de Biache-Saint-Vaast*, Vol. 1. MSPF 21.

Ulrix-Closset, M.
1975   *Le Paléolithique moyen dans le bassin Mossan en Belgique*. Éditions Universa. B-9200 Wetteren. Université de Liège.

Valladas, H.; Chadelle, J.; Geneste, J.; Joron, J.; Meignen, L.; and Texier, P.
1987   Datations par la thermoluminescence de gisements moustériens du Sud de la France. *L'Anthropologie* 91:211-226.

Valladas, H.; Joron, J.; Valladas, G.; Arensburg, B.; Bar-Yosef, O.; Belfer-Cohen, A.; Goldberg, P.; Laville, H.; Meignen, L.; Rak, Y.; Tchernov, E.; Tillier, A.; and Vandermeersch, B.
1987   Thermoluminescence Dates for the Neanderthal Burial Site at Kebara in Israel. *Nature* 330:159-160.

Valladas, H.; Reyss, J.; Joron, J.; Valladas, G.; Bar-Yosef, O.; and Vandermeersch, B.
1988   Thermoluminescence Dating of Mousterian "Proto-Cro-Magnon" Remains from Israel and the Origin of Modern Man. *Nature* 331:614-616.

Valoch, K.
1982   The Lower/Middle Palaeolithic Transition in Czechoslovakia. Pp. 193-201 in *The Transition from Lower to Middle Palaeolithic and the Origin of Modern Man*, ed. A. Ronen. BAR International Series 151. Oxford: BAR.

Verjux, C.
1988   Les denticulés moustériens. Pp. 197-204 in *L'homme de Néandertal*, ed. M. Otte. Vol. 4: *La technique*, eds. L. Binford and J.-P. Rigaud. ERAUL 31. Liège: Université de Liège.

Vertes, L.
1964   *Tata—eine Mittelpalaolithische travertin-siedlung in ungarin*. Budapest: Akadémiai Kiadó.

1965   Typology of the Buda Industry: A Pebble-Tool Industry from the Hungarian Lower Palaeolithic. *Quaternaria* 7:185-195.

Veyrier, M.; Beaux, E.; and Combier, J.
1951   Grotte des Nerons, à Soyons (Ardèche): les fouilles de 1950—leurs enseignements. *BSPF* 48:70-78.

Weniger, G.
1987   Magdalenian Settlement Pattern and Subsistence in Central Europe. The Southwestern and Central German Cases. Pp. 201-215 in *The Pleistocene Old World Perspectives*, ed. O. Soffer. New York: Plenum Press.

Whallon, R.
1989   Elements of Cultural Change in the Later Palaeolithic. Pp. 433-454 in *The Human Revolution: Behavioural and Biological Perspectives on the Origins of Modern Humans*, eds. P. Mellars and C. Stringer. Edinburgh: Edinburgh University Press.

White, J.
1969   Ston naip bilong tumbuna: The Living Stone Age in New Guinea. Pp. 511-516 in *La préhistoire: problèmes et tendances*, ed. D. de Sonneville-Bordes. Paris: CNRS.

White, R.
1982   Rethinking the Middle-Upper Paleolithic Transition. *CA* 23(2):169-192.

Wilmsen, E.
1968   Functional Analysis of Flaked Stone Artifacts. *AmAnt* 33:156-161.

Wobst, H.
1976   Locational Relationships in Palaeolithic Society. *JHE* 5:49-58.

Wolliard, G.
    1978   Grande Pile Peat Bog: A Continuous
             Pollen Record for the Last 140,000
             Years. *QR* 9:1-21.

Zeuner, F. E.
    1963   *History of Domesticated Animals.* New
             York: Harper & Row.

II

Technological Change in the Mousterian of Southwest France

Paul Mellars

INTRODUCTION

As Dibble and Rolland have pointed out (this volume) one of the most notable features of the Middle Paleolithic is the remarkably long span of time which it covers. Even if we restrict the notion of the "Mousterian" in its narrowly defined sense to the earlier part of the last glaciation, this still leaves a total time-range of approximately 80,000 years—i.e., extending from the start of the last glacial cooling at around 115,000 B.P. to the appearance of formally Upper Paleolithic technologies at ca. 35-40,000 B.P. At a conservative estimate, this period covers almost three times the time-span represented by the entire sequence of Upper Paleolithic industries within both the eastern and western zones of Europe.

The second notable feature is the remarkable scale and rapidity of the climatic and ecological fluctuations which took place during this period. From the ocean-core records alone it is clear that the earlier stages of the last glacial sequence were characterized by a highly complex, oscillatory pattern of climatic changes, ranging from almost fully temperate conditions during isotope stages 5c and 5a, to extreme full glacial conditions during isotope stage 4 (Shackleton and Opdyke 1973; Beaulieu and Reille 1984). In the northern periglacial fringes of Europe, these changes were reflected in shifts from predominantly dense deciduous woodland to almost barren, arctic tundra or steppe (Van der Hammen et al. 1967; Woillard and Mook 1982; Guiot et al. 1989). Commensurate changes in the character and composition of the contemporary animal populations were associated, directly and inevitably, with these climatic and vegetational shifts (Bordes and Prat 1965; Guadelli 1987; Delpech 1988).

The central point to be emphasized in the present context is that environmental changes of this scale and intensity can hardly have taken place without some kind of radical "adaptations" on the part of the contemporaneous human populations, and without some reflection of these changes in the character and composition of the associated stone tool technologies. Assessed in *a priori* terms, of course, these changes could have assumed a variety of different forms. Shifts in subsistence patterns could have necessitated changes in either the specific forms of stone tools, or the relative frequencies with which different tools were used (and discarded) on the occupation sites. Shifts in settlement patterns could have necessitated similar changes, perhaps accompanied (as suggested by Dibble and Rolland, this volume) by variations in the rates at which tools were successively reworked or resharpened in the course of prolonged use. Variations in the character or accessibility of local raw material supplies could have impinged on all aspects of technology, ranging from the choice of different core-reduction strategies, to the precise forms of the tools produced (Geneste 1985, 1988; Fish 1981; Turq, in press). Finally, and perhaps most significantly, these dramatic ecological changes could well have led—in at least some contexts—to major shifts in the ecological and geographical ranges occupied by different human populations, and accordingly to episodes of apparent population replacement in the documented archaeological records in particular regions (Mellars 1969, 1985; David 1973).

The existence of major changes in stone-tool technology during the course of the Middle Paleolithic period is therefore not merely plausible, but in many ways predictable, or even inevitable, when seen in these terms. In many regions of the Old

World, the reality of these technological shifts is now accepted as a well documented feature of the archaeological record—as, for example, in the Middle East, in various parts of Africa, and in many parts of Central and Eastern Europe (Copeland 1975; Jelinek 1982; Marks, this volume; Bosinski 1967; Clark 1982, 1983). Only in the extreme western fringes of Europe has the recognition of time-related patterning in lithic technology proved to be an issue of vigorous and continuing debate (Laville et al. 1980:208-215).

The various arguments in favor of a well-defined chronological pattern within the Mousterian industries of southwestern France have been outlined in too many earlier publications to require detailed documentation here (Mellars 1965, 1969, 1986a, 1986b, 1988, etc.). The main point to recall is that these arguments have been applied specifically to three of the major industrial variants of the Mousterian as defined in the studies of François Bordes (i.e., the Ferrassie, Quina, and Mousterian of Acheulian Tradition [MTA] variants), which are generally recognized as the most distinctive and sharply characterized of Bordes' variants in a general typological and technological sense (Bordes 1981, 1984). The chronological arguments rest primarily on the documented stratigraphic positions of these industries within the total range of stratified sites. In this context, four observations are especially significant:

1. The sharp localization and total segregation of the three industrial variants in question within the exceptionally long and continuous Mousterian succession (55 distinct levels) at Combe Grenal (see Fig. 2.1);

2. The consistent tendency for MTA levels to be stratified clearly above levels of either Quina or Ferrassie Mousterian;

3. The *general* tendency for MTA levels to occur within the uppermost stratigraphic levels of Mousterian sequences—usually (in at least twelve documented cases) stratified directly beneath levels with early Upper Paleolithic industries;

4. The striking consistency of the technological and typological shifts documented within the various stratified sequences of Ferrassie and Quina Mousterian industries (see below).

By comparison with the clarity of the stratigraphic patterning exhibited by the Ferrassie, Quina, and MTA industries, the position of the various occurrences of "Denticulate" and "Typical" Mousterian assemblages is demonstrably more complex, and evidently cannot be accomodated within any simple

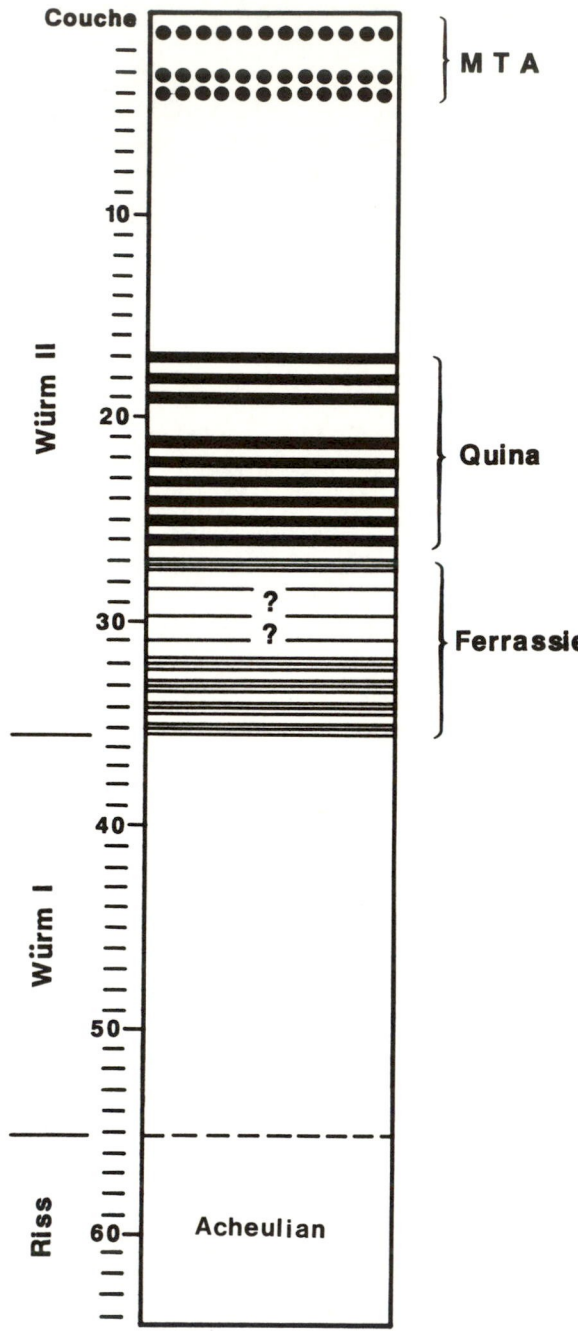

Figure 2.1   Stratigraphic distribution of Ferrassie, Quina, and Mousterian of Acheulian Tradition (MTA) industries at Combe Grenal (after Bordes and Prat 1965; Bordes 1972). The industries from Layers 28-30 were originally classified by Bordes (1955:428) as representing an "attenuated Ferrassie" variant.

linear developmental scheme (Mellars 1969:158-161). Nevertheless, the particular intepretative problems posed by these very poorly characterized variants of the Mousterian (cf. Bordes 1981:79; see below) should not be used to obscure the very much clearer chronological and stratigraphic patterns exhibited by the much more distinctive and sharply defined occurrences of the Ferrassie, Quina, and MTA industries.[1]

Potentially one of the most significant new contributions to understanding the general patterns of industrial variability within the Middle Paleolithic has been made by Rolland and Dibble, in their recent studies of potential effects of resharpening on the forms and relative frequencies of different retouched tool forms (Rolland 1977, 1981, 1988; Dibble 1983, 1984, 1987; Dibble and Rolland, this volume). In many respects, this represents a major breakthrough in some of the long debated issues of "cultural" versus "functional" interpretations of Middle Paleolithic variability. The main point to emphasize in the present context, however, is that these models are designed explicitly to account for variations in two specific aspects of the assemblages: on the one hand, the relative frequencies of *racloirs* versus notched and denticulated forms within the retouched tool component of the industries (Rolland 1977, 1981, 1988); and on the other hand, the varying frequencies of certain specific sub-types of *racloirs* (transverse, double, convergent, etc.) within the *racloir* category as a whole (Dibble 1983, 1984, 1987, etc.). In neither case are these models designed to account for the fundamental contrasts which separate the three major industrial variants under discussion here—i.e., the Ferrassie, Quina, and MTA variants. As Bordes repeatedly emphasized (1953, 1961, 1981, etc.), the distinction between the Ferrassie and Quina variants is based not purely on the "typological" features of the industries (though these play a role in his definitions, as discussed below) but rather on the fundamental contrasts in the basic techniques by which the primary flake blanks for tool production in the two industries were produced. In the case of the MTA, the definition is based almost entirely on two distinctive "type fossils" which are held to be specifically diagnostic of these industries—namely, typical cordiform handaxes, and typical (i.e., extensively retouched) backed knives (Bordes

1953:460-463; 1961:804-805; 1968:101-102; 1981:77-79; Bordes and de Sonneville-Bordes 1970:61-64). The recent "tool reduction" models of Dibble and Rolland are clearly not designed (and have never been claimed) to account for these specific aspects of industrial variation within the French Mousterian. As discussed further below, the tool reduction models may well have crucially important light to shed on the significance of some of the Denticulate and Typical Mousterian industries, and potentially on the relationships between some of these industries and those of the Ferrassie, Quina, and MTA groups. But it is important to bear in mind that these models have never been seen as a way of accounting for the specific technological and typological features which serve to differentiate between the Ferrassie, Quina, and MTA variants within the Bordes taxonomic scheme.

The last general point to emphasize here is that the stratigraphic distribution of the Ferrassie, Quina, and MTA industries outlined above provides strong support for Bordes' contention that these three variants do indeed represent significant taxonomic and behavioral entities within the specific context of the southwest French industries. The industrial sequence documented at Combe Grenal is particularly significant in this context. In this case, as noted above, it can be seen that each of these three variants occupies a specific and sharply localized segment of the industrial succession, with no indication of any stratigraphic overlapping of the three variants (Fig. 2.1). Statistically, the likelihood of this stratigraphic pattern arising entirely by chance is almost vanishingly small—less than one in a million. The consistent stratigraphic positions of the Quina, Ferrassie, and MTA industries documented in many other sites in the region (Mellars 1969, 1988), and the remarkably uniform patterns of technological development documented within the stratified sequences of "Charentian" (i.e., Ferrassie-Quina) assemblages (now documented in at least seven different sites, as discussed below) provide further support for this conclusion. It is hard to imagine how these stratigraphic patterns could be reconciled with the notion that the Ferrassie, Quina, and MTA variants represent essentially fortuitous associations of technological and typological features which lack any clear significance in broader taxonomic or behavioral terms.

TECHNOLOGICAL DEVELOPMENT
WITHIN THE CHARENTIAN INDUSTRIES

Within southwest France, by far the clearest evidence for a well-defined pattern of technological change over time is provided by the sequence of industries which Bordes referred to collectively under the term "Charentian." In Bordes' terms, of course, the Charentian was always seen as a strictly composite entity, comprising two major industrial variants—the Quina and Ferrasie Mousterian (Bordes 1953:461; 1961:806; 1968:101-102; 1972:53; 1981:79; 1984:160). Although distinguished by a range of individual features, Bordes nevertheless felt that these two variants shared sufficient elements in common to justify grouping them together under the broader "Charentian" label. The defining characteristics, in his terms, lay in three major quantitative features of the industries; first, a high overall percentage of sidescraper forms (invariably higher than 50%, and usually above 60%); secondly, an unusually low percentage of denticulated tools (invariably below 15%, and often as low as 2-5%);[2] and thirdly (and perhaps most significantly), a consistently high relative frequency of tools carrying distinctive "Quina-type" retouch. According to Bordes, the latter feature could invariably be used to differentiate the Quina and Ferrassie industries from the other industrial variants even when (as in some of the Typical assemblages) overall *racloir* frequencies may have overlapped with those at the lower end of the Charentian range (Bordes 1981:79; Bordes and de Sonneville-Bordes 1970:79).

Although defined by Bordes primarily in these quantitative terms, Bordes himself pointed out that there were several other more qualitative features which could be used to separate the Charentian industries from most of the other industrial variants of the Mousterian—including, for example, the presence of typical, double-pointed *limace* forms, and the presence of tools shaped by extensive bifacial "plano-convex" retouch (Bordes 1953:461; 1961:805; 1968:101; 1981:78). Later research has revealed other potentially equally distinctive features of the industries, including high frequencies of heavily convex *racloir* forms, unusually low frequencies of discarded cores, and (in at least many sites) high frequencies of bone *compresseurs* or *retouchoirs* (see Mellars 1967:104-109; also Rolland 1977:252). Potentially one of the most significant features of the Charentian grouping as a whole, of course, is the apparently total absence of typical cordiform handaxes and the

extreme scarcity (if not total absence) of typical backed knives (Bordes 1961:805; 1968:101-102; 1981:78; Bordes and de Sonneville-Bordes 1970:63).

The features used by Bordes to differentiate between the Ferrassie and Quina variants of the Charentian were based partly on technological and partly on typological features of the industries (Bordes 1953:461; 1961:806-807; 1968:101-102; 1981:78-79; 1984:160; Bordes and de Sonneville-Bordes 1970:62-63, 71). The core of the Ferrassie/Quina distinction, of course, lay in the character of the basic primary flaking techniques employed for tool production. While these were oriented strongly towards Levallois techniques in the case of the Ferrassie industries, they were largely replaced by much simpler (but technologically no less distinctive) non-Levallois techniques in the Quina industries (Turq, in press). With this basic technological division were associated general contrasts in the frequencies of both faceted striking platforms and elongated, blade-like flakes (both generally higher in the Ferrassie than in the Quina variant). In terms of tool morphology, Bordes emphasized three major contrasts between the Ferrassie and Quina variants: first, a sharply increased frequency of tools with typical "Quina" retouch in the Quina assemblages; second, a similar increase in the relative frequencies of transverse as opposed to lateral *racloir* forms in the Quina industry; and third, generally reduced frequencies of both double-edged *racloirs* and various forms of pointed tools (i.e., both "true points," and convergent and *déjeté racloirs*) in the Quina as opposed to the Ferrassie industries. The whole distinction between the Ferrassie and Quina variants, as defined in Bordes' terms, lay therefore in this relatively complex matrix of both strictly "typological" and more general "technological" features of the industries.

A close reading of Bordes' papers leaves no doubt that Bordes himself was well aware of the very close linkages between many of these essentially technological and typological features of the Quina and Ferrassie industries. As Bordes pointed out on several occasions (e.g., 1961:806; 1968:101; 1977:38; 1981:78-79; Bordes and de Sonneville-Bordes 1970:61) the sharply contrasting frequencies of transverse as opposed to lateral *racloir* forms can be seen as a direct, almost inevitable reflection of the variations in the forms of the initial flake blanks available for tool production in the two variants: the relatively elongated forms of flake blanks produced by most Levallois flaking techniques are clearly more suitable for the production of lateral *racloir* forms than are the shorter, broader flakes characteristic of most of the distinctively Quina-type flaking strategies—purely as a response to the need to secure the maximum potential length

of working edge on the finished tools. The strong correlation between the overall frequencies of transverse as opposed to lateral *racloir* forms and the Levallois indices of the industries illustrated in Figure 2.2 leaves little room for doubt on this score, and suggests that the documented contrasts in *racloir* form between

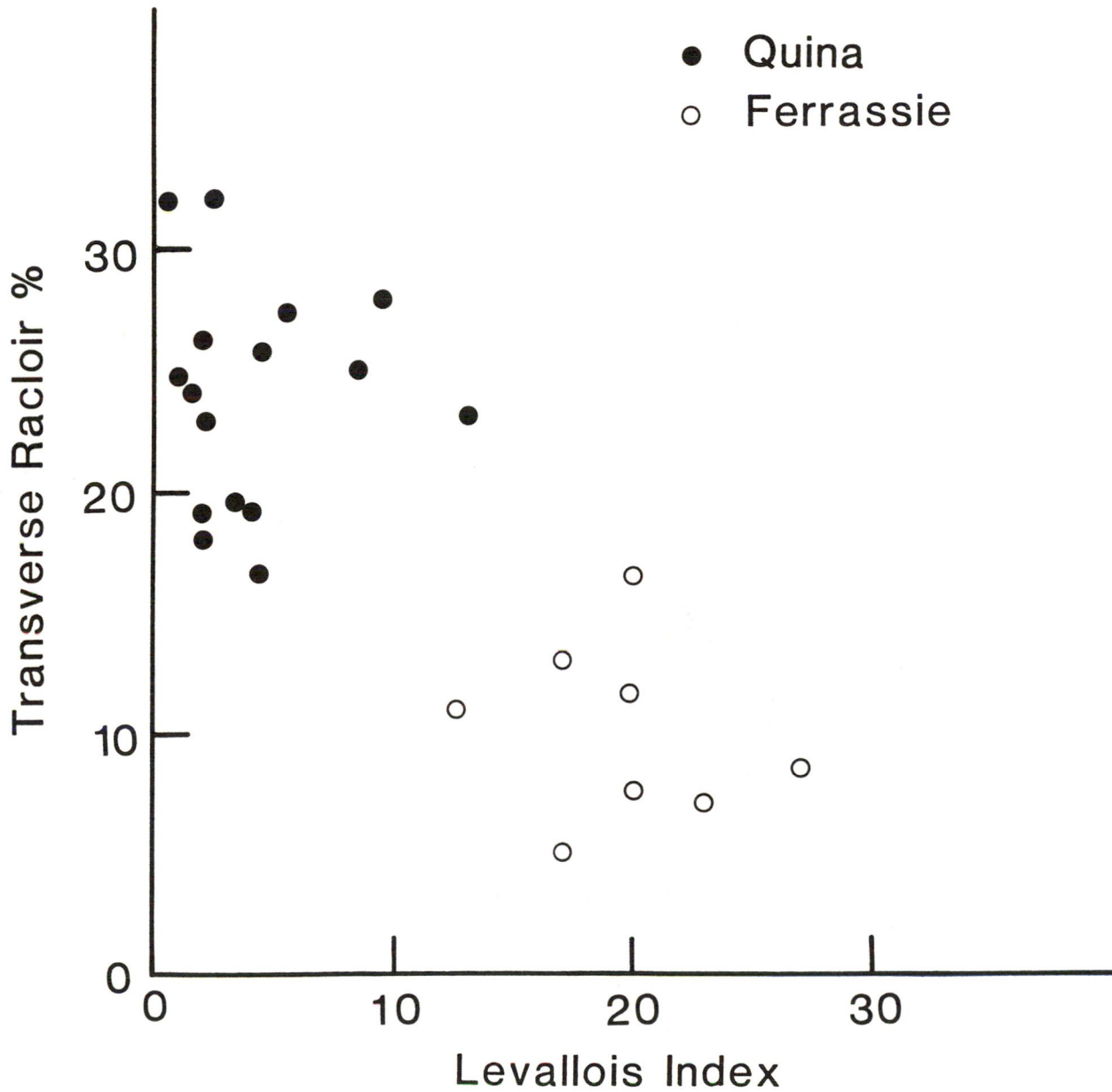

Figure 2.2   Relationship between Levallois indices and relative frequencies of transverse racloirs (as a percentage of all single-edged racloirs) recorded in Ferrassie and Quina Mousterian industries from southwest France. (Based on the assemblages from Combe Grenal, Abri Chadourne, Roc de Marsal, Mas Viel, Hauteroche, L'Ermitage, and La Rochette.)

the Ferrassie and Quina industries can be attributed, very largely if not entirely, to this basic technological contrast between the two variants. Similar arguments can be applied to the sharply increased frequencies of tools with typically heavy, invasive Quina-type retouch in the Quina assemblages (potentially a direct response to the constraints of applying retouch to the edges of relatively thick, heavy flakes: Bordes 1961:806; 1968:102; 1977:38; 1981:79; Bordes and de Sonneville-Bordes 1970:71); and, with slightly more reservations, to the variable production of more complex forms of double-edged and convergent *racloir* forms. As Dibble and Rolland (this volume) have pointed out, both of the latter forms are inherently more likely to be produced (or at least can be produced more easily) from relatively elongated, regular Levallois-type flakes than from the much thicker, less regular flakes encountered in Quina industries. It would seem, in other words, that when viewed in these terms, at least the majority of the apparent "typological" contrasts documented between the Ferrassie and Quina variants can be related very largely if not entirely to the underlying contrasts in the basic primary flaking strategies employed in the initial stages of flake production in the two variants.

If this line of reasoning is correct, then we are left with the impression that the documented contrasts between the Ferrassie and Quina Mousterian industries within the southwest French sites reflect, predominantly if not entirely, a basic shift in the primary techniques of flake production within these industries. The arguments for believing that this technological shift follows a fairly simple chronological pattern within this region have been set out on several occasions (Mellars 1965, 1967, 1969, 1988). The arguments rest essentially on a total of seven stratified sequences of Ferrassie and Quina assemblages, all of which reveal a regular, step-by-step decrease in the Levallois component of the industries between the lower and upper levels (see Fig. 2.3). In at least four of these sites it is possible to document levels of Quina-type Mousterian lying directly above levels of Ferrassie Mousterian—notably at Combe Grenal, Abri Chadourne, Abri Caminade-est and (further to the north) at Roc en Pail (Maine-et-Loire). Similar sequences may well exist at several other sites in the same region such as Pech de Bourre, Chez Pourré, Regourdou, Roc de Marsal, and Pech de l'Azé IV, but as yet the published data on these sites are not sufficient to document these patterns in detail (see

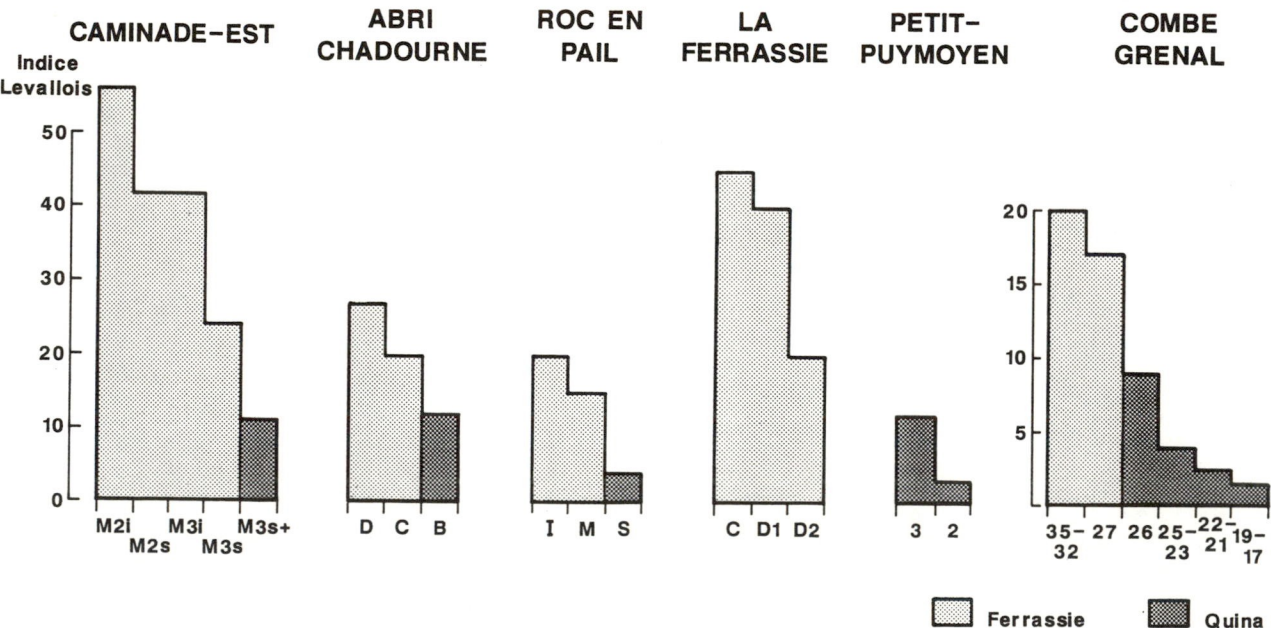

Figure 2.3   *Levallois indices recorded in stratified sequences of Ferrassie and Quina Mousterian industries in southwest France. For details of sequences, see Mellars 1969:153-154 and 1988:fig. 5. Note that the Levallois indices for the three industries from la Ferrassie have almost certainly been artificially raised by selective recovery of unretouched flakes during excavation (see note 3).*

Mellars 1988:106-107). Potentially far more significant is the clear pattern of technological "evolution" which can be seen within the individual sequences of both Ferrassie and Quina industries in these sites. Thus a pattern of progressive decrease in the Levallois index can be seen clearly *within* the stratified sequences of Ferrassie-type industries at Combe Grenal, La Ferrassie, Abri Chadourne, Abri Caminade-est, and Roc en Pail, and *within* the stratified sequences of Quina industries at Combe Grenal, Petit-Puymoyen and Plateau Baillard (Fig. 2.3). In other words, the pattern of reduction in the Levallois component is apparent not only *between* the main groupings of Ferrassie and Quina assemblages but also *within* each of these groupings. As pointed out elsewhere, the probability of these patterns arising entirely by chance is almost impossibly small—approximately one in 30,000 (Mellars 1988:107). It is hard to imagine how one could document a pattern of technological "evolution" from one industrial variant to another in any more convincing terms—either stratigraphically, or in terms of the statistical probabilities (i.e., improbabilities) involved.

The general chronology of these industries within the overall climatic sequence of the early Würm has been discussed on several occasions (e.g., Mellars 1969:155-156; 1986a, 1986b; Turq 1988; Assassi 1986; Guadelli and Laville 1990). In many sites (Combe Grenal, Roc de Marsal, Regourdou, La Quina, Marillac, Petit-Puymoyen, Hauteroche, Abri Chadourne, etc.) there is evidence that typical Quina-type assemblages date from a period of extremely severe climatic conditions, apparently correlated with the pleniglacial maximum of the Würm II phase—probably equivalent to isotope stage 4 in the ocean-core sequence (cf. Turq 1988:8; Guadelli and Laville 1990). The Ferrassie-type industries stratified below the Quina levels, by contrast, usually are associated with evidence of substantially milder climatic conditions (reflected, for example, by much lower frequencies of reindeer in the faunal assemblages), most probably reflecting the initial, less rigorous conditions of the earlier Würm II phase. The whole sequence of technological development therefore would appear to correlate with a period of progressively deteriorating climatic conditions— though perhaps with some significant amelioration of conditions during the final stages of the industrial sequence (as, for example, in the uppermost Quina levels at Combe Grenal and Roc de Marsal: cf. Turq 1988:10-11; Mellars 1988:fig. 6).

EXPLANATORY MODELS FOR TECHNOLOGICAL VARIATION

If the general outline of the "evolutionary" scheme of the Ferrassie and Quina industries described above is accepted, this still leaves two further questions to be addressed. First, how far can this be regarded as a rigid, invariable pattern of technological development within the southwest French sites, and how far can we identify any local variations or exceptions to this general pattern of development? And second, what sort of mechanisms can be invoked to explain why this kind of technological development should have occurred, apparently throughout a relatively wide geographical area and over a relatively long span of time?

The first question of localized variation to the general pattern of technological development raises some interesting issues. A close scrutiny of the available data suggests that certain variations of this kind can in fact be identified in the technological records from particular sites. Potentially the most significant variations are those in the relative and absolute values of the Levallois index. From Figure 2.3, for example, it can be seen that while the pattern of a gradual, progressive decline in the Levallois index can be documented consistently in all of the southwest French sites, the precise *range* over which these indices shift varies to some extent in the different sites. At Combe Grenal, for instance, the overall range of the indices seems to be slightly lower than that recorded in some other sites such as the Abri Chadourne or La Ferrassie.[3] Conversely, the assemblages from the Abri Caminade-est show exceptionally high values of the Levallois index, clearly above the normal range for the Charentian sequence as a whole. The explanation of these discrepancies probably lies in a combination of at least two separate factors. As Dibble and Rolland (this volume; Dibble, in press) have pointed out, the character of local raw material supplies is almost certainly a crucially important variable. Several studies have suggested that the nature and quality of local raw material (i.e., both its inherent flaking qualities and the shape and size of available nodules) can have a significant effect on the degree to which Levallois techniques can be effectively practiced, with poor quality or smaller-sized nodules generally favoring the adoption of simpler flaking techniques (Fish 1981:377-379; Dibble 1985:392). In this context, the relatively poor quality of the local raw materials available in the immediate neighborhood of the Combe Grenal site may well have had some effect in limiting the relative degree of utilization of this technique. A second crucial factor, of course, is the extent to which the systematic reduction of nodules was carried out actually *within* the occupation sites, and how far fully prepared flakes were deliberately introduced into the sites from other locations. Studies by Geneste and others have clearly demonstrated this kind of movement of Levallois flakes (and other artifacts) between different sites, and emphasized the potential influence of this effect on the overall frequencies of Levallois technology documented in particular sites (Geneste 1985, 1988; de Sonneville-Bordes 1969). In the case of Abri Caminade-est this is almost certainly the explanation for the unusually high Levallois indices recorded in the two Ferrassie-type assemblages at the base of the sequence: as de Sonneville-Bordes (1969) has pointed out, the overall composition of the lithic assemblages from these levels suggests that relatively little in situ flaking of flint nodules was carried out within the site itself, and that the majority of both the retouched tools and unretouched primary flakes were apparently imported into the site from elsewhere. All of the factors discussed above would inevitably influence the absolute values of the Levallois indices recorded within particular site sequences, and should perhaps be regarded not so much as "aberrations" to the general patterns of technological development recorded within the Ferrassie-Quina industries as a whole, but rather as predictable consequences of the normal patterns of technological behavior within different activity locations.

Similar localized variations can be seen in some of the typological features of the industries—most notably those of the relative frequencies of transverse *racloirs*, and perhaps also those of double and convergent *racloir* forms. As shown in Figure 2.2, the overall correlation between transverse *racloir* percentages and the Levallois index of the various assemblages is remarkably clear cut and (as discussed above) leaves no doubt that by far the dominant factor in controlling the varying production of transverse (as opposed to lateral) *racloirs* was closely related to variation in the basic technological strategy of primary flake production. Nevertheless, some of the minor variations in this relationship could well reflect the impact of successive tool-resharpening factors of the kind outlined by Dibble and Rolland (this volume). The clearest illustration of this effect has been provided by Meignen (1988) in her study of the Quina-type

assemblages from Marillac in the Charente. Here she was able to demonstrate that the sidescrapers manufactured from relatively high-quality raw materials derived from some distance away from the site included a significantly higher proportion of transverse forms than those manufactured from the much poorer quality, local raw materials. As she points out, this could reflect either the heavier degree of resharpening and reduction of the tools made on the better quality (more distant) raw materials or (alternatively) the selective use of particular, imported kinds of flake blanks specifically for the production of the transverse *racloir* forms (see also Turq 1988, in press). But in either case it is clear that essentially local effects, related either to variations in raw material supplies or to variable patterns of reduction of tools on the site, could influence the overall frequencies of transverse versus lateral *racloir* forms in specific industries (i.e., within the particular limits reflected in Fig. 2.2). As Dibble and Rolland (this volume) have pointed out, broadly similar factors could influence the variable degrees to which more complex double or convergent *racloir* forms were produced and discarded on particular sites. Nevertheless, the scale of these local variations should not be exaggerated. Overall, the most impressive feature is the way in which all of these specific typological and technological features of the Charentian industries conform to relatively well defined chronological patterns, clearly reflecting a *general* pattern of typological and technological development throughout the Charentian sequences as a whole.

The second question of *why* this general pattern of technological development should have occurred within the Charentian industries, is of course, the most crucial to the present discussion and ultimately, no doubt, to much wider issues of technological and typological variability within the Middle Paleolithic as a whole. The problem, in essence, is to identify why some kind of consistent shift in the technological aspects of the industries should have occurred, leading to a gradual, progressive reduction in the Levallois component of the technology. Since this pattern seems to have persisted throughout the entire chronological span of the Charentian development (i.e., over a period of at least ca. 10,000 years), it is reasonable to think in terms of some kind of continuous "pressure" or "constraint" on technological development which was apparently in operation throughout at least the greater part of this period.

Explanations for long-terms patterns of technological change in prehistory are notoriously difficult, and usually open to a variety of different explanatory models (see Rolland 1988; Jelinek 1988; Dibble and Rolland, this volume). The present case is certainly no exception. From the literature which has appeared over the past few years it is clear that one could propose at least three or four different explanatory frameworks to account for the shifts in Middle Paleolithic technology, all invoking varying degrees of emphasis on different "environmental" or "socio-economic" factors, and all encountering a variety of different theoretical or methodological difficulties in the procedures for systematic testing of the different models. All that will be attempted here is to spell out some of these potential models and to indicate—briefly—how they might potentially be applied in the present case.

1. One of the most obvious and perhaps seductively easy explanations would be to account for long-term patterns of technological change primarily in terms of variable constraints on the character or relative accessibility of local raw material supplies. In the case of Levallois technology, for example, it has often been suggested (as noted above) that for the effective, large-scale application of these techniques it is necessary to have access not only to relatively high-quality raw materials (i.e., relatively fine-grained materials, in which the strategies of flaking can be accurately controlled), but also to relatively large, fairly regular nodules (Fish 1981:377–379; Dibble 1985:392). Both of these generalizations can be questioned from specific archaeological contexts (e.g., Turq, in press; Tavoso 1984), but in broad terms the generalizations may well be valid. If these generalizations *are* valid, then of course it would be reasonable to look for explanations of long-term reductions in Levallois strategies in terms of continuing constraints on either the quality or local availability of raw material supplies. Two main scenarios could be visualized in the present context. In the first place it could be suggested that the initial, high-Levallois phases of Charentian technology were developed in contexts in which raw materials were relatively abundant (and of high quality), either within specific geographical contexts within the Perigord region itself (e.g., the Bergerac region), or alternatively in some other area (such as northern France) from which groups subsequently shifted to areas of generally poorer quality and/or less abundant materials (as, for example, in most of the Cretaceous and Jurassic outcrops of the southwest French region: Geneste 1985; Demars 1982). Under these conditions it could be argued that groups would "adapt" to the generally poorer quality sources of raw materials by gradually phasing out the

reliance on typically Levallois techniques in favor of technologically simpler or more "economical" non-Levallois techniques (Turq 1988, in press). The alternative possibility, suggested by Dibble and Rolland (this volume; Dibble, in press) is that a decline in Levallois technology could be related more simply to a progressive over-exploitation of the available raw material resources within the Perigord region itself. While the latter possibility may be difficult to visualize on a broad, regional scale, it could (as they suggest) be a significant factor in some of the more intensively occupied locations such as Combe Grenal, which are known to have been occupied, and presumably heavily exploited for raw materials, over a large part of the Mousterian period. What this model cannot explain, of course, is why some of the demonstrably *later* Mousterian industries in the same locations should have been able to revert (apparently rapidly) to the use of much more extensive Levallois techniques (see, for example, Rolland 1988:fig. 9.2).

2. A second alternative discussed by Dibble and Rolland is that a progressive decline in the use of Levallois techniques could have been related to increasingly intensive or sedentary patterns of occupation in particular sites, leading to increased pressures towards the most economical use of the available raw materials. In the case of the Ferrassie/Quina industries, for example, they argue that the sharp deterioration in climatic conditions towards the peak of the Würm II climatic episode (i.e., equivalent to isotope stage 4 of the ocean-core sequence) could have discouraged large-scale mobility of the human groups, and tended to concentrate economic activities within a relatively short radius of the major occupation sites (perhaps related in part to the use of more aggregated resources such as migrating reindeer herds: see also Jelinek 1988). This in turn would place further constraints on the patterns of access to raw material supplies, and would have provided a further incentive towards the use of the most economical (arguably non-Levallois) flaking strategies.

3. A totally different explanation, of course, would be to place the primary emphasis not so much on the character of the primary flaking techniques themselves, but rather on the specific forms and functions of the different retouched tools that were produced by the different techniques (e.g., Turq, in press). For example, it could no doubt be argued that typically Quina sidescrapers (i.e., relatively thick, convex forms, shaped by heavy, invasive retouch) might well be appropriate for much more heavy-duty hide-

working or skin-scraping activities than were the thinner, more lightly retouched forms encountered in Ferrassie-type industries, and could reflect simply a shift towards the greater use of animal skins (for clothing, rugs, shelters, etc.) during the increasingly harsh conditions of the main Würm II phase. Unfortunately, the available data on microscopic use-wear studies in this context are notoriously inconclusive, and can hardly be used to provide any clear test for this hypothesis (Beyries 1987, 1988; Anderson-Gerfaud 1990). If this pattern were to be substantiated, however, it would provide a potentially entirely separate line of interpretation for the documented shifts from predominantly Levallois to essentially non-Levallois techniques over the period of the Ferrassie-Quina transition. As Turq (1988, in press) has pointed out, the characteristically heavy, thick forms of flakes employed for tool production in Quina assemblages could be seen as entirely deliberate, preconceived products, designed specifically for the production of particular forms of retouched tools. The whole thrust of this hypothesis would therefore reverse the normally assumed relationships between "technology" and "typology," and imply that in at least some cases it was the changing *morphology* of stone tools that dictated shifts in the character of the associated flaking strategies and not *vice versa*. Clearly, much more explicit data on the actual functions of Quina versus non-Quina *racloirs* would be needed to evaluate this hypothesis further.

4. Finally, the progressive tool-reduction models of Dibble and Rolland could be invoked, in a slightly different guise, to account for documented shifts between Levallois and non-Levallois flaking techniques. If Dibble (1984, 1987) is correct in suggesting that typical Quina-type *racloirs* are in fact systematically more heavily reduced and resharpened tool forms than most of the other sidescraper forms, one could well ask how far the relatively thick, steep-edged flakes that were employed for the production of Quina scrapers may have been deliberately produced and selected for the production of these tools (Turq 1988, in press). In other words, if the need for repeated, intensive resharpening of sidescrapers became more pronounced during the course of the Ferrassie-Quina development (as a result of increased intensity and sedentism of occupation in the sites: Jelinek 1988:208), this could perhaps have provided a powerful incentive for the production of relatively thick, heavy flakes that were particularly well adapted to this kind of repeated resharpening. Here again, the entire thrust of the argument would reverse the usually-assumed relationships between technology and typology, and suggest that changes in tool morphology (and/or function) were acting as the primary determinants of changes in the associated flaking strategies.

The various interpretative scenarios outlined above are unlikely to be exhaustive. The aim is simply to show that in terms of current models of technological variability in the Middle Paleolithic there are in fact a range of different models which could, potentially, be invoked to account for systematic, long-term shifts in the relative use of Levallois versus non-Levallois flaking techniques. The essential problem, of course, lies in the difficulty of adequately testing these different scenarios against the available archaeological data. To document a major shift in lithic technology is one thing. To formulate and test different explanatory models for such changes is, unfortunately, a much more difficult and less readily achievable goal.

CONCLUSIONS

The aim of this paper has been to outline one particularly well documented case of chronologically-patterned technological and typological development within the Middle Paleolithic industries of western France, and to discuss some of the potential mechanisms by which this transition could have come about. The much more general issues of industrial variability posed by some of the other Mousterian variants within the same region—particularly those of the "Denticulate" and "Typical" Mousterian—cannot be discussed at length here. Briefly, my own view is that these industries are likely to reflect a variety of different factors, including at least some substantial component of technological change over time, but no doubt incorporating other factors related either to the specific economic functions on the sites (cf. Binford and Binford 1966, 1969) or to the kinds of successive tool-reduction processes discussed by Dibble and Rolland (cf. Mellars 1969:158-161). Clearly, one of the central questions in the present context is whether certain occurrences of either Typical or even Denticulate Mousterian industries may have been produced effectively simultaneously with the Ferrassie and Quina assemblages, purely in response to these kinds of localized "functional" variations in the specific patterns of activity in the different sites.

Interestingly, there is as yet remarkably little direct stratigraphic evidence for this, with only a single really well documented case of "interstratification" so far recorded within any of the long and multi-layered sequences of Ferrassie and Quina industries within the southwest French sites (i.e., the single level of Denticulate Mousterian stratified within the upper-most levels of Quina Mousterian in Layer 20 at Combe Grenal).[4] Nevertheless, the whole issue of the "functional," "cultural," or chronological significance of the Typical and Denticulate industries remains, to me, a largely open question in the present state of research.

The situation represented by the MTA industries, by contrast, seems much more sharply defined. In the first place there is now clear evidence that these industries belong, largely if not entirely, to a very late stage in the overall Mousterian succession within southwest France, entirely later than that occupied by the sequence of Ferrassie and Quina Mousterian industries (Mellars 1969, 1988). As noted earlier, MTA industries seem invariably to occupy the upper levels in stratified Mousterian sequences in this region, usually stratified directly beneath early Upper Paleolithic levels. It is equally significant that there is no trace whatever of these industries throughout the whole of the lowermost 50 levels of Mousterian occupation (spanning the greater part of both the Würm I and Würm II climatic phases) at Combe Grenal. Secondly, the typological and technological features of the MTA industries contrast in almost every documented respect with those of the Charentian industries. This applies not only to the overall composition of the industries (in terms of relative frequencies of sidescrapers, denticulates, tools showing typical Quina retouch, etc.) but above all to the presence in the MTA industries of two highly distinctive and idiosyncratic "type fossil" forms—i.e., typical cordiform handaxes, and equally typical (i.e., extensively retouched) backed knives (Bordes 1953:460-463; 1961:804-805; 1968:101-102; 1981:77-79; Bordes and de Sonneville-Bordes 1970:61-64). Even if some of the general quantitative features of the MTA industries might, in principle, be explicable in terms of the tool-reduction models proposed by Dibble and Rolland, it is clear that the presence of these highly idiosyncratic type fossils cannot be explained in these terms. Equally significant is the fact that the Levallois aspect of the industries (especially in the earliest stages of the MTA sequence) reverts to very much higher values than those recorded in the later (i.e.,

Quina) stages of the Charentian sequence (Mellars 1965, 1967). All of the present indications are therefore that the relatively sudden and abrupt appearance of the MTA industries within the southwest French sites represents a fundamental and wide-ranging change in the whole character of lithic technology within this region.

Exactly how one should account for the appearance of the MTA industries in the later stages of the Mousterian sequence is still a largely open question. At present we have very little information on the specific functions of the most distinctive tool forms in these industries (i.e., handaxes and backed knives: Beyries 1987, 1988; Anderson-Gerfaud 1990) and only very generalized information on the character of the associated settlement and subsistence strategies. In broad terms, perhaps, the Mousterian of Acheulian Tradition seems to represent an adaptation to variable but generally relatively mild ecological conditions (equivalent to isotope stage 3 of the ocean-core sequence) favoring the exploitation of predominantly bovid, horse, and red deer resources rather than the highly specialized exploitation of reindeer documented during the greater part of the Charentian sequence (Mellars 1969:145). But whether the particular features of the MTA industries can be related in any simple "functional" way to these shifts in ecological and economic patterns is at present an entirely open question. The alternative, of course, is that the appearance of the MTA industries reflects a much more fundamental change in the whole trajectory of Middle Paleolithic occupation in this region, representing the demographic replacement of the earlier populations by an entirely new human group. I would argue that population replacements of this kind are not only conceivable within the demographic frameworks of Middle Paleolithic communities, but probably to be predicted under certain conditions of combined ecological and demographic change (see Mellars 1969:150; 1985:287-289; David 1973:295-300).

To summarize, I would suggest that two major parameters have been consistently underestimated in earlier discussions of the character and significance of variability in Middle Paleolithic industries: on the one hand, the existence of clear, chronologically patterned changes in technology over time; and on the other hand, the occurrence of major changes in both basic technology and associated tool manufacturing patterns which are not related in any simple, direct fashion to shifts in the ecological or environmental context of the industries. The latter point perhaps is illustrated most clearly by some of the striking variations which can now be documented in the geographical distribution of several distinctive industrial variants of the Middle Paleolithic. As Dibble and Rolland (this volume) have pointed out, there is at present no convincing ecological or environmental explanation for the strikingly limited geographical distribution of bifacial leaf points in the Mousterian assemblages of Central and Eastern Europe; for the peculiar distribution of "Vasconian" industries in the Pyrenees and Cantabrian region; for the presence of tanged points in the North African Aterian industries; or for the peculiar restriction of MTA industries to the extreme western fringes of Europe (Bordes 1981; Mellars 1989:361; Otte, this volume). All of these features appear at present as strangely idiosyncratic features of Middle Paleolithic technology, without any simple or clear-cut explanation in either climatic, ecological, or other "environmental" terms. Exactly how these technological idiosyncrasies arose, and exactly what they may signify in social or demographic terms, is still a matter for debate (Mellars 1989:361). But until this aspect of essentially "non-functional" variation within the Middle Paleolithic is recognized, our perceptions of the significance of industrial variability within the Middle Paleolithic are likely to remain at best incomplete, and at worst potentially seriously misleading.

NOTES

1. As I have emphasized on several occasions (1969:136, 161; 1988:113-115) these observations apply strictly to the industrial sequence in southwest France, and purely to the industries dating from the earlier stages of the last glaciation. Clearly there is no reason why the sequence or chronology of industries in northern France or southeastern France should correspond exactly with that documented in the Perigord region. In addition, the status of certain so-called "Proto-Charentian" or "Proto-Quina" industries dating from the penultimate ("Riss") glaciation remains to be clarified (Mellars 1988:113-115).

2. As Le Tensorer (1978) and Turq (1988) have pointed out, the frequency of denticulates seems to increase significantly towards the end of the Charentian sequence—notably in the uppermost Quina levels at Combe Grenal (Layers 19-17) and Roc de Marsal (Layers IXb-XII).

3. As Meignen et al. (1977:289) have emphasized, the relatively high values of the Levallois index recorded for the industries from La Ferrassie are almost certainly due in part to the selective collection of unretouched flakes during the excavations of Peyrony. Unfortunately, the Levallois index recorded for the series collected during the recent excavations of Delporte cannot be compared directly with those for Peyrony's series, since it is not clear exactly how the layers excavated by Delporte correlate with those excavated by Peyrony (cf. Tuffreau 1984).

4. The significance of the three "Typical Mousterian" industries documented in Layers 28-30 at Combe Grenal is of debatable significance in this context: in the original publication by Bordes (1955:428) these industries were classified as representing simply an "attenuated Ferrassie" variant.

REFERENCES CITED

Anderson-Gerfaud, P.
    1990   Aspects of Behaviour in the Middle Paleolithic: Functional Analysis of Stone Tools from Southwest France. Pp. 389-418 in *The Emergence of Modern Humans: An Archaeological Perspective*, ed. P. Mellars. Edinburgh: Edinburgh University Press.

Assassi, F.
    1986   Recherches sédimentologiques sur la climatologie du Würm ancien et de l'interstade würmien en Périgord. Thesis, Université de Bordeaux.

Beaulieu, J. L. de, and Reille, M.
    1984   The Pollen Sequence of Les Echets (France): A New Element for the Chronology of the Upper Pleistocene. *Géographie physique et quaternaire* 38:3-9.

Beyries, S.
    1987   *Variabilité de l'industrie lithique au Moustérien: approche fonctionelle sur quelques gisements français*. BAR International Series 328. Oxford: BAR.
    1988   Functional Variability of Lithic Sets in the Middle Paleolithic. Pp. 213-223 in *Upper Pleistocene Prehistory of Western Eurasia*, eds. H. Dibble and A. Montet-White. Philadelphia: University Museum, University of Pennsylvania.

Binford, L. R., and Binford, S. R.
    1966   A Preliminary Analysis of Functional Variability in the Mousterian of Levallois Facies. *AA* 68:238-295.

Binford, S. R., and Binford, L. R.
    1969   Stone Tools and Human Behavior. *SciAm* 220(4):70-84.

Bordes, F.
1953   Essai de classification des industries "moustériennes." *BSPF* 50:457-466.
1955   La stratigraphie de la grotte de Combe-Grenal, Commune de Domme (Dordogne): note préliminaire. *BSPF* 52:426-429.
1961   Mousterian Cultures in France. *Science* 134:803-810.
1968   *The Old Stone Age.* London: Weidenfeld and Nicolson.
1972   *A Tale of Two Caves.* New York and London: Harper and Row.
1977   Time and Space Limits of the Mousterian. Pp. 37-39 in *Stone Tools as Cultural Markers,* ed. R. V. S. Wright. Canberra: Australian Institute of Aboriginal Studies.
1981   Vingt-cinq ans après: le complexe moustérien revisité. *BSPF* 78:77-87.
1984   *Leçons sur le Paléolithique.* Vol. 2: *Le Paléolithique en Europe.* CQ 7. Paris: CNRS.

Bordes, F., and Prat, F.
1965   Observations sur les faunes du Riss et du Würm I en Dordogne. *L'Anthropologie* 69:31-46.

Bordes, F., and Sonneville-Bordes, D. de
1970   The Significance of Variability in Palaeolithic Assemblages. *WA* 2:61-73.

Bosinski, G.
1967   *Die Mittelpaläolithischen Funde im Westlichen Mitteleuropa.* Fundamenta A4. Cologne: Herman Böhlau.

Clark, J. D.
1982   The Cultures of the Middle Palaeolithic/Middle Stone Age. Pp. 148-341 in *The Cambridge History of Africa.* Vol. 1: *From the Earliest Times to c. 500 BC,* ed. J. D. Clark. Cambridge: Cambridge University Press.
1983   The Significance of Culture Change in the Early Later Pleistocene in Northern and Southern Africa. Pp. 1-12 in *The Mousterian Legacy: Human Biocultural Change in the Upper Pleistocene,* ed. E. Trinkaus. BAR International Series 164. Oxford: BAR.

Copeland, L.
1975   The Middle and Upper Paleolithic of Lebanon and Syria in the Light of Recent Research. Pp. 317-350 in *Problems in Prehistory: North Africa and the Levant,* eds. F. Wendorf and A. E. Marks. Dallas: Southern Methodist University Press.

David, N. C.
1973   On Upper Palaeolithic Society, Ecology and Technological Change. Pp. 277-303 in *The Explanation of Culture Change,* ed. C. Renfrew. London: Duckworth.

Delpech, F.
1988   Les réponses des ongulés du Pléistocène supérieur aux changements climatiques en Aquitaine (sud-ouest de la France): quelques exemples. *Geobios* 21(4):495-503.

Demars, P.-Y.
1982   *L'utilisation du silex au Paléolithique supérieur: choix, approvisionnement, circulation: l'exemple du Bassin de Brive.* CQ 5. Paris: CNRS.

Dibble, H. L.
1983   Variability and change in the Middle Paleolithic of Western Europe and the Near East. Pp. 53-71 in *The Mousterian Legacy: Human Biocultural Change in the Upper Pleistocene,* ed. E. Trinkaus. Oxford: BAR International Series 164. Oxford: BAR.
1984   Interpreting Typological Variation of Middle Paleolithic Scrapers: Function, Style, or Sequence of Reduction. *JFA* 11:431-436.
1985   Raw Material Variation in Levallois Flake Manufacture. *CA* 26:391-393.
1987   The Interpretation of Middle Paleolithic Scraper Morphology. *AA* 52:109-117.
in press   Local Raw Material Exploitation and its Effects on Lower and Middle Paleolithic Assemblage Variability. In *Raw Material Exploitation among Prehistoric Hunter-Gatherers,* eds. A. Montet-White and S. Holen. Lawrence: University of Kansas Press.

Fish, P.
1981 Beyond Tools: Middle Paleolithic Debitage Analysis and Cultural Inference. *JAR* 37:374-386.

Geneste, J.-M.
1985 Analyse lithique des industries moustériennes du Périgord: une approche technologique du comportement des groupes humains au Paléolithique moyen. Thesis, Université de Bordeaux.
1988 Economie des resources lithiques dans le Moustérien du sud-ouest de la France. Pp. 75-97 in *L'homme de Néandertal*, ed. M. Otte. Vol. 6: *La subsistance*. ERAUL 33. Liège: Université de Liège.

Guadelli, J.-L.
1987 Contribution a l'étude des zoocenoses préhistoriques en Aquitaine (Würm ancien et interstade würmien). Thesis, Université de Bordeaux.

Guadelli, J.-L., and Laville, H.
1990 L'environnement climatique de la fin du Moustérien à Combe Grenal et à Camiac. Confrontation des données naturalistes et implications. Pp. 43-52 in *Paléolithique moyen récent et Paléolithique supérieur ancien en Europe*, ed. C. Farizy. Mémoires du Musée de Préhistoire d'Ile de France 3. Nemours: Association pour la Promotion de la Recherche Archéologique en Ile de France (A.P.R.A.I.F.).

Guiot, J.; Pons, A.; Beaulieu, J. L. de; and Reille, M.
1989 A 140,000-Year Continental Climate Reconstruction from Two European Pollen Records. *Nature* 338:309-313.

Jelinek, A.
1982 The Middle Paleolithic in the Southern Levant, with Comments on the Appearance of Modern *Homo sapiens*. Pp. 57-101 in *The Transition from the Lower to Middle Paleolithic and the Origins of Modern Man*, ed. A. Ronen. BAR International Series 151. Oxford: BAR.
1988 Technology, Typology, and Culture in the Middle Paleolithic. Pp. 199-212 in

Upper Pleistocene Prehistory of Western Eurasia, eds. H. Dibble and A. Montet-White. Philadelphia: University Museum, University of Pennsylvania.

Laville, H.; Rigaud, J.-P.; and Sackett, J. R.
1980 *Rock Shelters of the Perigord: Geological Stratigraphy and Archaeological Succession*. New York: Academic Press.

Le Tensorer, J.-M.
1978 Le Moustérien type Quina et son évolution dans le sud de la France. *BSPF* 75:141-149.

Meignen, L.
1988 Un exemple de comportement technologique différentiel selon les matières premières: Marillac, couches 9 et 10. Pp. 71-79 in *L'homme de Néandertal*, ed. M. Otte. Vol. 4: *La technique*, ed. L. Binford and J.-P. Rigaud. ERAUL 31. Liège: Université de Liège.

Meignen, L.; Chech, M.; and Vandermeersch, B.
1977 Le gisement moustérien d'Artenac a Saint Mary (Charente). *GP* 20:281-291.

Mellars, P. A.
1965 The Sequence and Development of Mousterian Traditions in South-Western France. *Nature* 205:626-627.
1967 The Mousterian Succession in South-West France. Ph.D. dissertation, Cambridge University.
1969 The Chronology of Mousterian Industries in the Perigord Region of South-West France. *PPS* 35:134-171.
1985 The Ecological Basis of Social Complexity in the Upper Paleolithic of Southwestern France. Pp. 271-297 in *Prehistoric Hunter-Gatherers: The Emergence of Cultural Complexity*, eds. T. D. Price and J. A. Brown. New York: Academic Press.
1986a A New Chronology for the French Mousterian Period. *Nature* 322:410-411.
1986b Dating and Correlating the French Mousterian (reply). *Nature* 324:113-114.
1988 The Chronology of the South-West French Mousterian: A Review of the Current Debate. Pp. 97-119 in *L'homme de Néandertal*, ed. M. Otte. Vol. 4: *La*

technique, ed. L. Binford and J.-P. Rigaud. ERAUL 31. Liège: Université de Liège.

1989 Major Issues in the Emergence of Modern Humans. *CA* 30:349-385.

Rolland, N.
1977 New Aspects of Middle Palaeolithic Variability in Western Europe. *Nature* 266:251-252.
1981 The Interpretation of Middle Palaeolithic Variability. *Man* 16:15-42.
1988 Observations on Some Middle Paleolithic Time Series in Southern France. Pp. 161-179 in *Upper Pleistocene Prehistory of Western Eurasia*, eds. H. Dibble and A. Montet-White. Philadelphia: University Museum, University of Pennsylvania.

Shackleton, N. J., and Opdyke, N. D.
1973 Oxygen Isotope and Paleomagnetic Stratigraphy of Equatorial Pacific Core V28-238: Oxygen Isotope Temperatures and Ice Volumes on a 10^5 and 10^6 Year Scale. *Journal of Quaternary Research* 3:39-55.

Sonneville-Bordes, D. de
1969 Les industries moustériennes de l'abri Caminade-Est, commune de La Canéda (Dordogne). *BSPF* 66:293-310.

Tavoso, A.
1984 Réflexions sur l'économie des matières premières au Moustérien. *BSPF* 81:79-82.

Tuffreau, A.
1984 Les industries moustériennes et Castelperroniennes de la Ferrassie. Pp. 111-144 in *Le Grand Abri de la Ferrassie: Fouilles 1968-1973*, ed. H. Delporte. Mémoire 7. Paris: IPH.

Turq, A.
1988 Le Moustérien de type Quina du Roc de Marsal à Campagne (Dordogne): contexte stratigraphique, analyse lithologique et technologie. *Documents d'Archéologie Périgourdine* 3:5-30.
in press Approche technologique et économique du facies Moustérien de type Quina: étude préliminaire. *BSPF*.

Van der Hammen, T.; Maarleveld, G. C.; Vogel, J. C.; and Zagwijn, W. H.
1967 Stratigraphy, Climatic Succession and Radiocarbon Dating of the Last Glacial in the Netherlands. *Geologie en Mijnbouw* 46:79-95.

Woillard, G. M., and Mook, W. G.
1982 Carbon-14 Dates at Grand Pile: Correlation of Land and Sea Chronologies. *Science* 215:159-161.

III

The Significance of Variability in the European Mousterian

Marcel Otte

THE ACTOR AND HIS TIMES

The branch of *Homo erectus* which occupied Europe between 1 and 0.5 million years ago evolved locally into the type of archaic *Homo sapiens* characteristic of that continent, the Neandertals (Hublin 1989). There is no marked anatomical difference between these two evolutionary grades in Europe. Outside Europe, the Neandertal form is only known in the Levant, and there it arrived late (Vandermeersch 1989). Thus Europe was populated by a single biological group before the Upper Paleolithic, with no significant outside input.

The Middle Paleolithic represents a crucial phase in human evolution. It was during this time that the role of anatomical change as the key adaptive mechanism was greatly reduced and thus the balance between biological and cultural change was tipped in favor of the latter (Leroi-Gourhan 1964). In other words, culture finally becomes the paramount means of human adaptive change in the Middle Paleolithic.

The appearance of prepared flake core reduction techniques, characteristic of this period, goes back to about 300,000 years ago: 240 kyr at Pontnewyd (Wales) (Green 1984) and 280 kyr at Mesvin (Belgium) (Cahen 1984). The next shift in lithic reduction techniques took place in Europe between 40-35 kyr, depending on the region. In fact, in some regional technological traditions of the early Upper Paleolithic, blank preparation processes typical of the Mousterian continued to be used for some time (e.g., in the Chatelperronian, Szletian, and other leaf-point industries). The duration of the Mousterian is thus extremely long, and there are no notable changes in it through time. Although some internal developments are possible, they were probably ephemeral, specific, local adaptive reactions to climatic fluctua-

tions (cf. Rolland 1981; contra Mellars 1986). No one has yet been able to assign exclusively chronological meaning to any of the aspects of Middle Paleolithic assemblage variability.

This general pattern of uniformity characterizes the Mousterian in the geographical sense as well. The same basic technical processes for stone tool manufacture are found from the Near East to the Urals and to the Atlantic: prepared flake cores to create the same general morphological classes of tools, such as sidescrapers, knives, and denticulates. Across a vast geographical extension, there is such technological similarity that a researcher accustomed to the materials of western Europe can quickly find the same processes present in upper Egypt, Israel, Turkey, or the Balkans.

The immense time range and very broad geographical extent of the Mousterian testify to the adaptive success of these hominids and their behavior. Whatever it represents in behavioral terms, this technology certainly allowed for adaptations to widely varying environments among the different inhabited regions and among the greatly differing climatic regimes that occurred throughout the course of the late Middle and early Upper Pleistocene of Europe. Thus, the apparently simple technology of the Middle Paleolithic, through its capacity for producing a wide variety of solutions from a limited number of techniques (Boëda 1986), was able to deal flexibly with an extreme variety of conditions imposed on human groups by the physical environment.

Aside from the lithic technology, there are many other aspects of behavior that seem to characterize the Middle Paleolithic. Wear traces on stone tools show that they were frequently used on vegetal matter, such as wood. This suggests that non-lithic materials were often utilized as artifacts, even though such objects are themselves only rarely preserved. Stakes, beams, and shafts were probably used in a complex technology that involved distinct sequences of actions even more flexible than those suggested by the lithic inventory alone. Traces of hafting on some stone tools constitute additional evidence of a complementary technology consisting of other materials (skins, sinews, vegetal resins) applied to the lithic elements. Handles aided in tool use, permitting the application of greater force and different kinds of motions during use.

Elaborate, and in some cases even specialized, hunting methods have been suggested on the basis of recent excavations at some Mousterian sites. For example, Neumark (East Germany) exhibits separate specialized activity areas for the butchering of different species, namely bison and red deer (Mania 1987). The site of Zwollen (Poland) shows a similar type of specialized hunting, in this case of horse and bison (Schild and Sulgostowska 1988). Additionally, there seems to be no difference in terms of hunting between the Mousterian and the Aurignacian (Simek 1987; Straus and Heller 1988).

Similarly, the sharing of food at camps, described by Chase (1983), shows the existence of a division of labor within human groups, and implies as well a kind of social solidarity—probably as a result of a long period of socialization. Non-technological, non-subsistence types of behavior have been documented by Marshack (1988) and Poplin (1988), including the Mousterian collection of curious objects such as fossils and minerals, suggesting the existence of esthetic or spiritual considerations even in this remote period.

Cutting and hammering marks on human bones, principally at Krapina in Yugoslavia (T. White 1988), but also at some other Europe sites (Le Mort 1988), suggest the existence of funerary rituals, perhaps of anthropophagic nature. Similarly, the presence of several unquestionable, systematically organized burials as at La Ferrassie (*pace* Gargett 1989) implies, if not religious practices, then at least a feeling of respect for or fear of the dead (Chase and Dibble 1987). Ever since this period, the systematic association of animal remains (horns, antlers, bones) with human burials gives an indication of the troubled and ambiguous relationship between humanity and the animal world, a phenomenon which resurges intensely in the form of animal images in the art of the Upper Paleolithic.

The few traces of structures (e.g., Molodova [Chernysh 1961]), hearths (e.g., Kebara [Meignen et al. 1989]), and spatial organization of living floors (e.g., Biache [Tuffreau and Somme 1988]; Cueva Morín [see Freeman, this volume]; Tonchesberg [Conard 1990]; and Sclayn [Otte 1988]), provide some evidence of a distribution and organization of activities that becomes even more well documented in the Upper Paleolithic. However, the more permanent occupations in the Mousterian resulted in a kind of amalgamation which makes the separation of Mousterian activities more difficult than in the Upper Paleolithic, which may have been a period of greater mobility. In fact, the huge Mousterian sites of the Rhineland, where large excavations have been conducted, show that specialized activity areas did exist during this period, including distinct butchering areas where only a few tools are associated with animal remains (Bosinski 1986).

LITHIC ASSEMBLAGE VARIABILITY

MEASURES OF VARIABILITY

The fastidious descriptions of European lithic assemblages have led to different and often contradictory interpretations—lyric or pathetic—that seem ultimately to be reflections of irreconcilable personal obsessions. Strangely, the criteria for measuring Mousterian variability are very limited in number, just as are the criteria for defining the period itself. In effect, they amount to just three categories of variables:
1. The general character of flake debitage, as measured by the complexity of the reduction sequence, aspects of flake shape, and the relative frequencies of

different forms (e.g., the "Levallois Index," the percentage of centripetal flakes, etc.). This first criterion for describing variability is concerned with the degree and quality of blank preparation.
2. The differing percentages of retouched tools observed among assemblages. Three major classes are distinguished: knives, sidescrapers, and denticulates. Within these classes minor morphological variations often appear at random (perhaps as the result of the intensity of reuse (cf. Dibble 1983). There also exist "vestiges" of early types of tools (i.e., bifaces and discs).
3. Discrete "stylistic" criteria, which are more rarely evoked: particular techniques for tool manufacture

(e.g., inverse retouch, special forms such as cleavers, etc.) or blank production (i.e., shapes, proportions, position of preparatory removals).

These criteria for describing Mousterian variability, apparently very simple, recombine in an infinity of ways, such that no one assemblage is identical to another in all respects.

TRADITIONAL EXPLANATIONS

There are also many diverse explanations for the assemblage variability measured according to these criteria, such as:

1. The cultural paradigm (Bordes 1968), which seeks to explain the differences in percentages of tool groups by assuming the existence of neighboring, contemporaneous traditions. This paradigm is incapable of explaining "mixed" assemblages and it is contradicted by the evidence of overlapping geographical areas for supposedly very distinct "cultural traditions." In fact, numerous assemblages containing "Quina" sidescrapers, Levallois debitage, and bifaces show that a single human group was fully capable of using a variety of techniques (Otte 1988).

2. An hypothesis of different activities has also been proposed to explain the same variation of tool percentages described by Bordes (Binford 1968). This hypothesis supposes a close relationship between the form and function of the tools, something that has been disproven by microwear analyses (e.g., Beyries 1987). Furthermore, it would imply that in some regions of Europe the Mousterians were mostly hunting bears, whereas in other regions they were mostly scraping hides, since different assemblage groups, or facies, are found concentrated in certain regions, sometimes to the exclusion of others.

3. The hypothesis of diachronic evolution (Mellars 1969; see Mellars, this volume), which does not explain cases of stratigraphic inversion among some of the facies, their reoccurrence, or the immense temporal duration of some of them.

NEW EXPLANATIONS

More recently other criteria of variability have been described and put to use in explanation: the role of lithic raw materials (Geneste 1985), the intensity of resharpening (Dibble 1988), settlement locations (Barton 1988), and relationships to the physical environments (Rolland 1981; and see Dibble and Rolland, this volume). Based on these and other works, one can deduce other factors that may have influenced the variability seen among Mousterian lithic assemblages.

THE ROLE OF RAW MATERIAL

At the site of Sclayn (Belgium), the main layer, dated to 130 kyr and attributed to the Last Interglacial, contains pieces made on diverse raw materials, which are strictly contemporaneous (Otte et al. 1988). If separate analyses were made on the different raw material types, one would conclude that different assemblage groups were present, namely, a Denticulate Mousterian, a Charentian, or, just as easily, a "Typical Mousterian." The role of raw materials has an impact not only on mechanical phenomena, but also in other ways that are much more complex and subtle. For example, the chert, which is local in origin, fell from the cave walls and ceiling in natural flakes, just like limestone spalls. It was retouched without preparation into simple denticulates. The quartz of this layer, which is of only slightly more distant origin (it was collected from the river a few hundred meters away) was knapped in situ to produce some crude perforators and becs. The flint of non-local origin (from about thirty km distant) was knapped in the cave in a centripetal manner ("para-Levallois") and yielded massive cortical flakes that were made into "Quina" sidescrapers by scalariform retouch. And large Levallois flakes made on a fine-grained sandstone are represented in their last preparatory stage, having been manufactured elsewhere and brought into the site.

Depending on the distance to and nature of raw materials, the same Mousterian knappers used different flaking schemes appropriate not only to the desired kind of tool (thus to function) and to their "style," but also to the ease of transport and the needs likely to be encountered at the site. Thus, different technical behaviors were combined within one single technological assemblage, this composite entity being left behind for the archaeologist to find. Because all of these behaviors were associated in the same creative cultural context, the various technical schemes should not to be mistaken for separate cultural traditions.

The interdependence between form and technique in exploiting raw materials has also been shown by Callow (1986) to exist on a diachronic axis at the site of La Cotte de Saint Brelade. During the different occupation phases, which were separated by sea level fluctuations, raw materials were differentially accessible at the site. What is interesting is that typological changes in the lithic industry followed the marine fluctuations. During periods of difficult access to materials, the artifacts were smaller, made on thick flakes using inverse or bifacial retouch, and altogether constituted a kind of impoverished "Charentian" industry. But with marine regression, these traits diminished as large nodules of good raw materials became more accessible.

THE REDUCTION SEQUENCE

The scheme of successive actions used to work a given block of stone can be experimentally reconstructed from the flake scars observed on lithic remains. Each phase of a proposed reduction sequence can then be compared with objects found at a site (Geneste 1985) and can thereby show which elements were produced in situ and which were transported to the sites. Such variations can, in turn, modify the appearance or facies of assemblages completely independent of any notion of cultural "traditions."

The case of Maestricht-Belvédère (Netherlands) includes an example of this sort of behavior broken down into different temporal episodes. A block of flint, derived from a Cretaceous outcrop, was exported, roughed out, and then knapped at this temporary workshop site, from which appropriate blanks for tools were in turn exported. Thus, Maestricht-Belvédère represents an intermediate step in the planned, organized transport of stone (Roebroeks et al. 1988). Conversely, the nearby site of Liège Saint-Walburge, which is located right on a flint outcrop, contained very numerous knapping debris, tools, and massive bifaces (De Puydt et al. 1913). In this case, the abundance of good quality material lends a "Levallois" or "Acheulian" appearance to what is, in fact, the same kind of industry.

MOUSTERIAN "FACIES" REVISITED

The groups of tool assemblages described originally by Bordes (1968), as facies of the Mousterian, can now be examined in a different light.

The Quina Mousterian, with many thick tools, mostly sidescrapers, now seems to be not only a grouping of special tools, but more importantly, the result of a succession of actions. These actions began with the choice of a raw material, then continued with the preparation of thick flakes used as special

blanks, which were then successively deeply retouched and frequently resharpened in such ways as to modify the shape of the tool (Turq 1989; Dibble 1987). Thus, these assemblages represent a particular succession of actions and so have no validity in defining a cultural "tradition." In another site or even at another spot in the same site, one could just as easily have used the Levallois technique on a different raw material for an equally specific purpose: the preparation of standardized flakes. The discards from this preparation can be found at a distant location simply because they were involved in a different system of articulation of technical stages in space and time. Thus one can see a typical Mousterian transformed into a Mousterian of Acheulian tradition by the discovery of just a handful of bifaces.

The case of the "Denticulate Mousterian" is probably different, since it seems to be related to specific activities and to a completely different type of technical behavior vis à vis raw materials which are often coarser (Geneste 1985; Beyries 1987).

SPATIAL EXTENT

The classic typological aspects of the Mousterian are found far from its "promised land" of the Perigord, in Belgium and Germany (Ulrix-Closset 1975; Bosinski 1986). But other means of production, notably inverse flat retouch and bifacial retouch, can also be observed in these assemblages with regard to the three main classes of tools (knives, sidescrapers, and points). Superimposed on the early traditions in the Belgian "Lotharingia," these technological traditions get stronger as one goes eastward: Konigsaüe in East Germany (Mania 1987), Prodnik in Poland (Kozlowski 1977), and Russia (Gábori 1976).

In fact, in any given period, one can perceive the appearance of minor stylistic differences of significant duration that possess genuine value as regional traditions—not just as the result of technique. Such regional stylistic differentiation, already observed by Bordes in the center of France, becomes more marked as one goes outward from there: a concentration of bifaces in the west, cleavers to the south, and an increase in foliate tools to the east. The recognition of cultural traditions thus becomes clearer as a clustering of sites, both geographically and in terms of their means of manufacturing common types of tools.

THE NEW ERA

With the Upper Paleolithic, everything suddenly changed, probably for no other reason than fashion, since the former deeply implanted type of adaptation to the European environments required no change. The concomitant appearance of a new subspecies of *Homo* and new technologies strongly suggests either a process of invasion or gene flow across the continent from an external source. One can propose three different but simultaneous processes and histories to account for these phenomena (Otte 1988):

1. The Aurignacian was entirely independent and autonomous, inventing the idea of making art images and using pendants as decoration. For these people, the definition of cultural identification transcends the exclusively technological domain (the industry) and is manifested in specific types of objects that mark the individual and his group (R. White 1988). It seems that particular functions became separated as activities became specialized, and adaptive potential was *reduced* by this specialization. Based on its common repertoire found over a very broad geographical area, it seems that the Aurignacian represents a process of *diffusion*.

2. The Chatelperronian was the product of Neandertals (at least at St. Césaire) imitating the blade and bone working techniques and site structural organization of the incoming Aurignacian (Pelegrin 1986), as well as elements of their symbol system (represented by pendants, such as those found at Arcy-sur-Cure). As has been shown by Harrold (1988), the Chatelperronian range shrank as the Aurignacian territory expanded. It thus represents the product of *acculturation* processes, whose ultimate result (extinction versus some contribution by the Western European Neandertals to later populations) is still hotly debated.

3. The vast region of the northern European plain, stretching from England to Russia, witnessed a separate, independent evolutionary trajectory. Developing out of the Mousterian traditions of Central Europe and moving northward during the Würm Interpleniglacial, the makers of the leaf-point industries created their own blade techniques. These techniques are somewhat older (40-35 kyr) than the earliest Aurignacian there and also outside the sphere of their influence. This technological innovation, based on local regional traditions, constituted a third kind of process leading to leptolithization, and was an independent invention of the techniques characteristic of the Upper Paleolithic.

CONCLUSIONS

Each one of the factors considered earlier (time, activities, cultural traditions) does play a part in causing the overall variability of the Middle Paleolithic assemblages. None, however, has exclusive explanatory power. In addition to them, taphonomic processes and behavioral factors intervene in significant ways to condition the nature of variability that we see and measure. Notably the relationships of sites to raw material sources, the partitioning of reduction sequences among sites, the relationships between particular kinds of techniques and specific types of tools, and the effects of resharpening, all have significant impact on the composition of Mousterian assemblages. Thus, the observed variability is at the same time both simpler in nature and more complex in causation than had been thought until now.

It is on the basis of inter-regional comparisons that we are most likely to see evidence for the development of cultural traditions. These regional traditions in the Mousterian gave rise to the different forms of adaptation that characterized the transition to the Upper Paleolithic: the Aurignacian in the Southeast, the Chatelperronian in the West, and the foliate point industries in the more northern and eastern areas as a result of migration of the Middle European groups into the plains.

ACKNOWLEDGMENTS

I wish to thank L. G. Straus, Department of Anthropology, University of New Mexico, the translator of this paper.

REFERENCES CITED

Barton, M.-C.
1988   *Lithic Variability and Middle Paleolithc Behavior: New Evidence from the Iberian Peninsula.* BAR International Series 408. Oxford: BAR.

Beyries, S.
1987   *Variabilité de l'industrie lithique au Moustérien, approache fonctionnelle sur quelques gisements français.* BAR International Series 328. Oxford: BAR.

Binford, S. R.
1968   Variability and Change in the Near Eastern Mousterian of Levallois Facies. Pp. 49-60 in *New Perspectives Archeology.* Chicago: Aldine.

Boëda, E.
1986   Approche technologique du concept levallois et évaluation de son champ d'application: étude de trois gisement saaliens et weichséliens de la France septentrionale. Thesis, Université de Paris.

Bordes, F.
1968   *Le Paléolithique dans le monde.* Paris: Éditions Hachette.

Bosinski, G.
1986   *Archäologie des Eiszeitalters, Vulkanimus und lavaindustrie am mittelrhein.* Mainz: Römisch Germainisches Zentralmuseum.

Cahen, D.
1984   Paléolithique inférieur et moyen en Belgique. Pp. 133-156 in *Peuples chasseurs de la Belgique Préhistorique dans leur cadre naturel,* eds. D. Cahen and P. Haesaerts. Brussels: Institut des Sciences Naturelles.

Callow, P., and Conford, J.-M.
1986   *La Cotte de St. Brelade 1961-1978.* Norwich: Geo Books.

Chase, P.-G.
1983   *The Hunters of Combe Grenal: Approaches to Middle Paleolithic Subsistence in Europe.* BAR International Series 286. Oxford: BAR.

Chase, P. G., and Dibble, H.
1987   Middle Paleolithic Symbolism: A Review of Current Evidence and Interpretations. *JAA* 6:263-296.

Chernysh, A. P.
1961   *Paleolitichna stoianka Molodave.* Kiev: Akad. Nauk.

Conard, N. J.
1990   Tönchesberg and its Position in the Paleolithic Prehistory of Northern Europe. Ph.D. dissertation, Yale University, New Haven, CT.

De Puydt, M.; Hamal-Nandrin, J.; and Servais, J.
1913   *Le gisement de Sainte-Walburge dans le limon Hesbayen.* Liège: Institut Préhistorique Liégeois.

Dibble, H. L.
1983   Variability and Change in the Middle Paleolithic of Western Europe and the Near East. Pp. 53-71 in *The Mousterian Legacy,* ed. E. Trinkaus. BAR International Series 164. Oxford: BAR.
1987   The Interpretation of Middle Paleolithic Scraper Morphology. *AmAnt* 52(1):109-117.
1988   Typological Aspects of Reduction and Intensity of Utilization of Lithic Resources in French Mousterian. Pp. 181-198 in *Upper Pleistocene Prehistory of Western Eurasia,* eds. H. L. Dibble and A. Montet-White. Philadelphia: University Museum, University of Pennsylvania.

Gábori, M.
1976   *Les civilisations du Paléolithique moyen entre les Alpes et l'Oural: Esquisse historique.* Budapest: Akadémiai Kiadó.

Gargett, R.
1989   Grave Shortcomings: The Evidence for Neandertal Burial. *CA* 30:157-190.

Geneste, J.-M.
1985   Analyse lithique d'industries moustériennes du Périgord: une approche technologique du comportement des groupes humains au Paléolithique moyen. Thesis, Université de Bordeaux.

Green, S. H.
1984 *Pontnewydd Cave, A Lower Palaeolithic Hominid Site in Wales.* Cardiff: National Museum of Wales.

Harrold, F. B.
1988 The Chatelperronian and the Early Aurignacian. Pp. 157-191 in *France, The Early Upper Paleolithic Evidence from Europe and the Near East.* BAR International Series 437. Oxford: BAR.

Hublin, J. J.
1989 La transition Néandertaliens/Hommes de type moderne en Europe occidental: aspects paléontologiques et culturels. Pp. 23-38 in *L'homme de Néandertal*, ed. M. Otte. Vol. 7: *L'extinction.* ERAUL No. 34. Liège: Université de Liège.

Kozlowski, J.
1977 *Epoka Kamienia Na Ziemiach Polskich.* Warsaw: Panstwowe Wydawnictwo Naukowe.

Le Mort, Fr.
1988 Le décharnement du cadavre chez les néandertaliens: quelques exemples. Pp. 43-45 in *L'homme de Néandertal*, ed. M. Otte. Vol. 5: *La pensée.* ERAUL No. 32. Liège: Université de Liège.

Leroi-Gourhan, A.
1964 *Le Geste et la Parole, Technique et langage.* Paris: Albin Michel.

Mania, D.
1987 Das Mittelpal olithikum van Neumark-Nord, eine besondere ökologis-chökonomische Fazies Beute-und Schlachtpl tze am Ufer eines Sees. *Colloque Halle* (August 23-28) (preprint).

Marshack, A.
1988 The Neanderthals and the Human Capacity for Symbolic Thought: Cognitive and Problem-Solving Aspects of Mousterian Symbol. Pp. 57-91 in *L'homme de Néandertal*, ed. M. Otte. Vol. 5: *La pensée.* ERAUL No. 32. Liège: Université de Liège.

Meignen, L.; Bar-Yosef, O.; and Goldberg, P.
1989 Les structures de combustions moustéri-ennes de la grotte de Kébara (Mont Carmel, Israel). Pp. 141-146 in *Nature et fonction des foyers préhistoriques*, ed. M. Olive and Y. Taborin. Mémoires du Musée de Préhistoire d'Ile de France No. 2.

Mellars, P.
1969 The Chronology of Mousterian Industries in the Périgord Region of South-West France. *PPS* 35:134-171.
1986 A New Chronology for the French Mousterian Period. *Nature* 322:410-411.

Otte, M.
1988 Du Paléolithique moyen au supérieur: la nature de la différence. *Colloque de Cambridge*, in preparation.

Otte, M.; Evrard, J.-M.; and Mathis, A.
1988 Interprétation d'un habitat au Paléolithique moyen: La grotte de Sclayn, Belgique. Pp. 95-124 in *Upper Pleistocene Prehistory of Western Eurasia*, eds. H. L. Dibble and A. Montet-White. Philadelphia: University Museum, University of Pennsylvania.

Pelegrin, J.
1986 Technologie lithique une méthode appliquée à l'étude de deux séries du Périgordien ancien. Thesis, Université de Paris.

Poplin, F.
1988 Aux origines néandertaliennes de l'art. Matiére, forme, symétries. Contribution d'une galène et d'un oursin fossile taillé de Merry-sur-Yonne (France). Pp. 109-116 in *L'homme de Néandertal*, ed. M. Otte. Vol. 5: *La pensée.* ERAUL No. 32. Liège: Université de Liège.

Roebroeks, W.; Kolen, J.; and Rensink, E.
1988 Planning Depth, Anticipation and the Organization of Middle Palaeolithic Technology: The "Archaic Natives" Meet Eve's Descendants. *Helinium* 28/1:17-34.

Rolland, N.
1981 The Interpretation of Middle Palaeolithic Variability. *Man* 16:15-42.

Schild, R., and Sulgostowska, Z.
1988   Le Paléolithique moyen de la plaine nord européenne à Zwollen, premiers résultats. Pp. 149-167 in *L'homme de Néandertal*, ed. M. Otte. Vol. 8: *La mutation*. ERAUL No. 35. Liège: Université de Liège.

Simek, J. F.
1987   Spatial Order and Behavioural Change in the French Palaeolithic. *Antiquity* 61:25-40.

Straus, L., and Heller, C.
1988   Explorations of the Twilight Zone: The Early Upper Paleolithic in Cantabria and Gascony. Pp. 97-133 in *The Early Upper Palaeolithic*, eds. J. Hoffecker and C. Wolf. BAR 437. Oxford: BAR.

Tuffreau, A., and Somme, J.
1988   *Le gisement paléolithique moyen de Biache-Saint-Vaast (Pas-de-Calais)*. Vol. 1: *Stratigraphie, Environment. Etudes Archéologiques* (1st part).

Turq, A.
1985   Le Moustérien de type Quina du Roc de Marsal (Dordogne). *BSPF* 82(2):46-51.
1989   Approche technologique et économique du faciès Moustérien du type Quina: étude préliminaire. *BSPF* 86(8):244-256.

Ulrix-Closset, M.
1975   *Le paléolithique moyen dans le bassin mosan en Belgique*. Wetteren: Universa.

Vandermeersch, B.
1989   L'extinction des Néandertaliens. In *L'homme de Néandertal*, ed. M. Otte. Vol. 7: *L'extinction*. ERAUL No. 34. Liège: Université de Liège.

Verjux, C., and Rousseau, D.-D.
1986   La retouche Quina: une mise au point. *BSPF* 83(11-12):404-415.

White, R.
1988   Production Complexity and Standardisation in Early Aurignacian Bead and Pendant Manufacture: Evolutionary Implications. Pp. 366-390 in *The Human Revolution: Behavioural and Biological Perspectives on the Origins of Modern Humans*, eds. P. Mellars and C. Stringer. Edinburgh: Edinburgh University Press.

White, T.
1988   *The Minimum Number of Neandertals in the Krapina Assemblage*. Zagreb: 12th International Congress of Anthropological and Ethnological Sciences.

IV

The Place of the Mousterian of the Charente in the Middle Paleolithic of Southwest France

André Debénath

The Charente basin experienced a great density of human occupation during the Lower and Middle Paleolithic, evidenced by a number of occupied sites yielding important asemblages of both lithic and hominid remains. However, the richness of this area masks the fact that its prehistory is still not well understood, principally because many of the most important sites, such as La Quina, Chateauneuf-sur-Charente, and other sites in the valley of the Eaux-Claires, were excavated many years ago. Recent excavations have been more restricted in scope and have tended to concentrate on sites which have suffered from varying amounts of destruction, such as La Cave, Montgaudier, St. Césaire, etc. The new exca-vations at La Quina, involving the Universities of Bordeaux, Arizona, and Pennsylvania, are only begin-ning and do not yet permit any definitive conclusions. Moreover, the geological history of the region is only beginning to be outlined and so it is difficult to have a precise view of the chronology of the industries. There are also problems concerning the definition and origin of the Mousterian industries here, due largely to the differential quality of available data and the fact that only a few sites, notably Artenac, Fontéchevade, and La Chaise, have yielded evidence of industries prior to the last glaciation. We shall begin, then, with a brief review of the industries of the last of these sites.

THE RISSIAN INDUSTRIES OF LA CHAISE

At La Chaise, Bordes et al. (1953) noted the pres-ence of at least two different industries, a Denticulate Mousterian and what he called an attenuated Mouste-rian of Acheulian Tradition. Signficantly, these two industries were completely different from the assem-blage group more characteristic of the region, i.e., the Quina Mousterian named after the site of La Quina. My own controlled excavations at La Chaise (Debé-nath 1974, 1983, 1988) have, in fact, differentiated three industrial facies at La Chaise, the first two of which date to the end of the Riss glaciation and the third from the beginning of the Early Würm (based on sedimentological and palynological studies, as well as absolute dates). These facies are:

1. Facies A, with Levallois debitage, a high unre-stricted faceting index (IFs), and well-developed use of platform rejuvenation or *reprise du talon* (see Debénath 1988). This industry comes from the lower levels dated to the Riss III, i.e., Couches 51-53.

2. Facies B, with a less marked use of Levallois and a lower IFs than is seen in Facies A, but a higher restricted faceting index (IF). This facies comes from the upper Riss III levels, Couches III-VIII.

3. Facies C. In this facies, most of the technical char-acteristics are attenuated, with little Levallois debitage, and only sporadic use of the *reprise du talon* technique; only the unrestricted faceting index is similar to that seen in the other facies. This industry is associated with the Early Würm layers of the Abri Suard (Couches I and II) and can also be ascribed to Couch-es 9 and 10 of the Abri Bourgeois-Delaunay.

While the Charentian Index (IC) is moderate in Facies A and B (IC = 17 and 15, respectively), it is clearly more elevated in Facies C (IC = 30). In con-

DEBÉNATH

trast, the Quina Index (IQ), whether computed as a restricted or unrestricted index, is in all cases very low. There is always weak representation of bifaces (the Biface Index reaches a maximum of only 8, rising in a general fashion from Facies A to C in Suard, but decreasing to almost 0 in the Early Würm of Bourgeois-Delaunay). Moreover, the bifaces are almost always very small and generally of poor quality (most are atypical, partial, and often with a cortical backing). All of these characteristics are reminiscent of the Meridional Acheulian of the Perigord. Of the flake tools, scrapers constitute the dominant group, with a large proportion of simple convex types. The proportions of denticulates vary inversely with the *racloirs*.

The typological originality of these industries resides partly in the presence of tools that are otherwise rare in Western Europe in the final Riss and Early Würm: pedunculates, bifacial foliate pieces, and numerous Kostienki knives (which are sometimes atyp-

ical). There is also one Chatelperron point and numerous composite tools often associated with the *racloirs*, denticulates and notches, and other types of tools.

As is true for other Rissian industries that have few or no bifaces, it is difficult to make direct comparisons between these early industries from La Chaise and those of the "classic" Acheulian. The techniques used in the manufacture of the La Chaise tools, as well as the overall typological aspects, suggest that these industries were, in fact, closer to the Mousterian than to the Acheulian. Probably these Rissian industries represent the deep roots of at least a portion of the Mousterian industries of the Charente basin.

Mousterian industries that date to the beginning of the Early Würm are definitely recognized only in the Facies C industries of La Chaise, though there is a possibility that the Mousterian from Montgaudier also dates to this time. Clearly, evidence from other sites of this time is badly needed.

A BRIEF REVIEW OF THE
MOUSTERIAN COMPLEX IN THE CHARENTE

Attention will now be turned to the later Mousterian industries of the Charente. This review will focus primarily on those assemblages that come from the more recent excavations, though, unfortunately, the earlier collections sometimes represent the only available evidence.

THE TYPICAL MOUSTERIAN

The Typical Mousterian is almost unknown in the Charente, except perhaps at Fontéchevade and Le Placard. At the latter site, the excavations of Roche (from 1958-1968) exposed a very small portion of the site and the amount of material recovered is insufficient to make a precise diagnosis (Roche 1965). At Fontéchevade, the upper part of Couche C (Level C1) yielded about 40 objects, which Henri-Martin (1957) attributed to a "Moustérien pointes," but which could also represent a Typical Mousterian. Again, however, the small number of objects prevents any definitive attribution.

THE DENTICULATE MOUSTERIAN

A good example of a Denticulate Mousterian from the Charente comes from the site of Hauteroche—the Grotte-à-Melon at Chateauneuf-sur-Charente. Exca-

vations here were carried out first by Chauvet, followed by M.-C. Cauvin, and later by myself. The material recovered from the upper levels by Cauvin is not very abundant (less than 100 identifiable tools), which means that the interpretation must be tentative. However, it exhibits a slightly Levallois debitage (the Levallois Index, or IL, is 13.09) and the typological Levallois index is low. Faceting is equally low (IF = 29.5, IFs = 15.8). Naturally backed knives are well represented, but there are no typical backed knives. In spite of the small number of tools, Cauvin states that "nonetheless, it presents the characteristic feel of a Denticulate Mousterian . . . typologically, what seems to stand out in this industry is the abundance and variety of scrapers . . . but still the denticulates are very numerous (Group IV real = 23.59, essential = 32.8)."

In my own excavations, Couche 3 yielded more than 1300 objects, with 143 and 119 of them represented in the real and essential counts, respectively. In this assemblage, the Levallois Index is very weak (5.88), the ILty is low, and the unrestricted and restricted faceting indices are low (14.0 and 11.52, respectively). The Backed Knife and Biface Indices are zero, while the Blade Index is nearly so. While the Scraper Index is moderate (29, based on the essential count), the Charentian Index is low. The cumulative diagram for this sample approaches those of other Denticulate Mousterian assemblages, although the rise in the scraper group is higher than that seen in Cauvin's diagram.

Overall, the tools, which are manufactured in a greyish yellow or greyish blue flint, are small and the quality of workmanship is not high. There are several examples of pieces with double patina and naturally backed knives are fairly numerous (15% of the tools). The scrapers are of various types, though simple convex scrapers represent almost one-half of the types and simple straight scrapers are also well represented. The remaining scrapers are distributed among practically all of the types, except for *déjetés*, and, for the most part, transverse varieties. Denticulates and notches (especially the latter) represent about 40% of the tools.

Thus, as evidenced in the excavations by Cauvin, Pradel (see Bordes 1957), and myself, the Denticulate Mousterian of Hauteroche is characterized by an enrichment of scrapers, which distinguishes it somewhat from the Denticulate Mousterian of the Perigord.

The new excavations at La Quina have shown the presence of a Mousterian industry with denticulates in the upper levels of 6C through 2 (lower to higher). While there is a gradual decrease in lithic elements through these levels, almost 85% of the tools are notches and denticulates. This industry probably corresponds to the *Moustérien final* of Germaine Henri-Martin, though she did not extensively report on it. She did mention in several contexts, however, that it preceded a Chatelperronian horizon. A Denticulate Mousterian is also noted by F. Lévêque at La Roche à Pierrot at Saint-Césaire.

THE CHARENTIAN MOUSTERIAN

As its name implies, the Charentian Mousterian is the facies most well represented in the Charente. Compared, for example, with the Perigord, it is more appropriate here to emphasize the distinction between the Quina and Ferrassie subgroups.

THE FERRASSIE TYPE

Two recently excavated sites can be considered here: Artenac and the Abri Lartet at Montgaudier.

The excavations by Vandermeersch at Artenac concentrated on the upper sequence of the site, in which five couches were identified. Couche 2 is the richest (almost 1300 pieces) and was the subject of detailed studies by Meignen et al. (1977). The debitage is slightly Levallois (IL = 18.13), with moderate faceting (IF = 42.23). The different typological components (with a high percentage of scrapers, usually lateral types, and an absence of bifaces and backed knives) led these authors to assign the industry to the the Ferrassie variant of the Charentian Mousterian. Meignen et al. also note that this industry is similar to that of the Abri Commont, located in the Eaux-Claire valley. However, Artenac is technologically distinct from Pons, in which the Levallois character is more evident, and from Couche C of La Ferrassie, for which this facies was defined.

The Abri Lartet of Montgaudier is the only Mousterian locus of that site where the industry is in situ (Debénath and Duport 1987). While all of the beds of this locus have yielded material, only the upper two (1 and 2) are sufficiently rich to afford us a detailed view. These two levels are grouped together for reasons discussed elsewhere (Debénath and Duport 1987).

The material from the Abri Lartet totals 3144 objects, of which there are 402 tools in the complete count and 305 in the essential. The Levallois technique was moderately employed (IL = 13.81) and faceting is generally developed (IF = 25.85; IFs = 18.7). While the strict Blade Index (i.e., the percentage of true blades relative to the total of blades and flakes) is weak (5.74), one notes a laminar tendency in the industry in the unrestricted Blade Index (i.e., percentage of blades and bladey flakes relative to the total), which reaches almost 12.0. The Charentian Index is around 22.0. Moreover, the Quina aspect is modest (IQ large = 15.4, IQ strict = 5.9). Typologically, the Mousterian Group is dominant (62.68 real, 82.63 essential). Groups III and IV (Upper Paleolithic types and denticulates, repectively) are weak. The scrapers represent the principal types made on flakes (IR = 60.12, real, and 79.34, essential). In general they are of average workmanship, quite regular and with light retouch. Like that of Artenac, this industry can be assigned without any doubt to the Charentian group, but it seems that it is somewhat intermediate in form between the Ferrassie and Quina types.

It is also worth noting that all of the technological phases proposed by Geneste (1985) are represented here and that there are also a few unworked (or simply tested) nodules of raw material, mostly cobbles. Cortical flakes constitute almost 20% of the debitage, and are the most common of the ordinary flakes. There is also a high proportion (more than 40%) of retouch flakes. All of this implies that the raw material, probably in the form of small nodules of flint, was collected in the proximity of the site, and that the manufacture of tools took place on site. The small exposure of the excavation does not permit any recognition of specific activity zones.

THE QUINA TYPE

The Quina Mousterian is the assemblage group most represented in the Charente and is the one associated with almost all of the human remains known from this region. Paradoxically, it is still relatively poorly known, since the excavations in the Eaux-Claire valley were done long ago; the material from the sites of Bois du Roc and La Cave is still be studied; the upper shelter of La Vauzelle has yielded a typical, though poor series; the excavations by G. Henri-Martin at La Quina are still not published; and our own work in these layers of this site is just beginning.

The earlier excavations at Chateauneuf-sur-Charente uncovered a Quina Mousterian in which the Levallois Index is practically zero, as are the Blade and Faceting indices. The Scraper Index is around 90, but some reserve should be exercised regarding the sample. Within the scrapers, 38% are simple convex types and 20% are transverse. Bifacial scrapers also exist in small numbers, but they are atypical and may have been confused with actual bifaces in the earlier studies. Biface and Backed Knife Indices are practially zero, but the Charentian Index (40) and the strict Quina Index (30) are both high.

My own controlled excavations in the Quina levels from Chateauneuf have recovered only a small number of objects, but among them scrapers dominate and Quina retouch is well developed. In both series the tools are small and there are none of the very large pieces such as those described earlier by Henri-Martin from La Quina.

An interesting series of Quina Mousterian comes from the recent excavations by Vandermeersch (1967-1980) at Marillac. The section here is about 4 meters and the deposits are constituted of limestone blocks and rubble often in a clayey matrix. These deposits are characterized by a certain homogeneity and their "cold" character is confirmed by the constant presence of reindeer.

Couches 9 and 10, from the lower part of the sequence, were studied by Meignen and Vandermeersch (1987). On the basis of 238 tools, their study shows a high proportion of scrapers (70% and 53% in Couches 9 and 10, respectively). The strict Quina Index is 18 in Couche 9 and 29 in Couche 10, which is close to that from Chateauneuf. Transverse types make up between 35% and 22% of the scrapers, although simple convex scrapers dominate (37% and 55% for the two couches). True denticulates are rare, but there are a number of notches. It is also interesting to note that certain scrapers were frequently resharpened. As at Chateauneuf, there are no very large scrapers.

THE MOUSTERIAN OF ACHEULIAN TRADITION (MTA)

This assemblage group is relatively rare in the caves and rockshelters of the Charente. It may have been present in Level C2 at Fontéchevade. This level, which yielded only about 20 tools, nonetheless had three bifaces, of which at least one could be representative of an MTA industry.

At La Quina, G. Henri-Martin suggested that an MTA existed in the "derniers habitats moustériens" of the upper levels of the site. During the 1987 season of the new excavations, Level 6D produced evidence of an intense fabrication of bifaces not only in the form of many biface retouch flakes, but also in the presence of two complete and four partial bifaces. The two complete examples are small and triangular. A tip of a plano-convex biface of probably large dimensions was also found. Although it is too early to conclude definitively, it seems that this industry represents an MTA, Type B.

The Grotte Clouet, at Cognac, has given the best information about the MTA in the Charente. This site is a small rock shelter 4 m wide and 5 m deep, which opens onto the valley of the Antenne. It was the object of numerous clandestine excavations before Burnez began limited excavations in the upper levels in 1958. These levels also furnished Upper Paleolithic material, including a Perigordian with Noailles burins and perhaps some Aurignacian, *senso lato*. In addition, two Solutrean *pointes à cran* were also found. The MTA comes from Couche 4. Close to 200 objects came from this level, 114 of which make up the real count, but only 58 the essential count. The debitage is Levallois (IL = 30). Faceting is well marked (IF = 75, IFs = 56). The Blade Index is very weak (about 4). The Scraper Index is 24 (essential) and the Acheulian Index is around 7. The Upper Paleolithic Group is moderate (14), but the Group IV (denticulates) is weak. Moreover, the Charentian and Quina indices are low. Of the two bifaces, one is triangular with a broken tip, and the other is oval. It should be noted that all of the handaxes from Clouet, including several found out of stratigraphic context, exhibit virtually identical workmanship: all are made on flakes and preserve the platform surface as a base.

CHRONOSTRATIGRAPHY
OF THE MOUSTERIAN OF THE CHARENTE

The first remark to be made regarding the chronology of the Mousterian of the Charente is that wherever the two industries occur together, the MTA always precedes the Denticulate. The second is to note the general lack of absolute dates for the Middle Paleolithic, especially when compared to the number available for the Upper Paleolithic. For the earlier sites, only La Chaise has been dated absolutely, and for the Mousterian, only La Quina. Dates from the latter, of which there are only two, were obtained for the "Final Mousterian" of La Quina: 34,100 ± 700 (GrN 4494) and 31,000 ± 400 (GrN 4499), the first of which is judged by the laboratory to be the better. We do not know, however, if this date corresponds to the Denticulate Mousterian or to the MTA levels. New dates for the Denticulate Mousterian and MTA based on the new excavations at La Quina are currently being processed.

At the present time we have no hard data that would allow us to place the Mousterian levels of Fontéchevade in the sequence of the Early Würm. Based on geological and faunal data, we can reasonably suggest that the "atypical" Ferrassie from Artenac and the MTA from Clouet date to the first part of the Early Würm, and that the Mousterian of the Abri Lartet at Montgaudier, Hauteroche, Marillac, La Quina, and Saint-Césaire all date to the second part of the Early Würm. This is as precise as we can be for the moment.

REFERENCES CITED

Bordes, F.
1957   Le Moustérien de Hauteroche. Comparisons statistiques. *L'Anthropologie* 61:436-441.

Bordes, F., et al.
1953   Station de La Chaise, comune de Vouthon, grotte Suard, fouilles David. *Bulletin et Memoirs de la Société Archéologique et Historique de la Charente*, 20 pp.

Debénath, A.
1974   Recherches sur les terrains quaternaires Charentais et les industries qui leur sont associées. Thesis, Université de Bordeaux.
1983   Quelques particularités techniques et typologiques des industries de La Chaise-de-Vouthon (Charente). *Actes du 105ème Congres* CNSS (Caen, 1980): 239-247.
1988   Recent Thoughts on the Riss and Early Würm Lithic Assemblages of La Chaise de Vouthon (Charente, France). Pp. 85-89 in *Upper Pleistocene Prehistory of Western Eurasia,* eds. H. Dibble and A. Montet-White. Philadelphia: University Museum, University of Pennsylvania.

Debénath, A., and Duport, L.
1987   Le Moustérien de la Grotte de Montgaudier (Charente), note preliminaire.

Geneste, J.-M.
1985   Analyse lithique d'industries moustériennes du Périgord: une approche technologique du comportement des groupes humains au Paléolithique moyen. Thesis, Université de Bordeaux.

Henri-Martin, G.
1957   La Grotte de Fontechevade. *Annales Institut Paleontologie Humaine.* Memoir 28. Paris.

Meignen, L.; Chech, M.; and Vandermeersch, B.
1977   Le gisement moustérien d'Artenac a Saint-Mary (Charente). *GP* 20(1):281-291.

Meignen, L., and Vandermeersch, B.
1987   Le gisement moustérien de Marillac (Charente) couche 9 et 10. . . . Outillages. Economie de matiéres premières. Pp. 135-144 in *Préhistoire de Poitou-Charentes: problèmes actuels.* Editions du C.T.H.S. Paris.

Roche, A.
1971   La grotte du Placard. *BAFEQ* 1965(3-5):245-250.

V

Middle Paleolithic Settlement in Northern France

Alain Tuffreau

INTRODUCTION

The north of France, which includes the regions of Nord, Pas-de-Calais, and Picardie, and especially the Somme Valley, has played a primary role in the study of Prehistory since the mid-nineteenth century when Boucher de Perthes first advanced the notion of the antiquity of man. Subsequently, several Lower and Middle Paleolithic industries were defined on the basis of lithics recovered from quarries along the Somme and incorporated into the chrono-typological classifications of V. Commont, H. Breuil, F. Bordes, and F. Bourdier. Unlike other regions, especially southern France, which underwent profound reevaluation in the 1960s based on intense excavation of Middle Paleolithic sites, northern France remained comparatively stable. However, the discovery of Biache-Saint-Vaast in 1976 initiated a number of salvage excavations encompassing large areas, and the results from this multidisciplinary operation have revealed a great deal of new information concerning the prehistoric inhabitants, their relationship with the environment, occupation strategies, and tool industries of the loess regions of northwestern Europe at the end of the Middle and beginning of the Upper Pleistocene.

THE NATURAL SETTING

The chalky substrate of northern France (at Bas-Artois, Picardie), which contains an abundance of flint in chalky taluses and alluvial stream deposits, constitutes the northern extension of the Parisian basin. This region, consisting of the Somme basin and the high basins of Escaut and Oise, is between the Atlantic coast and the great northern European plain. Numerous valleys in the chalky plateau, covered locally by tertiary sands, facilitated human migration towards the northeast (Haut-Escaut, Haine basin, and the Sambre-Meuse channel) and England when it was connected to the continent during glacial periods, and towards the southwest (access to the Seine basin through the Oise valley). While this region of northern France belongs to the northernmost part of Europe not covered by the Scandinavian glacier (Figs. 5.1 and 5.2), it was exposed to periglacial conditions during unfavorable climatic phases and marked by the presence of permafrost and, during the coldest periods, polygonal formations created by large ice wedges. Loess was deposited in sites with favorable morphological conditions, downwind and oriented towards the southeast. Only with the advent of the Weichselian periglacial did these loess deposits form a blanket that almost completely covered the substrate (Sommé 1976, 1989). Alluvial sediments composed of gravels from cold phases and fine fluviatile sediments deposited during interglacials are a result of periglacial conditions (Antoine 1989; Sommé et al. 1984) which occurred cyclically, alternating with interglacials and short warming episodes (early glacial phases and interstadials). Recent tectonic movement most likely caused the terracing of the alluvial sediments, which can be seen at Biache-Saint-Vaast in the Scarpe valley (Colbeaux et al. 1988).

A regional chronostratigraphy has been established using the terrace system of the Somme valley (which begins prior to the Bruhnes-Matuyama paleomagnetic boundary) and stratigraphical markers such as paleosurfaces and ice wedges which occur in the loess layers. The Middle Paleolithic covers a vast period of

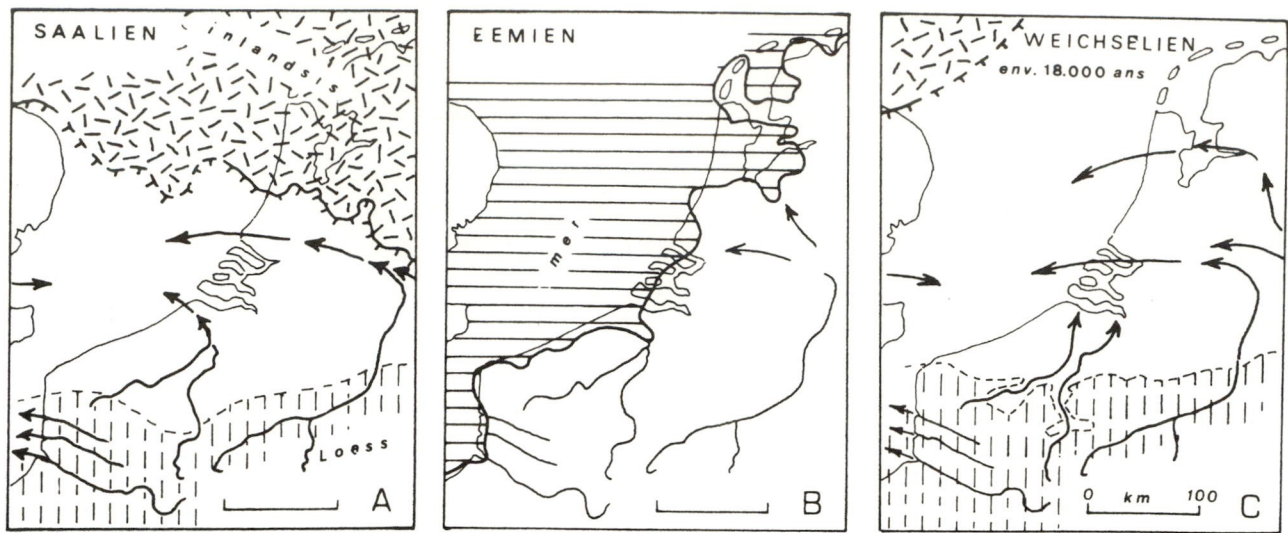

Figure 5.1 *A paleographic map of northwest Europe. (A) Saalian; (B) Eemian Interglacial; (C) Upper Weichselian pleniglacial. (After J. Sommé.)*

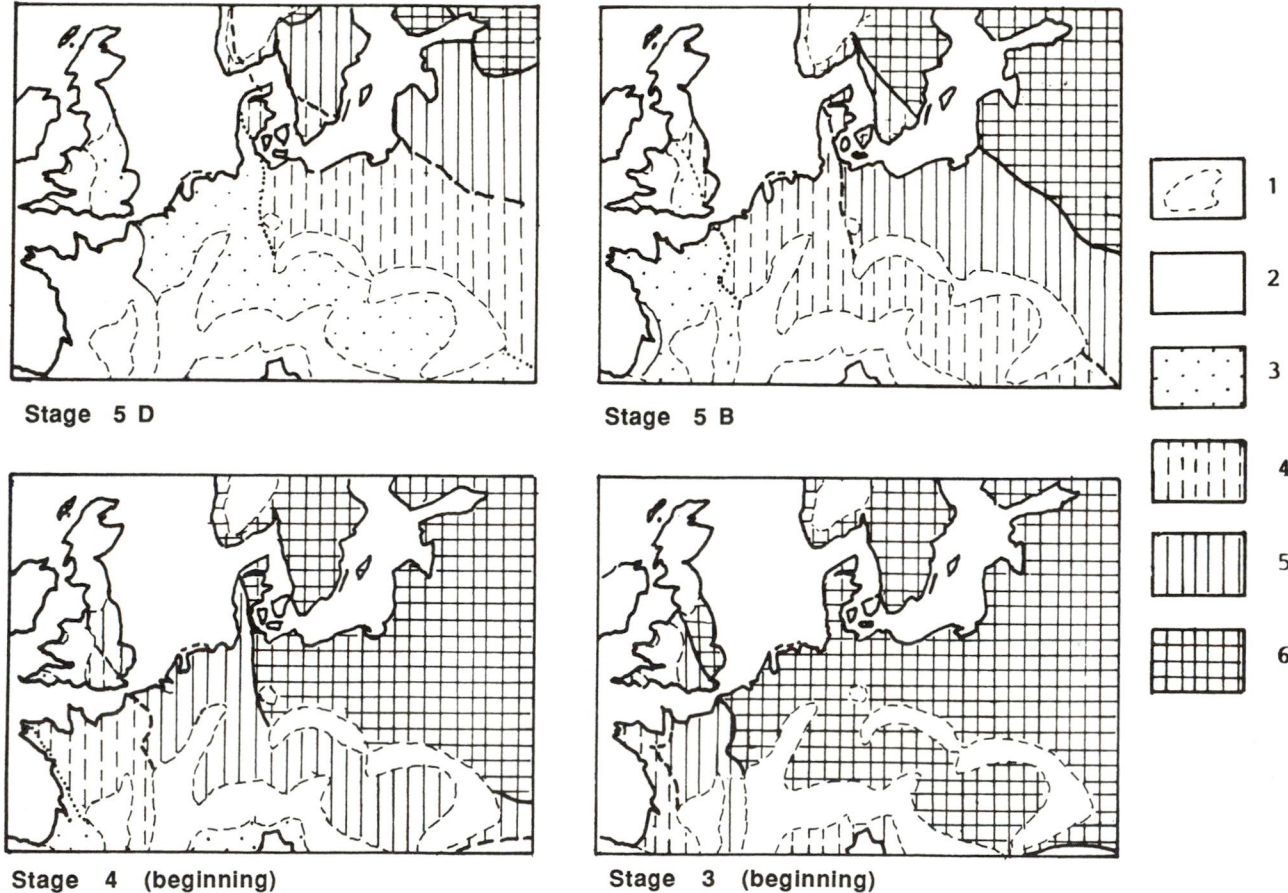

Figure 5.2 *Graphic representations of climatic conditions during upper Pleistocene stages 5d, 5b, 4, and 3. 1: Mountainous zone not considered; 2: permafrost to a depth less than 1 m; 3: permafrost to a depth greater than 1 m; 4: sporadic permafrost; 5: discontinuous permafrost; 6: continuous permafrost.*

time comprising several glacials and interglacials from isotope stage 8 to the first half of stage 3. Middle Paleolithic remains occur in alluvial deposits of lower terraces, in the last loess layers of the Middle Pleistocene and in the first part of the Last Glacial (Weichselian). In the Somme valley, the lower terrace complex, which consists of three depositional units (the Argoeuves, Montières, and Etouvie), dates to the end of the Middle Pleistocene based on its loess covering and relationship with previous terraces. The oldest of these units, the Argoeuves terrace, which contains Levallois industries, dates to isotope stage 8 (Antoine 1989; Haesaerts and Dupuis 1986). The Montières unit (Boutmy-Muchembled quarry) as well as the Biache layer (Scarpe valley) are older than two glacial cycles, the latter formed from the Eemian and Weichselian (Tuffreau et al. 1981). The fluviatile formations at the end of the alluvial sequence are covered by the last of the early loess deposits (Saalian) which was altered by pedogenesis during the Eemian. Thermoluminescence of burnt flint has yielded an absolute date of 175,000 ± 13,000 years, which would place the fine fluviatile sequence of Biache at the beginning of isotopic stage 6.

The fine fluviatile deposits provide the most favorable conditions for conservation of human occupation remains. Pollen and bone are well preserved, which facilitates the interpretation of spatial organization and paleoenvironment of the inhabitants. This is not always the case for loess which, in northern France, is frequently decalcified. However, the sites are always open-air, whether they are found in loess or fluviatile deposits.

The North of France, therefore, is part of a vast paleogeographic domain of Europe and the Northwest, occupying a marginal position at the westernmost part of Eurasia. It was profoundly affected by climatic fluctuations during the Middle and Upper Pleistocene. The other two great paleogeographic regions of western Europe are the middle altitude (*Mittelgebirge* of German workers) areas of Britain, the Massif Central, eastern France, and Central Europe; and southern Europe including the Iberian peninsula, the Midi of France, and Italy. The meridional location of southern Europe resulted in less extreme climatic variations, and the presence of karstic cavities and quasi-absence of loess created a completely different sedimentary context. Loess deposits containing stratigraphic markers in northern France enable correlations to be made with certain areas in the middle altitude regions (Central Europe), although Central European loess is somewhat different, deposited in more sheltered conditions (Haesaerts 1985).

Northern France is therefore an ideal area in which to explore relations between man and his environment in response to extreme, cyclical climatic fluctuations.

CLIMATE AND PALEOENVIRONMENT
IN HUMAN OCCUPATION SITES

Layers containing artifacts such as stone tools and bone fragments with cut marks are conserved in fine fluviatile deposits formed above alluvial gravels. Palynological and faunal analyses (large fauna, micromammals, and mollusks) as well as micromorphological data consistently reveal the presence of very cold, temperate climates (Sommé et al. 1984), without the recognition of an interglacial *sensu stricto*. The archaeological sequence at Biache, for example, indicates fluctuations from cold temperate to warm continental conditions, with marked seasonal changes such as freezing in the winter. The principal human occupation with the most remains, including the two human crania, coincides with the bioclimatic optimum. Archaeological layers are still present at the base of the loess sequence, which has indicated a second cold temperate stage prior to the establishment of full glacial conditions. Similar paleoclimatic conditions have been determined at the Acheulian site of Cagny-l'Epinette, where the archaeological layers are likewise in fine fluviatile sediments (Tuffreau et al. 1986).

Artifacts from downslope loess sequences also come from occupations during cold temperate climates of Early Glacial type, as can be seen at Riencourt-les-Bapaume (salvage excavations on the North TGV track), at Seclin, which dates to the beginning of the Last Glacial (Tuffreau et al. 1985), and the upper levels (D, D1) of Biache-Saint-Vaast. There is as yet no evidence for the presence of man during a full glacial, but instead all remains of human occupation occur in interstadial contexts. Artifacts found in loess deposits can usually be correlated with intraloess surfaces demonstrating slight alteration, as is the case at Corbehem (first pleniglacial before the Weichselian pleniglacial, isotope stage 3; Tuffreau 1979). Likewise, the presence of humans during full interglacials has not been clearly established. This could be due in part to the short duration of interglacials, on the order of tens of thousands of years, in relation to an entire glacial cycle. For example, the early Weichselian Glacial (substages 5d-5a), which covers about 40,000 years, contains numerous remains of human occupation. In addition, stable interglacial conditions are not very favorable for downslope sedimentation processes and furthermore, archaeological remains from these times were not protected by a thick sedimentary layer and so were washed away during erosion of the upper part of the Bt horizon. This is in contrast to glacial periods, especially their beginnings, as indicated by the pedocomplex of the early Weichselian Glacial (Sommé et al. 1986; Van Vliet-Lanöe 1986). The development of such a pedocomplex, locally important in downslope loess sequences, resulted from unstable morphoclimatic fluctuations favorable for entrapment of human artifacts.

However, the cold, temperate nature of fine fluviatile sediments from different layers in the Somme basin (the Upper, Middle, and Lower terrace complex), determined on the basis of palynological analyses, could be due to climatic conditions resulting from ancient atmospheric conditions. Peat bogs extending into Northern France during the Holocene have left traces of an oceanic climate which are not found in prior interglacials. In effect, these peat bogs are absent from alluvial sequences in the Middle and Upper Pleistocene of the Somme. If Munaut's (1988) hypothesis is confirmed, such palynologically based climatic conditions would in large part be interglacial, with continental sylvo-steppe environments, rather than interstadial. In this case, certain artifacts included in fine fluviatile sediments would reflect human occupation during interglacials. However, this type of occupation has not been confirmed outside of alluvial contexts because of the absence of sedimentary deposits (loess layers) on slopes, and many of the stone tools found there are in disturbed, secondary gravels eroding from the interglacial pedocomplex.

The distribution of Middle Paleolithic sites is closely linked to the hydrographic network (Tuffreau 1988). Sites are situated in valleys, sheltered from northwestern winds, around or slightly above riverbeds. Nearby chalk taluses, providing shelter from wind as well as an abundant source of flint, were one attraction. But the preference for valley occupation can also be explained by the presence of wooded prairies and, as has been observed at Seclin, gallery forests which provided favorable conditions for large mammals such as bovines, rhinoceroses, deer, and bears, of which numerous remains have been found at Biache-Saint-Vaast. As suggested by de Heinzelin (1984), this type of mosaic environment is also favorable for the exploitation of plant resources by humans, although evidence for this has not been preserved in the archaeological record to the same degree as faunal remains have been. However, the lack of permanent water resources on plateaus, due to the depth of the water tables, would most likely have provided rather hostile environments. The highest sites all have a sandy, Tertiary substrate. Conditions there must have been similar to those in the valleys, due to water tables close to the surface that fed springs at the contact between sand and impermeable clay layers. The richness of archaeological remains in the early last glacial pedocomplex is therefore due to the importance of the biomass as well as the favorable preservation conditions.

THE NATURE OF THE SITES

It is a fact that the walls of caves and rock shelters act as natural limits to constrain human activity and the distribution of archaeological remains. Thus, such topographical constraints in these kinds of sites render the observation of separate occupations rather difficult, especially given also that boundaries between occupations are rarely provided by sterile sediments. The situation is completely different for open-air sites, however. There, remains of human activity extend over a surface of at least a few hundred square meters, a situation which corresponds to occupations in natural sites without limits discernible during excavation. In order to study internal organization of open-air sites, then, it is necessary to conduct large-scale horizontal excavations using *décapage* methods in order to expose as many occupation floors as possible, these being defined by Bordes (1975:142) as "an observable surface on which paleolithic man lived during a period of time short enough that the position of artifacts may be correlated to his activities." During areal excavation of these sites, sterile sedimentary levels frequently separate archaeological layers, or they can be discerned by the relative positions of artifacts, especially if there are adequate numbers of remains.

The total accumulation of lithic remains is the result of specialized activities that have taken place in separate locations, an observation which has been substantiated at Riencourt-les-Bapaume (Early Weichselian Glacial), where excavations covered a surface of 10,000 sq. m. The products of different phases of the *chaîne opératoire*, or lithic reduction sequence, are often found scattered throughout the layer over several tens of square meters, as is the case at Biache-Saint-Vaast (Tuffreau and Sommé 1988). It is therefore necessary to determine the *chaîne opératoire* phase to which lithic material belongs before classifying it according to industry.

THE LITHIC ASSEMBLAGES

The Middle Paleolithic seems to appear suddenly in Northern France, without evidence for continuity with the Lower Paleolithic (Figs. 5.3 and 5.4). This interpretation is reinforced by the fact that lower terraces and the last loess deposits of the recent Middle Pleistocene always contain assemblages with Levallois debitage and tools made on standardized flakes that differ from assemblages of the upper and middle terraces (Champ du Mars and Stade à Abbeville quarries; Cagny-la-Garenne and Cagny-l'Epinette, respectively). These earlier industries usually contain Acheulian-type bifaces and tools made on more variable flakes, and they are dominated by notches and denticulates (Tuffreau 1987, 1989).

Levallois debitage is present in all industries of Northern France. Quantitative differences in Levallois debitage seem to result primarily from spatial localizations. Of greater significance are the changes in lithic technology that took place in the late Middle Pleistocene, which permitted the development of the Levallois technique. In fact, the technological analysis of material from recent excavations has revealed an important variability in Levallois debitage. Besides classical Levallois flake production, where a single flake is removed from a prepared core, another technique involves the removal of several predetermined flakes from the same core (Fig. 5.5). This is the recurrent flaking method that is present at Biache-Saint-Vaast (Boëda 1988a and b).

It is possible to subdivide the Middle Paleolithic into two phases, one from the late Middle Pleistocene (isotope stages 6–8), the other from the Upper Pleistocene (isotope stages 5–first half of 3). This division is not only chronologic, but also corresponds to the lithic industries, not all of which are present in the same climatic-sedimentary deposits. This is the case, for example, in Acheulian biface industries from the recent Middle Pleistocene and for the MTA and Micoquian, from the Weichselian.

THE EARLIER PHASE OF THE MIDDLE PALEOLITHIC

Very different assemblages are present during this phase, consisting of Mousterian industries and biface industries termed Epi-Acheulian and Middle Paleolithic of Cambresian facies.

The Middle Paleolithic of Cambresian facies consists of lithic assemblages characterized by the presence of tools on evolved flakes, associated with numerous bifaces. This is the case at the Atelier Commont, which contains morphologically varying bifaces, asso-

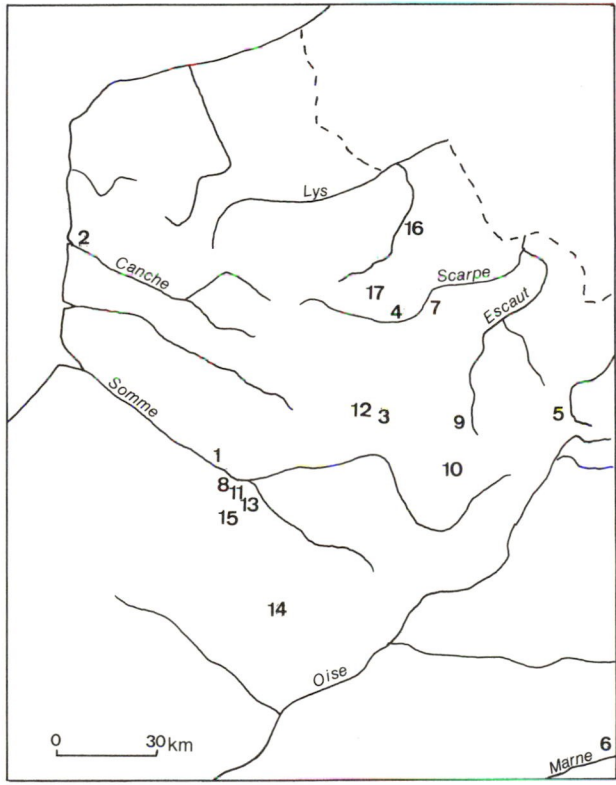

Figure 5.3   A map of Middle Paleolithic sites in northern France that are cited in the text. 1: Argoeuves; 2: Bagarre (Etaples); 3: Bapaume; 4: Biache-Saint-Vaast; 5: Busigny; 6: Champvoisy; 7: Corbehem; 8: Etouvie; 9: Gouzeau-court; 10: Longavesnes; 11: Montières; 12: Riencourt-les-Bapaume; 13: Saint-Acheul (Atelier Commont); 14: Saint-Just-en-Chaussée; 15: Salouel; 16: Seclin; 17: Vimy.

ciated with evolved flakes and a variety of scrapers (over one-third of the tools are on flakes) as well as a significant number of Upper Paleolithic types such as backed knives and endscrapers (Bordes and Fitte 1953; Tuffreau and Fagnart 1986/87). The lithic series from Gouzeaucourt (Marcy 1989; Tuffreau and Bouchet 1985) contains over 500 flat bifaces, which account for over one-third of the tools recovered from an excavation of 120 sq. m. Oval and cordiform types dominate, while elongated types are completely absent. Most flake tools are notches and denticulates, but the scrapers, with very scaled retouch which is unusual for this part of France, are very well made. Levallois debitage is rare. Morphologically different bifaces are found at Vimy, Longavesnes, and in layer 5 of Bagarre.

These data, primarily from Gouzeaucourt, indicate a persistence of bifaces into a Middle Paleolithic setting, without clear evolutionary links with the preceding classic Acheulian industries. These industries, which are late Acheulian on the basis of the bifaces and Mousterian on the basis of the flake tools, were previously named Upper Acheulian, although they could have been named Mousterian of Acheulian Tradition (MTA) if this term had not already been used in a different sense. Instead, they have been named Middle Paleolithic of Cambresian facies (PMC).

Age B. P.	Oxygen Isotope Stage	Alluvial terrace formations (nappes) or silt deposits (loess)	Sites	Industries
	3	Recent Loess	Corbehem	Typical Mousterian
	4	Humiferous Complex	Riencourt	Micoquian
	a	Humiferous Complex	Seclin	Blade Industries
	5 b			
	c			Typical Mousterian MTA
115 000	d			
127 000	e	Interglacial Soil		
	6	Nappe d'Etouvie older loess		
	7		Biache	Ferrassie Mousterian
			Bapaume Salouel	Epi - Acheulian Denticulate Mousterian
	8	Nappe de Montières older loess	Gouzeaucourt Atelier Commont	
		Nappe d'Argoeuves		

Figure 5.4   *Chronostratigraphic table for the principal Middle Paleolithic sites in northern France.*

The Epi-Acheulian includes assemblages from Bapaume-Osiers, Montières, and Boutmy-Muchembled quarry which contain rare Acheulian biface types and tools on Mousterian flakes. The few bifaces present do not belong to any specific type, but pointed forms are most frequent. The utilization of Levallois debitage is generalized and there is a variety of standardized flake tools.

Finally, numerous assemblages containing all the technological and typological characteristics of certain classic Mousterian industries of the Last Glaciation are present in the recent Middle Pleistocene of northern France. This is especially true for the Ferrassie assemblages (Champvoisy, cf. Tuffreau 1989). For example, the Biache-Saint-Vaast assemblage (Levels IIA and II base) is characterized by convergent tools such as Mousterian points and convergent scrapers. These tools occur in much greater frequency than in any other Mousterian series typed by the Bordian

method. They are very elongated, often with an asymmetrical cross-section (Fig. 5.6), and resemble Rheindahlen tools found in a similar chronostratigraphic context (Bosinski 1986). Another unique feature of this assemblage is the lightness of retouch on double scrapers, which sometimes makes them difficult to differentiate from simple retouched flakes. All of the Mousterian tool types are well differentiated, as the strong correlation between certain tool types and blanks demonstrates. The standardization of the convergent pieces (Mousterian points, convergent scrapers) is perhaps due to a hafting mechanism (Beyries 1988). The features of the assemblages in these levels of Biache-Saint-Vaast are unique enough that they have been labeled "Mousterian of Ferrassie type of Biache facies."

Assemblages containing denticulates are present at Salouel and at Biache-Saint-Vaast, Level H (Ameloot-Van der Heijden 1989).

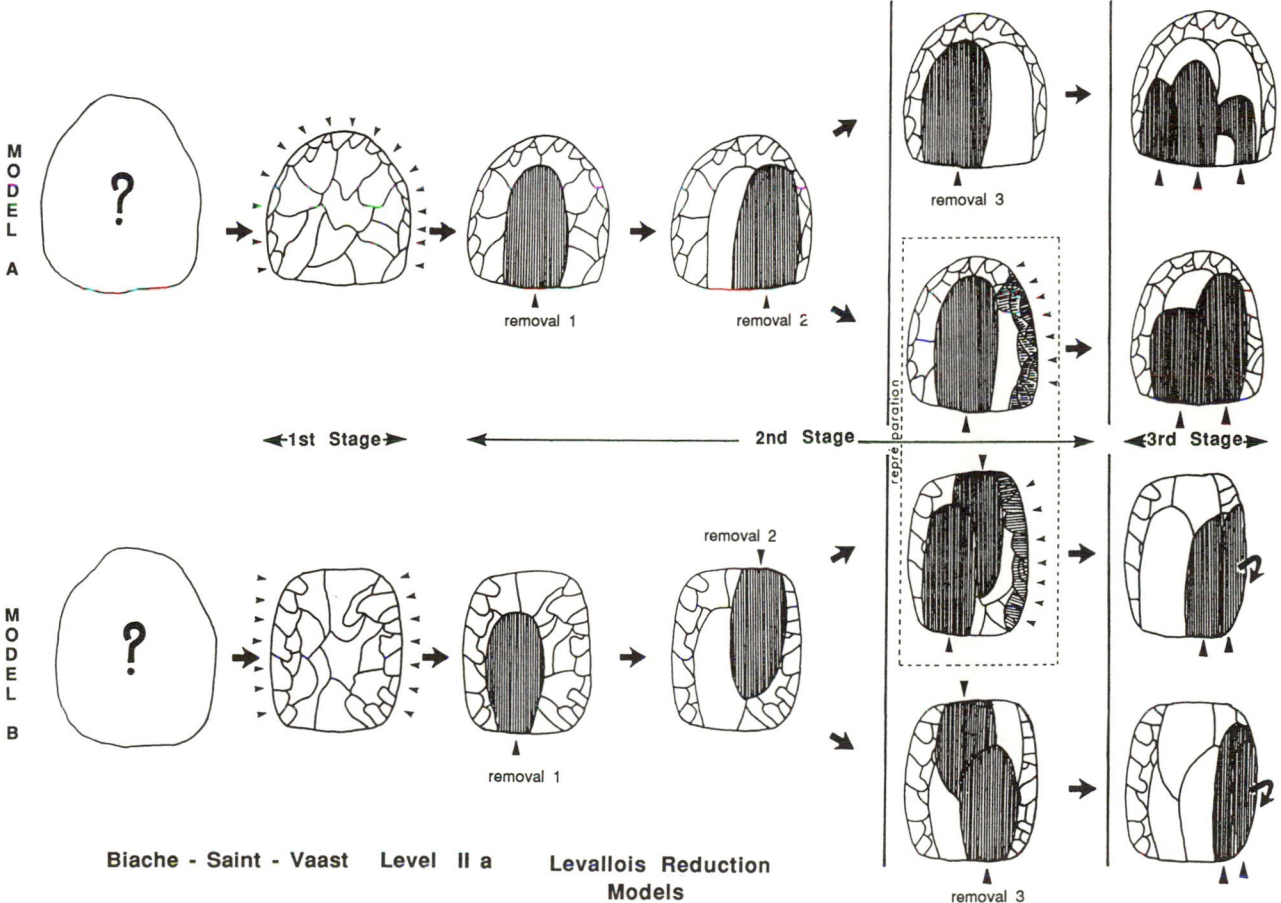

Figure 5.5   Levallois technology (méthode récurrente) for Biache-Saint-Vaast (after E. Boëda).

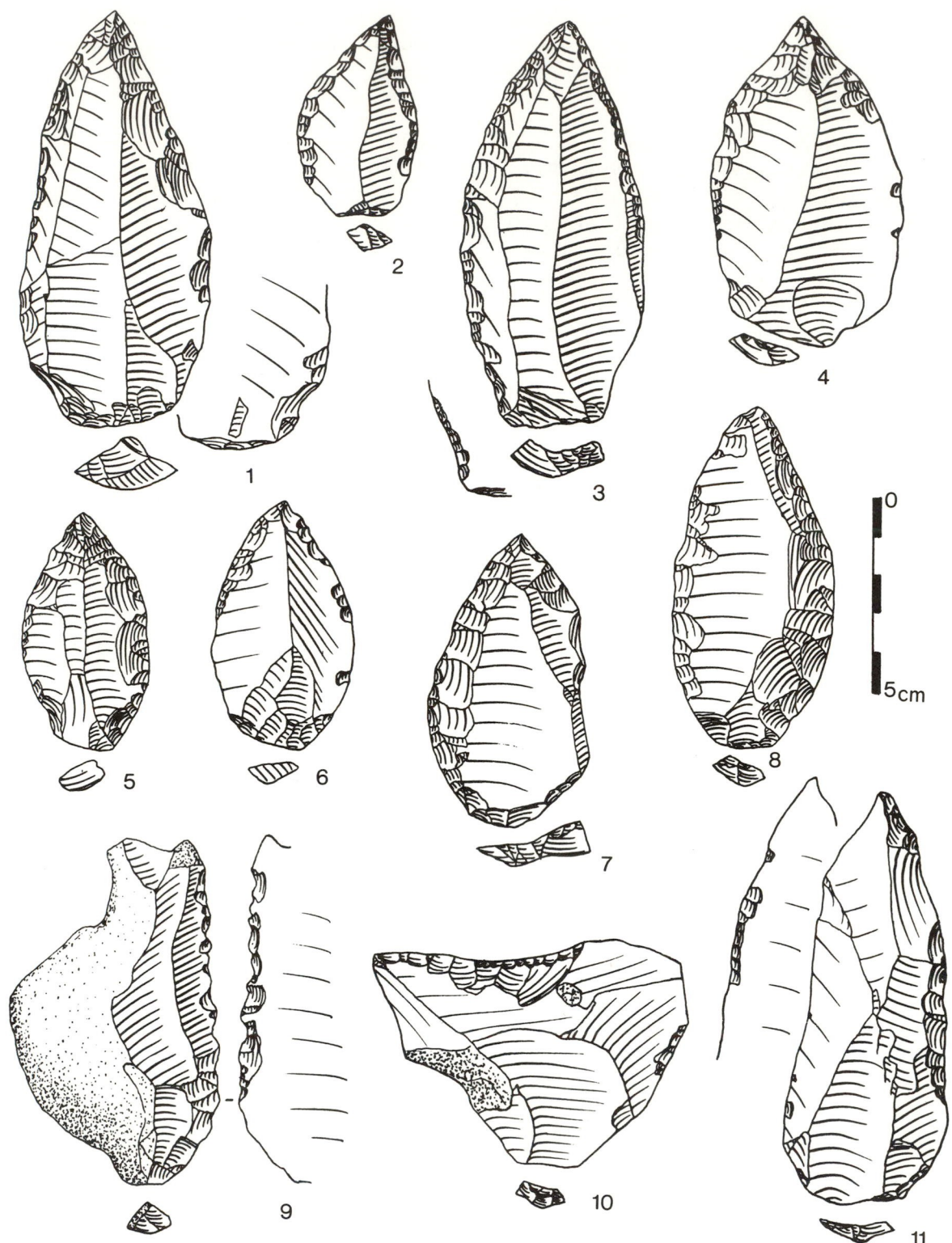

Figure 5.6   Biache-Saint-Vaast, level IIA: Ferrassie Mousterian. 1-8: Convergent tools; 9: denticulate; 10: transverse scraper; 11: backed knife.

THE RECENT PHASE
OF THE MIDDLE PALEOLITHIC

The assemblages of the recent phase of the Middle Paleolithic are found most often in wet deposits of the Weichselian Early Glacial (substages 5c to 5a). Worked flint has also been recovered from even more recent levels: humid gley from stage 4 (upper level with Micoquian industries at Riencourt-les-Bapaume), humid levels from Moershofd, dated to around 45,000 B.P.), and above the first Weichselian loess at Corbehem. All the classic industries recognized by Bordes, except the MTA-B and Charentian of Quina type, are present. We will present the principal ones as well as a blade debitage group which has recently been discovered.

The Mousterian of Acheulian Tradition (MTA) type A, with its flat, triangular bifaces made on flakes, is one of the most unique assemblages. Contrary to its name, however, the MTA-A has no links with the Acheulian. It occurs only during the recent phase of the Middle Paleolithic and, in the North of France, always from the Weichselian Early Glacial pedocomplex, as has been shown by numerous discoveries made in brickyards. The flake tool component is unique, with a moderately high Mousterian Group Index, typologically varied, with few bifacially retouched scrapers and convergent tools. Upper Paleolithic types, including backed knives, are often abundant, sometimes exceeding the number of notches and denticulates.

The Typical Mousterian, found at Corbehem, the "2nd humid layer" of Saint-Just-en-Chaussee, and at Riencourt-les-Bapaume, includes non-biface assemblages which have a varied typological composition. Actually, certain of these assemblages which contain a significant Upper Paleolithic tool component could be MTA-A industries from a location in which bifaces were not recovered. This could be the case for the assemblage of Saint-Just-en-Chausee and for that of Houppeville, in the Seine basin (Farizy and Tuffreau 1986).

The Mousterian of Ferrassie Type is present at the sites of Bapaume (Fig. 5.7) and Busigny, where the assemblages contain the characteristic technology and typology of Levallois facies and a strong Mousterian group with numerous convergent tools.

The term "Seclin Facies" has been used for assemblages with blade debitage which are present at Seclin (Tuffreau et al. 1985) and Riencourt-les-Bapaume at the beginning of the Last Glacial (substage 5a). They are characterized by the presence of blades obtained from Upper Paleolithic cores (Fig. 5.8). According to Boëda (1988c), the entire volume of the core is utilized, rather than a single flaking surface as in the Levallois technique. The management of this volume is variable. There are examples of transition from a core with a Levallois flaking surface to one with semi-circular debitage using overshot blades which create a blade core. In other cases flaking is entirely circular from the beginning, and the core takes shape with the removal of *lames à cretes*. Levallois cores with preferential flaking or centripetal debitage are present as well. Flake tools include Upper Paleolithic types such as burins and backed pieces associated with scrapers.

These assemblages represent a technological transition from Middle to Upper Paleolithic, although the context remains Middle Paleolithic. The appearance of the Upper Paleolithic during the Weichselian Interpleniglacial is accompanied by other manifestations in adornment and habitat suggesting changes in comportment exceeding the observable technological changes.

It is interesting to note the presence of similar technological phenomena in the Near East and in South Africa at roughly the same time (Mellars 1989; Singer and Wymer 1982). These industries have no relationship to the Upper Paleolithic since the Mousterian industries are found between them and the later blade industries of the Near East and Northern France. It would be interesting to try to understand why this technological innovation appears in such distant paleogeographic regions (perhaps due to a convergence in responses to changing environments in regions susceptible to climatic changes).

The recent excavations at Riencourt-les-Bapaume have revealed a Micoquian industry with foliate pieces (*Faustkeilblätter*) at the top of an archaeological sequence (Fig. 5.9). This discovery confirms the western extension of certain central European Micoquian industries which have traces in Belgium ("Mousterian with bifacial retouch" in the cave of Docteur a Huccorgne; Ulrix-Closset 1975). *Prondniks* are also present in an old collection from the Bethune region in Northern France (Marcy 1991).

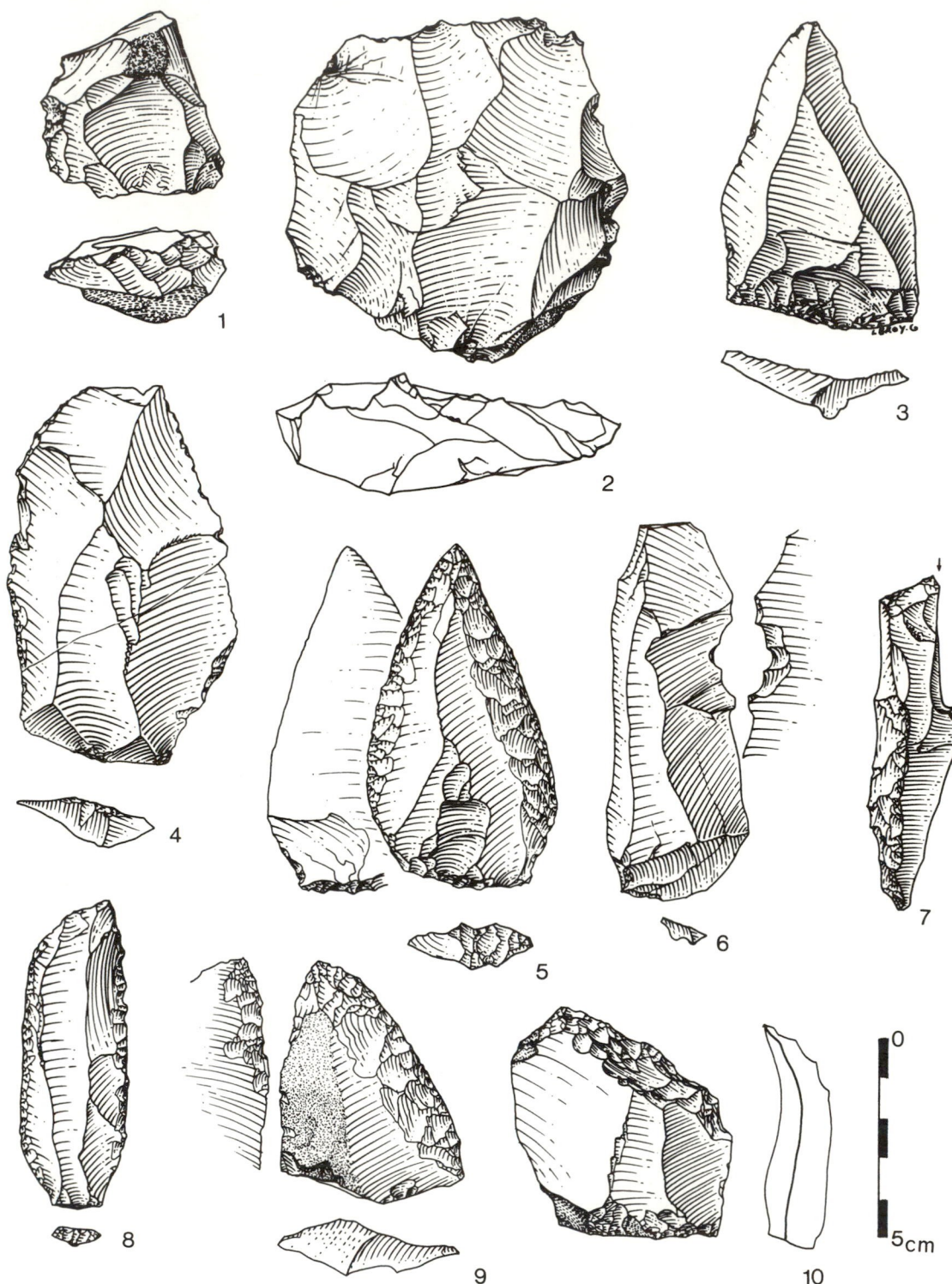

Figure 5.7   *Riencourt-les-Bapaume, level C. 1: Levallois core (méthode préférential); 2: Levallois core (débitage centripète); 3: Levallois point; 4: Levallois flake with irregular retouch; 5: Mousterian point; 6: notch; 7: burin on a blade (débordant); 8: single straight sidescraper; 9: convergent scraper with alternate retouch; 10: transverse scraper.*

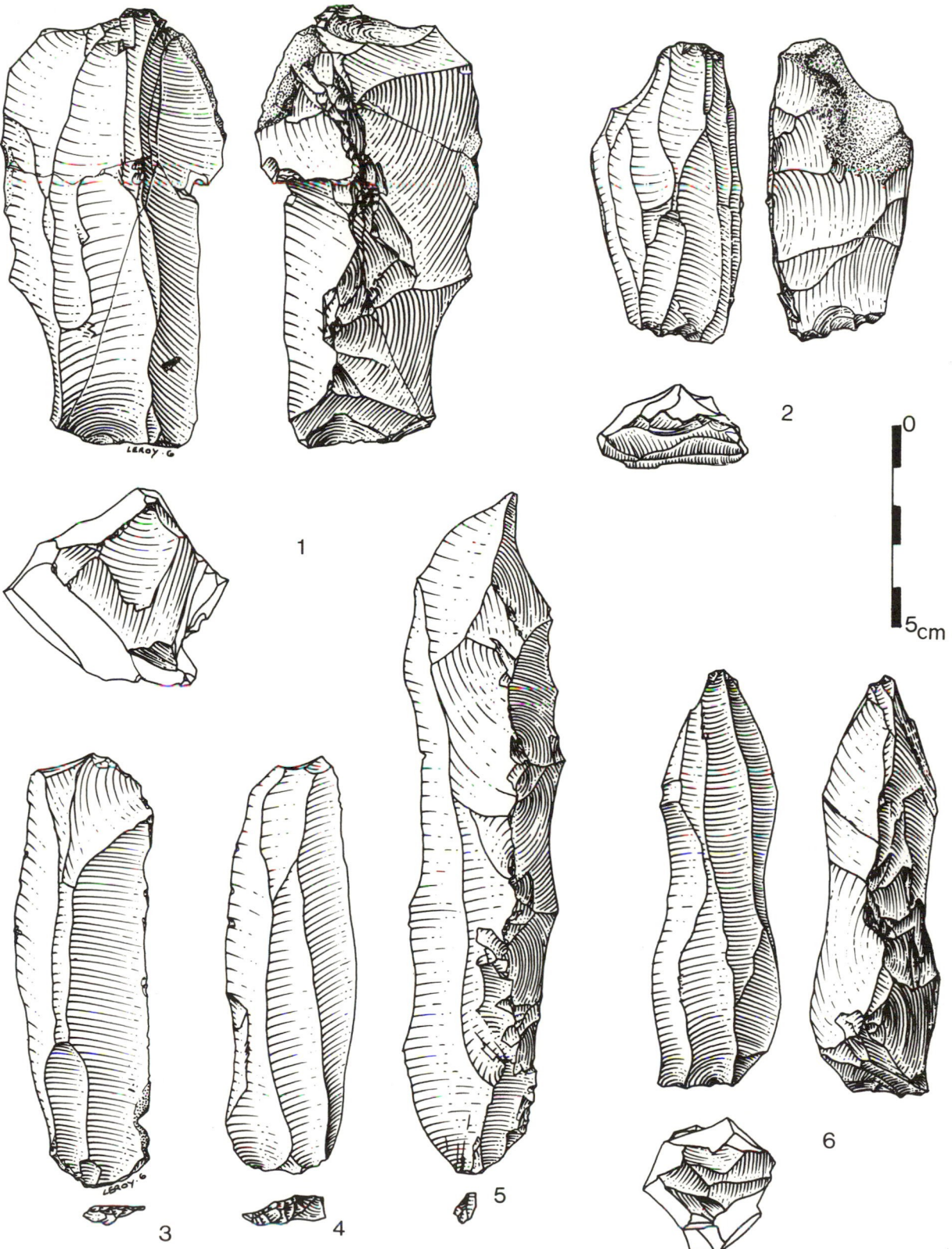

Figure 5.8   *Riencourt-les-Bapaume, level C. 1, 2, and 6: Blade cores; 3 and 4: blades; 5: crested blade.*

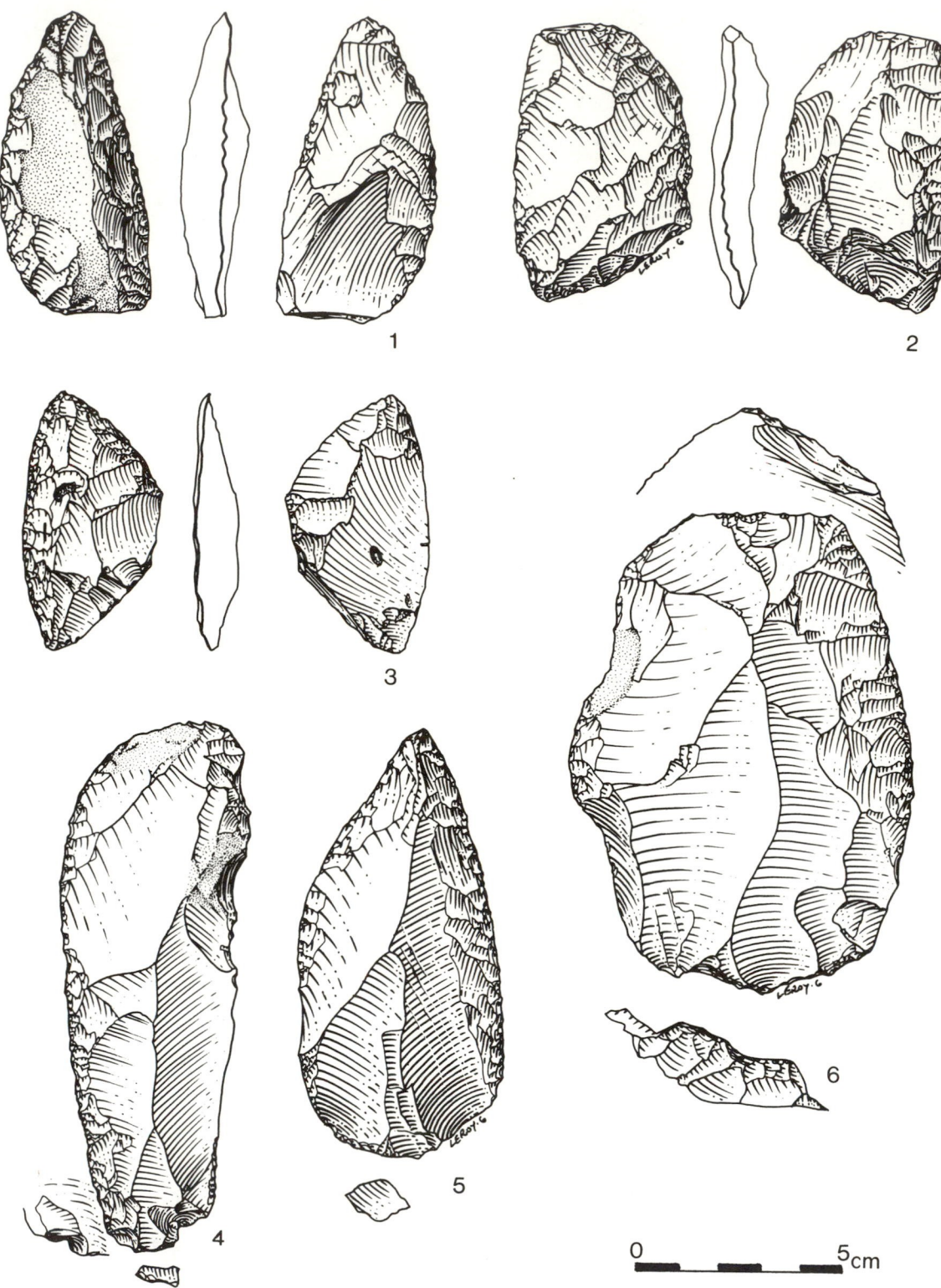

Figure 5.9   *Riencourt-les-Bapaume, level D. 1-3: Bifacial leaf-shaped point; 4 and 6: single sidescrapers; 5: Mousterian point.*

CONCLUSIONS

The North of France appears to be a marginal region that was abandoned during harsh climatic phases and reoccupied during temperate or moderately cold periods. It would thus be illusory to attempt to find a local evolution of industries there. Its geographical position makes it a passage zone between England and the Continent as well as between central Europe and the southern edge of the great northern European plain in the east and the Atlantic Ocean to the west. This is why Middle Paleolithic assemblages are often linked to the Levallois facies of industries in Southwestern France and often show indications of influence from the east (such as the Micoquian). The uniqueness of certain assemblages, which for the most part do not have extensive reduction of retouched types, is probably due to the abundance of raw material and to activity in open-air sites, which is more dispersed than in cave or rock shelters (see Dibble and Rolland, this volume). Certain original facies, such as the Biache-Saint-Vaast elongated convergent scrapers and the blade facies of the Early Weichselian Glacial can be interpreted as a response to particular environments, the nature of which is yet to be elucidated.

REFERENCES CITED

Ameloot-Van der Heijden, N.
1989   Les séries lithiques des niveaux E et de la couche DO du gisement paléolithique de Biache-Saint-Vaast (Pas-de-Calais). Pp. 43–50 in *Paléolithique et Mésolithique du Nord de la France. Nouvelles recherches*, ed. A. Tuffreau. Publications du CERP 1. Lille.

Antoine, P.
1989   Les terrasses quaternaires du bassin de la Somme: étude géologique et géomorphologique. Contribution à la connaissance du paléoenvironnement des gisements paléolithiques. Thesis, Univ. Sc. Techn. de Lille.

Beyries, S.
1988   Etude tracéologique des racloirs du niveau IIA. Pp. 215–230 in *Le gisement paléolithique moyen de Biache-Saint-Vaast (Pas-de-Calais)*, Vol. 1, eds. A. Tuffreau and J. Sommé. MSPF 21. Paris.

Boëda, E.
1988a   Le concept Levallois et évaluation de son champ d'application. Pp. 13–26 in *L'homme de Néandertal*, ed. M. Otte. Vol. 4: *La technique*, eds. L. Binford and J.-P. Rigaud. ERAUL 31. Liège, Université de Liège.
1988b   Le concept laminaire: rupture et filiation avec le concept Levallois. Pp. 41–59 in *L'homme de Néandertal*, ed. M. Otte. Vol. 8: *La mutation*, ed. J. K. Kozlowski. ERAUL 35. Liège, Université de Liège.
1988c   Analyse technologique de débitage du niveau IIA. Pp. 185–214 in *Le gisement paléolithique moyen de Biache-Saint-Vaast (Pas-de-Calais)*, Vol. 1, eds. A. Tuffreau and J. Sommé. MSPF 21. Paris.

Bordes, F.
1975   Sur la notion de sol d'habitat en préhistoire paléolithique. *BSPF* 72:139–144.

Bordes, F., and Fitte, P.
1953   L'Atelier Commont. *L'Anthropologie* 57:1–45.

Bosinski, G.
1986   Chronostratigraphie du Paléolithique inférieur et moyen en Rhénanie. Pp. 15–35 in *Chronostratigraphie et faciès culturels du Paléolithique inférieur et moyen dans l'Europe du Nord-Ouest*, eds. A. Tuffreau and J. Sommé. *BAFEQ* Supplément 26. Paris: AFEQ.

Colbeaux, J. P.; Sommé, J.; and Tuffreau, A.
1988   Tectonique. Pp. 61–67 in *Le gisement paléolithique moyen de Biache-Saint-Vaast (Pas-de-Calais)*, Vol. 1, eds. A. Tuffreau and J. Sommé. MSPF 21. Paris.

Farizy, C., and Tuffreau, A.
1986   Industries et cultures du Paléolithique moyen récent dans la moitié Nord de la France. Pp. 225–234 in *Chronostratigraphie et faciès culturels du Paléolithique*

inférieur et moyen dans l'Europe du Nord-Ouest, eds. A. Tuffreau and J. Sommé. *BAFEQ* Supplément 26. Paris: AFEQ.

Haesaerts, P.
1985   Les loess du Pléistocène supérieur en Belgique: comparaison avec les séquences d'Europe centrale. *BAFEQ* 22:105-115.

Haesaerts, P., and Dupuis, C.
1986   Contribution à la stratigraphie des nappes alluviales de la Somme et de l'Avre dans la région d'Amiens. Pp. 171-186 in *Chronostratigraphie et faciès culturels du Paléolithique inférieur et moyen dans l'Europe du Nord-Ouest*, eds. A. Tuffreau and J. Sommé. *BAFEQ* Supplément 26. Paris: AFEQ.

Heinzelin, J. de
1984   Essai sur archéologie et régions naturelles. Pp. 101-106 in *Peuples chasseurs de la Belgique dans leur cadre naturel*, eds. D. Cahen and P. Haesaerts. Brussels.

Marcy, J. L.
1989   L'outillage sur éclat du gisement acheuléen de la vallée du Muid à Gouzeaucourt (Nord): premiers résultats. Pp. 31-41 in *Paléolithique et Mésolithique du Nord de la France*, ed. A. Tuffreau. Publications du CERP 1. Lille.
1991   *Les prondniks du Mont de Beuvry à Béthune (Pas-de-Calais)*. Publications du CERP 2. Lille. In press.

Mellars, P.
1989   Technological Changes across the Middle-Upper Palaeolithic Transition: Economic, Social and Cognitive Perspectives. Pp. 338-365 in *The Human Revolution: Behavioural and Biological Perspectives on the Origins of Modern Humans*, eds. P. Mellars and C. Stringer. Princeton, NJ: Princeton University Press.

Munaut, A. V.
1988   L'environnment végétal de quelques dépôts quaternaires du Bassin de la Somme (France). *Revue archéologique Picardie* (special number):45-56.

Singer, R., and Wymer, J.
1982   *The Middle Stone Age at Klasies River Mouth in South Africa*. Chicago, IL: University of Chicago Press.

Sommé, J.
1976   Les limons quaternaires dans les plaines du Nord. Pp. 173-176 in *La Préhistoire française*, Vol. 1, ed. H. de Lumley. Paris.
1989   La stratigraphie des loess. *Le temps de la Préhistoire*, Vol. 1, ed. J. P. Mohen. Paris.

Sommé, J.; Fagnart, J. P.; Léger, M.; Munaut, A. V.; Puisségur, J. J.; and Tuffreau, A.
1984   Terrasses fluviatiles du Pléistocène moyen en France septentrionale: signification dynamique et climatique. *BAFEQ* 21:52-58.

Sommé, J.; Lautridou, J. P.; Heim, J.; Maucorps, J.; Puisségur, J. J.; Rousseau, D. D.; Thévenin, A.; and Van Vliet-Lanöe, B.
1986   Le cycle climatique du Pléistocène supérieur dans les loess d'Alsace à Achenheim. *BAFEQ* 23:97-104

Tuffreau, A.
1979   Le gisement moustérien du château à Corbehem (Pas-de-Calais). *GP* 22:371-389.
1987   Le Paléolithique inférieur et moyen du Nord de la France (Nord Pas-de-Calais, Picardie) dans son cadre stratigraphique. 2 vols. Thesis, University of Lille.
1988   Les habitats du Paléolithique inférieur et moyen dans le Nord de la France (Nord, Pas-de-Calais, Somme). *Revue archéologique Picardie* (special number):91-104.
1989   (ed.) *Livret-guide de l'excursion dans la vallée de la Somme*. Colloquium: L'Acheuléen dans l'ouest de l'Europe (Rome).

Tuffreau, A., and Bouchet, J. P.
1985   Le gisement acheuléen de la vallée du Muid à Gouzeaucourt (Nord). *BSPF* 82:291-306.

Tuffreau, A.; Bouchet, J. P.; Moigne, A. M.; and Munaut, A. V.
1986   Les niveaux acheuléens de la moyenne terrasse du Bassin de la Somme à Cagny-l'Epinette (Somme). *L'Anthropologie* 90:9-27.

Tuffreau, A., and Fagnart, J. P.
198-87   Nouvelles recherches à la carrière Bul-
          tel-Tellier de Saint-Acheul (Amiens,
          Somme). *Antiquités Nationales*
          18/19:47-54.

Tuffreau, A.; Munaut, A. V.; Puisségur, J. J.; and
Sommé, J.
1981   Les basses terrasses dans les vallées du
          Nord de la France et de la Picardie.
          BSPF 78:291-305.

Tuffreau, A.; Révillion, S.; Sommé, J.; Aitken, M. J.;
Huxtable, J.; and Leroi-Gourhan, A.
1985   Le gisement paléolithique moyen de
          Seclin (Nord, France). *Archéologisches
          Korrespondenzblatt* 15:131-138.

Tuffreau, A., and Sommé, J., eds.
1988   *Le gisement paléolithique moyen de Biache-
          Saint-Vaast (Pas-de-Calais)*, Vol. 1.
          MSPF 21. Paris.

Ulrix-Closset, M.
1975   *Le Paléolithique moyen dans le bassin
          mosan*. Wetteren.

Van Vliet-Lanöe, B.
1986   Le pédocomplexe du dernier inter-
          glaciaire (de 125 000 à 75 000 BP).
          Variations de faciès et signification
          paléoclimatique du Sud de la Pologne à
          l'Ouest de la Bretagne. *BAFEQ*
          23:139-150.

VI

Raw Material and Technological Studies of the Quina Mousterian in Perigord

Alain Turq

A method of analysis linking lithic technology, typology, and technology (Turq and Dols 1988) has been applied to industries from 13 Quina Mousterian layers in the Perigord region of southwest France (Fig. 6.1): Roc de Marsal (7 layers, deriving from Lafille's excavation: Bordes and Lafille 1962; Turq 1979, 1985, 1988b); Las Pelenos (Coulonges' excavation: Coulonges et al. 1952; Le Tensorer 1969); Mas Viel (Niederlender's excavation: Niederlender et al. 1956); L'Ermitage (Faux 1986); Moulin du Milieu upper layers (Turq's excavation: unpublished and Turq 1988a); Chinchon (Sireix and Bordes 1972); and Combe Grenal, layer 22, (Bordes' excavation: Bordes 1955, 1972). On the basis of these analyses we can present a new technological and economic evaluation of this facies of the Mousterian.

RAW MATERIAL PROCUREMENT

Between 90 and 98% of the raw material utilized in Quina industries is local in origin, derived from a radius less than 5 km from the sites. A rational and efficient choice is indicated by the selection of good quality material from local alluvial deposits and out- crops. The remainder of the raw materials were pro- cured from a zone ranging from ca. 10 to ca. 100 km from the sites (Turq 1988b). The variety and quanti- ties of these non-local materials are very restricted.

TECHNOLOGICAL AND ECONOMIC STUDY OF THE DEBITAGE

The preferred form of flake blank in Quina indus- tries is typically asymmetrical in section (Turq 1988b and 1989), in which the morphological axis of the flake may or may not coincide with the main flaking axis. The maximum thickness of this preferred blank is always located opposite the longest cutting edge of the flake. This particular morphology may occur in the case of cortically or naturally backed knives, as well as in flakes with a thick and wide butt, or on flakes with a single prominent ridge. In the case of thick-butted blanks, this butt is often "Clactonian" in character, and usually unfaceted.

The advantage of this type of blank lies partly in the ease with which it could be produced and partly in its suitability for the application of typically Quina retouch and for the application of successive phases of resharpening (Fig. 6.2).

TYPICAL QUINA PRODUCTION AND PROCESSES OF MANUFACTURE

Typically, Quina flakes can be grouped into four categories:
1. Naturally backed knives: these include flakes pro- duced by the so-called "*en tranche de saucisson*" technique (Cheynier 1953; Bourlon 1907, 1910) (Fig. 6.3:3), 'cov- ering' naturally backed pieces (Fig. 6.3:1 and 4), and sim- pler cortical-backed knives (Fig. 6.3:2 and Fig. 6.4:2);
2. Flakes whose back is formed by the butt of the flake (Fig. 6.4:1, 3, and 6);
3. *Debitage*-backed flakes (Fig. 6.3:6 and 7);
4. Asymmetric flakes (Fig. 6.3:5 and Fig. 6.4:5).

Three schemes may be proposed for the produc- tion of the various forms of "naturally backed knives" listed in (1) above, based partly on the archaeological material, and partly on experimental replication. These are illustrated graphically in Figures 6.5-7.

OTHER TECHNOLOGICAL OBSERVATIONS

Two important points are emphasized by the global technological study of Quina-type flaking strategies (Fig. 6.8):

1. The general scarcity of core maintenance products (Fig. 6.8:column 5), which reflects the very limited degree of preparation of both the striking platforms and main flaking surfaces of the cores;

2. The abundance of small chips and fragments (Fig. 6.8:column 8). Since these clearly do not derive from the faceting of striking platforms, they must indicate the extensive retouching and resharpening of retouched tools on the sites.

It appears, from an examination of the totality of the knapping products, that the occasional specimens of morphologically "Levallois" flakes do not occur in association with other characteristic by-products of the Levallois production scheme (Boëda 1986). These flakes therefore almost certainly represent fortuitous Levallois products, resulting either from the occasional centripetal flaking of cores, from the manufacture of large scrapers, or from the collection of pieces from earlier Middle Paleolithic sites.

The Quina production scheme described here may be regarded as economical, in the sense that the number of desired blanks produced in the production scheme is relatively high. From personal experiments it is clear that these techniques can produce between 60 and 77% of "desired" blanks. By contrast, similar experiments with Levallois techniques produced only 11-30% of desired blanks (in the studies by Schelinskii 1983 and Plisson 1988) or between 5 and 25% (in the studies by Geneste 1985).

STRATEGY OF MODIFICATION

The patterns of use and modification of primary flake blanks in Quina industries may be summarized as follows.

1. A high percentage of the flakes (55 to 76%) were retouched into tools. It should also be noted that in the case of scrapers a substantial length of the available edge was normally retouched. The percentage of composite tools is also high (10 to 26%).

2. There are varying degrees of correspondence between the forms of flake blanks and the types of tools produced. In the case of notched and denticulated tools, the tools are produced on very variable forms

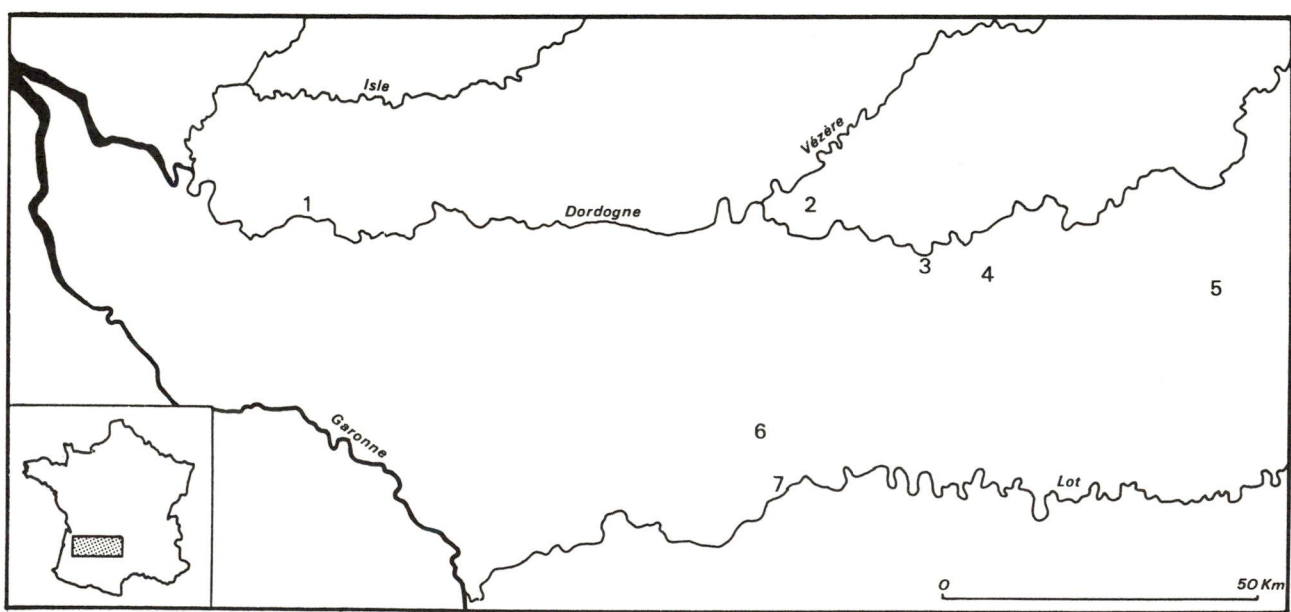

Figure 6.1.   *Geographic location of studied sites. 1: Chinchon; 2: Roc de Marsal; 3: Combe Grenal; 4: L'Ermitage; 5: Mas Viel; 6: Moulin du Milieu; 7: Las Pelenos.*

of blanks, as in other facies of the Mousterian (Geneste 1989). In the case of scrapers, on the other hand, the type of blank chosen seems to vary with the type of tool produced (Turq 1988b).

Overall, it would seem that all of the observations on both the techniques of debitage and the use and retouching of flakes point to our emphasis on the economical, parsimonious use of lithic raw material. In several cases it can be seen that broken fragments of either cores or tools were frequently reused for tool manufacture.

THE *CHAÎNE OPÉRATOIRE*

The distinctiveness of the Quina production scheme lies in the fact that a variety of relatively simple, alternative methods can be used to produce a range of clearly predetermined products. The basic reduction sequences (*chaînes opératoires*) for flint nodules can be summarized as follows:

1. Introduction of raw material to the site in the form of previously tested blocks;

2. The removal of one or two primary "trial" flakes from the nodule (either uni-polar or bi-polar);

3. The production of cortical knives. The occasional waste elements produced at this stage are normally due to knapping accidents (including *outrepasse* removals and 'Siret' fractures);

4. The remainder of the nodule (either its center or one of its extremities) is transformed into a core through the preparation of several striking platforms, or by limited removal of cortex;

5. The production of debitage-backed knives, Clactonian flakes (Breuil 1932), and asymmetrical flakes. Undifferentiated flakes, as well as fragments, may also be obtained. Certain of these flake products (such as the *en tranche de saucisson* flakes) may be transformed into cores and exploited in the same manner;

6. In the final stages of flaking, some cores (either on flakes or on nodules) may be further modified into tools;

7. The majority of the produced flakes are transformed into tools. This transformation, by retouch, into notches, denticulates or scrapers, results in characteristic by-products.

SIGNIFICANCE OF THE QUINA MOUSTERIAN FACIES

The Quina Mousterian facies is known essentially from rockshelter sites, with very few known occurrences of open-air sites (Sireix and Bordes 1972; Le Tensorer 1973; Airvaux and Chollet 1975). The few documented open-air sites are not located in the main areas of flint exploitation sites (such as the Bergerach region: Geneste 1985) and evidently do not represent a workshop facies of the Mousterian.

Chronologically, the Quina Mousterian is known principally from isotope stage 4, and possibly 3 (Lav-

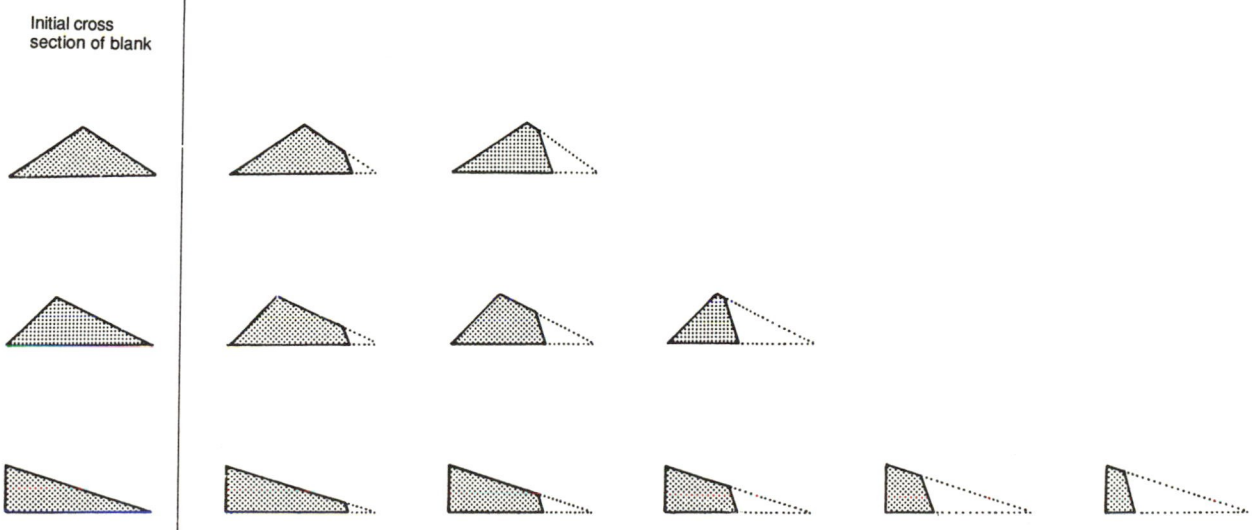

Figure 6.2. *Relationship between the initial cross-section of blanks and the potential number of resharpening phases.*

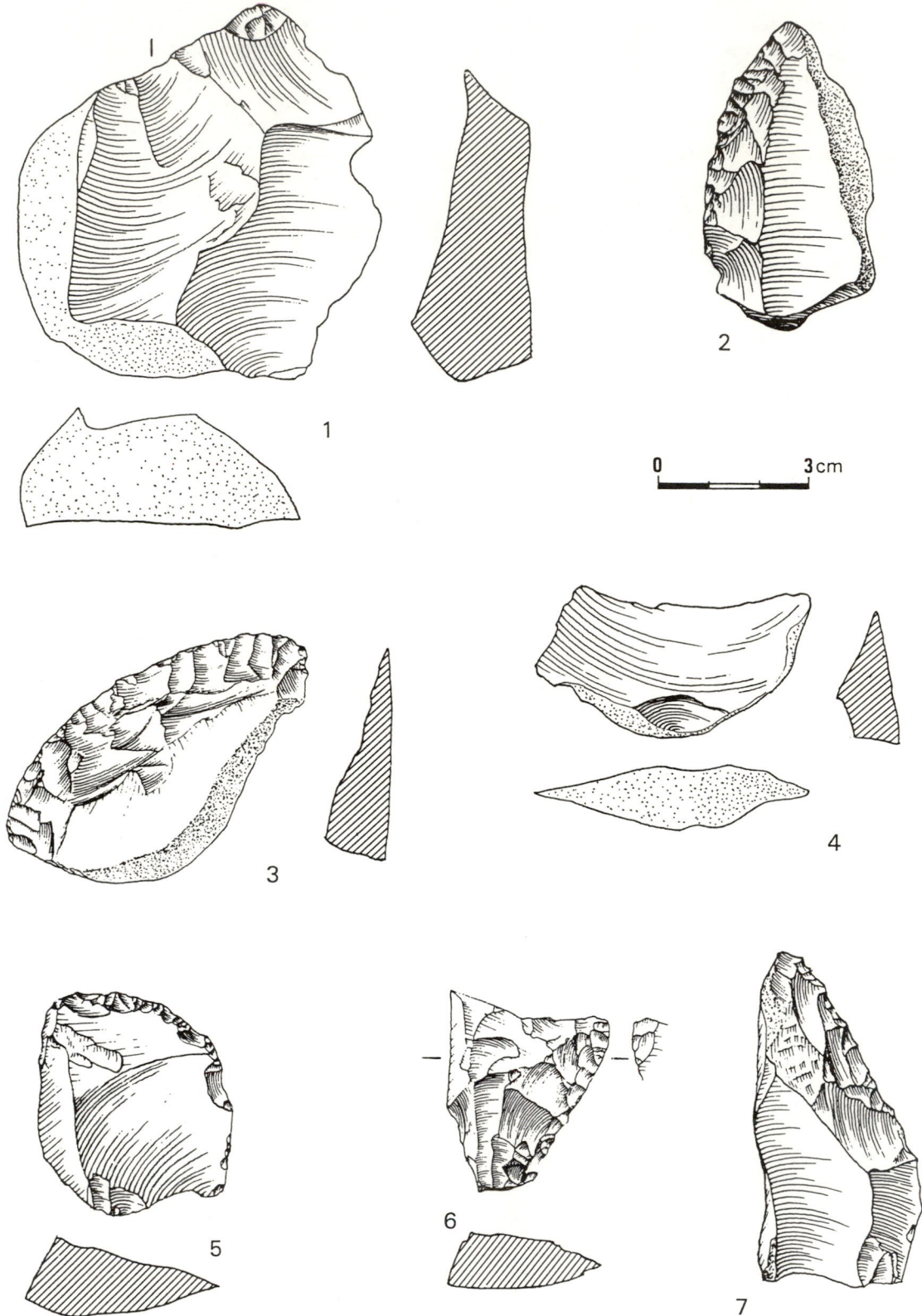

Figure 6.3.   Typical Quina products.

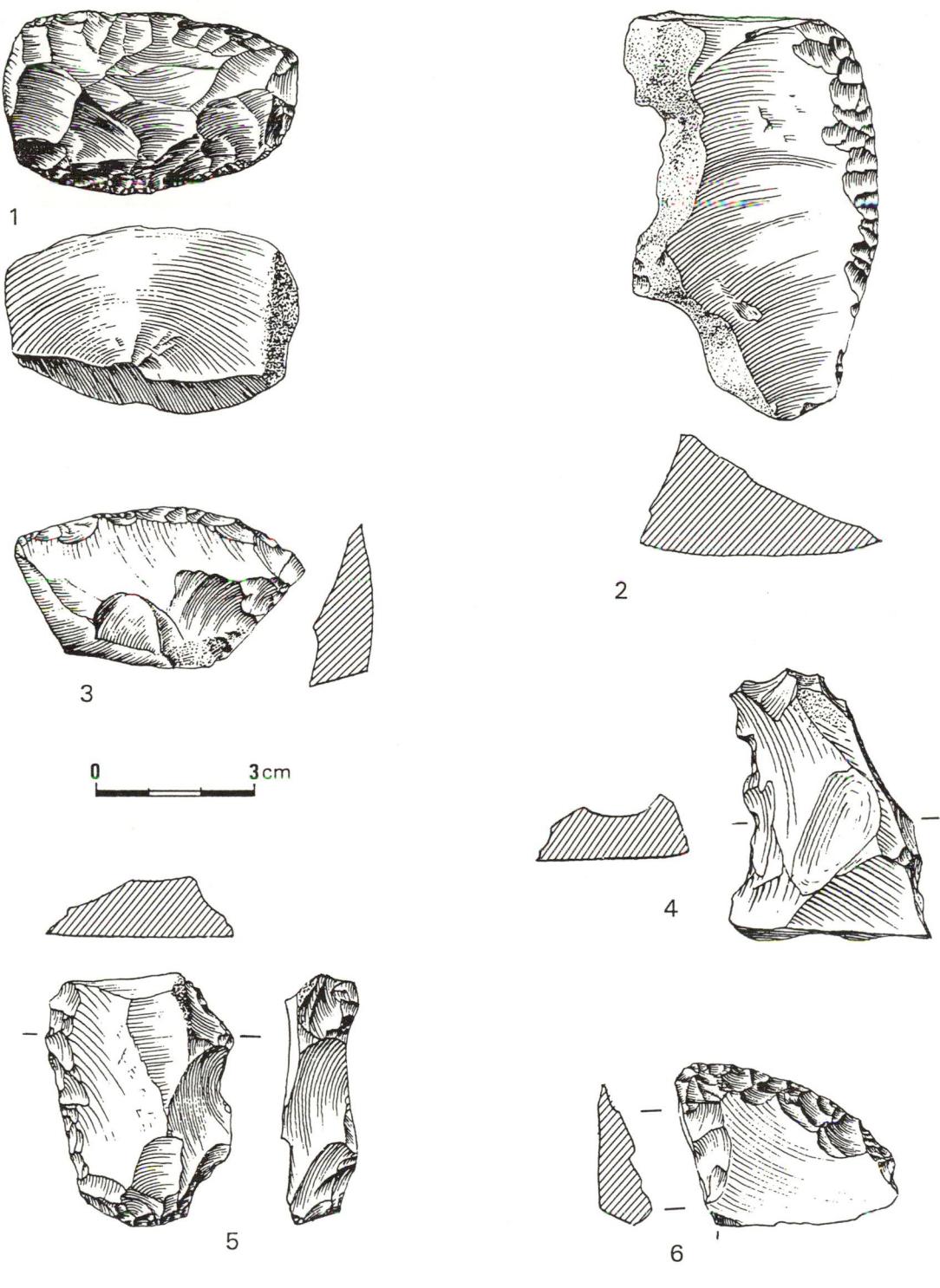

Figure 6.4.   Typical Quina products.

ille 1975; Bordes 1984; Guichard 1976). In the Aquitaine basin, related but not identical industries may exist at the end of stage 5 (as at Combe-Capelle: Bourgon 1957; Texier 1968; Laville et al. 1983) and even before that time, as at Les Tares (Rigaud and Texier 1981) and La Micoque layer 3 (Bourgon 1957). In most of the Quina levels the available paleobotanical and paleontological evidence (Paquereau 1974-75a and b; Van Campo and Bouchud 1962; Guadelli 1987) indicates a severe climate and a steppe-like landscape.

The lack of evidence for chronological continuity between these occurrences, together with an apparent lack of highly specific site functions (knapping site, home base, temporary camp) seems to rule out the possibility that the Quina type represents a single cultural facies. On the other hand, all these observations are compatible with the hypothesis of a group repeatedly using locations in the landscape for the performance of specialized activities, during harsh climatic conditions. The strategies for the procurement of raw materials and for the production and transformation of tools all suggest an emphasis on time-economizing procedures. It would therefore seem, on the basis of the technological study presented here, that the activity in which the Quina groups were engaged was time-consuming, and necessitated a quickly produced and highly specific, but not very diversified, tool kit for its performance.

ACKNOWLEDGMENTS

I particularly wish to thank all the people who have allowed me to study the lithic industries in their

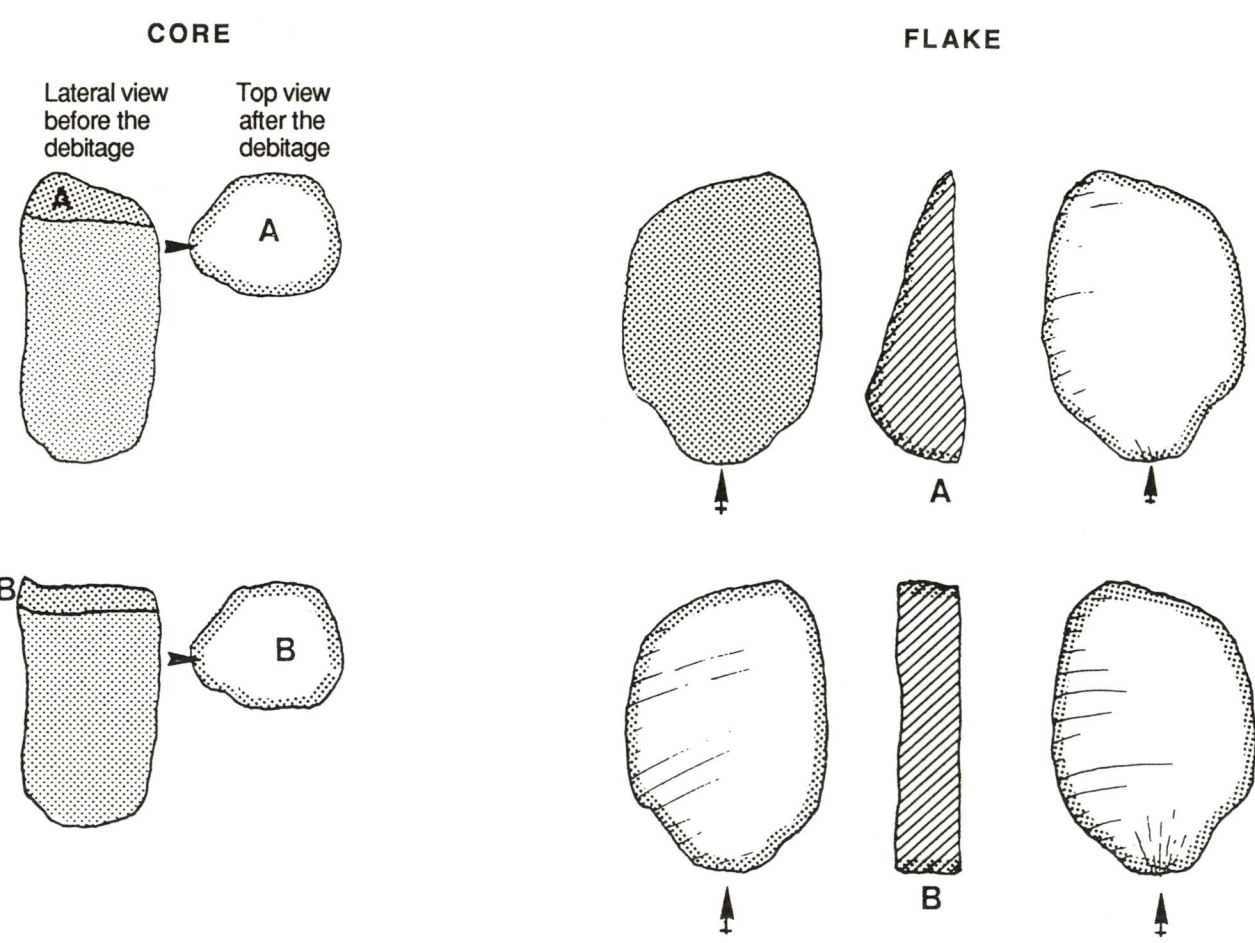

Figure 6.5.   *Scheme for the production of flakes called "en tranche de saucisson": (A) primary flake* (entame); *(B) flake called* en tranche de saucisson.

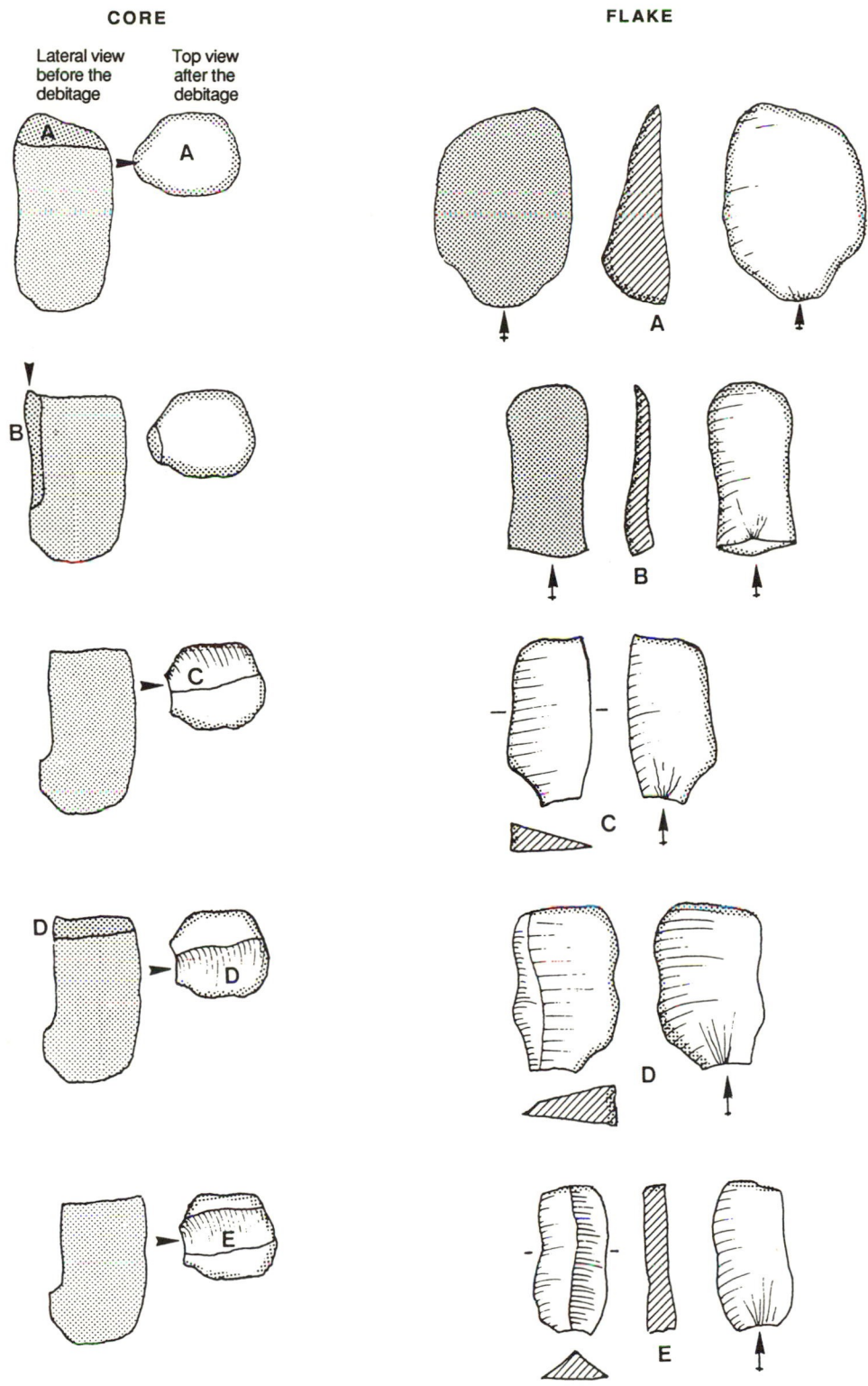

Figure 6.6. Scheme for the production of 'covering' cortical-backed knives: (A) primary flake (entame); (B) cortical flake; (C, D) 'covering' cortical-backed knives; (E) flake for the preparation of debitage surface.

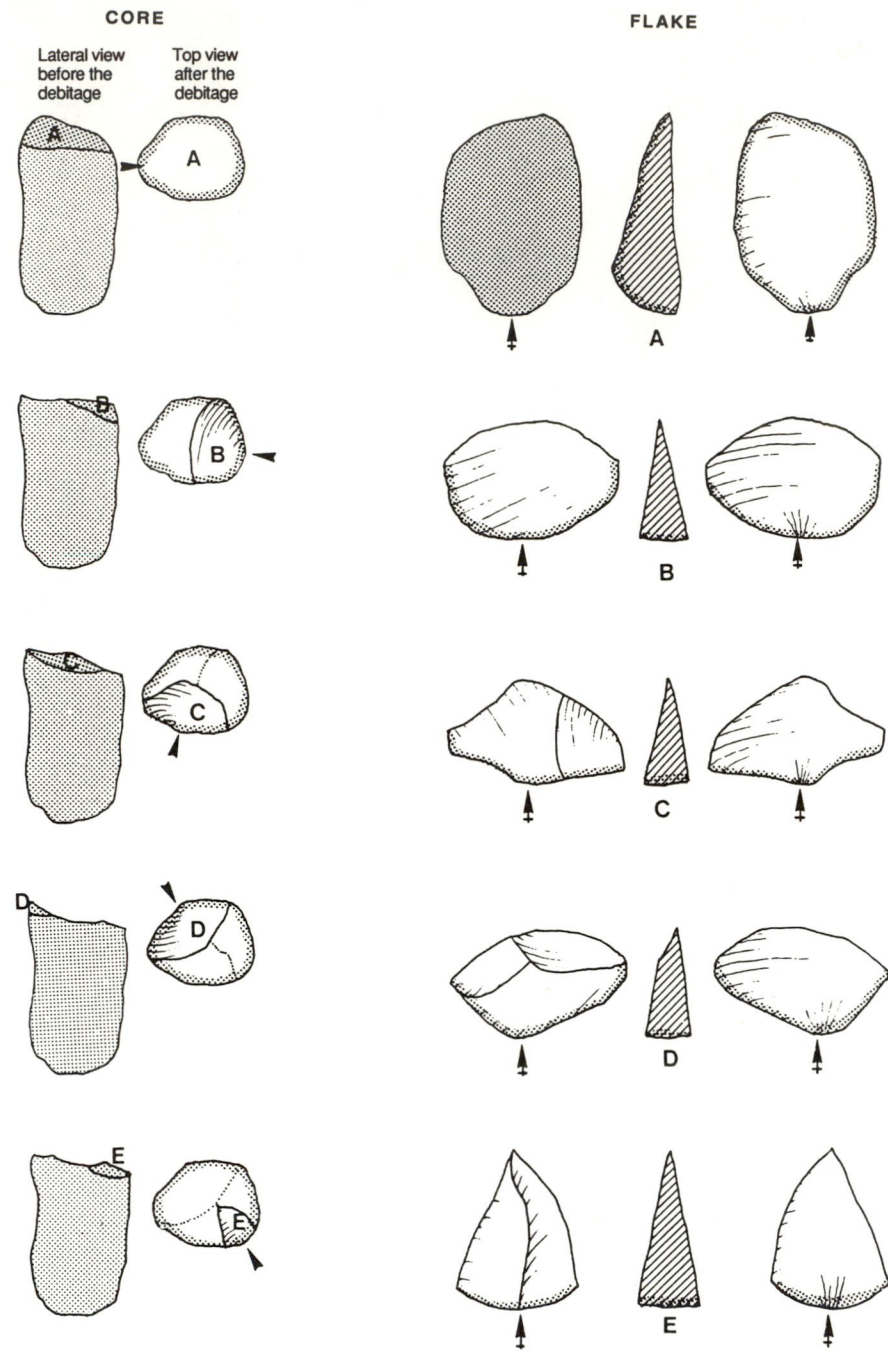

CORE

Lateral view before the debitage

Top view after the debitage

FLAKE

Figure 6.7. Scheme for the production of cortical-backed knives: (A) primary flake (entame); (B) cortical flake; (C, D) cortical-backed knives; (E) flake for the preparation of debitage surface.

charge: F. Bordes and D. de Sonneville-Bordes, M. J. Guichard and M. J. J. Cleyet-Merle, curators in the National Museum of Prehistory in Les Eyzies, Mme. Lafille, widow of the late J. Lafille, M. Lorblanchett and M. Hameau, curators in the A. Lémozi Museum in Cabrerets, and M. Sireix. I also thank Mr. N. Schlanger and Mr. M. Sigaud for translating this paper.

REFERENCES CITED

Airvaux, J., and Chollet, A.
1975   Le site moustérien de la Fontaine à Scorbé-Clairvaux (Vienne). *BSPF* 72:209–217.

Boëda, E.
1986   Approche technologique du concept levallois et évaluation de son champ d'application: étude de trois gisements saaliens et weichséliens de la France septentrionale. 2 vols. Thesis, Université de Paris.

Bordes, F.
1955   La stratigraphie de la grotte de combe Grenal, commune de Domme (Dordogne): note préliminaire. *BSPF* 52:425–429.
1972   *A Tale of Two Caves*. New York: Harper and Row.
1984   *Leçons sur le Paléolithique*. Vol. 2: *Le Paléolithique en Europe*. CQ 7. Paris: CNRS.

Bordes, F., and Lafille, J.
1962   Découverte d'un squelette d'enfant moustérien dans le gisement du Roc de Marsal, commune de Campagne du Bugue (Dordogne). *CRASP* 254:714–715.

Bourgon, M.
1957   *Les industries moustériennes et pré-moustériennes du Périgord*. AIPH Mémoire 27. Paris: Masson.

Bourlon, M.
1907   Débitage des rognons de silex en traches parallèles. *BSPF* 4:330–332.
1910   L'industrie des foyers supériers au Moustier. *Revue Préhistorique* 5:157–167.

Breuil, H.
1932   Les industries à éclats du Paléolithique ancien, I: Le Clactonien. *Préhistoire* 1:125–190.

Cheynier, A.
1953   Stratigraphie de l'abri Lachaud et les cultures des bords abattus. *Archivo de Prehistoria Levantina* 4:25–55.

Coulonges, L.; Lansac, A.; Piveteau, J.; and Vallois, H.
1952   Le gisement préhistorique de Monsempron (Lot-et-Garrone). *AIPH* 38:83–120.

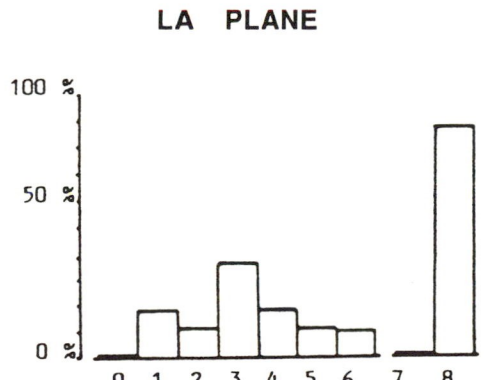
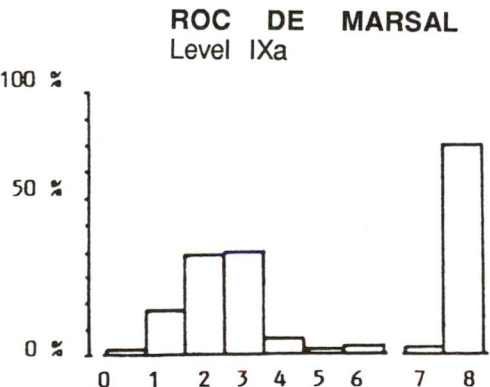

Figure 6.8.   *Comparison between the global technological composition of a Mousterian of Acheulian Tradition (La Plane) and a Quina Mousterian (Level IXa of Roc de Marsal): 0: tested blocks; 1: decortication; 2: naturally backed knives; 3: ordinary flakes; 4: Levallois flakes; 5: primary and secondary trimming flakes; 6: cores; 7: retouch chips; 8: fragments and little chips.*

Faux, M. F.
1986 *Le peuplement préhistorique dans la région de Gourdon, Lot.* Maîtrise: Histoire de l'Art et Archéologie (préhistoire). Toulouse: Université de Toulouse Mirail.

Geneste, J. M.
1985 Analyse lithique d'industries moustériennes du Périgord: une approche technologique du comportement des groups humains au Paléolithique moyen. Thesis, Université de Bordeaux.
1989 Economie des ressources lithiques dans le Moustérien du Sud-Ouest de la France. Pp. 75-97 in *L'homme de Néandertal*, ed. M. Otte. Vol. 6: *La subsistance.* ERAUL 33. Liège: Université de Liège.

Guadelli, J. L.
1987 Contribution à l'étude des zoocénoses préhistoriques en Aquitaine (Würm ancien et interstade wurmien). Thesis, Université de Bordeaux.

Guichard, J.
1976 Les civilisations du Paléolithique moyen en Périgord. Pp. 1053-1069 in *La Préhistoire Française: les civilisations paléolithiques et mésolithiques de la France.* Paris: CNRS.

Laville, H.
1975 *Climatologie et chronologie du Paléolithique en Périgord. Etude sédimentologique de dépôts en grottes et sous abris.* Etudes Quaternaires, Géologie, Paléontologie, Préhistoire 4. Marseilles: Université de Provence, Laboratoire de Paléontologie Humaine et de Préhistoire.

Laville, H; Turon, J. L.; Texier; J. P.; Raynal, J.-P.; Delpech, F.; Paquereau, M.-M.; Prat, F.; and Debénath, A.
1983 Histoire paléoclimatique de l'Aquitaine et du golfe de Gascogne au Pléistocène supérieur depuis le dernier interglaciaire. Pp. 219-241 in *Paléoclimats: actes du Colloque de l'AGSO* (Bordeaux, May). CQ no. hors série; BIGBA 34. Paris: CNRS.

Le Tensorer, J. M.
1969 Le Moustérien de Las Pélénos (Lot-et-Garonne): étude statistique. *BSPF* 66:232-236.

1973 Les industries moustériennes du plateau Baillard (Lot-et-Garonne). *BSPF* 70:73-79.

Niederlender, A.; Lacam, R.; Cadiergues, D.; and Bordes, F.
1956 Le gisement moustérien du Mas-Viel (Lot). *L'Anthropologie* 60:211-235.

Paquereau, M.-M.
1974-75a Le Würm ancien en Périgord: étude palynologique. Part 1: Les diagrammes palynologiques, la zonation climatique. *Quaternaria* 18:1-49.
1974-75b Le Würm ancien en Périgord: étude palynologique. Part 2: L'évolution des climats et des flores. *Quaternaria* 18:67-160.

Plisson, H.
1988 Technologie et tracéologie des outils moustériens en Union soviérique: les travaux de U. E. Shchelinskii. Pp. 121-168 in *L'homme de Néandertal*, ed. M. Otte. Vol. 4: *La technique*, eds. L. Binford and J.-P. Rigaud. ERAUL 31. Liège: Université de Liège.

Rigaud, J. P., and Texier, J. P.
1981 A propos des particularités techniques et typologiques du gisement des Tares, commune de Sourzac (Dordogne). *BSPF* 78:109-117.

Shchelinskii, V. E.
1983 Kizoutcheniiou techniki, technologii izgotovleniia founktsii oroudii moust'erskoi eophou (Vers une étude de la technique de fabrication et de la fonction des outils de l'époque moustérienne). Pp. 72-133 in *Technologiia proizvodstva y epohy paleolita.* Leningrad: Naouka.

Sireix, M., and Bordes F.
1972 Le Moustérien de Chinchon (Gironde). *BSPF* 69:324-336.

Texier, J. P.
1968 Etude sédimentologique des dépôts de pente de la vallée de la Couze (Dordogne). Thesis, Université de Bordeaux.

Turq, A.
1979 *L'évolution du Moustérien de type quina au Roc de Marsal et en Périgord: modification de l'équilibre technique et typologique.* Mémoire, Ecole des Hautes Etudes en Sciences Sociales. Toulouse.
1985 Le Moustérien de type Quina du Roc de Marsal (Dordogne). *BSPF* 82:46-51.
1988a Le Paléolithique inférieur et moyen en Haut-Agenais: état des recherches. *Revue de l'Agenais* 115 (Jan.-Mar.):83-112.
1988b Le Moustérien de type Quina du Roc de Marsal à Campagne (Dordogne): context stratigraphique, analyse lithologique et technologique. *Documents d'Archéologie Périgourdine* 3:5-30.
1989 Approache technologique et économique du faciés moustérien de type Quina: étude préliminare. *BSPF* 86:244-256.

Turq, A., and Dols, Y.
1988 Le site moustérien de Tour de Faure, Lot. *Bulletin de la Société des Etudes du Lot* 4:189-219.

Van Campo, M., and Bouchud, J.
1962 Flore accompagnant le squelette d'enfant moustérien découvert au Roc de Marsal, commune du Bugue (Dordogne), et première étude de la faune du gisement. *CRASP* 254:897-899.

VII

Subsistence and Behavioral Patterns of Some Middle Paleolithic Local Groups

Catherine Farizy

Francine David

It is one thing to show how the distribution of archaeological debris reflects the use of site space, but it is another to demonstrate how the formation of archaeological assemblages can be expected to reflect a group's settlement and subsistence activities. When archaeologists describe their sites, they commonly use interpretive vocabulary such as "settlements," "camps," "home bases," or "living floors" without knowing or caring what the reality was. However, it might be possible to use the archaeological records to find out the choices of which these assemblages are the result; that is to say, to determine not only the activity which took place but also the stage of this action (in any technical sequence) and the way it is predictably associated with a global strategy.

Clearly, any discussion of these issues must be related to the chronological and geographical contexts involved. We cannot be certain whether local groups shared activities during the earliest phases of the Paleolithic in France, because there is no true hominid site prior to one million years ago. Those dating from between 800,000 and 400,000 years ago are few and poorly studied, and we know nothing about subsistence from these periods. When does strategic hunting begin? How long did scavenging alone predominate (if it ever was exclusive)? What role did fire play?

With the appearance of "Neandertal" hominids in the Riss and early Würm we begin to know much more about these questions—especially concerning land use. For example, mobility-based behavior seems to be directly linked to the structure of the natural environment. Neandertals did not wander about nature at random (nor indeed do animal species), and had to combine their need for subsistence with their technological needs and with their social requirements. In contrast to some recent characterizations, we believe that Neandertals are in no way comparable to Australopithecines, and should not be forced into some kind of pre-human model which does not concur with the available archaeological and technological evidence.

If earlier generations of French prehistorians failed to understand the behavior of Neandertal populations it is mainly because their models were based upon the behavior of recent *H. sapiens sapiens* (e.g., Magdalenian) populations, or modern hunters and gatherers. However, between Oldowan hominids and Magdalenian men there is the Neandertal world which is something quite different. Neither the models for the Australopithecines nor those for modern hunter-gatherers are sufficient for understanding the Middle Paleolithic. There is a need for new models which more appropriately fit the unique status of the Neandertals—more complex than earlier hominids, with highly constraining traditions, but different from the variability of modern cultural adaptations. Either these European Middle Paleolithic people were at the end of one "ancient" trajectory of behavior or at the beginning of a modern one.

With regard to the study of Middle Paleolithic sites we need to know the kind of unit at our disposal: the more we know about the units we analyze the further we shall go towards an explanation of behavior.

The central problem in the study of Middle Paleolithic sites is a severe lack of contextual documents. Very little information can be expected from the early excavations in cave and rockshelter sites, since the excavated areas were generally too small and too poorly recorded to reveal if the site was a home base or a temporary hunter's camp. Until 1970 most archaeologists were primarily interested in chronological sequences rather than studies of economic or social organization; and those who looked for spatial organization on Middle Paleolithic living floors were generally unsuccessful, especially since this was not the primary goal of the excavations. Hardly any living floors from these periods are preserved. What we have is, at best, accumulated artifacts produced by the same human group over a period of time that may range from a few weeks or years to perhaps a century or more. Some of the recently discovered open-air sites when they are well enough preserved may provide valuable data to add to those from cave and rock shelter sites. The possibility of some natural disturbance of these sites need not prevent us from securing useful information, as long as we keep in mind that it is multi-time units, and not a one-week, one-family living floor, that are being investigated.

The first problem of course is linked to the preservation of material remains. Any Middle Paleolithic archaeological database is a biased one, but since there are so few sites we need to work on most of them—though a primary geological deposition is a necessary condition; and we must try to reconstruct what has been lost.

Faced with dense aggregations of Middle Paleolithic materials we can usually assume that we are dealing with areas where one or more families shared, at one or several times, a given range of activities. If so, we have the accumulation of the use of the same place for simi-

lar purposes over different lengths of time. Of course, that most Middle Paleolithic archaeological units are mixed may not be the only explanation for the fact that faunal remains, lithic tools, and debris often seem to be randomly distributed in the archaeological deposits. Even so the cumulative and mixed aspect of Middle Paleolithic archaeological deposits should carry some information about the organization of the human groups who were at least partly responsible for creating them, and may provide important information on some of the organization strategy involved.

Even with relatively poorly preserved archaeological material it is possible to go beyond mere descriptions of the archaeological material itself. Detailed studies of the spatial distribution of material can frequently shed important light on the internal organization of the sites. If we can discern some kind of repeated patterning in the material (the same activity repeated at the same place several times) for which several technical responses were available, then we may be closer to decoding essential patterns of behavior.

Our purpose here is to isolate repeated activities and to explore their level of significance in regard to expedient versus planned human behavior, through the study of two open-air Middle Paleolithic accumulations.

MAURAN (PETITS PYRENEES)

This site extends at least 80 m from east to west and at least 10 m from north and south. The richest archaeological level is at an average of 4 m below ground surface and is over 30 cm thick. Although only 25 sq. m have been excavated so far, the archaeological material seems to be generally representative of that from the other areas that have been tested. The archaeological accumulation consists of bones, lithic artifacts, and burnt bones (Fig. 7.1). The faunal remains include bones of bison (*Bison* cf. *priscus*) and a very limited number of bones of horses and cervids. The lithic industry includes small tools, such as flint denticulates, and a few scrapers and heavy tools such as quartzite choppers (Fig. 7.2). Though the lithic industry is not as rich as the fauna and seems to be very specialized, it nevertheless shows that the cores were prepared on site, and that the tools were also manufactured here. Some pebbles were brought into the site, and show no visible trace of use. Despite the clayey, calcareous nature of the deposit, the bones must have been in contact with air or water for an extended period of time since their surfaces are often smoothed. As a result, it is difficult to see clear cut marks or gnawing on the majority of the

faunal remains. Post-depositional fracture is common but it is generally easy to separate those fractures from original breakage patterns. On chronostratigraphic grounds the site appears to date either from a Riss interstadial or from the beginning of the early Würm.

Faunal remains were studied using the entire faunal assemblage as a single entity. The bones have been tabulated by Francine David according to minimum number of elements (MNE), minimum animal units (MAU) and standardized MAU values (MAU%), following the method of L. Binford (1984). The MNI for bison calculated using mandibular teeth is 136. The relative percentages (MAU%) for bison bones are illustrated in Figure 7.3. The most common elements are the calcaneum, proximal metatarsal, mandible, astragalus, distal tibia, proximal radio-cubitus, distal humerus, and tarsals. Meaty bones from around the shoulder and fore limb are well represented, while innominate bones are missing, as well as some hind limbs (Fig. 7.4). We cannot explain the low frequency of femora solely by the fact that they were systematically broken for marrow processing and consequently less likely to survive. And we must also note that there is a lack of the pelvis, which is not a particularly weak bone.

Different stages in the butchering process can be established at Mauran, including the dismemberment of carcasses, removal of muscle masses from the bones, and breakage of the bones for marrow extraction.

The distribution plans indicate the existence of heavily disarticulated carcasses, with hardly any feet connections. Further analysis of the bones strongly suggests that the carcasses were dismembered.

Cut marks are infrequent because of the previously mentioned problems with preservation, but have been recorded clearly on many of the humeri. Several cut marks are also present on the radio-cubitus, on the atlas, and on phalanges. On the humerus, cut marks are situated either on the shafts (possibly reflecting filletting of meat from the bones) or on the proximal part above

the articulation (suggesting dismemberment). Such cut marks indicate that muscle masses were removed from the bones in addition to dismembering them.

Systematic fracture of the long bones for marrow extraction is evidenced by hundreds of fragments of bison long bones (Figs. 7.5-6). Breakage of the humeri shows a classic pattern: they have been broken at the distal extremity just above the trochlea on the internal edge, by means of a heavy blow. An impact point is visible on this side and a secondary impact on the opposite side. A second blow may have been struck at the proximal end below the articulation. Radio-cubitus or metapodial bones were often broken for marrow, while the femur and humerus and, to a lesser extent, the tibia were systematically broken.

What can we infer from these patterns about foraging techniques and meat procurement?

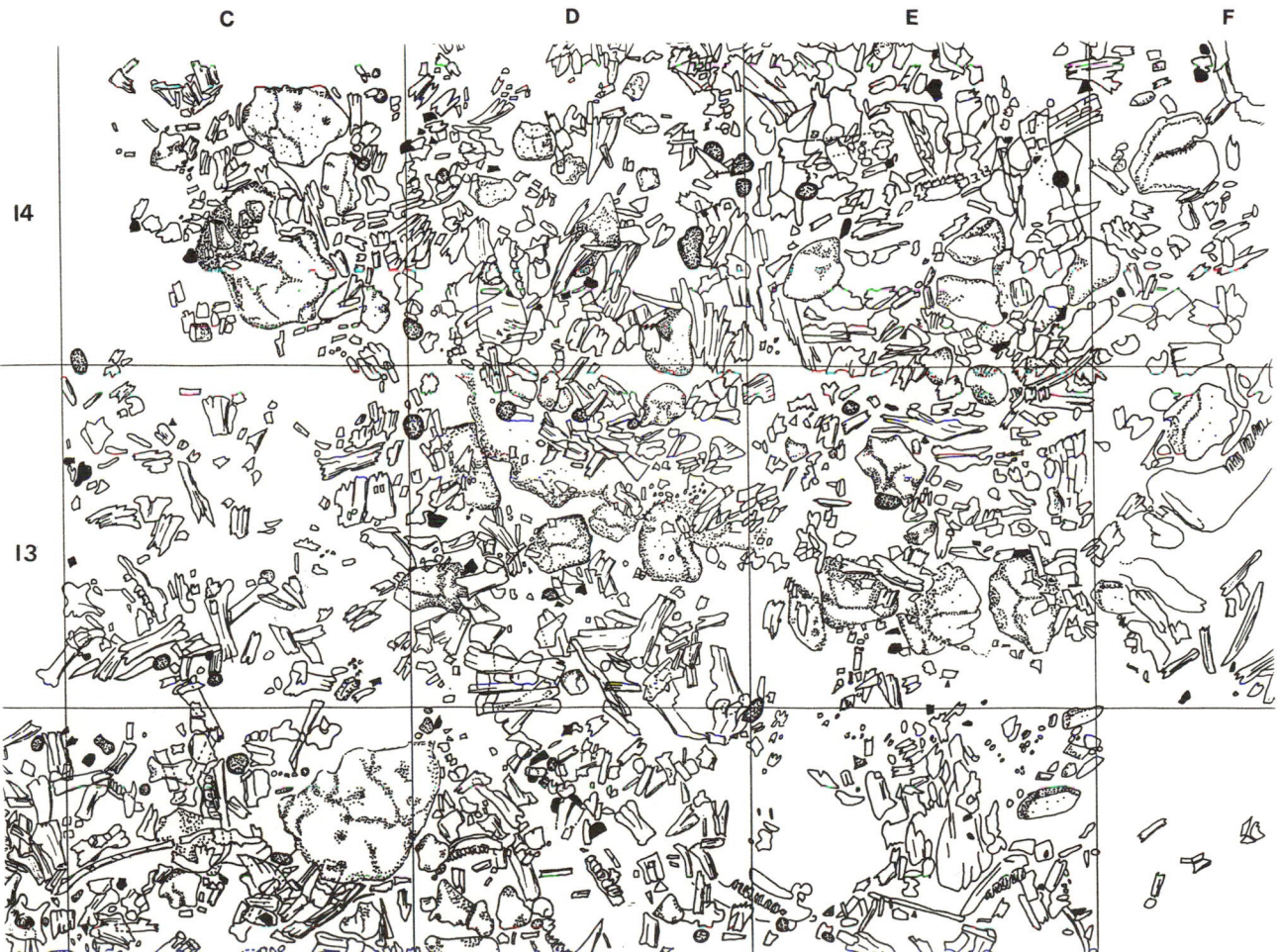

Figure 7.1   Mauran. An example of the prehistoric accumulation (white = bones; black = lithic industry; stippled = pebbles).

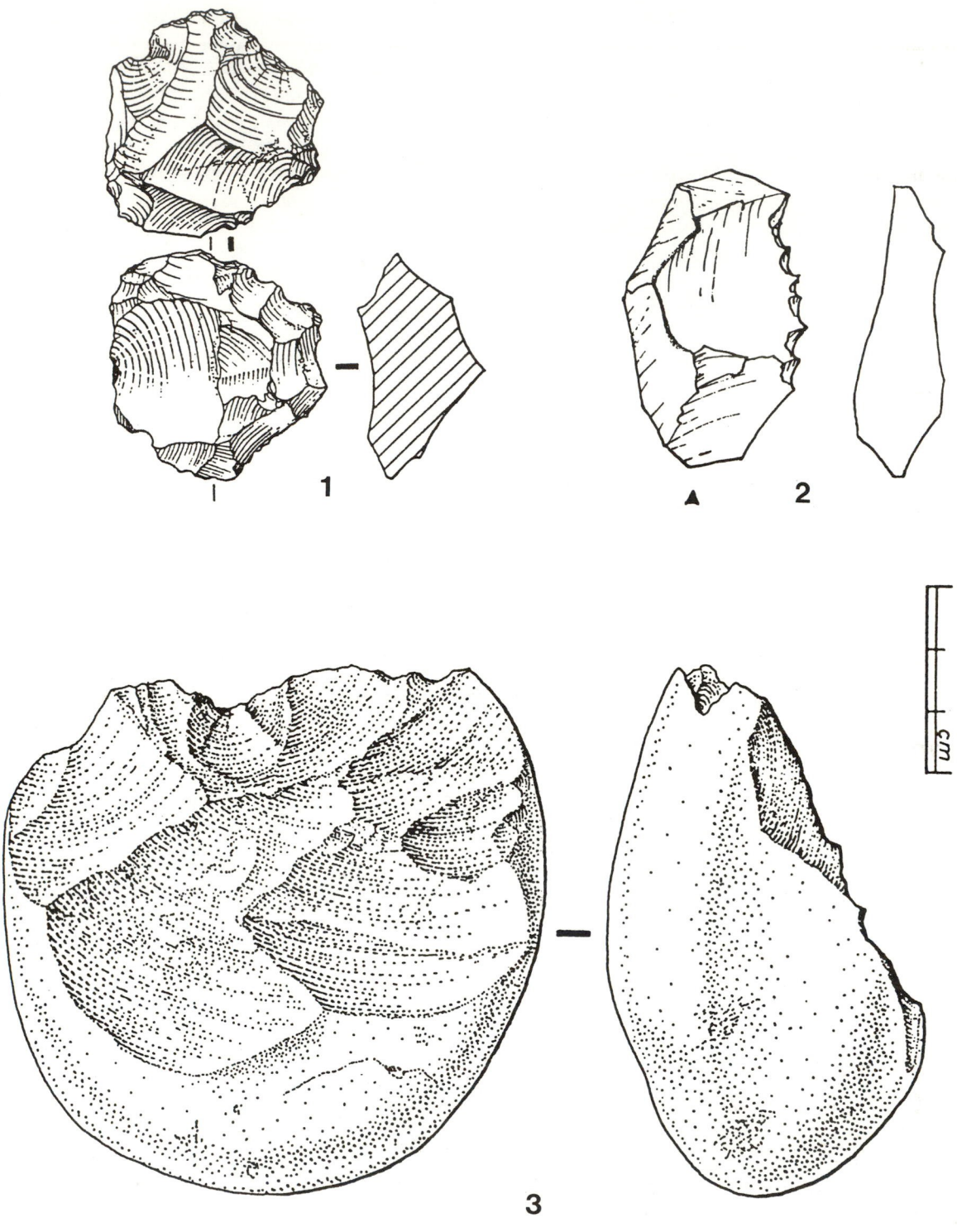

Figure 7.2   *Mauran lithic industry. 1: Flint core; 2: flint denticulate; 3: quartzite chopper.*

The age distribution of the animals killed reveals curves similar to those obtained for Upper Paleolithic sites where hunting is well documented. There are relatively few remains of very young individuals (less than 3 months in age). There are two series of ages for milk teeth; several individuals at around 6 months or less and several at around 18 months. Could this be related to a pattern of seasonal exploitation or simply to poor conservation? These question have yet to be resolved, though the available data suggest interrup-

tions in the seasonal use of the site. What we observed at Mauran is a site which seems to have been selected for certain specific activities. Animals, particularly small herds with females and young, were hunted close to the excavated area. While large-scale hunting would no doubt have been possible with driving techniques, the fact that all of the carcasses seem to have been processed in the same manner would suggest that relatively few animals were killed at any one time.

CHAMPLOST (NORTHERN BURGUNDY)

Two areas of this site have so far been excavated. The major excavation exposed an area of 120 sq. m, while the second excavation (40 m away) comprised only 20 sq. m.

The whole of the material from this site is strikingly different from that at Mauran. Stone tools are numerous as well as cores and debitage. Accumulations of burned bones and ash are present in addition

to many faunal remains. But these faunal remains are completely different from those at Mauran, though the species are the same. Once again bovid remains are dominant, associated with some horse and cervid. Whole axial skeletons are not present, nor are heads or feet (Fig. 7.7). Only fragmented long bone shafts were found in the first excavated area, while the same

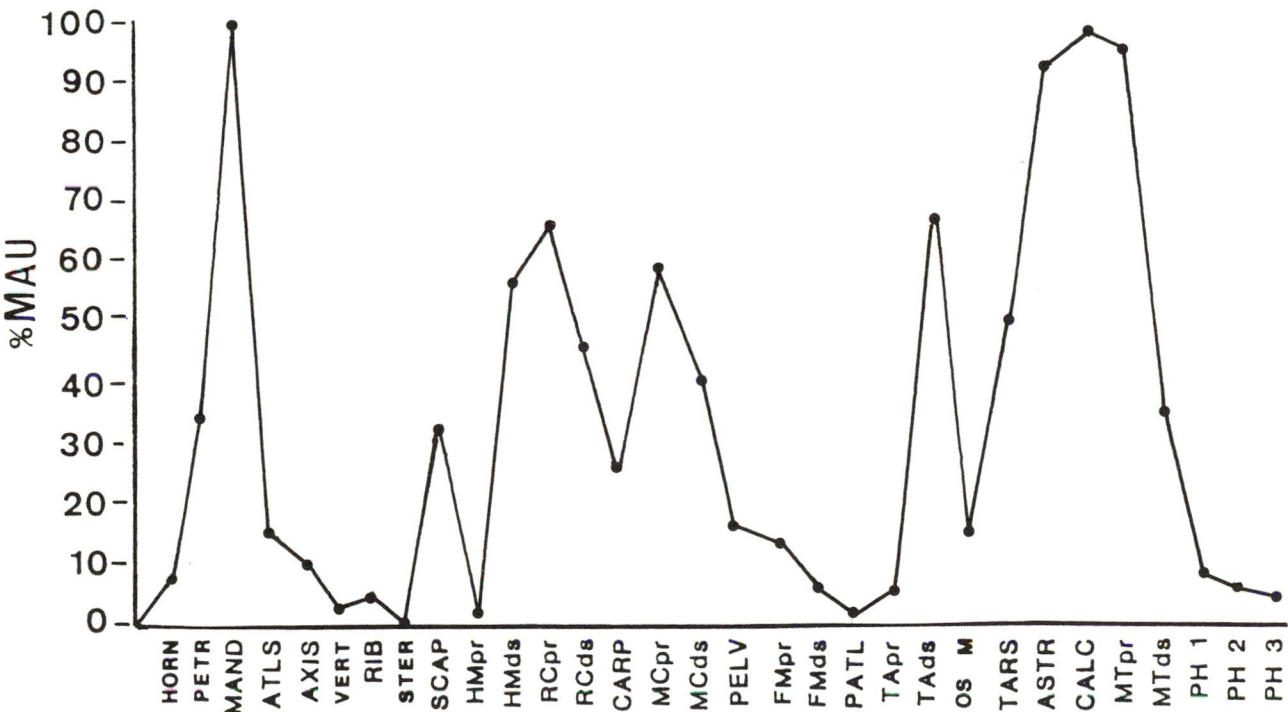

Figure 7.3   *Indexed minimal animal unit values (MAU%) for Mauran bison bones. In this diagram, good preservation of the bones may explain the high frequency of jaws, astragali, and calcanea, while vertebrae and ribs are infrequent. Two striking elements are apparent: the fore limbs rich in meat are numerous, while the hind ones (equally as rich) are few. The scarcity of the femora cannot be totally explained by the fact that its high rate of breakage for marrow is conducive to a rapid destruction of epiphysis; and one would expect more pelves. It may be that the pelvis (meaty) part of the skeleton was taken away—with part of the hind limbs—for later processing.*

remains plus a few vertebrae and teeth were found in the second. It would appear in this case that the site was located at some distance from where the animals were killed. Only parts of the carcasses were selectively brought to the site for further processing, and for the consumption of meat and marrow.

The lithic assemblage from the site includes numerous specialized highly retouched scrapers. The distribution of the lithic material appears to show some spatial patterning, though there is no indica-

tion of any specialized areas or concentrations of specific forms of debitage or tools. The relative frequencies of different varieties of lithic materials appear to be similar across the excavated area. There are, however, important differences among some lithic remains which still remain to be explained. More detailed studies of these artifacts may reveal some significant spatial patterning, but we still need suitable models in order to derive an explanation from them.

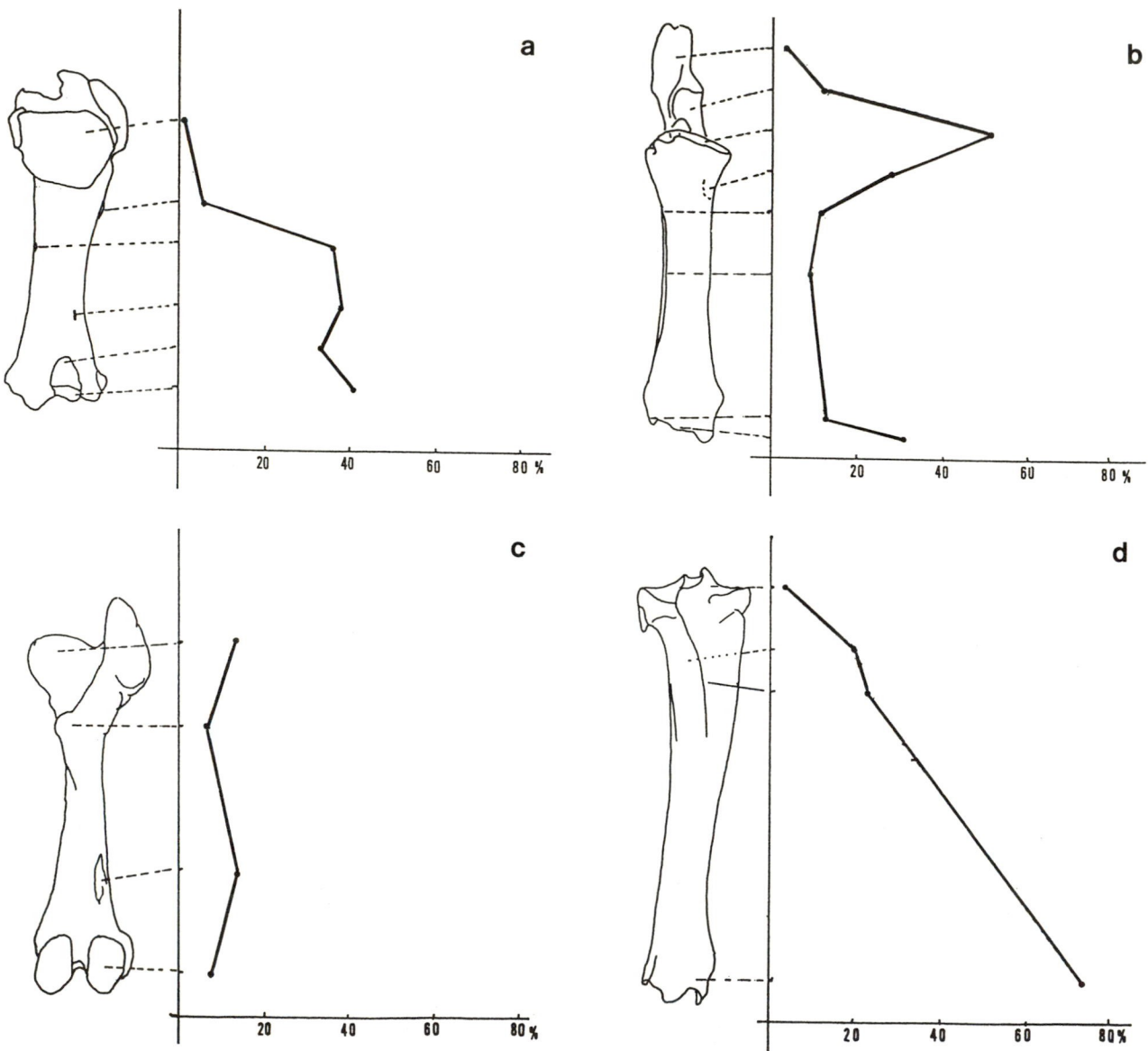

Figure 7.4   Relative frequencies of the different portions of bison long bones at Mauran: (a) humerus, (b) radius, (c) femur, (d) tibia. On the fore limb, the distal humerus and proximal radius are rather well represented. The femur is poorly preserved, while the distal tibia is often present.

CONCLUSION

In this paper we have examined two specific Middle Paleolithic sites, each one apparently utilized by the same human group over an extended time-span. These two very different butchering sites allow us to infer the existence of specialized patterns of mammal hunting repeated through time. The pattern of long-bone breakage at Mauran shows highly distinctive patterns, and the absence of certain bison hind limbs and pelves might be explained by the systematic transport of these meaty parts away from the site. Champlost seems instead to represent a camp where parts of the animals killed were brought back and consumed on the site itself.

Middle Paleolithic data often appear monotonous, and such monotony may be the result of mixed activities, mixed times, or both combined, perhaps with an absence of specialization. Two things must be kept in mind. We failed to show any functional distinction of particular areas of the sites in the way we find them in Upper Paleolithic settlements. But this does not mean that Middle Paleolithic groups were not able to plan short- or even long-term foraging strategies. Their behavior seems to be highly dependent on social constraints, and this could explain why behavioral patterns appear to change so slowly. Neandertals may have practiced short-term foraging subsistence strategies

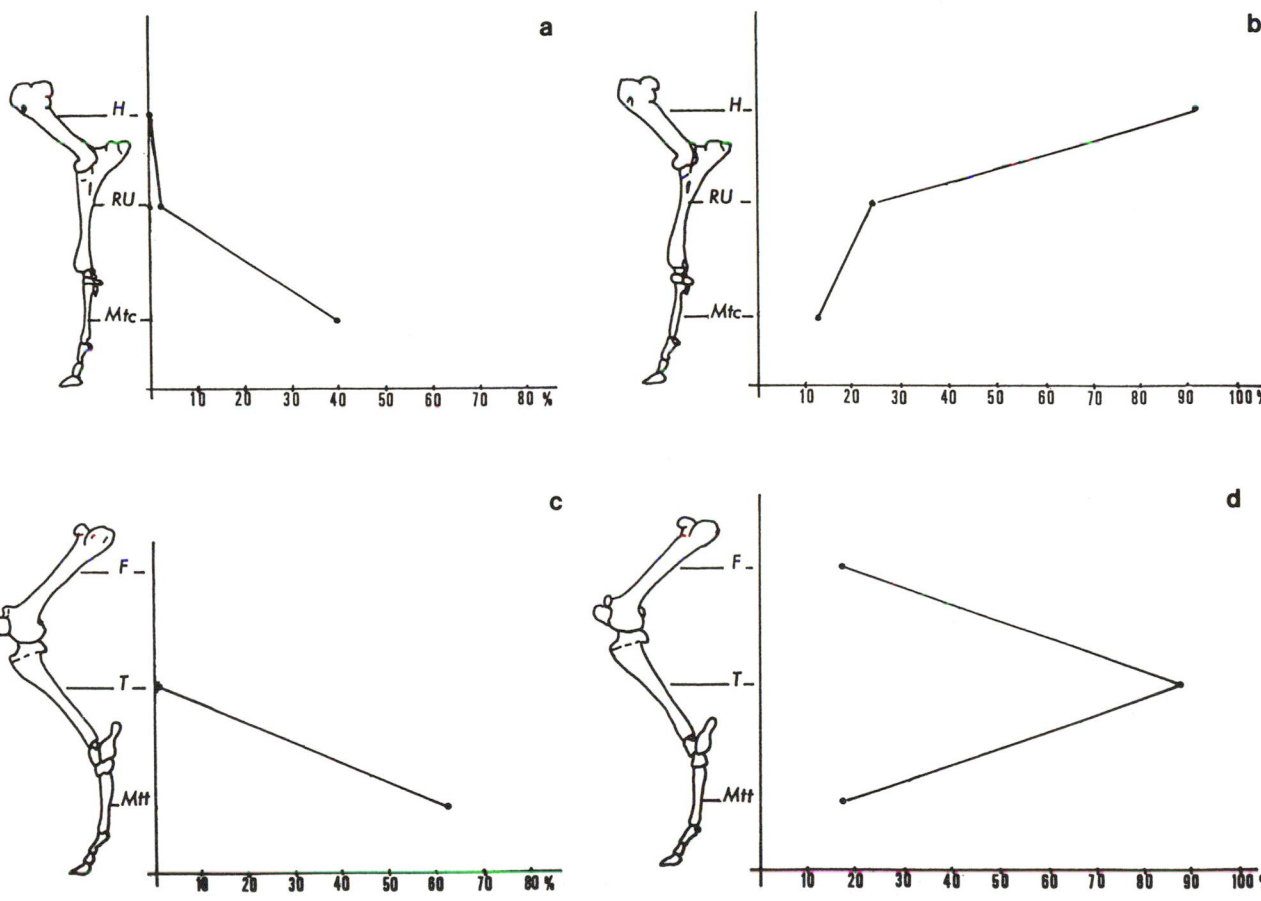

Figure 7.5   Frequencies of complete bones of bison from Mauran: (a) upper limb, (c) hind limb; and comparison between the fragmentation of the different bones (b, d) (after Todd and Rapson 1988). In the case of complete bones, only metatarsal and metacarpal bones are rarely broken by heavy percussion; humeri, femora, and tibiae are never complete, and a few radii are ever complete. As for fragmentation, radii, metacarpals, femora, and metatarsals show fewer differences in the frequency between proximal and distal ends, whereas the distal portions of humerii and tibiae are significantly better preserved than the proximal portions of these bones.

which included both hunting and scavenging—though scavenging from abandoned and scattered carcasses is inevitably difficult to prove in contexts (like northern Europe) where the primary scavenging localities themselves are difficult to find.

ACKNOWLEDGMENTS

We are grateful to James Enloe for his help in the preparation of the English version of this paper.

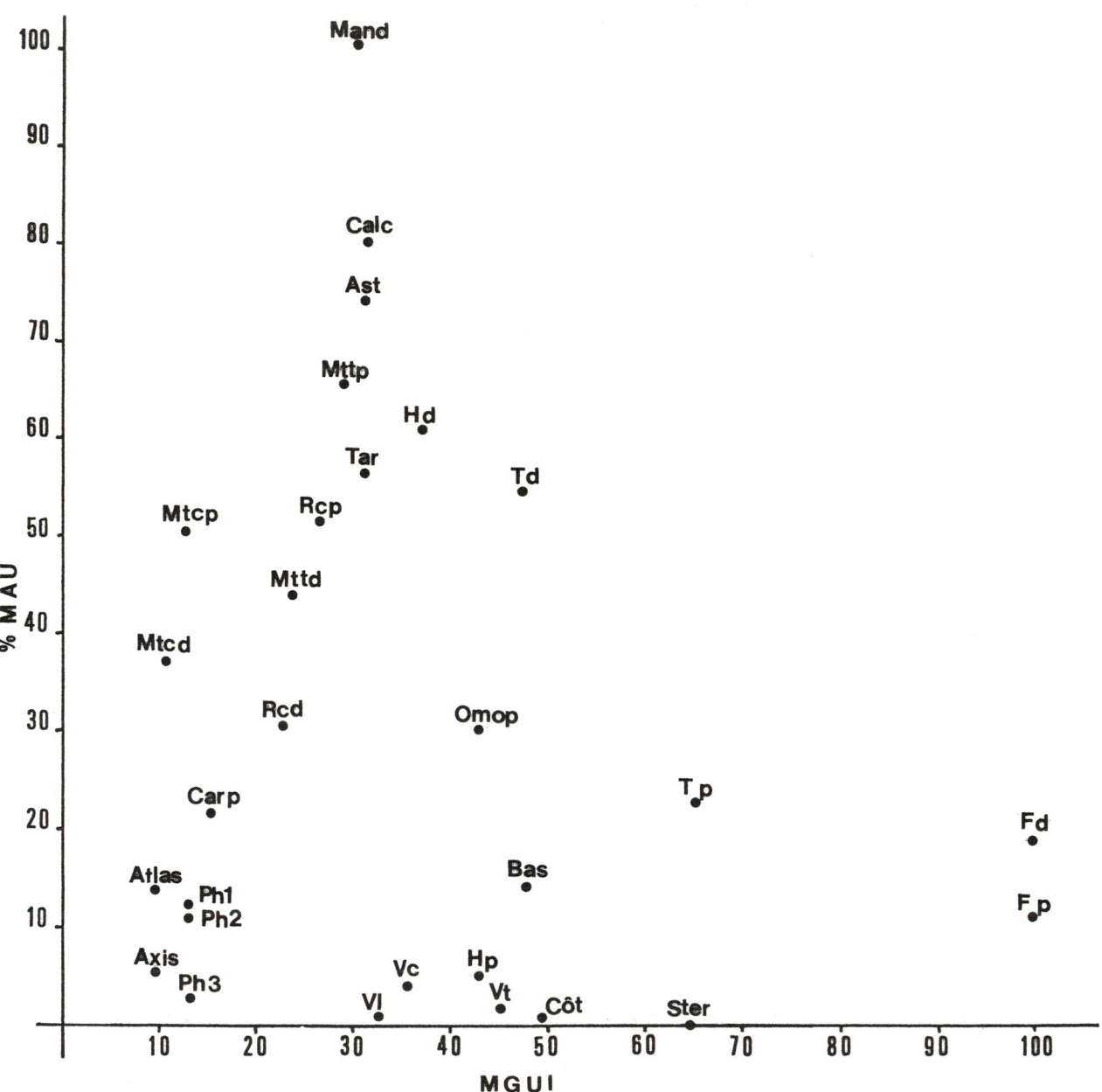

Figure 7.6   Relationships between the Modified General Utility Index (MGUI, Binford 1978) and Mauran bison bones. This figure confirms the low frequency of some meaty parts such as the femur and to a lesser extent the innominates. On the other hand, bison humeri, which provide more meat than those of the reindeer, are frequent. The less fractured bones such as tarsal, mandibular, metapodial, are over-represented.

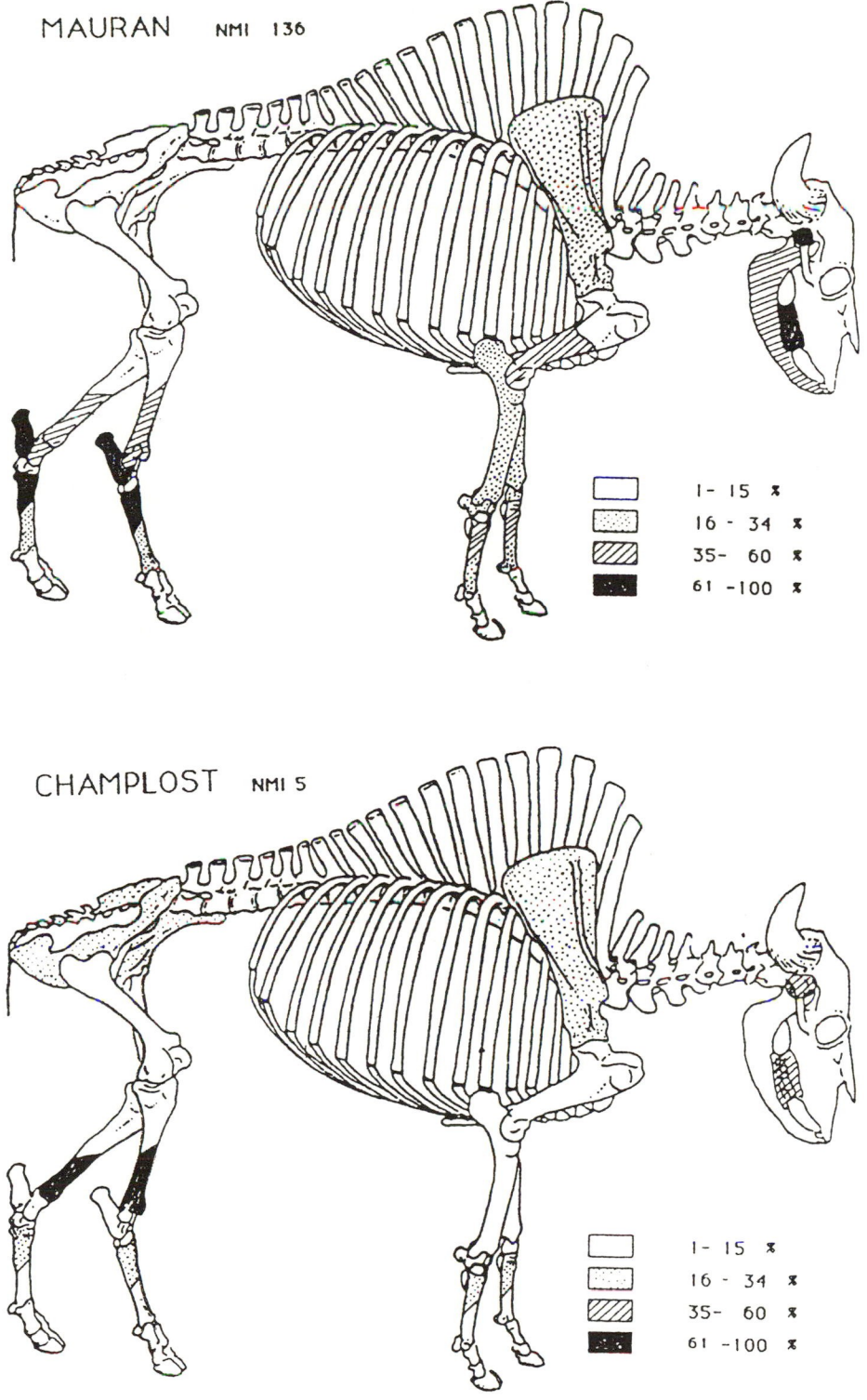

Figure 7.7   *Minimal animal unit (MAU) values for Mauran and Champlost bison bones.*

BIBLIOGRAPHY

Binford, L. R.

1978   *Nunamiut Ethnoarchaeology*. New York: Academic Press.

1981   *Bones: Ancient Men and Modern Myths*. New York: Academic Press.

1984   *Faunal Remains from Klasies River Mouth*. New York: Academic Press.

1988   Fact and Fiction about the Zinjanthropus Floor: Data, Arguments and Interpretations. *CA* 29:123-155.

David, F.

1972   Témoins osseux. Pp. 295-320 in *Fouilles de Pincevent. Essai d'analyse ethnographique d'un habitat magdalénien (La section 36)*, eds. A. Leroi-Gourhan and M. Brézillon. GP Supplément 7. Paris: CNRS.

in press   La faune de Pincevent et Verberie. In *Environnements et habitats magdaléniens. Le centre du Bassin parisien*, ed. Y. Taborin. Paris: DAF.

Farizy, C.

in press   Spatial Organization and Middle Paleolithic Open Air Sites. Paper presented at the international symposium of Origini "L'interpretazione funzionale dei dati in paletnologia" (Rome, June 1988).

Farizy, C., and David, F.

1988   Chasse et alimentation carnée au Paléolithique moyen, l'apport des gisements de plein air. Pp. 59-62 in *L'homme de Néandertal*, ed. M. Otte. Vol. 6: *La subsistance*. ERAUL 33. Liège: Université de Liège.

Frison, G., and Todd, L.

1986   *The Colby Mammoth Site. Taphonomy and Archaeology of a Clovis Kill in Northern Wyoming*. Albuquerque: University of New Mexico Press.

Rapson, D. J., and Todd, L. C.

1989   Body Size, Season, Sex and Butchery: Inference about Storage and Transport through Faunal Analysis. Paper presented at the 54th Annual Meeting of the SAA (Atlanta, April).

Speth, J. D.

1983   *Bison Kills and Bone Counts: Decision Making by Ancient Hunters*. Chicago: University of Chicago Press.

1987   Early Hominid Subsistence Strategies in Seasonal Habitats. *JAS* 14:13-29.

Todd, L. C., and Rapson, D. J.

1988   Long Bone Fragmentation and Interpretation of Faunal Assemblages: Approaches to Comparative Analysis. *JAS* 15:307-325.

Todd, L. C.; Rapson, D. J.; and Ingbar, E.

1985   Glimpses of Organization: Integrating Site Structure with Analysis of Assemblage Content. Paper presented at the 50th Annual Meeting of the SAA (Denver, May).

VIII

Approaches to the Middle Paleolithic in Northern Spain

Victoria Cabrera Valdes

Federico Bernaldo de Quirós

INTRODUCTION

While many different types of archaeological deposits are found along the coastal fringe of Cantabrian Spain, caves sites are especially important because of their deep stratigraphic accumulations. In Cantabria, almost all of these sites are found in valleys, or areas of low altitude, or near the coast. The coastal plain constitutes a narrow horizontal corridor extending from the Pyrenees to the Asturian region. Few sites are encountered toward the interior of the peninsula, although some, like El Conde in Asturias, Axlor in the Basque region, and Lezetxiki in Guipúzcoa, are situated at higher altitudes. Others lie toward the interior in longitudinal valleys. A good example is El Castillo, which is situated about 30 km from the coast, midway up a mountain of the same name. The best known cave deposits in the Cantabrian region are El Conde, Cueva Morín, El Pendo, Castillo, Hornos de la Peña, La Flecha, Cobalejos, La Fuente del Francés, El Linar, and the rockshelters of San Vitores (Freeman 1966) in Cantabria, Venta de la Perra and Axlor (Altuna 1980;

Barandiarán 1980) in the Basque Country, and Lezetxiki (Barandiarán 1978) in Guipúzcoa (Fig. 8.1). Of these, Morín, Pendo, and Castillo provide the deepest stratigraphic sequences. The degree to which we understand these sites varies greatly, relying almost always on the lithic industry and occasionally on faunal analysis.

There have been two attempts to reconstruct the chronostratigraphy of this area, one by Kornprobst (1967), who focused on the cave of Lezetxiki, and another by Butzer (1981), who correlated the sequences of Castillo, Morín, and Pendo. According to these studies, Level VII from Lezetxiki, the levels below XXII in Morín, and Levels XVIII and XVI at Pendo, resemble each other and correspond to the Würm I. According to Butzer, Castillo's Level 22 and the rest of Morín and Pendo's strata date to Würm II. However, according to our more recent analyses, the lower levels of Castillo display a clearer continuity with the Riss-Würm, and thus Level 22 of this site probably dates to Würm I.

THE INDUSTRIAL ASSEMBLAGES AND THEIR INTERPRETATION

The series described here are among the richest assemblages of the region and allow for a variety of technological and typological studies. In general, it can be said that the Mousterian assemblages of Cantabria display a certain typological monotony.

RAW MATERIALS

There appears to be selection of raw material according to local accessibility. At Castillo, for exam-

ple, a typological distinction occurs between quartzite and flint, although the latter represents a greater exhaustion of supply than does the quartzite, because of the greater difficulty in access to it. However, for special pieces like flake cleavers, there is a clear utilization of materials such as ophite and coarse-grained quartzite, which are rarely utilized in other pieces. We will return to this later (see Fig. 8.2).

The following patterns are apparent in relation to the use of raw materials.

Flint comes from diverse sources in Morín and Pendo, sites that are situated closer to coastal outcrops. At Morín, the proportion of flint is very high, in both the retouched and unretouched material. The only exception to this is in Level 15, where the proportion of quartzite is equal to that of flint. At Pendo, flint is also well represented. At Castillo the proportion of flint reaches 40% in the Mousterian strata (Levels 20 and 22), while it drops in the strata below the Acheulian level (30% for Level 25a and 7.82% for Level 25b). In the cave of El Conde, the percentage of flint is almost zero and in La Flecha it reaches only 2.46%. At Axlor and Lezetxiki, it is very typical to encounter flint given the accessibility of raw material sources. These facts reinforce current notions that are now offered on the Upper Paleolithic of the region, since tools found in the Basque areas are more often made on flint than those found in areas progressively further west on the Cantabrian shelf.

Quartzite usually occurs as rolled pebbles, except in El Conde, where there are veins located nearby. Its presence overall is low to moderate in Morín and Pendo, high in Castillo (45%) and Hornos de la Peña, and very high in El Conde and La Flecha (78%). The high quality of the Cantabrian quartzite, which is very fine grained, leads to its frequent utilization in some deposits thoughout the Paleolithic sequences. The use of ophite is also well represented at the sites of Pendo, Morín, and Castillo, and outcrops close to the latter two sites. Its use is emphasized in the manufacture of flake cleavers, but is also represented among the flake tools, as in Level 17 of Morín. Quartz and black Jurassic limestone appear as consistent elements, as well as schist at Axlor.

TECHNOLOGICAL AND TYPOLOGICAL CONSIDERATIONS OF THE CANTABRIAN FACIES

In general, the Middle Paleolithic assemblages of Cantabria exhibit low indices of Levallois technique (IL = 6 or 7%), an absence of blades, and a predominance of flakes. Platform faceting is also limited, usually not observed on more than 10% of the pieces, and dihedral platforms vary between 15 and 25%. Thus, plain and cortical platforms are predominant, which correlates with the use of pebbles as the primary source of raw material.

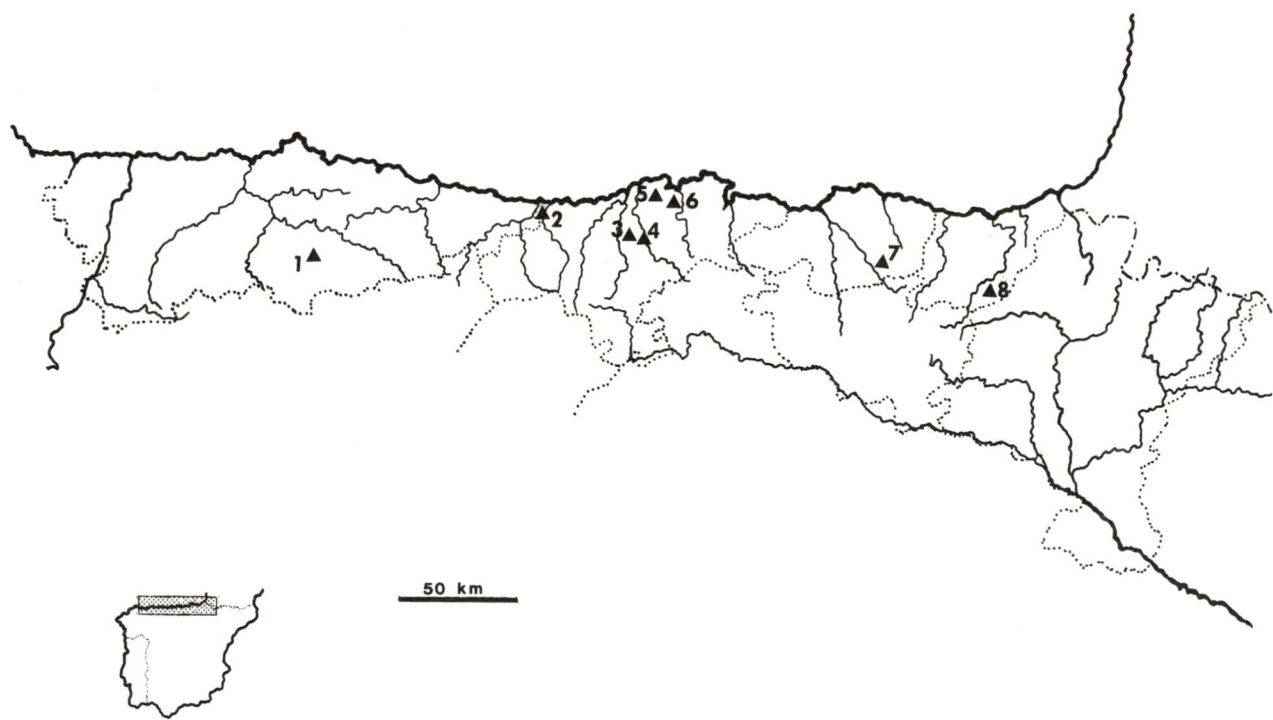

Figure 8.1   *Location of the main Mousterian sites mentioned in text. 1: El Conde; 2: Unquera; 3: Hornos de la Peña; 4: Castillo; 5: Pendo; 6: Morín; 7: Axlor; 8: Lezetxiki. The dotted lines are modern regional boundaries.*

Sidescrapers and denticulates are the dominant types, with limited representation of Upper Paleolithic elements such as perforators, dihedral burins, endscrapers on flakes, and carinated scrapers. The proportion of flake cleavers is even smaller, in lower limits being barely represented. It is important to note that in some cases the presence of denticulates may reflect geological disturbances, and thus may depend on which part of the site was excavated. At El Conde, for example, the excavated area is at the back of the cave, where the Aurignacian levels also exhibit a high degree of denticulate pieces (see also Freeman, this volume).

The various assemblages from Cantabrian cave deposits have been assigned to three classic Mousterian assemblage groups, as shown in Table 8.1. To some extent these assignments are somewhat arbitrary, since the assemblages present only tendencies toward one group or another. It is also necessary to define those series with flake cleavers as a special facies that encompasses the Cantabrian region and the western Pyrenees. Bordes (1953) called this regional facies the "Vasconian," basing its significance on its Charentian tendency and its presence in areas that surround the Bay of Biscay. However, there has since been a great deal of discussion of this group and its definition. Even the term itself is not very accurate, since this facies extended well into the central valleys of the Cantabrian coast, which is neither historically nor culturally Basque.

Aside from this terminological consideration, there are also technological and typological aspects of these industries that should be reviewed. Bordes based his original judgements primarily on two deposits, the Abri Olha (in the French Pyrenees) and Level 20 of Castillo. Subsequently the analysis of Freeman of the Cueva Morín material (Freeman 1964; González Echegaray et al. 1971, 1973; González Echegaray and Freeman 1978) and that of

TABLE 8.1.

ASSIGNMENT OF THE INDUSTRIES OF VARIOUS SITES AND LEVELS TO MOUSTERIAN ASSEMBLAGE GROUPS. (H) INDICATES THE PRESENCE OF FLAKE CLEAVERS (*HENDEDORES*) IN THE ASSEMBLAGE.

Charentian	Denticulate	Typical
Castillo 20 (H)	El Conde 5	Cobalejos?
Castillo 22	El Conde 6	Lezetxiki VI
Axlor	Morín 11	Lezetxiki VII
Lezetxiki IVa	Morín 12	Morín 17 (H)
Lezetxiki IVc	Morín 17inf.	Morín 16 (H)
	La Flecha	Morín 15 (H)
	Pendo VIIId	Pendo XIII (H)
	Pendo XI	Pendo XIV
	Pendo XII	Pendo XVI
	Lezetxiki Vb	Hornos de la Peña

El Pendo (González Echegaray et al. 1980) significantly broadened the view of this assemblage group, though creating at the same time a certain degree of confusion. Freeman originally felt that the cleaver assemblages of Morín and Castillo resembled a peculiar form of the Mousterian of Acheulian Tradition (MTA), though later, after his examination of the El Pendo material, he decided that these assemblages could not be truly considered as the MTA and instead assigned them to the Typical Mousterian, though one somewhat rich in sidescrapers.

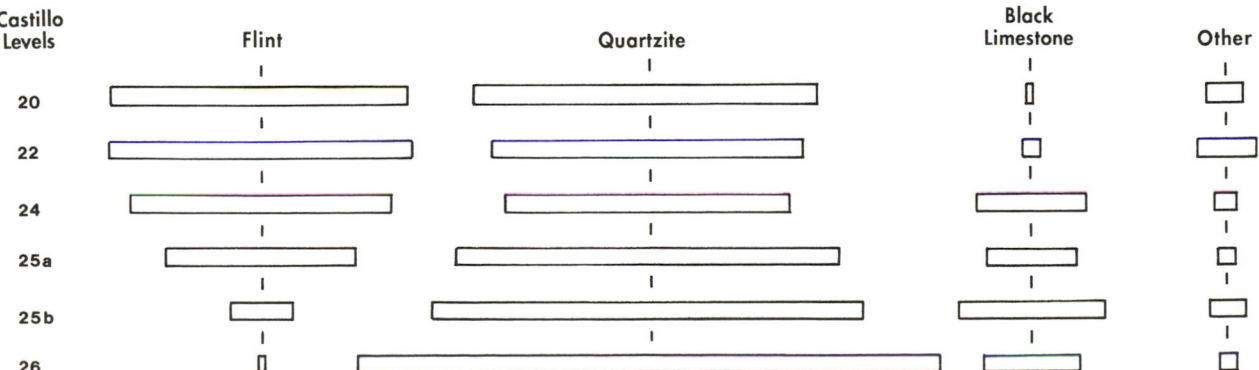

Figure 8.2   Distribution of raw materials in Castillo lower levels.

In our revision (Cabrera Valdes 1983) based on the more significant classic Vasconian assemblages, we observed significant variability in this industry, from assemblages that are similar to the MTA to those that are like the Typical Mousterian of Freeman. However, certain assemblages analyzed by us (Cabrera Valdes 1978, 1984), such as Level 20 of Castillo, cannot fit into a classification of Typical Mousterian rich in sidescrapers, given the Charentian characteristics among the scrapers. We attributed this particular assemblage to an evolved Charentian, which is in agreement with the opinion of Bordes. Hoping to avoid confusion and eliminate erroneous nomenclature, we proposed that the assemblages with flake cleavers should not be treated as a special facies. Given their variability, we consider it more appropriate to assign them to other Mousterian groups which encompass more of their characteristics, though acknowledging always the presence of flake cleavers.

On the other hand, recent work in the region of the French Basque region associates assemblages with flake cleavers with a regional subtype of the MTA, in which cleavers seem to substitute for handaxes (Santamaria 1984; Chauchat 1985). In the slope south of the Pyrenees—in the Spanish Basque region and Navarra—cleavers are found in open-air deposits. The lithic context in which they appear is similar culturally to the Late Upper Acheulian and/or to the MTA, which is true also for Murba in Alava (Baldéon 1974), and the assemblage of Balsa de Aranzaduya on the Navarra slope of the Urbasa sierra (Barandiarán and Vallespí 1980).

The issue of Mousterian facies appears confused, but in our opinion the confusion need not be amplified. When we move away from the geographic areas where the facies were first defined, the distinctions become blurred and appear more as tendencies than as representative assemblages containing certain attributes. In fact, the assemblages are better seen as collections of variables to which cultural elements are associated in relation to determined economic activities (Cabrera Valdes 1988).

THE SIGNIFICANCE OF FLAKE CLEAVERS AS A CULTURAL ELEMENT

A special relevance is often attributed to flake cleavers, seeing them in certain contexts as a cultural/chronological marker of some importance. However, their presence is witnessed in numerous Lower and Middle Paleolithic contexts and is not restricted to the regions bordering the Cantabrian Sea or the Bay of Biscay (i.e., Gascony) and their neighbors. The presence of flake cleavers in classic Würmian Middle Paleolithic cave deposits of the Pyrenees and the Cantabrian shelf should probably be interpreted in relation to aspects of the raw materials, which appear in diverse assemblages, and to certain technological traits related to specific, but as yet unknown, activities. It is quite possible that the cleavers constitute a cultural element that is important from the micro-regional point of view for the recognition of relations between settlements and activities accomplished in distinct occupations. However, it is important to point out that we do not consider that they should be considered as a type fossil.

In the Cantabrian shelf, cleavers are present in assemblages of three sites with deep stratigraphies: El Castillo, Cueva Morín, and El Pendo. Geographically they form a triangle between the Bay of Santander and the valley of the Pas River, with no side of the triangle longer than 25 km (Fig. 8.3). In these three deposits flake cleavers are always made on ophite and coarse-grained quartzites and never on flint. The use of ophite versus quartzite is variable: at El Pendo ophite was used exclusively; at Morín it is predominant (84.61%); and in Castillo only about 21% of the cleavers are made on ophite, compared with about 79% on quartzite. Given the lack of flint cleavers, we propose that there was an intentional selection of ophite and quartzite for the production of cleavers, especially given that these same materials were only occasionally used for the rest of the widely varying lithic assemblages. Moreover, it must be taken into account that, as already noted for Castillo and Morín, veins of ophite occur within a two-km radius. Some samples display a cortex characteristic of rolled pebbles, however, which may suggest that the catchment territory was situated in fluvial watersheds that traversed these veins. The proximity of ophite sources to Morín was previously noted by Conde de la Vega del Sella (1921).

In the Atlantic Pyrenees, at Abri Olha, Isturitz, and Gatzarría, cleavers also are encountered on raw materials only mediocre for knapping, suggesting again an expedient use of the nearest sources (Bahn 1983). In the case of the Abri Ohla, the recent study of Chauchat (1985) shows that flake cleavers on sandstone and coarse-grained quartzite are abundant in layer Fi4, typical in Fi3, and almost disappear in Fi2 (Fig. 8.4). Quartzite also appears in the last Mousterian level of the sequence at Gatzarría (Laplace 1966).

At Castillo, the flint materials in the classic Mousterian levels appear reserved for the manufacture of tools that vary in size between 4.5 and 7 cm, i.e.,

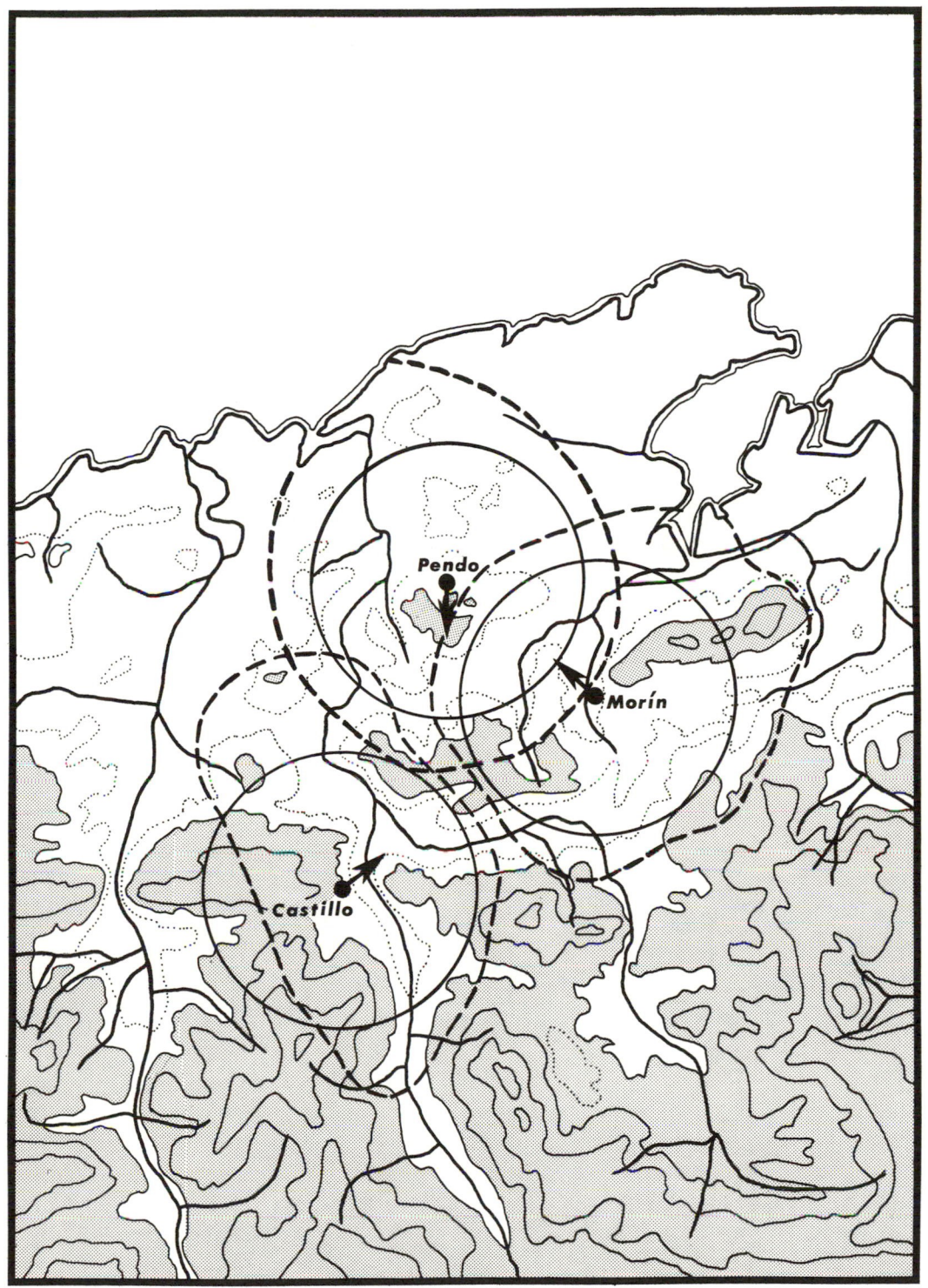

Figure 8.3   Situation of sites of Castillo, Morín, and Pendo in central Cantabria. Arrows show orientation of mouth. Contour interval 200 m. Dashed lines indicate possible territorial distributions (following natural relief).

smaller than the cleavers. An approximately equal number of tools are made on fine-grained quartzite. Also, a large number of flint cores were found, including many fragments or chunks, but only a few flakes (Cabrera Valdes and Bernaldo de Quirós 1985). This could relate to the necessity of transporting the nodules of flint from more distant zones than for the quarztite and/or the size of the flint nodules. At Morín, flint is the predominant raw material among the tools. At El Pendo, the tools from different levels are most often made on flint, with the exception of Level XIII, which has ophite cleavers, and in which the percentages of flint and quartzite are equal.

The selection of the ophite for the making of flake cleavers appears evident in the levels of occupation of these three deposits. The reason for this selection is probably due to the smaller size of the flint nodules, which, at least in Castillo, resulted in the saving of the flint nodules for other pieces. The volume of the pebbles of fine-grained quartzite does not appear to be as restrictive as that of the flint, although the structural characteristics of the quartzite would not be amenable to its transformation into flakes designed to be

cleavers. Few other raw materials were used in the manufacture of cleavers, regardless of the size or availability of the nodules or even their frequent use for non-typological pieces. One example is the black Jurassic limestone that is very abundant in the debitage at Castillo, but not used for the cleavers. It seems that this material is very plastic and may not have been suitable for whatever functions cleavers served.

The technological aspects of cleaver manufacturing at these sites has been studied by Benito del Rey (1972-73), and it is useful to review his work. At Castillo, he recognized three size classes with the following dimensions (expressed as length x width x platform thickness):

maxima: 15 x 14 x 5 cm
           12 x 19 x 3/4 cm
minima: 6 x 5 x 2 cm

One special characteristic observable on some of the cleavers, also noted by other investigators, including H. Breuil and H. Obermaier, is the presence of cortex on the dorsal surface along the transverse edge. These would be assigned to Type 0 in the classification of Tixier (1956), as a special subtype, or to Type

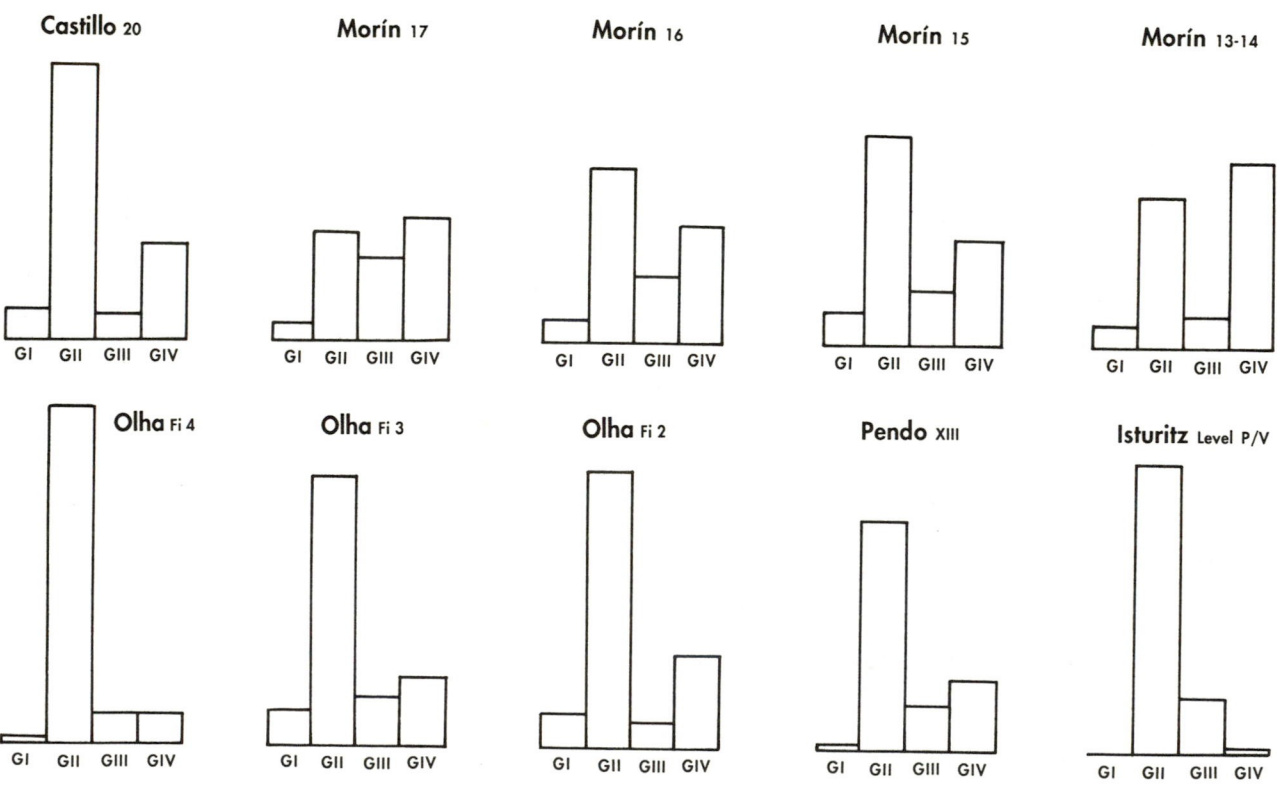

Figure 8.4   *Relative frequencies of major typological groups (Groups I-IV) for sites with cleaver flakes.*

7 in the classification of Benito del Rey (1972-73), which builds on the series established by Tixier. In the level of Castillo where this type is best represented, the percentage of Type 0 totals 27 (the percentage of Type 7 is 12.2). In the material excavated at Morín during the 1969 season, one cleaver of this type was found in Level 17 and another in Level 16. However, in the 1953/57 collections of El Pendo not one can be counted. Although this type is characteristic in this region, the most represensive types are those from Castillo and Morín which are classifiable as Type 2, while El Pendo yielded exclusively Type 3 cleavers.

The stratigraphic position of the Cantabrian group of sites is correlated to the final fluctuations of the Würm II (Butzer 1981). At Castillo, these fluctuations occur at the end of the Mousterian sequence, with Level 20 (which contains cleavers) assigned by Butzer to the Hengelo. However, the dates recently obtained through C-14 mass spectrometry (Cabrera Valdes and Bischoff 1989) for the lower levels of the Early Upper Paleolithic, separated from the surface of Level 20 by a thick stratum of sterile silts, suggest that Level 20 could be placed in the final moments of Würm II, prior to the Hengelo and not as far from this phase as had been supposed. The layer of sterile silts, which marks the Middle to Upper Paleolithic transition could then imply contemporaneity with the last levels of the Mousterian occupations of Morín and Pendo, attributed to Denticulate Mousterian. Thus, the Mousterian occupations that yield flake cleavers in the three caves could have been contemporary. If this is confirmed by new dates, one could suppose a narrow temporal relation among the several occupations, significant with reference to alternation of occupations within a territory framed by some 25 km of activity.

To summarize, the flake cleavers appearing in cave deposits attributed to the end of Würm II suggest the following points: First, the cleavers cannot be considered as type fossils of a Mousterian type, since they are found in a very wide cultural/chronological radius in Lower Paleolithic contexts, and even sporadically in the Upper Paleolithic. Second, their morphotechnic characteristics in distinct regional contexts and chronological/cultural horizons signify particular activities. Third, the cleavers are also associated with the selection of particular raw materials, which generally occur close to the occupations, and which, at least in the case of the area circumscribed by these three Cantabrian sites, are practically never used for the manufacture of other pieces. In these cases the cleavers appear as cultural elements, which relate to the limits of exploitation in the catchment area of each occupation. Fourth, if chronostratigraphic interrelation of the three cave deposits is confirmed, and given the other characteristics just mentioned, then these pieces could be valuable in microregional cultural terms (within a chronological/cultural horizon delimited by other factors). They could thus possibly be used for detecting the effects of individual behavior input on aspects of the lithic industry, the mobility of groups (perhaps even the same group), as well as for the delimitation of their territory linked to other contextual factors.

STATISTICAL ANALYSES

The only statistical analyses performed on Mousterian materials of this region are those of Freeman (1971, 1973) and our own (Cabrera Valdes 1988). The work of Freeman is based on the application of the Kolmolgorov-Smirnov test, which ultimately resulted in a three-dimensional interlinked chain of levels. In the graphic representation (Freeman in González Echegaray et al. 1980:fig. 23) two clusters are apparent. In one direction, the chain begins with Castillo Beta (Level 22), linked through Pendo XIV to Morín 15, Morín 16, and Pendo XIII. The other significant, and more complete cluster, is composed of Pendo XII/XI, Pendo VIII, Pendo XVI, Morín 17, Morín 11, Morín 12, and Morín 17inf. These two major groups are linked by Morín's Level 13/14, which in turn draws in Castillo's Level 20 (Alpha).

Our work is based on large assemblages, selected for their provenience in very representative deposits. Among those that stand out are Morín (González Echegaray et al. 1971, 1973; González Echegaray and Freeman 1978), El Pendo (González Echegaray et al. 1980) and Castillo (Cabrera Valdes 1978, 1984). Complementing these sites are those of La Flecha (Freeman and González Echegaray 1967), El Conde (Freeman 1977) and Lezetxiki (Altuna 1972). For comparisons with the Cantabrian strata, recently published works on cave deposits of other regions of Spain have been used as well, including the caves of Los Casares (Barandiarán 1973) and Ermita (Moure Romanillo and Delibes 1972) in the North Meseta, Eudoviges (Barandiarán 1979) in the valley of the Ebro, and the stratigraphically deep site of Cova Negra (Villaverde Bonilla 1984) in Valencia. The purpose of our analysis is to examine the structure of the Cantabrian Middle Paleolithic independently of Freeman, using a series of variables and analyses different from his, in order to compare results.

MULTIVARIATE ANALYSES

At first, a Principal Components Analysis (using the ACOPRI system: see Mallo 1985) was run on four variables corresponding to the Mousterian group indices. On the first pass the results were obvious: four principal components which corresponded to the four input variables. However when these results were submitted to the Kaiser reduction method (for which only the most important component was retained), the first Principal Component (F1) yielded an eigenvalue greater than 50%. In order to be more graphic we also retained a second component (F2), which together explained a total of 80% of the variance (Fig. 8.5).

This analysis was carried out in two phases: first on Cantabrian assemblages and then with other peninsular assemblages. In both cases the results were similar. For the first series of sites, only the most important deposits were selected, including those of Morín (7 levels), Pendo (5 levels), and Castillo (5 levels). Two different clusters resulted, one containing assemblages with a predominance of denticulated pieces and the other assemblages in which the highest loading variable is Group II, or principally the sidescrapers. Typical Mousterian assemblages are included in both clusters, except those sufficiently close to one or another group that they conform to the fundamental assemblage groups. Only Level 24 of Castillo remains isolated from the series. This level has been considered as

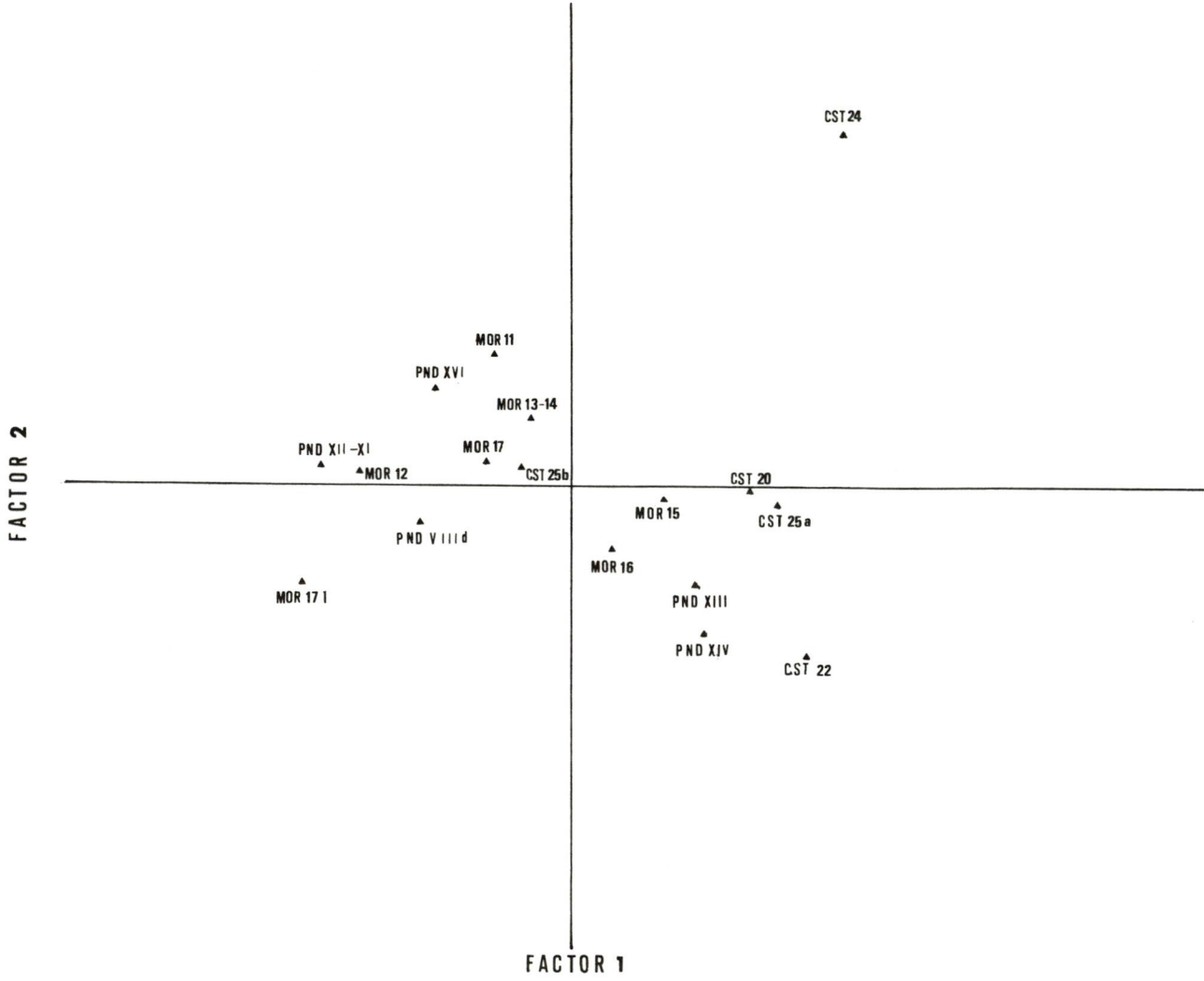

Figure 8.5   *Scatter of factor analysis of Cantabrian sites. MOR: Morín; PND: Pendo; CST: Castillo.*

Middle Acheulian by some investigators and Upper Acheulian by us (Cabrera Valdes 1984).

The assemblages characterized by the denticulated pieces are Conde 6 and 5; Morín 17inf., 12, and 11; all the levels of La Flecha; Pendo XI–XII and VIIId; and Lezetxiki Vb. Some deposits, such as Cobalejos and Hornos de la Peña, lie close to the assemblages for which the Group II variable is dominant. Of similar form and very clear style are Lezetxiki VI and VII and Morín 17, 16, 15, and 13/14. El Pendo's Level XVI has a tendency toward denticulates and its Levels XIV and XII are intermediate, thus differing in some cases from the results of the Kolmolgorov-Smirnov analysis. It is also possible to observe in the diagram (Fig. 8.5) a cluster of Castillo's Levels 20, 22, and 25a with Morín's 15 and 16 and Pendo's Levels XIII and XIV. Yet another cluster is composed of Level 25b of Castillo, Levels 11, 12, 13/14, and 17 of Morín, and Levels XI–XII and XVI of Pendo. Finally, Morín

17inf. and Pendo VIIId show a markedly distinct cluster, having always been interpreted as corresponding to assemblages of the Denticulate facies.

In order to compare the Cantabrian assemblages with those of other areas, data from Eudoviges, Casares, Ermita, and Cova Negra (14 levels) were added. The material from these sites has been assigned to the Charentian, Typical Mousterian, and MTA assemblage groups. The results were similar to those obtained with the Cantabrian sites, but the clustering is not as clear (Fig. 8.6). There is one cluster of assemblages where the loading of denticulates is very strong, and another opposite cluster of assemblages rich in sidescrapers. The assemblages that had been previously considered as MTA and scraper-rich Typical Mousterian show a greater integration in the A1 cluster than had occurred previously with Castillo's Level 24. This level remains isolated and contrasts with Levels 25a and 25b stratigraphically below it and the strata con-

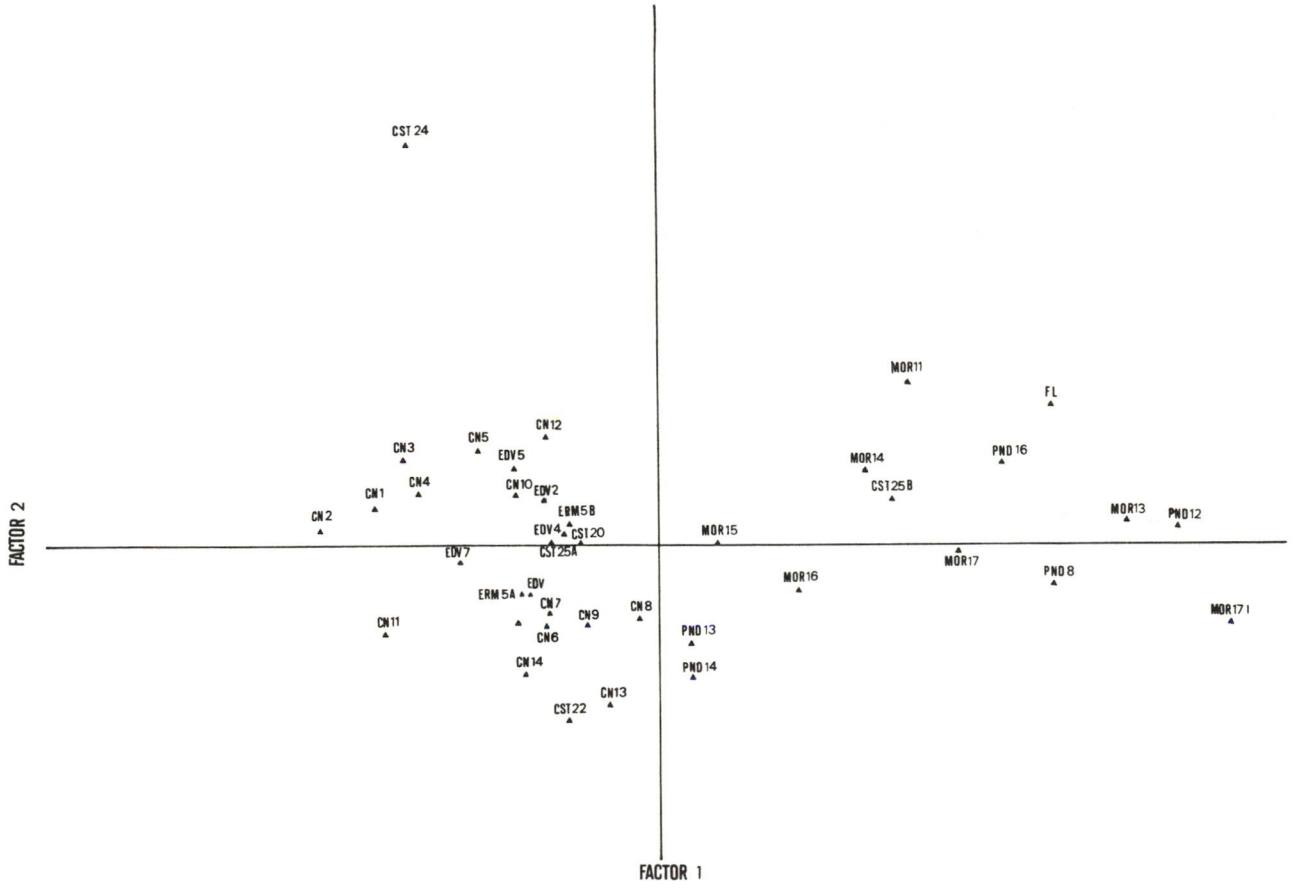

Figure 8.6   *Scatter of factor analysis of main Mousterian sites in Spain. MOR: Morín; PND: Pendo; CST: Castillo; EDV: Eudoviges; ERM: Ermita; CN: Cova Negra; FL: La Flecha.*

sidered classic Würm Mousterian which lie above. Similarly, Morín 17inf. and Pendo VIII are grouped with greater clarity than in the previous analysis. The long stratigraphy of Cova Negra, with most of its 14 levels considered as Quina Mousterian, and some MTA and Typical Mousterian, suggests a stratigraphically linked helicoidal evolution like that at Castillo.

In order to compare these sites on the basis of a greater number of variables, a cluster analysis was performed on a reduced number of types, compressing Bordes' type list into 15 variables. These composite variables were extracted from the dendrogram which pooled the sequences of the three principal deposits of Castillo, Morín, and Pendo (Fig. 8.7).

The results obtained are similar to the previous analysis, with two main clusters and the isolation of Castillo, Level 24. The lowest level of this site (Level 26) has been included and also demonstrates a lack of concordance with the two groups (though it must be taken into account that it has a very limited number of pieces). Thus, this analysis, which is based on typological characteristics, clearly demonstrates the existence of two contrasting structures characterized by the representation of only two characteristic pieces, namely denticulates and sidescrapers (see also Dibble and Rolland, this volume), though it must be emphasized again that neither bifacial pieces nor cleavers were taken into account. In this case, some of the assemblages that were not clearly aligned with the others in the earlier analyses are now more clearly placed in one or the other of the two principal clusters.

Thus, the two clusters combine assemblages that were previously classified as different Mousterian assemblage groups. In one cluster, Denticulate Mousterian assemblages are linked with Morín 13/14 and Morín 17, usually considered as Typical Mousterian. Included also in this group is Level XVI from Pendo, defined by Freeman as a very anomalous Typical Mousterian "rich in denticulates." Grouped together in the second cluster are those assemblages that have high frequencies of sidescrapers and which traditionally have been considered as Charentian or Typical Mousterian.

Included in the second cluster are the lower levels of Castillo, which can be assigned to the Riss/Würm. These levels are situated below a series of stalagmitic caps and a formation of cave pearls. Their most probable age is 92,800 B.P., obtained by Rainer Grün of the University of Koln (R. Grün, pers. comm.) and similar to two ages calculated by J. Bischoff. Level 24 is defined as Acheulian and is the unit that was responsible for the grouping seen in the cluster analysis. Levels 25a and 25b nevertheless fall together in the groups of the Würmian Middle Paleolithic strata. In this sense the Acheulian level acts to cluster the others, as much in the principal component analyses as in the cluster analysis. Layer 24 presents the most elevated index of flint utilization, as well as of Levallois technique. In typological terms, the presence of bifaces (a variable that has not been included in the analysis) also contrasts with the Mousterian assemblages. It should emphasized again that cleavers were also not included in the dendrogram and were not considered when assigning various levels to particular assemblage groups. The cleavers in general appear as pieces able to associate with different assemblages of variables, acting as a qualitative characteristic and not a diagnostic one.

PALEOECOLOGY AND SUBSISTENCE

Since the only major paleobotanical study concerning the Middle Paleolithic was done by Arlette Leroi-Gourhan (González Echegaray et al. 1971) for the uppermost Mousterian level of Cueva Morín, faunal remains provide the bulk of the evidence for paleoenvironment. However, most of the faunal studies that have been done are fragmentary and based on very scarce remains. While various investigators have studied these remains over the past several decades, the principal research has been done by Altuna, though we should also call attention to the now classic work of Freeman (1973) on human exploitation of environmental resources. In some cases where the faunal representation is substantial, such as at Castillo, the dating should be viewed with some caution and, while the old faunal collection is valuable from a purely paleontological point of view, it is not valid for zooarchaeological analyses.

Among the large mammals, three herbivores occur with the greatest frequency: red deer, which in some cases are quite large; bovids, including bison in Castillo 22 and Lezetxiki VII and VI that have yielded some dates; and equids, which appear in more minor proportion, though some large individuals with Stenonian traits have been observed at Lezetxiki. These species are present in more or less constant proportions in most Mousterian deposits (except in Level 17 of Morín, where bovids are the most abundant species) and do not indicate any specialization of hunting.

Remains of *Rhinocerontidos* also occur, especially represented by molars. However, it is necessary to restudy these collections, since these forms are divided between the *Dicerorhinus kirchbergensis Merck*, found in the early levels of Castillo, and the *Dicerorhinus hemitoechus* which appears in Morín and Cobalejos (Altuna 1972). Lastly, *Coelodonta antiquitatis*, which is particularly adapted to the frigid steppe, appears in Unquera and Lezetxiki.

Chamois and caprids appear, though infrequently, at Lezetxiki, Level 5 of El Conde, and in Level 22 of

Castillo—sites situated in areas of steep topography. *Sus scrofa* is also very scarce as well as *Capreolus capreolus*. Reindeer, *Rangifer tarandus*, has been found only in the deposit at Axlor.

While the spectrum of species is varied, it is rather restricted to a very few species which contribute the highest levels of protein to the human diet. These economic fauna include essentially five species of ungulates, the proportions of which vary in accordance to their prevalence in the natural environment surround-

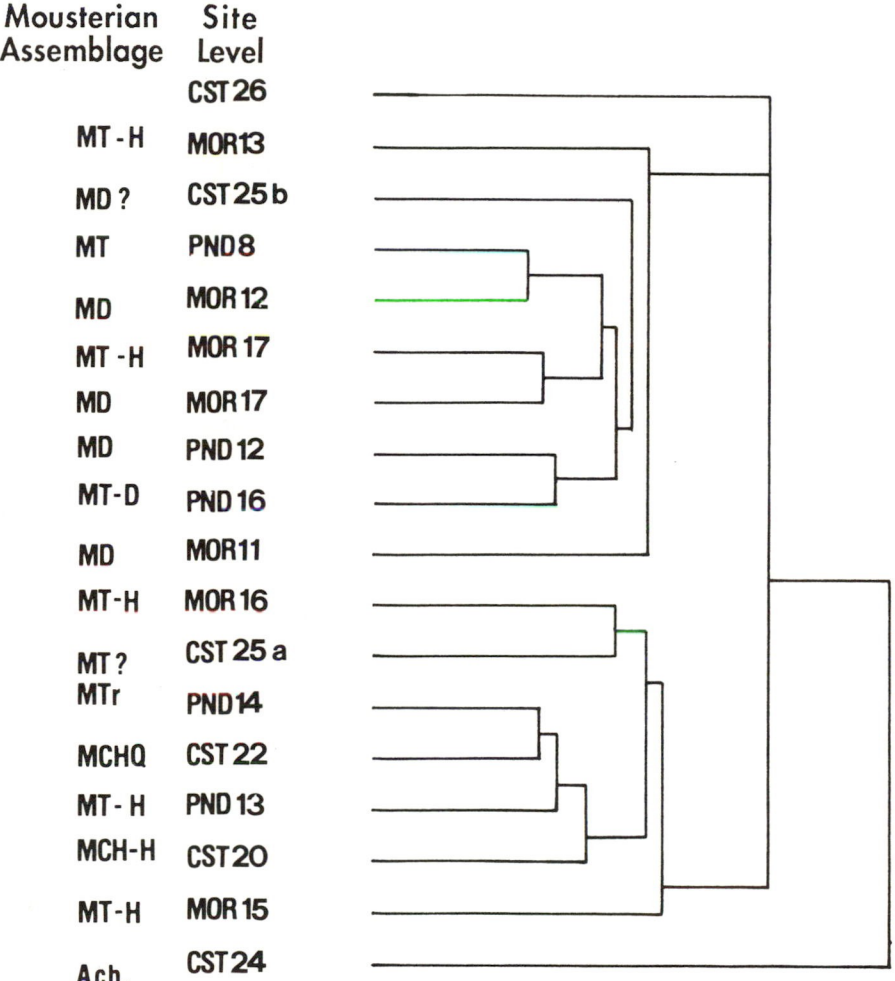

Figure 8.7 *Dendrogram of cluster analysis of Cantabrian sites. The assigment to the various Mousterian groups are shown in two columns. MT: Typical Mousterian; MTr: Typical Mousterian rich in sidescrapers; MD: Denticulate Mousterian; MCH: Charentian Mousterian (Q = Quina); Ach.: Acheulian. The abbreviation '-H' indicates the presence of flake cleavers (hendedores) in the assemblages, although they have not been taken as a group of variables in the statistical analysis. MOR: Morín; PND: Pendo; CST: Castillo.*

ing the sites. Red deer, horses, and the large bovids, all of which are associated with transitional environments of parkland/forest and open plains, make up three basic groups. However, the proper identification of bison constitutes a significant problem, since distinguishing between *Bison* and *Bos* is difficult in the absence of certain parts of the skeleton. Bison is found more frequently in forest zones than is the aurochs.

To these large ungulates the small bovids are added, such as goat and chamois. Both of these species require more rugged environments and are more numerous in those sites situated in very steep and rocky environments or sometimes those of great altitude, such as Lezetxiki. Although in the minority, other ungulates such as the roe deer and wild boar also appear, species that are related principally to environments of forest and/or parkland. Although these latter species are associated with the same environment as red deer, they occur more infrequently, which suggests a particular preference for the latter and only sporadic capture of the roe deer and wild boar. Of course, boar is a very dangerous species to hunt compared to the red deer or the roe deer (which are more gregarious, at least at certain times of the year), and its economic value is also less.

Due to the danger and difficulty of hunting rhinocerontids, exacerbated by their non-gregarious social behavior (they usually occur as adult pairs accompanied by individual young), arguments have been made that their presence suggests that the Mousterians hunted them in order to gain social prestige. However, it is also quite possible that they may not have been hunted at all, but rather scavenged (Guerin and Faure 1983). The environment of these animals varies from grassy plains to frigid steppe.

The non-economic fauna include carnivores, the remains of which are commonly present in Mousterian strata, but then gradually disappear in the archaeological record. Among them, though it is actually an omnivore, is the cave bear, which has been the subject of numerous cultural explanations. It appears most certainly in the site of Lezetxiki, though it also occurs in levels of sites where cultural remains are either rare or absent (Altuna 1972); thus a cynegetic relation does not always appear probable. On the other hand, there may be some problems in assessing the actual distribution of these remains due to a lack of care in the recovery of material during the old excavation. This may be the case at Castillo, where cave bear remains appear in sterile layers as well as in the occupations attributed to the Mousterian, though the thickness of

levels such as Level 22 make the distinction of occupation surfaces very difficult. In this case, *Ursus spelaeus* may actually be alternating with the human occupation, though this disassociation may be masked by the intensity of occupation of the cave in the Mousterian levels.

Among the true carnivores, the presence of scavengers like the hyena stands out, though its presence is indicated more on the basis of coprolites, phosphates, and traces of the animals' activity on bone material than on actual skeletal remains. As in the case of the cave bear, the frequency of this species is greater in the Mousterian layers than in those of later Paleolithic stages.

Other fauna include birds, for example *Pyrrhocorax* sp., which is present in the cave of El Conde and in Level 22 at Castillo, the latter from old identification and corresponding to a cliff habitat. The black vulture, which is a raptor native to forest habitats, is present in the same layer. From Level 20 of Castillo two migratory species have been identified, *Coccothrastes coccothrastes*, which presently occurs in September and October, and cliff-nesting *Corvus monedula*, which today occurs during the spring and autumn but rarely nests. Another cliff form from this same level, but one that is more sedentary, is *Falco tinnunculus*.

INTERPRETATIONS ABOUT SUBSISTENCE

A current topic of debate concerns the nature of Mousterian subsistence strategies, that is, whether they were "specialized," "generalized," or "opportunitistic." As was just described, three herbivore groups, red deer, bovids, and equids, tend to dominate the assemblages but in very similar proportions to one another. As noted, they seem to reflect a spectrum of adaptations to the environment surrounding the sites and their similar proportions suggest a concept of an opportunistic (in the biological sense) strategy.

The conclusion of opportunistic strategy is based largely on the work of Altuna (1989), who compared the Mousterian fauna with that of recently analyzed Magdalenian deposits. For other authors, notably Straus (1983), hunting strategies in the Mousterian are seen to be more generalized, aimed at large ungulates of open environments. However, these comparisons are based on the much later adaptations in the Magdalenian, which actually represent an extreme specialization.

There are data that suggest at least some preferences in the Mousterian. Based on Vaufrey's estimates of the minimum number of individuals for two traditional strata at Castillo (Cabrera Valdes 1984:table 48), it is apparent that red deer predominates in both levels (Level 20: 184 MNI; Level 22: 78), followed by large bovids (Level 20: 133; Level 22: 58), and finally by equids (Level 20: "abundant"; and Level 22: 35). Although there are dangers inherent in studies of older collections, we believe that nonetheless there is a clear predominance of red deer. Likewise, in the revised sequence at Morín there is a higher percentage of large bovids in Level 17 compared with other levels of the site, followed by red deer and equids. In the cave of El Conde the small bovids (*Capra* and *Rupicapra*) are the dominant species followed by the equids. In Vizcaya and Guipúzcoa, the red deer appears also to be less important, likewise in some levels of Lezetxiki. On the other hand, the reasons for these varying percentages may be found in the nature of the environment surrounding the deposits, as seems to be the case with the lithic raw materials.

A more detailed study of food niches has been examined by Clark (1986) based on 14 assemblages. He concluded that an absence of mollusks implies no exploitation of the littoral zone. Actually, such resources are not significantly exploited until the Lower Magdalenian, a period in which significant accumulations of mollusks were collected in deposits such as El Juyo, Altamira, and even Castillo, which is 20 km distant from the coast.

However, when studying niche exploitation it is important to distinguish between economic fauna and non-economic fauna, since the faunal content of a cavity is a palimpsest on which the cumulative effects of various processes are seen, including but not limited to human activities. Although the presence of scavengers is observed in some levels (Straus 1982), it is difficult in other cases to separate out their actions from those of the hominids. To do so requires a broad knowledge of the geologic processes affecting the deposits, along with observations of marks and fractures on bones and the recovery of scavenger coprolites. Since such observations were not consistently made in the earlier analyses, conclusions drawn from them may not be entirely accurate. Further problems with the earlier studies stem from the lack of recording and stratigraphic control; and the more limited excavations at either the mouth of the cave or against the back of the site, where sedimentary processes may have altered the traces of human occupations even more.

TECHNOLOGICAL CHARACTERISTICS AND GROUP MOBILITY

Based on technological characteristics in the assemblages of the Cantabrian shelf, there are indications concerning the distribution of habitable space which may reflect the activity or activities which took place. These indications result primarily from the spatial analysis of Cueva Morín (Freeman 1976) and the visible remains of hearths in the deep stratigraphic section of Castillo.

In the east sector of Level 17 at Morín, which was 5 to 10 cm thick, an interruption of the accumulated remains corresponded with an alignment of stones. These followed a pattern which enabled them to be interpreted as a wall. This alignment isolated an enclosure of some 6.6 sq. m of arched contours, which closed the access to the interior. The materials inside this enclosure indicated an activity related to specific materials. This conclusion is based on associations of particular materials in three distinct areas. One zone presented a concentration of cleavers and bone remains ("tools of retouched bone" [González Echegaray and Freeman 1978]), another near the entrance of the cave yielded an association of sidescrapers, notches, and flakes, and the third zone showed an assemblage of blades, small flakes, and perforators. In the bottom of the layer an intense coloration was present due to the decomposition of organic materials. These characteristics were interpreted by the investigators of the deposit as evidence for the treatment of skins. The enclosure within the cave could not have contained a large group of persons. Shed antlers found among the bone remains were interpreted as an indication of a seasonal occupation in spring or summer. The remains of the human occupation were probably not affected by the passage of scavengers since only one coprolite was found in the enclosure itself.

Castillo is another deposit where clear remains of human habitation have been found. Although Obermaier commented on the presence of continuous "hearths" in the previous excavation, we originally assumed that these were probably due to the presence of dense occupation levels and that they did not therefore correspond to the presence of clear structures related to combustion. The new excavations, based on horizontal exposure of the levels, did find large areas of combustion of vegetable material—probably indicating the presence of real hearths—laid down in distinct tracts within the Mousterian strata. These layers are separated from the overlying Upper Paleolithic levels by a level (up to 50 cm thick) which consists of layers of sterile silt. This find will undoubtedly yield very valuable data in the future.

Although based on some approximations, available data indicate a very low population density during the Mousterian of Cantabria (Butzer 1986). Typically, the settlements are found concentrated on the coastal plain and low hills. Expansion from these settlements is local, consisting of radii from 5 to 10 km in the wide valleys of the low-altitude hilly region. Deposits also appear along rivers in the interior valleys at altitudes between 30 and 100 m. These sites are in the minority and are where the most specialized subsistence strategies are observed. According to Butzer, the proportions of these two settlement types are similar for both the Upper and Middle Paleolithic: in each case one-third of the sites are interior settlements (9 of 27 sites of the Upper Paleolithic and 3 of 9 sites of the Middle Paleolithic).

On the other hand, calculations by Straus (1983) and Clark (1986) of tool density (per volume of sediment) and site frequency do show some changes over time. According to them, the Mousterian corresponds to a low site frequency of 0.2 (14 deposits and 75,000 years), with a progressive increase until the Asturian, where this measure reaches an average of 25.7 (77 deposits in an average of 3000 years). However, as Butzer suggests, erosion and removal of sediments could have biased the number of known deposits. To this comment we would also add that there has been a more intense investigation of Upper Paleolithic sites and that open air settlements are very difficult to detect, which would considerably skew these figures.

Nonetheless, in general one tends to consider the Mousterian groups as few in number and dispersed. In supporting this conclusion, Butzer also notes a spatial organization of areas non-overlapping in terms of their seasonal definition. It is important to note that the presence of particular cultural characteristics, such as cleavers, may help to clear up this topic, in conjunction with a broad series of absolute dates. An increase in use of the deposits through time is often interpreted as being due to an increase in the population, in the sense of either an increase in the number of groups or an increase in group size. We would also suggest progressive increase in group mobility and an increase in the level of social organization required for the territorial control.

Thus, in the Middle Paleolithic of Cantabria, niche exploitation is established primarily on the littoral fringe and in the selective exploitation of wide valleys in the band of low hills. The high mountains and the periphery of the central plateau do not seem to have been utilized, or, if so, only sporadically. Again, however, surveys of the north plateau have not been carried out with the same intensity as those on the Cantabria shelf, which is a problem that some investigators have addressed in recent years.

ACKNOWLEDGMENTS

We thank Stephen L. Kluskens for his valuable assistance in translating this paper.

REFERENCES CITED

Altuna, J.
  1972   Fauna de mamíferos de los yacimientos prehistóricos de Guipúzcoa. *Munibe* 24:1-464.
  1980   Fauna del yacimiento de Axlor (Dima, Vizcaya). *Vasconia Antiqua. Obras completas de D. J. M. de Barandiarán* 17:207-209, 219-266, and 273-279.
  1989   Subsistance d'origine animale pendant le Moustérien dans la région cantabrique (Espagne). In *L'homme de Néandertal*, ed. M. Otte. Vol. 6: *La subsistance*, eds. L. Freeman and M. Patou. ERAUL 33. Liège: Université de Liège.

Bahn, P. G.
  1983   *Pyrenean Prehistory*. London: Aris and Phillips.

Baldéon, A.
  1974   El yacimiento del paleolítico inferior de Murba. *Estudios de Arqueologíca Alavesa* 6:17-31.

Barandiarán, J. M. de
  1978   Exploracion de la Cueva de Lezetxiki (Mondragon). *Vasconia Antiqua. Obras completas de D. J. M. Barandiarán* 14:7-132.
  1980   Excavationes en Axlor (Dima) 1967-

1974. *Vasconia Antigua. Obras completas de D. J. M. Barandiarán* 17:127-134.

Barandiarán, I.
1973   *La Cueva de los Casares (Riba de Saelices, Guadalajara).* Excavaciones Arqueologicas en España 76. Madrid: Ministerio de Educación y Ciencia, Subdirección de Arqueología.
1979   Yacimiento musteriense del Covacho de Eduviges (Teruel). *Tabona* 3:5-11.

Barandiarán, I., and Vallespí, E.
1980   *Prehistoria de Navarra.* Pamplona: Diputación Foral de Navarra.

Benito del Rey, M.
1972-73   Los Hendidores de la Capa Musteriense "Alfa" de la Cueva del Castillo (Santander). Estudio Tipologico. *Zephyrus* 23-24:31-84.

Bordes, F.
1953   Essai de classification des industries "moustériennes." *BSPF* 50:457-466.
1961   *Typologie du Paléolithique ancien et moyen.* 2 vols. MIPUB 1. Bordeaux: Delmas.

Butzer, K. W.
1981   Cave Sediments, Upper Pleistocene Stratigraphy and Mousterian Facies in Cantabrian Spain. *JAS* 8:133-183.
1986   Palaeolithic Adaptations and Settlement in Cantabrian Spain. *Advances in World Archaeology* 5:200-252.

Cabrera Valdes, V.
1978   La Cueva del Castillo (Puente Viesgo, Santander). Ph.D. thesis, Universidad Complutense de Madrid.
1983   Notas sobre el Musteriense Cantabrico: el "Vasconiense." Pp. 131-141 in *Homenaje al Prof. Dr. Martin Almagro Basch*, Vol. 1. Madrid: Ministerio de Cultura.
1984   *El Yacimiento de la Cueva del Castillo (Puente Viesgo, Santander).* Bibliotheca Praehistorica Hispana 22.
1988   Aspects of Middle Palaeolithic in Cantabrian Spain. Pp. 27-33 in *L'homme de Néandertal*, ed. M. Otte. Vol. 4: La technique, eds. L. Binford and J.-P. Rigaud. ERAUL 31. Liège, Université de Liège.

Cabrera Valdes, V., and Bernaldo de Quirós, F.
1985   Evolution technique et culturelle de la grotte de El Castillo. Pp. 206-221 in *La Signification culturelle des industries lithiques.* BAR International Series 239. Oxford: BAR.

Cabrera Valdes, V., and Bischoff, J.
1989   Accelerator ^{14}C Ages for Early Upper Palaeolithic (Basal Aurigacian) at El Castillo Cave (Spain). *JAS* 16:577-584.

Chauchat, C.
1985   L'abri Olha, Cambo (Pyrenées Atlantique), la nouvelle étude de la collection Passemard. *BSPF* 82:237-238.

Clark, G. A.
1986   El nicho alimenticio humano en el Norte de España desde el Paleolitico hasta la Romanizacion. *Trabajos de Prehistoria* 63:159-184.

Freeman, L. G.
1964   Mousterian Developments in Cantabrian Spain. Ph.D. dissertation, Department of Anthropology, University of Chicago.
1966   The Nature of Mousterian Facies in Cantabrian Spain. *AA* 68:230-237.
1971   El Musteriense Cantabrico: nuevas perspectivas. *Ampurias* 31-32:55-69.
1973   The Significance of Mammalian Faunas from Paleolithic Occupations in Cantabrian Spain. *AmAnt* 38:3-17.
1976   Middle Palaeolithic Dwelling Remmants from Spain. *9th Congrès UISPP, Colloque 11* (Niza): 35-48.
1977   Contribucion al estudio de niveles paleoliticos en la Cueva del Conde (Oviedo). *Bol. del Instituto de Estudios Asturianos* 90-91:447-488.

Freeman, L. G., and González Echegaray, J.
1967   La industria musteriense de la cueva de la Flecha (Puente Viesgo, Santander). *Zephyrus* 18:61-63.

González Echegaray, J., and Freeman, L. G.
1978   *Vida y Muerte en Cueva Morín.* Santander: Institución Cultural de Cantabria.

González Echegaray, J.; Freeman, L. G.; Barandiarán, I.; Apellaniz, J. M.; Butzer, K. W.; Fuentes Vidarte, C.; Madariaga, B.; González Morales, J. A.; and Leroi-Gourhan, A.
1980   *El yacimiento de la cueva de "El Pendo" (excavaciones 1953-57).* BPH 17. Madrid: Instituto Español de Prehistoria/Universidad de Madrid.

González Echegaray, J.; Freeman, L. G.; Butzer, K. W.; Leroi-Gourhan, A.; Altuna, J.; Madariaga, B.; and Apellaniz, J. M.
1971   *Cueva Morín, Excavaciones 1966-1968.* Santander: Patronato de las Cuevas Prehistóricas de la Provincia de Santander.

González Echegaray, J.; Freeman, L. G.; Madariaga, B.; Butzer, K. W.; and Altuna, J.
1973   *Cueva Morín, Excavaciones 1969.* Santander: Patronato de las Cuevas Prehistóricas de la Provincia de Santander.

Guérin, C. and Faure, M.
1983   Les hommes du Paléolithique européen ont-ils chassé le rhinoceros? Pp. 29-36 in *La faune et l'homme préhistorique.* MSPF 16. Paris: SPF.

Kornprobst, P.
1967   Premiers resultats d'une étude geologique et paleoclimatique du remplisage paléolithique moyen et superieur de la grotte de Lezetxiki (Mondragon, Guipúzcoa). *Munibe* 19:247-260.

Laplace, J.
1966   Les niveaux castelperronien, protoaurignacien et aurignacien de la grotte de Gatzarría à Suhare Pays basque, fouilles 1961-1963. *Quartär* 17:117-140.

Mallo, F.
1985   *Analisis de Componentes Principales.* Universidad de León.

Moure Romanillo, A., and Delibes, M.
1972   El yacimiento musteriense de la Cueva de la Ermita (Hortiguela, Burgos). *Noticiario Arqueologico Hispana* 1:11-44.

Santamaria, R.
1984   Les hachereauz sur éclat dans le Moustérien: les pièces du niveau P sv d'Isturitz. *Bull. du Musée Basque.* Bayonne.

Straus, L. G.
1982   Carnivores and Cave Sites in Cantabrian Spain. *JAR* 38:75-96.
1983   From Mousterian to Magdalenian: Cultural Evolution viewed from Vasco-Cantabrian Spain and Pyrenean France. Pp. 73-11 in *The Mousterian Legacy*, ed. E. Trinkhaus. BAR International Series 164. Oxford: BAR.

Tixier, J.
1956   Les hachereaux dans l'Acheuléen nordafricain. Notes typologiques. *Congrès Préhistorique de Française* XVI session. (Poitiers-Anguleme): 914-923.

Vega del Sella, C. de la
1921   *El Paleolítico de Cueva Morín. Notas para la Climatología Cuaternaria.* Memoria 29. Madrid: Comisión de Investigaciones Prehistóricas y Paleontológicas.

Vega Toscano, L. G.
1983   Los problemas del Paleolitico Medio en España. Pp. 115-130 in *Homenaje al Prof. Dr. Martin Almagro Basch*, Vol 1. Madrid: Minsterio de Cultura.

Villaverde Bonilla, V.
1984   *La Cova Negra de Xativa y el Musteriense de la Region Central del Mediterraneo Español.* Trabajos Varios 79. Servicio de Investigaciones Prehistóricas.

IX

Mousterian Facies in Space: New Data from Morín Level 16

L. G. Freeman

INTRODUCTION

Similarity and difference; continuity and change: years before I began to study archaeology, I was taught how much of all intellectual endeavor is encompassed in the attempt to learn what those qualities are and how they are related.

How different are we skeletally from the Neandertals? What constraints did Neandertal morphology place on their behavior? Were they ancestors or just distant relatives of *Homo sapiens sapiens*? What is the nature of the process by which they were replaced by skeletally modern people? How different are we behaviorally from the Neandertals? Are there transitional Middle/Upper Paleolithic artifact industries? Is the Chatelperronian an attenuated Mousterian industry? Does it spring from some Mousterian facies, and if so, which one? What are the Mousterian facies, anyway, and what accounts for the differences between them? and why do they persist over such immense areas for such a long time? All are modern, topical questions, evidently. Yet none of them is new—some were leading themes of debate well before my graduate studies.

Of course, there has been progress in our field. In fact, we know a great deal more today about Neandertal skeletal variability and functional morphology, about Mousterian artifact assemblages, about the Upper Paleolithic, and about the origins of anatomically modern people than we did in the 1950s. But the same questions are still very much with us (though I hope that their meaning has changed, however subtly, and that the questioners are at least a little more sophisticated than graduate students were in the 1950s). Fundamental aspects of the similarity and difference, continuity and change, that characterize the relationships between the bodies and behavior of Neandertals and those of modern humans still remain to be clarified. I fear that unless we are still more careful and precise in framing our questions and searching for relevant information they will go unanswered, or we will not know the answers when we see them. The ongoing dialogue about the nature of Mousterian facies is very much a case in point.

I should make it clear that understanding the difference among Mousterian assemblages is one problem, and that of understanding Mousterian facies a quite separate issue. Despite the number of new Mousterian *assemblages* that have been excavated since 1960, and the many pages that have been devoted to detailed studies of their composition since then, we still do not fully understand what makes them sometimes similar, sometimes different. On the other hand, while debate about the nature of Mousterian facies is as common today as it was in the 1960s when it began, the "Facies Question" has in fact been essentially resolved (though most investigators are still unaware that that is so). The work of de Lumley in the French Midi, my own analyses of Spanish Mousterian collections, especially those from Morín and El Pendo, and investigations of others in France and Spain, have already provided sufficient evidence to close the debate, not by resolving all of the causes of inter-assemblage difference, to be sure, but by showing that discussion of the facies question is largely senseless and inconsequential (see articles by Dibble and Rolland, and by Otte, this volume). If that is still not generally realized by most prehistorians—though some of the supporting evidence is more than a quarter century old—it is due both to the immense prestige of François Bordes, and to the fact that too many prehistorians read little outside what is written in their native tongues. This paper will present evidence to support the claim that the facies question burns no longer.

I discuss only part of that evidence—to me a most convincing part—but I hope that those who are still not familiar with the evidence will find in this presentation the glimmerings of a new understanding of the meaning of differences between Mousterian assemblages. It poses new problems that cannot be resolved within the traditional framework in which the "Facies Question" was originally generated. The solution of those problems requires non-traditional approaches to artifact classification and new viewpoints concerning the nature of the investigation and relevance of different kind of data. Research by others has already carried us further toward the final resolution of these issues than can be suggested here. The observations I present have at least the merit of being first-hand observations from my own experience. I hope that readers will find in them the stimulus to open a new and productive chapter in the study of Mousterian artifact assemblages.

THE FACIES CONCEPT: STRENGTHS AND WEAKNESSES

My friend and teacher, Prof. François Bordes (though he would have given the late Maurice Bourgon a good deal of the credit), virtually single-handedly systematized the study of Mousterian stone tool assemblages, as everyone knows (Bordes 1961 and elsewhere). His accomplishment was truly masterful, as anyone with the least idea of the chaotic state of artifact classification (and of Lower and Middle Paleolithic studies generally) prior to his reformulation must admit. Bordes recognized a series of modal kinds of assemblages, which he called facies, that he found to be distinctive, traditional industrial ensembles with long-enduring coexistence in space and time. He conceived the facies to be independent lines of industrial development (rooted in "tribal" and perhaps "racial" distinctions), differentiated primarily on stylistic grounds (Bordes 1968:141-144). The facies concept truly instilled order into the study of Middle Paleolithic industries. It has informed and stimulated Mousterian research for four decades. Yet I believe that it must be abandoned.

Readers will already be aware from other publications that although Bordes taught me almost all I know about the Mousterian, I think, despite his opinion, that the load of functional and technological information in Mousterian types as he defined them is so great as to drown out most of the stylistic information he sought. The work of the Binfords (1966 and elsewhere), my own work (1966; González Echegaray

et al. 1971, 1973, 1980; González Echegaray and Freeman 1978), and that of others, already suggested in the 1960s that a great deal (though by no means all) of the difference between facies was probably due to functional/technological factors. Bordes, however, never found that argument convincing.

The first evidence challenging Bordes' characterization of the Mousterian facies as independent and stylistically distinctive industrial strains came from the discovery that they intergrade. At first it was thought that collections that looked like "blends" of different facies were mixed or badly excavated, or too small to be reliable. Soon, however, work in Spain and the Midi of France (de Lumley 1971, 1972, and elsewhere) showed that even large, well-stratified assemblages excavated by the most careful modern methods could have similarly "intermediate" characteristics. Bordes himself knew of such "blended" collections, but considered them the result of contact and inter-influence of different Mousterian "tribes," each of which under ordinary circumstances only produced the pure facies that was its traditional equipment. As he said: "if a woman from the Quina-type Mousterian was carried off by an Acheulean-tradition Mousterian man, she may perhaps have continued to make her tribal type of thick scraper . . ." (Bordes 1968:144-145), and for a while at least the couple and the group that sheltered them would therefore have made artifact assemblages that shared the characteristics of the Mousterian of Acheulian Tradition (MTA) and the Quina facies.

Others, including myself, found the idea that the facies were the stylistically different products of different "tribes" inherently improbable, based on what we knew of ethnography—a subject of which most prehistorians of the 1960s (and many today) were invincibly ignorant. No sociocultural groups I knew of from the ethnographic record distinguished themselves from their neighbors by making different proportions of the same kinds of tools those neighbors made. Yet that was the kind of "stylistic" difference Bordes supposed would have served to mark the identity of the "tribes" who made some of the facies from each other (there are of course other facies that have diagnostic tool types: in other respects they, too, intergrade).

Other evidence challenging Bordes' facies concept came from quantitative tests. Some large collections assigned by Bordes to different facies, when examined with standard statistical methods, proved not to be significantly different—while in other cases collections assigned to the same facies were shown to be very different indeed. (The first discovery was the more striking, since even relatively small differences between two large collections may be highly significant statistically).

Paradoxically, it may very well be our fault—the Binfords', Mellars', some others', and mine—that Bordes became so rigid in his conceptualization of the facies as mutually exclusive stylistic strains of industrial development. Bordes was, after all, an excellent paleontologist and geologist, and by baptizing the tool groups "facies" he consciously chose a term that in geology implies lateral intergradation. When the theoretical implications of his definition were challenged, he moved away from a more elastic definition of "facies" in the geological sense to an inflexible conception of mutually exclusive, non-overlapping compartments. Had he been left to gradually work out the implications of the facies concept by himself, without our interference, he probably would have done a better job. But what is past is done.

THE POTENTIAL IMPLICATIONS OF SPATIAL PATTERNING

Until the late 1960s all arguments that most of the difference between Mousterian facies might be due to "functional" (i.e., economic/technological) considerations rather than stylistic differences between distinct identity-conscious socio-cultural groups were based on comparisons of whole assemblages or old collec-

tions in museums, most of which lacked accurate data on spatial provenience. Many workers realized that the "Facies Question" could best be resolved by the examination of spatial distributions of different artifact types in a single archaeological level. Finding relationships between the distributions of particular formal tool types or wear traces and specific kinds of contextual data (plant remains, animal species, or skeletal parts) might lead to an understanding of the different functions of the different tools that went beyond pure speculation based on artifact shape. There was the possibility that artifact types characterizing different facies might be found spatially segregated in single levels.

The discovery of large assemblages representing different facies in a single, relatively short-term occupation level would be extremely important evidence favoring the "functionalist" position—it would be virtually impossible to explain such a discovery in traditional "Bordesian" terms. In fact, the discovery has been made, not just once, but several times, but most of the cases are unpublished or otherwise little known. At Cueva Morín in Cantabrian Spain, there were two such cases in our 1960s excavations: Upper Level 17 and Level 16. Both have been mentioned in previous publications, but neither is well-known. The most persuasive, that of Level 16, is the subject of the rest of this presentation.

EXCAVATIONS AT CUEVA MORÍN

Cueva Morín was discovered in 1910, and was extensively excavated in the early part of this century (Vega del Sella 1921; Carballo 1923). Excavations were renewed in 1966 by the Seminario de Prehistoria y Arqueología Sautuola under the direction of J. Gonzáez Echegaray and M. A. García Guinea, and continued in 1968 and 1969 under the direction of González Echegaray and myself. Our work is the subject of two monographs (González Echegaray et al. 1971, 1973) and a book (González Echegaray and Freeman 1978), as well as several shorter publications about particular aspects of the research (Cushman 1975; Freeman 1978a, 1978b; Freeman and González Echegaray 1970; Gleach 1987; Gleach et al. 1988).

In the new excavations, a relatively complete Upper Paleolithic sequence, beginning with a Chatelperronian horizon, was found to overlie a complex Middle Paleolithic stratigraphy, comprising nine Mousterian or probable Mousterian occupations. At base, Level 22, seen in a very small exposure in a deep sondage, yielded

only eight retouched artifacts, including two denticulates and a perforator. Its affinities cannot be determined with precision, and it is only noteworthy because it also produced a fragment of roe deer rib decorated with incised curved tally-marks arranged in pairs (see Freeman and González Echegaray 1983:144-155; González Echegaray 1988). The other eight levels include three Denticulate Mousterian horizons (Levels Lower 17, 12, and 11) and five levels now assigned to the Typical Mousterian: three (Upper 17, 13/14) relatively rich in denticulates, one "normal" (16), and one (15) sidescraper-rich (IR ess = 45.0). Some of the assemblages were substantial (373 "essential" flake tools in Upper Level 17, 307 in the part of Level 16 previously reported). All were non-Levallois and unfaceted. The regionally characteristic cleaver-flake type was also recovered from Levels Upper 17 (12 cleaver-flakes), 16 (12), 15 (2), and 13 (1). There are remnants of a structure in Upper Level 17 and well-marked patterns in the spatial distribution of residues there and in Levels 16 and 15.

MOUSTERIAN LEVEL 16

It is Level 16 that is of interest here. During 1968 and 1969, it was exposed in the cave over an area of some 7 sq. m (Table 9.1, left; Fig. 9.1). Using Bordes' diagnostics, the largest tool group in Level 16 was the Mousterian group (Group II ess = 37.8), predominantly because of the sidescraper categories (IR ess = 35.8); the so-called "Upper Paleolithic" group was reasonably well represented (Group III ess = 16.3); denticulates were not particularly numerous (Group IV ess = 20.5). The sidescrapers from this level were especially well-made. This part of the Level 16 assemblage was published in the monographs on Cueva Morín.

One would naively assume, following usual dicta, that stone artifacts from unexcavated parts of Level 16 ought to have similar characteristics. That is not the case, and for that reason the level is extremely interesting. In fact, had the complete flake tool assemblage been classified together, we would have diagnosed it as denticulate-rich (denticulates relatively abundant, just outnumbering sidescrapers) rather than as ordinary Typical Mousterian. That contrast is striking enough in itself. But the differences between two spatially segregated parts of the total assemblage are even more marked.

During the 1969 excavations, soil casts of several Aurignacian burials were found, in mound-capped trenches excavated into the uppermost Mousterian deposits. One of these unusual burials (Morín I) was removed *en bloc* and transported from Spain to the Smithsonian Institution for final excavation and preservation. In this process it was necessary to excavate a small part of Level 16 in trenching around the block. More of the level was included in the block itself, underlying the burial. The artifacts from that portion of Level 16 beneath the burial were recovered with all possible attention to horizontal and vertical provenience, in the course of excavation of the underside of the burial in 1971 in the U. S. Museum of Natural History in Washington. They were not studied with the rest of the collection, which remained in Spain, and until this time, they have not been published.

The area from which these artifacts were excavated is quite small (just over 5 sq. m all told, but most artifacts were found in an even smaller, 3-sq.-m space). Stone tools were very abundant, and isolated spatial concentrations of artifacts were noted during excavation (as they were in the rest of the level, too). One area about 40 cm in diameter in the middle of square 6H contained an accumulation of 14 Tayac points, a type represented by just one specimen in the assemblage previously published. Ten of these were found together in an even smaller area, less than 25 cm in diameter. This anomalous concentration (and a nearby hearth) was recognized during excavation, of course, but the exact number of Tayac points it contained was not known until the classification of the tools was completed.

The partial assemblage from that portion of Level 16 that underlay the Morín burial yielded 613 flakes and blades, 253 "Real" flake tools (in Bordes' terms), 5 cores, 34 miscellaneous broken stone chunks, 3 hammerstones, and 16 apparently unworked pebbles or cobbles. Some 70% of the artifacts are made of poor quality chert, with about 27% made of quartzite and another 3% of ophite and other raw materials. These figures are somewhat different from the rest of the level. At Morín, large tools are often made of ophite. There are 12 ophite cleaver-flakes and some waste in the rest of the level, but no large tools, and almost no ophite waste, under the burial.

Excluding all other pieces, unretouched flakes and blades constitute 71% of the collection and flake tools the remaining 29%. The assemblage is technically non-Levallois and unfaceted. Crushed or heavily utilized pieces are less than 10% of the "real flake tool" total. These figures are generally similar to those published for the rest of the level, though the proportion of flake tools to unretouched pieces is somewhat larger in the area under the burial.

When the characteristics of the "essential" flake tool assemblage are examined, however, striking differences from the earlier figures emerge (Table 9.1, right; Fig. 9.2). The "essential" flake tool inventory is, once more, substantial, numbering 227 pieces. Levallois types are very rare. So-called "Mousterian" types now number only about 18% of the essential count, and while most (16% of the "essential" total) are still sidescrapers, they are very much less abundant here than in the part of the level excavated earlier. So-called "Upper Paleolithic" types are also moderately represented, with about 18.5% of the total. Denticulate tools are as abundant as the other two major categories combined: 37.4% of essential tools. Bifaces (even cleaver-flakes) are totally absent, and backed knives very rare.

This part of the assemblage, found by itself, would present no classificatory problems. It is more than adequately large for trustworthy diagnosis. The percentage list, the indices, and the overall appearance of the

TABLE 9.1

MORÍN 16. COMPARISON OF TOOL ASSEMBLAGES.

TYPE #	MORÍN 16 NW			MORÍN 16 UNDER AURIGNACIAN BURIAL		
	FREQUENCY	REAL %	ESSENTIAL %	FREQUENCY	REAL %	ESSENTIAL %
1	4	0.0108	0.0000	0	0.0000	0.0000
2	15	0.0403	0.0000	1	0.0040	0.0000
4	1	0.0027	0.0033	0	0.0000	0.0000
5	4	0.0108	0.0130	0	0.0000	0.0000
6	5	0.0134	0.0163	2	0.0079	0.0088
7	0	0.0000	0.0000	2	0.0079	0.0088
8	1	0.0027	0.0033	1	0.0040	0.0044
9	11	0.0296	0.0358	4	0.0158	0.0176
10	51	0.1371	0.1661	16	0.0632	0.0705
11	2	0.0054	0.0065	2	0.0079	0.0088
12	0	0.0000	0.0000	1	0.0040	0.0044
13	1	0.0027	0.0033	5	0.0198	0.0220
15	3	0.0081	0.0098	2	0.0079	0.0088
19	3	0.0081	0.0098	0	0.0000	0.0000
21	8	0.0215	0.0261	1	0.0040	0.0044
23	11	0.0296	0.0358	2	0.0079	0.0088
25	7	0.0188	0.0228	1	0.0040	0.0044
26	1	0.0027	0.0033	1	0.0040	0.0044
27	3	0.0081	0.0098	0	0.0000	0.0000
28	2	0.0054	0.0065	0	0.0000	0.0000
29	7	0.0188	0.0228	1	0.0040	0.0044
30	7	0.0188	0.0228	1	0.0040	0.0044
31	8	0.0215	0.0261	3	0.0119	0.0132
32	2	0.0054	0.0065	0	0.0000	0.0000
33	6	0.0161	0.0195	8	0.0316	0.0352
34	6	0.0161	0.0195	1	0.0040	0.0044
35	17	0.0457	0.0554	28	0.1107	0.1233
37	1	0.0027	0.0033	1	0.0040	0.0044
38	5	0.0134	0.0163	6	0.0237	0.0264
39	2	0.0054	0.0065	2	0.0079	0.0088
40	3	0.0081	0.0098	0	0.0000	0.0000
42	37	0.0995	0.1205	28	0.1107	0.1233
43	63	0.1694	0.2052	85	0.3360	0.3744
44	7	0.0188	0.0228	4	0.0158	0.0176
45	4	0.0108	0.0000	1	0.0040	0.0000
46	10	0.0269	0.0000	3	0.0119	0.0000
47	10	0.0269	0.0000	3	0.0119	0.0000
48	9	0.0242	0.0000	9	0.0356	0.0000
49	10	0.0269	0.0000	9	0.0356	0.0000
50	3	0.0081	0.0000	0	0.0000	0.0000
51	1	0.0027	0.0033	14	0.0553	0.0617
52	2	0.0054	0.0065	0	0.0000	0.0000
54	5	0.0134	0.0163	0	0.0000	0.0000
59	4	0.0108	0.0130	0	0.0000	0.0000
61	2	0.0054	0.0065	0	0.0000	0.0000
62	8	0.0215	0.0261	5	0.0198	0.0220

	MORÍN 16 NW		MORÍN 16 UNDER AURIGNACIAN BURIAL	
TOTAL	372		TOTAL	253
TOTAL ESSENTIAL	307		TOTAL ESSENTIAL	227
BIFACES	16		BIFACES	0

INDICES

ILty	5.108	IR	29.570	IR(es)	35.831
IAu	0.269	IAu(e)	0.326	IB	4.124
IB(es)	4.954	GpI	5.376	GpII	31.183
GpII(e)	37.785	GPIII	13.441	GpIII(e)	16.287
GpIV	16.935	GpIV(e)	20.521		

INDICES

ILty	0.395	IR	14.229	IR(es)	15.859
IAu	0.395	IAu(e)	0.441	IB	0.000
IB(es)	0.000	GpI	0.395	GpII	16.206
GpII(e)	18.062	GPIII	16.601	GpIII(e)	18.502
GpIV	33.597	GpIV(e)	37.445		

cumulative percentage graph are quite characteristic of assemblages assigned by Bordes to the Denticulate Mousterian facies (variety non-Levallois, unfaceted).

The facies attribution of this part of the level contrasts markedly with that derived from the other 307 tools from this level. The rest of Level 16 was classified as Typical Mousterian, where well-made sidescrapers outnumbered denticulates substantially, and cleaver-flakes were also well represented. The differences are highly statistically significant—the odds are much more than a thousand to one that they are not due to chance alone.

The tools excavated from the burial area are so distinctive that when they are added to the rest of the pieces from the level, the combined assemblage becomes significantly different from either of its two "halves." The combined assemblage contains 534 "essential" flake tools, and its more significant characteristic indices are: Group II = 25.12; IR = 27.3; Group III = 17.2; Group IV = 27.7. There is less than one chance in 100 that the difference between the partial assemblage from beneath the burial and the total united assemblage is simply due to random sampling error, and less than one in 50 that the whole assemblage and the assemblage excavated in the cave differ by chance alone.

SPATIAL DIFFERENTIATION: THE EXCEPTION OR THE RULE?

The case of Morín Level 16 ought to drive home the fact that there is no reason to believe that in every site the proportional distribution of different types of stone artifacts over the whole of any specific occupation surface will necessarily be uniform or homogeneous. We ought, on the contrary, to expect that excavations in different areas of an occupation will often yield collections—even quite large ones—that differ substantially in their characteristics. When different collections from a single occupation level have the characteristics of different recognized facies, some of the postulated causes of inter-facies difference can conclusively and immediately be ruled out for that particular case, at least.

These very distinct partial assemblages from Level 16 were recovered from different parts of a single undisturbed occupation level. All evidence, including the spatial distribution itself, suggests that the occupation of Level 16 was of short duration (although the accumulation of the geological deposit that contains the occupation may have lasted indefinitely longer). In this case, the difference between the Denticulate and Typical Mousterian facies, as represented by the two

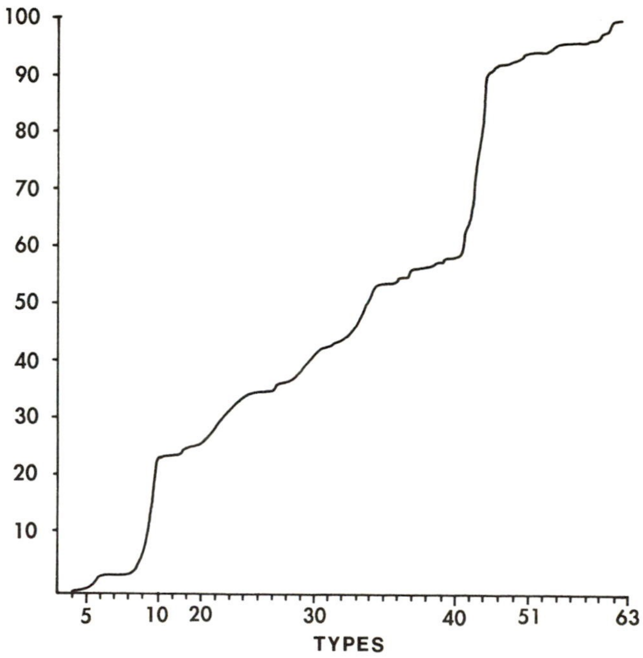

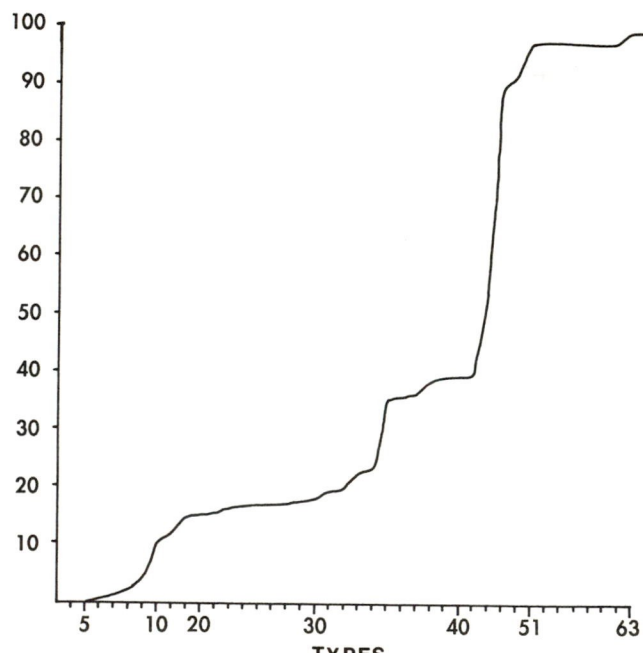

Figure 9.1   Graph of the frequency distribution of tool types in Morín Level 16 northwest of the burial.

Figure 9.2   Graph of the frequency distribution of tool types in Morín Level 16 underlying the burial.

parts of the collection, is almost certainly not related to the passage of time. Furthermore, for the difference to be related to occupation by culturally distinct groups, these groups would have had to be co-resident within a very small space. It is ridiculous to think that two different societies shared a total of 13 m of excavated space in Level 16. It might, of course, be suggested that the Denticulate-assemblage users and the Typical-assemblage users were different social segments of the same group, and that the tools reflect their separate status. But even in that case the space occupied by each segment would be impossibly small. It is most logical and parsimonious to suggest that this spatial patterning in Level 16 reflects different and very small-scale activities being performed by a very few members of the same group in different parts of the site.

I suppose that it is possible that someone might maintain that Morín Level 16 or the Cantabrian Mousterian in general are unique situations, and that spatial patterning of this kind never occurs in French Mousterian sites. Bordes himself would never have made such an assertion, as he had on several occasions found spatially differentiated distributions in his own excavations—for that reason he was always skeptical of classifications based on assemblages from very small exposures. Frankly, I do not see how the position could be seriously sustained by any excavator with experience in relatively undisturbed sites.

THE DEVITALIZATION OF THE FACIES CONCEPT

These observations return us to our general problem: that of the devitalization of the facies concept itself.

There is no doubt that the facies concept was useful for a long time. Debate about the causes of facies differences provoked a most rewarding inquiry into the nature and relationship of style and function. By posing such questions as whether all functional differences necessarily had a seasonal component, thus prompting us to think about the kinds of evidence that would indicate seasonality (botanical data, age profiles of young animals, wear and the presence of annuli in high-crowned herbivore teeth, oxygen isotope ratios in mollusk growth-rings, etc.) the facies debate refined our analytical toolkit even as we learned that functionality and seasonality played distinctly different roles in producing the archaeological toolkits. But it has led investigators down some blind alleys as well. We eventually began to ask such silly questions as what race of Neandertals were carpenters, or what tribe cut up its food! In hindsight one can see that those are just the sorts of questions implied by investigations of the nature of facies difference, as long as we thought of the facies as stylistically distinctive entities. Some investigators, accepting the equation of "style" and "race," are still intrigued with the issue of the genetic relationship between the authors of the Mousterian of Acheulian Tradition and Cro-Magnons.

Even if the facies concept had not outlived its usefulness, the secure attribution of an excavated assemblage to a particular facies would be an unattainable accomplishment. Our experience with Morín Level 16 shows that facies diagnosis based on a large sample of artifacts from an occupation level is not to be trusted. If the definition of a facies is based on a spatially restricted *sample* from an occupation level where different areas were the scenes of different activities, rather than on the level's *total contents*, there is no reason to believe that the classified assemblage will ever fairly represent the level as a whole—if it does, it will be purely accidental. We almost never excavate whole occupation levels, so we scarcely ever have *total* assemblages to classify. Random sampling might be suggested as a possible solution to this problem, but practical considerations oppose the excavation of randomly-placed pits. The difficulty of excavating small deep sondages is one major objection; their destructiveness of patterned horizontal distributions is another; the fact that one can never be sure one is sampling the same strata, even where stratigraphy is shallow, makes random pitting self-defeating in almost every case.

As I said earlier, my own work in Spain and that of de Lumley in the French Midi long ago suggested that the facies concept had become outmoded. De Lumley analyzed a number of well-excavated assemblages and found that they could not be assigned to any recognized facies without enlarging the facies definition. He resolved the problem to his own satisfaction by expanding the definition of the Typical Mousterian to accept those collections. His practice has prevailed, despite the fact that I believe it makes of the Typical Mousterian a sort of archaeological catchall into which to pile everything that will not fit elsewhere. But, as we say in Chicago, there is no sense in fighting City Hall, so I too use the expanded Typical Mousterian for purposes of communication with my colleagues. But I don't believe in it.

In fact, I do not believe in *any* of the facies in the same way Bordes did. In my own experience with Morín and El Pendo (González Echegaray et al. 1980), and Mousterian assemblages in other parts of Spain, I have found too many cases of well-excavated intermediate assemblages. In the El Pendo monograph, I set out the statistical evidence in support of the theory that Mousterian assemblages from Cantabrian Spain are points along a spectrum of continuous intergradation that has sidescraper-rich collections at one end and denticulate-rich assemblages at the other. Any segmentation of this continuum is arbitrary.

Of course, what Bordes identified as facies did exist—by definition, if for no other reason. Assemblages that fell to one side or another of fundamental threshold values Bordes recognized seemed to clump in particular places like modal concentrations along the continuum of variation in artifact proportions. As long as intermediate assemblages were dismissed as mixed or considered somehow anomalous, as was Bordes' practice, these apparent "modes" could be made to seem to be separated by absolute gaps. In light of later research, the "modes" do not seem to be nearly as marked as was once thought—some seem in fact to have disappeared, and it is quite likely that others are simply artifacts of the threshold values used to define them (see Dibble and Rolland, this volume). In Cantabria, there are no gaps between them, though apparent troughs do remain.

The reason why we find apparent multi-modality in assemblage makeup (there are both theoretical and practical reasons why this is expectable) is itself a fascinating topic to explore, but it cannot be explored using the facies concept. Evidently, the time has come when we have to realize that the Mousterian *facies* should no longer be our focus of inquiry. Instead we must turn our attention to Mousterian *assemblages* and, even more strongly, to the *subassemblages* (toolkits?—in the broadest sense) of which they are made up, and to areal differentiation in the spatial distribution of particular types and subassemblages (see, for more details, González Echegaray et al. 1980). The facies question is beside the point—we have learned that much—but we still do not have a sufficient understanding of what makes Mousterian assemblages different. And we will not go much further in that direction until we revise our analytical techniques.

FUNCTION, STYLE, AND THE AIMS OF CLASSIFICATION

One's approach to the study of stone tools has important implications for what may be learned from them. Even the best minds that have addressed these issues have shown some confusion on this point. There is no such thing as "*The* Ideal Artifact Classification." Any assemblage—in fact any single artifact—has an infinite number of attributes, and no classification, whether based on *a priori* pigeonholes or empirically defined attribute clusters, could possibly consider them all. Nor could any classification ever hope to answer all the possible questions about the nature of tools or assemblages that might ever be asked. Any satisfactory system of artifact classification must be designed to answer a specific set of questions about tools and assemblages. A classification is only satisfactory insofar as the attributes it selects for consideration are pertinent to the questions it asks. This is nothing new or startling—these observations should be familiar and obvious.

The larger issues of function versus style in artifact attributes simply cannot be addressed using Bordes' typology, no matter how much good service it has rendered. When Bordes formalized the type definitions many of us use in classifying Lower and Middle Paleolithic assemblages, his aim was to define types with stylistic as well as functional/technological validity. Yet at the same time, he deliberately defined the tool types so that his definitions would have the widest possible applicability—so each type would be a contrasting minimal constellation of attributes that could be recognized wherever in space or time it recurred, regardless of the inevitable minor variations between individual members of each type. A simple convex sidescraper should be recognizable as such whether it is markedly convex or not so convex, whether or not it is made on a Levallois flake, or has a "natural back." It should be recognizably "the same thing" whether it is found in France or Russia, whether it is 400,000 or 40,000 years old. A moment's thought should be enough to suggest that, in the Bordes classification, attributes sensitive to spatial and temporal difference are relegated to a secondary position. These "minor" attributes—recognized as such after Bordes' empirical examination of hundreds or thousands of similar pieces from many periods and regions revealed the more essential or invariant attributes of each type—are in fact ignored in the construction of the cumulative percentage graphs and indices used for comparison.

Since the 1950s, some investigators who use the Bordes typology have come to doubt the very existence of style in Mousterian assemblages. No wonder. In defining the types the way Bordes did, he excluded at the outset exactly those attributes that are inherently likely to bear the greatest load of information about style. They do not enter at all into the confection of the graphs used to define the supposedly "stylistic" ensembles. (Of course, Bordes discussed the range of formal variation in each type in the narrative portion of his assemblage descriptions, but facies diagnosis was based on the cumulative curves and indices, not the narrative description.)

Let me try to make the fallacy of this procedure clearer with an analogy. As I write, I have in my pocket both Spanish 5 peseta pieces and American nickels. They are both circular, about the same size, and as far as I can tell by eye, are made of the same silvery alloy. On one side, each has a man's head, an inscription, and a date, and on the reverse, another (geometric) motif, an inscription, and a stated value; neither has any attachment or perforation for suspension. (As it happens, similar pieces have seen use in past centuries, and they can be recognized in many countries.) If I have enough such pieces, I will see that they are all generally similar, and will be able to place them all in the same "type." The differences between the items in my "type" seem minor in comparison with their similarities.

Suppose that, in my classification, I do unite these items on the basis of the particular limited bundle of distinctive attributes they all share. The analogy to Bordes' practice is fair. What I am doing is just what Bordes did when he distinguished, say, simple convex scrapers as a type distinct from other stone tools. This is an appropriate procedure, for some purposes, but it would be quite inappropriate for others. I would not be wrong from one perspective to consider these coins (and many others like them) to be the same kind of thing, because both were made in about the same way, both serve as substitutes for value, and (though this is accidental) both can be exchanged for approximately the same kind and quantity of goods. From the standpoint of the way they were made, their use and value, the differences between the coins seem quite like the differences between simple convex sidescrapers—they are not as striking as the attributes that unite them.

While none of us knows much about what simple convex sidescrapers "meant" to their makers, we all know something about coins. It is easy to see that my classification reflects the functions and technological

characteristics of the coins quite adequately. But does it take stylistic characteristics into consideration? I believe not. If I think I have defined a stylistically sensitive type, as Bordes thought he was doing, I am very much mistaken. Everyone will recognize that I have suppressed most of the stylistic attributes in my classification of coins. In money it is precisely style that counts. If I try to spend the Spanish coin in the U.S., I will soon find that the "accidental" attributes I have relegated to a secondary position in my classification are major, not minor. The style that makes all the difference has been drowned out in my classification by attributes that reflect technological and economic considerations.

Had I wanted to produce a stylistically sensitive classification I should have given more importance to the differences in decoration of the coins. For those seemingly minor attributes—the language of the inscriptions, the fact that one contains the name "España," the other "United States of America," and that one of the heads is that of King Juan Carlos of Spain and the other is Thomas Jefferson—embody precisely those stylistic differences that mark coinage as being from one country and time as opposed to another. In fact, the stylistic difference is so important that it even constrains the function of the artifacts. My nickel may not be worth much in the U.S.A., but it is not even money in Spain.

Bordes' approach to the classification of Mousterian tools mistakes function for style, and for that reason whatever stylistic entities there may be will escape us as long as we use it. But there is a seeming contradiction between what I have said and the fact that, when an essentially similar approach is applied to Upper Paleolithic collections, it works. I have no doubt that the Upper Paleolithic typology devised by de Sonneville-Bordes and Perrot is sensitive to at least those aspects of style that are time-related. How can that be?

The answer seems to be that the adequacy of a classification depends as much on how obvious the toolmakers made patterning, and how much of each kind of information they incorporated in their types, as it does on the abilities of the typologist. Though I am sure it is present, stylistic information is neglected in the Mousterian typology partly because it is so difficult to find. Later Upper Paleolithic toolmakers—particularly after about 20,000 years ago—deliberately put a great deal more of "themselves" into the shapes of certain distinctive stone and bone tool types. If we can say that Mousterian assemblages are surprisingly "uniform" over a huge area for an immense time, that is not at all true for Upper Paleolithic industries, which are regionally distinctive, relatively short-lived, and often identified by the presence of idiosyncratic artifact types. Think, for example, of the quick turnover of Aurignacian bone point types, or of the marked differences in the kinds of Solutrean points that characterize various times and places. Of course, the introduction of a well-differentiated and often deliberately decorated bone industry in the Upper Paleolithic added greatly to the possibilities for stylistic variation. The de Sonneville-Bordes typology is sensitive to style in part because style has become so much more important in the collections. There is no paradox here.

NEW APPROACHES TO CLASSIFICATION

If we are to progress towards an understanding of similarity and difference among Mousterian artifact series, we need both more refined typological concepts and more carefully controlled assemblages. We must be very careful that our conceptual framework is clear, precise, and thorough, and that it does not confuse fundamentally different issues. "Style" and "function," as I have used the concepts above, are inadequate in this respect: they are too broadly defined and overlap too much to be of real utility, and in any case they do not exhaust the possible causes or correlates of difference between assemblages.

That there has been substantial progress in the study of lithic artifacts in the last two decades is undeniable. Despite these advances, the potential causes of difference between assemblages still remain the same. It is also true that no major classificatory system in current use in Paleolithic studies makes any realistic attempt to evaluate all the causes for inter-assemblage difference.

Some of that difference is always due to sampling error. Only relatively recently have statistical tests of significance that evaluate this factor been systematically applied in Paleolithic studies. Assemblages may differ because of the selective action of geological agencies or excavator bias, or because of undetected disturbance by burrowing animals or deliberate digging or housecleaning by prehistoric people. Greater care than was usual in earlier excavations is needed to control for some of these actions. Assemblages may differ because of the use of different raw materials, or differing extents of wear and resharpening of working edges (Dibble and Rolland, this volume). Assemblages contain toolkits used to perform different activities, one "functional" component in variation. A group of artifacts may have peculiar attributes because of individual differences in tool-making habits or personal idiosyncracies in the ways the tools were used. The artifacts we find may differ in part due to intra-group stylistic considerations—they might have been made or used by different groups within a single society, who wanted to stress their identity by using particular forms of artifacts, or peculiar toolmaking techniques. They might have been made by members of different societies—in this case, stylistic markers of the sort that differentiate contemporaneous societies from one another may well be present. Tools may differ because resources, techniques, or preferences have changed over time. Some of this time-related difference is due to changing technological functions—improved ways of doing things in an ever-changing environmental setting—while another part is due to stylistic factors, whether deliberate or unconscious.

Until we recognize what each of these factors may potentially contribute to inter-assemblage difference, and devise adequate means for controlling their relative contribution (either alone or in combination), so that some can be "held constant" while the effects of others are evaluated, the study of artifact assemblages will not get us much farther than we have already come. The problem is a knotty one. There is no way to decide *a priori* which attributes are likely to be primarily stylistic and which are likely to be functional when we begin classifying. In fact, ethnography teaches us that the ways artifacts are used may often be "styles" of doing things, and that the way items are decorated is often believed by the users to dictate the manner and context of their use. But the problems can be resolved with new and more sophisticated approaches. We need to adopt different methods of artifact classification, including more and different kinds of quantification, more detailed and reliable wear studies, and more attention to minimal details of the technical aspects of tool-making and reworking. Some of these approaches are already in use (see, for example, the chapters by Beyries, Dibble, Jelinek, and Rolland in Dibble and Montet-White 1988); what we need to do is improve them, combine them, synthesize them into more coherent and reliable systems.

Just as important, we must generate new sets of hypotheses about the meaning of variation in artifacts, assemblages, and subassemblages, and about other aspects of continuity and discontinuity in space and time. Nothing less than a complete overhaul of Mousterian classification is evidently needed. Until there is a satisfactory substitute, however, I have no doubt that the Bordes classification will continue to be employed, and to render good service within its limits to those who have been made aware of what they are.

IMPLICATIONS FOR THE STUDY OF THE NEANDERTAL TRANSITION

Can studies of Mousterian assemblages tell us anything about the replacement of Neandertals by *Homo sapiens sapiens*? Not directly. It is skeletons, not tools, that tell us about the evolution of the human body. There is no direct and non-trivial relationship between tool types and body form in the remote past any more than there is in the present. The discovery of a Neandertal in the Saint-Césaire Chatelperronian, or of skeletally "modern" people in the Qafzeh Mousterian, is important and interesting, but neither disturbing nor terribly illuminating, as far as its human evolutionary implications go; such co-occurrences in themselves add absolutely nothing to our knowledge of relationships between Neandertals and anatomically modern people.

Of course, if I am right in believing that differences among Mousterian assemblages that become apparent in using the Bordes typology are mostly reflections of the performance of different sets of activities, then there is really no sense in searching further for the affiliation of early Upper Paleolithic industries and particular Mousterian facies. Detailed typological similarities between them would only show that early Upper Paleolithic peoples continued to perform some of the same tasks as Mousterians. That would tell us nothing new about relationships between peoples or cultural affinities.

However, from a broader perspective, new approaches to the understanding of the reasons why Mousterian assemblages are variable cannot fail to throw more light on the nature of Mousterian cultural adaptations and capacities, the differences as well as the continuities between them, and the changes that transpired to make them so different from the later adaptations of the Upper Paleolithic. And those are topics of the greatest importance.

ACKNOWLEDGMENTS

The excavations in Morín Level 16 that are reported here were undertaken between 1968 and 1971, under the joint direction of J. González Echegaray and the author, with the financial assistance of grants from the National Science Foundation to the University of Chicago, of the Spanish Direction General of Fine Arts, the Wenner Gren Foundation for Anthropological Research, and the Lichtstern Fund for Anthropological Research of the Department of Anthropology, University of Chicago, to the senior author. The Smithsonian Institution and the U.S. Air Force also provided crucial support for our research in its later stages. To all of those organizations we wish once more to express our deepest gratitude.

The final classification of the previously unreported materials on which this article was largely based was performed in a course on stone tool typology taught at the University of Chicago during the winter of 1988. I thank the following for their essential contribution to that study: David O. Anderson, Patricia K. Anderson, Frederic W. Gleach, Suzette McInerney, Anthony Reich, and Matthew Seddon. The results of the classification are discussed in a similar framework in an article by Gleach et al. (1988). Minor errors in that presentation are corrected here.

REFERENCES CITED

Beyries, S.
1988   Functional Variability of Lithic Sets in the Middle Paleolithic. Pp. 213-223 in *Upper Pleistocene Prehistory of Western Eurasia*, eds. H. Dibble and A. Montet-White. Philadelphia: University Museum, University of Pennsylvania.

Binford, L. R., and Binford, S. R.
1966   A Preliminary Analysis of Functional Variability in the Mousterian of Levallois Facies. *AA* 68:238-295.

Bordes, F.
1961   *Typologie du Paléolithique ancien et moyen.* 2 vols. MIPUB 1. Bordeaux: Delmas.

1968   *The Old Stone Age.* New York: World University Library.

1972   *A Tale of Two Caves.* New York: Harper and Row.

Carballo, J.

1923   *Excavaciones en la Cueva del Rey, en Villanueva (Santander).* Memoria 9, Junta Superior de Excavaciones y Antiguedades 53. Madrid.

Cushman, K. A.

1975   Spatial Analysis of an Aurignacian Occupation Floor at Cueva Morín, Spain. M.A. thesis, Department of Anthropology, University of Chicago.

Dibble, H.

1988   Typological Aspects of Reduction and Intensity of Utilization of Lithic Resources in the French Mousterian. Pp. 181-197 in *Upper Pleistocene Prehistory of Western Eurasia*, eds. H. Dibble and A. Montet-White. Philadelphia: University Museum, University of Pennsylvania.

Freeman, L. G.

1966   The Nature of Mousterian Facies in Cantabrian Spain. *AA* 68:230-237.

1978a   The Analysis of Some Occupation Floor Distributions from Earlier and Middle Paleolithic Sites in Spain. Pp. 57-116 in *Views of the Past: Essays in Old World Prehistory and Paleoanthropology*, ed. L. G. Freeman. The Hague: Mouton Publishers.

1978b   Mousterian Worked Bone from Cueva Morín (Santander, Spain): A Preliminary Description. Pp. 29-51 in *Views of the Past: Essays in Old World Prehistory and Paleoanthropology*, ed. L. G. Freeman. The Hague: Mouton Publishers.

Freeman, L. G., and González Echegaray, J.

1970   Aurignacian Structural Features and Burials at Cueva Morín (Santander, Spain). *Nature* 226:722-726.

1983   Tally-Marked Bone from Mousterian Levels at Cueva Morín (Santander, Spain). Pp. 143-147 in *Homenage al Prof. Dr. Martin Almagro Basch*, Vol. 1. Madrid: Ministerio de Cultura.

Gleach, F. W.

1987   Factor Analysis as an Indicator of Spatial Distribution: An Example from the Cantabrian Mousterian. M.A. thesis, Department of Anthropology, University of Chicago.

Gleach, F. W.; Freeman, L. G.; Anderson, D.; Anderson, P.; McInerney, S.; Reich, A.; and Seddon, M.

1988   A Report on Previously Unanalyzed Material from Cueva Morín. *Chicago Anthropology Exchange* 17:61-68.

González Echegaray, J.

1988   Decorative Patterns in the Mousterian of Cueva Morín. Pp. 37-42 in *L'homme de Néandertal*, ed. M. Otte. Vol. 5: *La pensee*, ed. O. Bar-Yosef. ERAUL 32. Liège: Université de Liège.

González Echegaray, J., and Freeman, L. G.

1978   *Vida y muerte en Cueva Morín.* Santander: Institución Cultural de Cantabria.

González Echegaray, J.; Freeman, L. G.; Barandiarán, I.; Apellaniz, J.; Butzer, K.; Fuentes, C.; Madariaga, B.; González Morales, J.; and Leroi-Gourhan, A.

1980   *El yacimiento de la cueva de "El Pendo" (excavaciones 1953-1957).* BPH 17. Madrid: Instituto Español de Prehistoria/Universidad de Madrid.

González Echegaray, J.; Freeman, L. G.; Butzer, K.; Leroi-Gourhan, A.; Altuna, J.; Madariaga, B.; and Apellaniz, J.

1971   *Cueva Morín: Excavaciones 1966-1968.* Santander: Publicaciones del Patronato de Las Cuevas Prehistóricas de la Provincia de Santander.

González Echegaray, J.; Freeman, L. G.; Madariaga, B.; Butzer, K.; and Altuna, J.

1973   *Cueva Morín: Excavaciones 1969.* Santander: Publicaciones del Patronato de Las Cuevas Prehistóricas de la Provincia de Santander.

Jelinek, A.

1988   Technology, Typology and Culture in the Middle Paleolithic. Pp. 199-212 in *Upper Pleistocene Prehistory of Western Eurasia*, eds. H. Dibble and A. Montet-White. Philadelphia: University Museum, University of Pennsylvania.

Lumley, H. de
1971-72   *Le Paléolithique inférieur et moyen du Midi méditerraneén dans son cadre géologique. GP* Supplément 5e (1 and 2). Paris: CNRS.

Rolland, N.
1988   Observations on Some Middle Paleolithic Time Series in Southern France. Pp. 161-180 in *Upper Pleistocene Prehistory of Western Eurasia*, eds. H. Dibble and A. Montet-White. Philadelphia: University Museum, University of Pennsylvania.

Vega del Sella, C. de
1921   *El Paleolítico de Cueva Morín (Santander) y notas para la Climatología Cuaternaria.* Memoria 29. Madrid: Comisión de Investigaciones Paleontológicas y Prehistóricas.

X

Typological Variability
in the Levantine Middle Paleolithic

Anthony E. Marks

INTRODUCTION

In 1937, when Dorothy Garrod published the results of her excavations at Mugharet et Tabun on the Levantine coast, just south of Haifa (Fig. 10.1), she presented a view of the Levantine Middle Paleolithic quite different from the then prevailing understanding of the European Middle Paleolithic (Garrod and Bate 1937), namely, that the European dichotomy between the Levalloisian and the Mousterian did not seem to apply in the Levant. At Tabun, as at Shukba (Garrod 1928), there was an industry rich in both Levallois pieces and Mousterian retouched tools; reflecting this, she named it the Levalloiso-Mousterian. This was quite innovative and was a marked departure from the ideas being formulated in the region, given that Neuville (1934) had seen the European dichotomy in his excavations in the nearby Judean Desert, and that a Levalloisian had recently been reported from Egypt (Caton-Thompson and Gardner 1932). To Garrod, the Levalloiso-Mousterian was not paralleled in Europe, where she saw Mousterian and Levalloisian assemblages alternating (Garrod and Bate 1937:120).

Based on differences in both faunal and lithic assemblages (Garrod and Bate 1937:115), Garrod defined a Lower and an Upper Levalloiso-Mousterian. The Lower Levalloiso-Mousterian, occurring in Tabun Layers C and D, was characterized by triangular flakes and elongated blanks, as well as by a fair number of Upper Paleolithic tool types, such as burins, endscrapers, and backed knives. Additionally, there was a significant number of typical Mousterian tools, including sidescrapers and Mousterian points. The Upper Levalloiso-Mousterian, from Layer B and the Chimney of Tabun, was defined on the basis of more typical Mousterian attributes. The retouched tools were heavily weighted toward Mousterian

sidescrapers, while points were rare (Garrod and Bate 1937:115). There was little tendency toward blank elongation and triangular flakes (i.e., Levallois points), which were only moderately represented. In fact, the main differences between the Upper and Lower Levalloiso-Mousterian lay in the "relative abundance" of scrapers versus triangular Levallois points (Garrod and Bate 1937:115).

In spite of these major differences between the two phases, to Garrod they shared both typical Mousterian traits (sidescrapers and Mousterian points) and Levalloisian traits (i.e., the large number of Levallois flakes). She clearly believed that both of these phases truly belonged together in this context and, thus, that they could be distinguished as much by their technology as by their typology. Garrod's perceptions were generally accepted and both the concept of the Levalloiso-Mousterian and the distinctions between its phases became standard in the literature until well after World War II (Garrod 1957; Haller 1946; Ewing 1947; Weachter 1952), except for Wrescher (1967) and Neuville (1951) who remained committed to a "Levalloisian."

Since the 1930s, a number of changes have taken place. The Levalloiso-Mousterian is now called the Levantine Mousterian and, while two phases are still usually recognized, they include different groupings of the Tabun layers: a Late Levantine Mousterian includes Tabun, Layers C, B, and the Chimney, while an Early Levantine Mousterian is correlated with Tabun, Layer D (Jelinek 1981b; Marks 1981; Bar-Yosef 1980).

Although a number of different workers have examined aspects of the Levantine Middle Paleolithic since Garrod (Bordes 1955; Skinner 1965; Perrot 1968; Copeland 1975; Crew 1975; Jelinek 1975; Meignen and Bar-Yosef 1988; Marks 1990), almost all

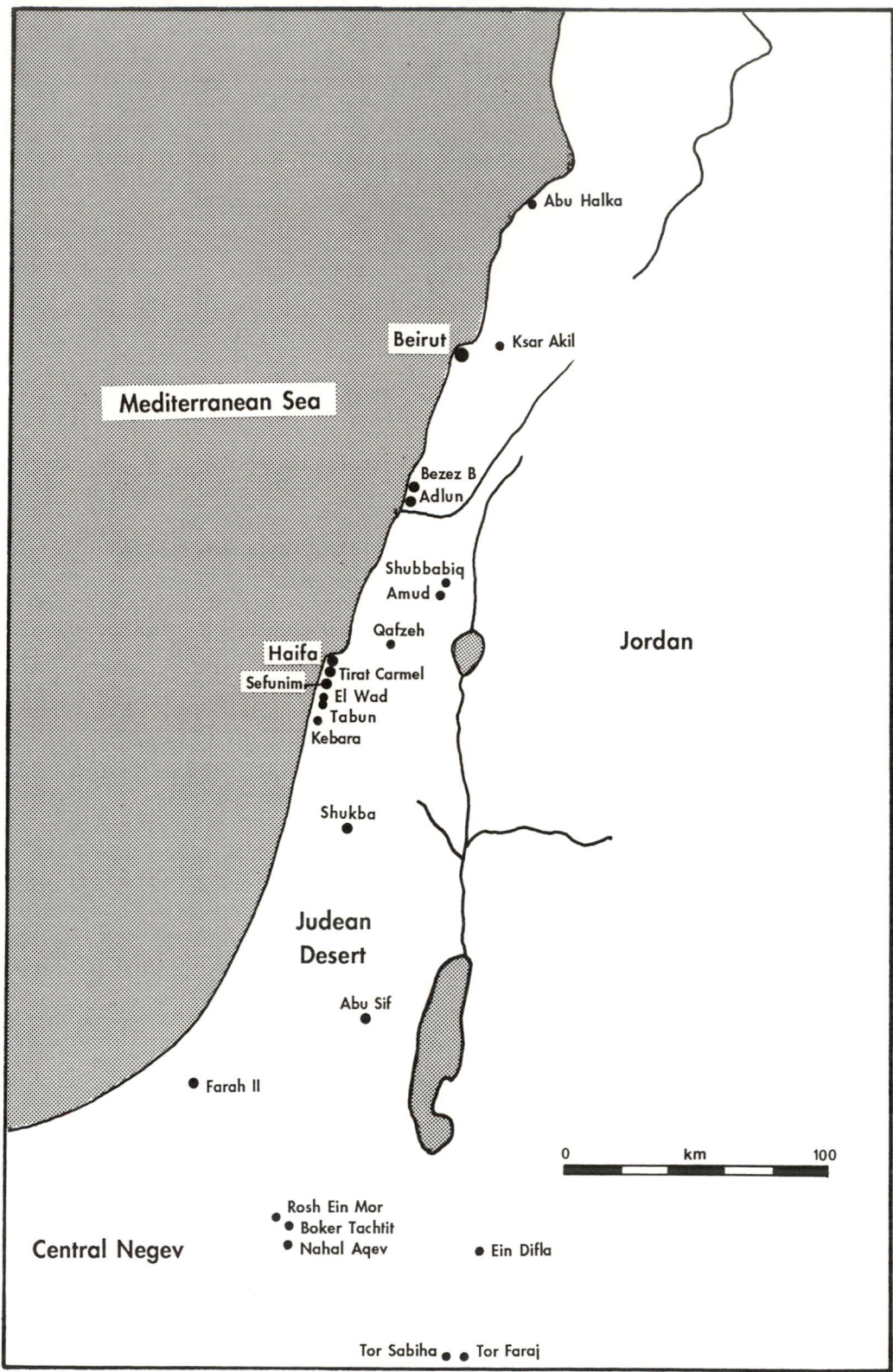

Figure 10.1   Map showing the main sites mentioned in the text.

have found that any organization of it tends to emphasize technological over typological variability. Thus, Skinner (1965) essentially divided the Levantine Mousterian into sub-groups based upon a clustering of Levallois indices. Moreover, Hours and Copeland, in proposing a three-phase developmental sequence for the Levantine Middle Paleolithic used technological criteria rather than typological ones (Hours et al. 1973; Copeland 1975). They suggested that Garrod's Lower Levalloiso-Mousterian be divided into a Phase 1, Levantine Mousterian (Tabun, Layer D) and a Phase 2 (Tabun, Layer C), while Garrod's Upper Levalloiso-Mousterian become Phase 3. Those proposed phases were based on changes in technological traits, such as blank elongation of both flakes and points in Phase 1, the absence of elongation and points in Phase 2, and the reappearance in Phase 3 of elongated blanks and points which were now mainly wide and short. On the other hand, Bordes (1955), in his study of Jabrud, matched its assemblages with the typological patterning that he had also seen in southwestern Europe, but recognized the importance of the technology by suggesting that a number of the Levalloiso-Mousterian levels there should be called "Levalloisien" (Bordes 1955:502). Perrot (1968) also tended to balance typological and technological traits in his definitions. Thus, while he recognized a "Typical Mousterian" in the European sense, he also defined a Mousterian facies of "elongated points," which was technologically rather than typologically based. Aside from Bordes and Perrot, no other worker found typologically based groupings to be more enlightening than those that emphasized technological criteria.

In the past 25 years, a good deal of attention has been paid to the Levantine Middle Paleolithic. In the central and northern Levant, there have been excavations of new sites, such as Douara Cave in Syria (Akazawa 1974, 1979) and Tirat Carmel (Ronen 1974), the re-excavations of old sites such as Tabun (e.g., Jelinek et al. 1973), and Kebara (Meignen and Bar-Yosef 1988), as well as the publication of studies of old excavations at Kebara (Boutié 1981), Adlun (Roe 1983), and the Mousterian levels of Ksar Akil (Marks and Volkman 1986). In the southern Levant, surveys in the Central Negev revealed new open-air Middle Paleolithic sites, such as Rosh Ein Mor (Crew 1976) and Nahal Aqev (Munday 1977), as well as numerous smaller sites (Munday 1976). Somewhat farther north another Middle Paleolithic site, Farah II, was located in the Beer Sheva plain (Gilead and Grigson 1984). In short, a great deal of new data has

become available which provides enough information to refine and improve Garrod's work.

The excavations at Tabun have confirmed Garrod's basic stratigraphic sequence (Jelinek 1975). Here, as at Ksar Akil and Jabrud, the Early Levantine Mousterian always underlies the Late Levantine Mousterian. Not only did these excavations point to the temporal priority of the Early Levantine Mousterian over the Late Levantine Mousterian, but at Tabun they also appeared to establish a stratigraphically positioned, technological data base to justify Garrod's idea that the Lower and Upper Levantine Mousterian were part of the same developmental sequence (Jelinek 1982). This perception, again, was based on vectored change in basic technology, not on shifts in retouched tool percentages. Thus, not only was the relative sequence confirmed by stratigraphy in the central Levant but so was the seeming developmental continuity of the two phases as first recognized by Garrod.

Large-scale surveys have indicated that only assemblages comparable to the Early Levantine Mousterian are present south of the Beer Sheva plain in Israel (Marks 1981; Marks and Freidel 1977), as well as to the east in southern Jordan (Henry 1988; Lindly and Clark 1987). In the north, on the other hand, there are only a very few Early Levantine Mousterian sites, except in the marginal zones of northeastern Syria (Copeland and Hours 1981), while Late Levantine Mousterian sites are common. Thus, only the Early Levantine Mousterian appears to be pan-Levantine.

In spite of all these new data, however, the traditional view of a pan-Levantine, Middle Paleolithic unilineal developmental sequence has not been confirmed. In fact, there is now some question both as to the necessary relative sequencing of the two assemblage types (the Early and Late Levantine Mousterian), as well as to their absolute dating (Bar-Yosef and Goldberg 1988; Marks 1990). For example, new dates from Qafzeh and Skhul (Stringer et al. 1989), apparently associated with Late Levantine Mousterian assemblages, fall at about 90,000 B.P., which is at least comparable if not older than the extrapolated dates from the Early Levantine Mousterian at Tabun (Jelinek 1982), and earlier than dated Early Levantine Mousterian associated springs in the Central Negev (Schwarcz et al. 1979). Assuming that all these dates are generally accurate, then both the Early and Late Levantine Mousterian can be dated to before ca. 80,000 B.P.

In addition, both the Early and Late Levantine Mousterian appear to continue until relatively late. A series of radiocarbon dates (Henry and Servello 1974) place a number of Late Levantine Mousterian occupations after 55,000 B.P., while recent TL dates place the Late Levantine Mousterian at Kebara between 60,000 and 48,000 B.P. (Valladas et al. 1987). In the south, a few Middle Paleolithic assemblages which are technologically Early Levantine Mousterian are associated with dry, cool conditions correlated with the late Middle Paleolithic (Henry 1988; Lindly and Clark 1987, with reservations), while a terminal Early Levantine Mousterian is dated to ca. 47,000 B.P. at Boker Tachtit in the Central Negev (Marks 1981).

Thus, present evidence strongly suggests that both the Early and Late Levantine Mousterian are temporally both early and late! Not only does this make the current nomenclature inappropriate, it makes Garrod and Copeland's interpretations inappropriate, as well.

It now seems certain that modern and archaic *Homo sapiens* both made assemblages definable technologically as Late Levantine Mousterian; modern *Homo sapiens* ("Proto-Cro-Magnon") at Qafzeh and Skhul (Vandermeersch 1981) and Neandertals at Kebara (Arensburg et al. 1985). Granted, if the dates are accurate, the modern hominids made their Late Levantine Mousterian some 30,000 years before the Neandertals made theirs. On the other hand, we have no hominid fossils associated with the Early Levantine Mousterian, temporally early or late in its development. This is unfortunate, since it is an example of the Early Levantine Mousterian which develops directly into the initial Levantine Upper Paleolithic about 45,000 B.P. (Marks 1988). This continuity clearly argues for a

modern *Homo sapiens* as the maker of, at least, the temporally late Early Levantine Mousterian.

Thus, the presently available data do not lend themselves well to a simple model of Levantine Middle Paleolithic development. Certainly, a unilineal pan-Levantine cultural development seems out of the question. It has already been suggested that Early Levantine Mousterian lithic technology was well adapted to the climatically marginal, steppic zones of the Levant and, therefore, retained its essential character over a long time in those marginal zones (Jelinek 1981a; Marks 1981); in fact, this adaptation reinforced those technological patterns which basically characterized it, such as blank elongation as an adaptation to mobility (Marks 1988; *contra* Munday 1979).

It has been posited that Neandertals arrived late in the Levant, after ca. 55,000 B.P. (Bar-Yosef et al. 1986), while modern *Homo sapiens* were only sporadic visitors (Stringer et al. 1989) If this was so, the Neandertals arrived carrying the same specific patterns of lithic technology and typology as already had been present in the Levant and some adjacent areas for at least 30,000 years. While all this is possible, it is certainly uncomfortable that our traditional systematics do not seem to distinguish between one Levantine/African (?) lithic tradition made by modern *Homo sapiens* and an historically unconnected lithic tradition made by immigrant Neandertals. This is particularly unfortunate, since the former would have been adapted to mild to dry climatic conditions, while the latter were apparently adapted to quite rigorous, cold conditions.

TYPOLOGICAL COMPARISONS

In this light it is perhaps useful to look again at the nature of the Early and Late Levantine Mousterian lithic industries. Technological studies have always insisted on significant differences between the two but always within the rubric of developed Levallois production (e.g., Garrod and Bate 1937; Jelinek 1975; Bar-Yosef 1980). The problem here, much discussed lately (Copeland 1983; Marks and Volkman 1983; Meignen and Bar-Yosef 1988; Boëda 1988), lies in the broad definition of Levallois. While it is impossible to deny that a wide range of blanks were produced by strategies which predetermined their shapes and sizes and, therefore, fall under the broad concept of Levallois (Bordes 1980; Meignen and Bar-Yosef 1988; cf. Boëda 1988), it is far from clear that such a broad concept, per se, has much analytic utility for interassemblage comparisons based on specific patterns of

reduction strategies. Even after Bordian systematics were generally adopted in the Levant, workers continued to distinguish between the Early and Late Levantine Mousterian using technological criteria mainly outside Bordian systematics—tendencies toward or away from blank elongation, on-axis versus using centripetal core preparation, converging versus ovoid flake forms, and short/wide versus long/narrow point forms. Bordian systematics (Bordes 1950, 1961) do not effectively differentiate among these various forms of core reduction, nor were they meant to. Thus, Levallois blades and flakes are not differentiated in the typology, and neither are flakes produced from unidirectional cores as opposed to those prepared centripetally. Given that Bordian systematics do not easily accommodate such distinctions, perhaps it is not surprising that Bordes (1955) himself emphasized the typology of the Jabrud Middle Paleolithic sequence rather than its technology.

But, aside from Bordes' work at Jabrud, little emphasis has been placed on Levantine Middle Paleolithic typological variability, beyond the general observation that the Early Levantine Mousterian has more Upper Paleolithic type tools than does the Late Levantine Mousterian (e.g., Copeland 1975; Bar-Yosef 1980). This bias away from typological criteria for defining industrial groups stems from a number of factors. In the Levant technological variability is very marked. Even with small retouched tool samples, there is always debitage to measure (e.g., Akazawa 1979; Ronen 1984), and the marked distinctions in specific Levallois reduction strategies between the Early and Late Levantine Mousterian makes assignment of an assemblage into one or the other relatively simple.

On the other hand, the non-systematic retention of retouched tools during the older excavations (e.g., those of Garrod, Neuville, Rust, etc.), makes it impossible to use such collections successfully in an analytic system such as Bordes', where a total tool configuration is the necessary working universe. To a large extent, this explains why Skinner's conclusions (1965) relied essentially on the Levallois and related indices, rather than on typological clustering.

In recent years, there has been a tendency to present Bordian typological indices, note that most are not reliable, and move quickly on to more detailed technological analyses (e.g., Akazawa 1979; Jelinek 1981b; Marks 1988). It also must be admitted that a number of workers, myself included, believe that under most conditions more may be learned from technology than from typology; or, at least, that the variables which control technology are more easily recognized and controlled than those which may affect a typology of retouched pieces. But, in spite of the obvious uncertainties inherent in using a typological approach, it is also clear that a good deal of information is potentially available from the retouched tools of any lithic industry.

Because of the problems inherent in analyzing assemblages that were acquired and studied by different workers over a long period of time, the concept of the total tool configuration as the only legitimate analytic universe must be abandoned. Therefore, for the purposes of this article, only those retouched tool types that have a high probability of having been identified consistently and distinguished from other tools by all workers will be used. I would suggest that, from Garrod on, everyone working in the Levant

probably distinguished equally well between sidescrapers and endscrapers and between backed knives and steeply retouched sidescrapers and therefore these tool groups are reliable for study. On the other hand, raclettes and pseudo-Levallois points, for example, have not always been recognized and still are not uniformly included in assemblage typologies. The same can be said of notches and Mousterian tranchets.

Much of the detailed morphological variability recognized in Bordian systematics, particularly for sidescrapers, has been shown to have little value in cultural interpretations. In fact, recent work by Dibble (1984, 1987) has suggested that specific morphology of the more extensively retouched tools— sidescrapers and Mousterian points—might best be understood not in typological terms but, rather, as reflections of differential resharpening intensity. Under this scenario, the specific form of heavily retouched tools would represent not any mental template carried by the maker of a desired form, either culturally or functionally determined but, at most, a generalized mental template of tool conditions which were not desirable, causing the tool's discard (Dibble 1989). Along with these considerations, work by Dibble and Rolland (see Dibble and Rolland, this volume) suggests that Bordian systematics and the resulting industrial groupings hardly monitor either general cultural or specific functional variability, as has been argued back and forth for many years (Binford and Binford 1966; Bordes 1973; Binford 1973). If their perceptions are accurate, the kinds of variability recognized by Bordian systematics more likely reflect the complex interaction between residential mobility, intensity of occupation, local raw material availability, and tendencies for the curation of desirable raw materials.

It is far from clear, however, that these interpretations are universally applicable. Partly to test this question and partly to see whether a new look at Levantine Mousterian typological variability might provide useful data, it was decided to approach the typological studies using only a few classes of tools: those which are well defined and usually recognized and saved by the archaeologists. Following the work of Dibble (1988) and Rolland (1981), sidescrapers (Bordes types 6-29), with Mousterian points included (there were relatively few cave bears in the Levant), and denticulates (Bordes type 43) were chosen for study, as well as a group comprising the Upper Paleolithic classes of endscrapers, burins, perforators, and backed knives (Bordes types 30-37). All other types were excluded.

The selection of these three variables (i.e., the percentages of scrapers/Mousterian points, denticulates, and Upper Paleolithic types) permitted the use of a tripolar graph to illustrate the relative importance of each in various Levantine Mousterian assemblages, independent of each assemblage's technological patterns (Fig. 10.2).

It should be noted that one serious problem in this approach is that many assemblages have only a limited number of relevant tools. Thus, some of these assemblages have too few of the needed retouched tools to be considered normally in a Bordian analysis (as noted even by Garrod [Garrod and Bate 1937:115]), though they can be classified by their technology. Assemblages such as that from Douara Cave are technologically characteristic but have only 20 appropriate retouched tools (Akazawa 1979:35). The same is true for the assemblage from Sefunim, with only 13 usable tools (Ronen 1984:519). There are a number of other sam-

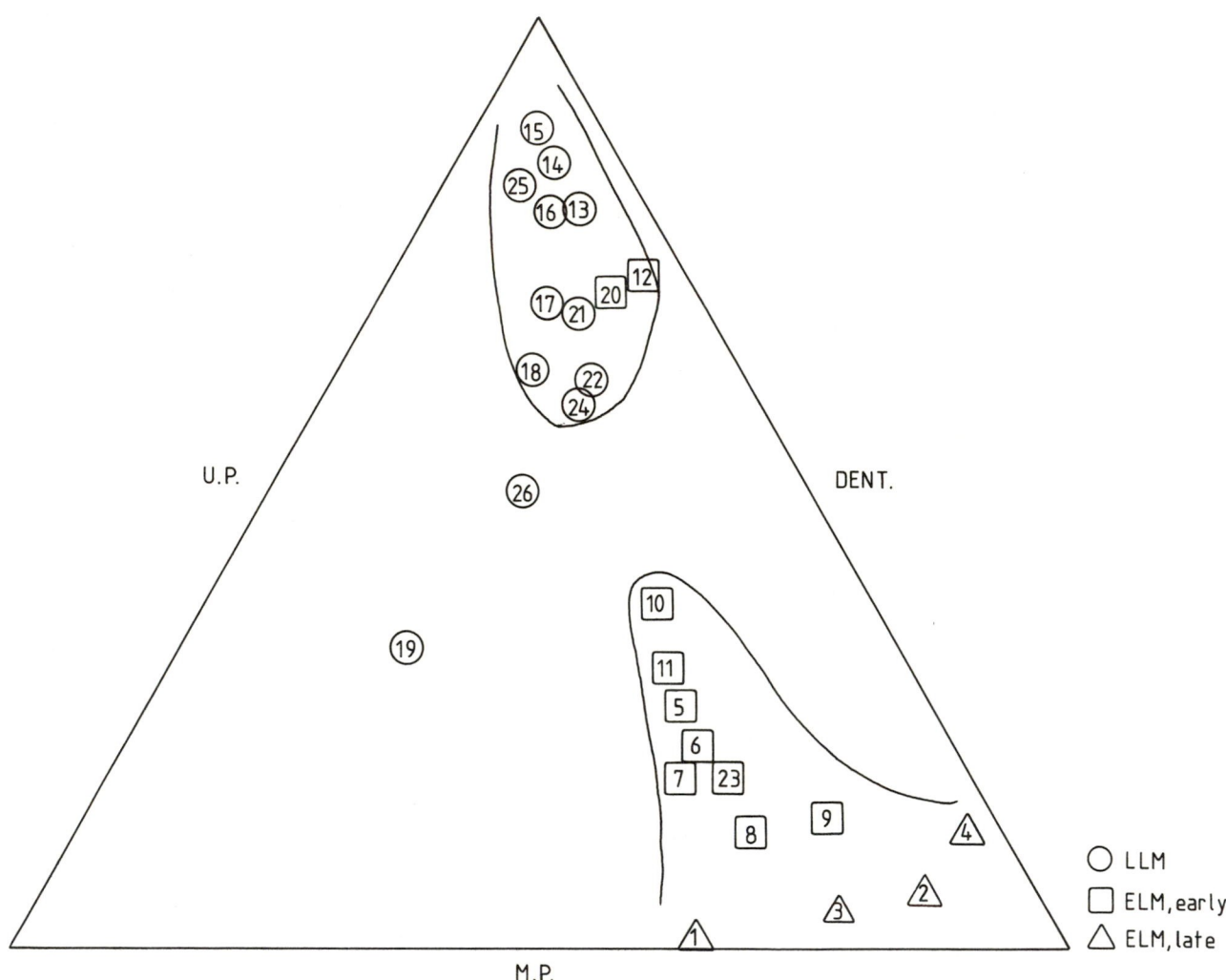

Figure 10.2   *Tripole graph of the three main classes of Levantine Mousterian typology (Middle Paleolithic tools—Bordes types 6-29; Upper Paleolithic tools—Bordes types 30-37; and denticulates—Bordes type 43) for sites of the temporally early Early Levantine Mousterian, the temporally late Early Levantine Mousterian, and the Late Levantine Mousterian. The site numbers are as follows: Ein Difla (1); Boker Tachtit, Level 1 (2) and Level 2 (3); Tor Faraj A (4); Rosh Ein Mor, Level 4 (5), Level 5 (6), Level 7 (7), Level 8 (8), and Level 9 (9); Nahal Aqev e-g (10) and a-d (11); Tabun, Unit IX (12); Kebara, Level II (13), Level III (14), Level IV (15), Level V (16), Level VI (17), Level VII (18), and Level VIII (19); Bezez B (20); Tabun 18-26 (21) and 1-17 (22); Ksar Akil XXVIII A/B (23), XXVII A/B (24), and XXVI A/B (25); Shubbabiq (26).*

ples with comparable sample problems. In certain cases where the samples come from arbitrary excavation levels of minimal depth, it is perhaps justifiable to group adjacent levels together to increase the usable retouched tool samples to above 50 and, in so doing, partly remove the chance for random swings in proportional occurrences. This has been done for the samples from Nahal Aqev (Munday 1977) and for the apparently arbitrary divisions of the Ksar Akil levels into A and B (Marks and Volkman 1986). Larger groupings were necessary for the samples from Tabun because the samples sizes from the natural levels were so small (Jelinek, pers. comm.). Finally, a few assemblages were excluded from the study because of the author's judgment that artifact condition was poor, owing either to long exposure at the surface (Rosh Ein Mor, Level 6) or to probable movement and crushing in situ (Tirat Carmel). In both cases, the number of irregularly edged blanks indicated artificially high occurrences of denticulate-like tools.

In spite of these problems and uncertainties, it is at once clear that of the three variables, denticulates account for the least variability. The lineal aspect of the plot in Figure 10.2 shows that the denticulate component does not control the clustering of the assemblages. Thus, denticulates are not a major factor in Levantine Mousterian typological variability, unlike the situation in Europe (Dibble 1988; Rolland 1981).

Also unlike the situation in Europe, most significant variability in these Levantine assemblages is seen in the relative proportions of "Middle Paleolithic," as opposed to "Upper Paleolithic" tool groups. The two clusters indicate that the assemblages, as a group, do not form a continuous distribution of shifting proportions from Middle to Upper Paleolithic retouched tools.

With three exceptions, the clustering shown in Figure 10.2 corresponds with the traditional assignments of these assemblages into an Early or Late Levantine Mousterian. The upper cluster, with two sub-clusters, contains all Late Levantine Mousterian assemblages used in this study, with the exception of Shubbabiq (26), which is a slight outlier, and Kebara Level VIII (19), which appears to be unlike any other assemblage. It may be of some significance that the uppermost sub-cluster includes the top four levels of Kebara, II through V (13 through 16), and the top level at Ksar Akil (25). Recent work at Kebara (Meignen 1988) indicates that the upper portion may be a relatively recent Late Levantine Mousterian, while the uppermost level of Ksar Akil may also represent a terminal Late Levantine Mousterian.

The second upper sub-cluster contains the equivalent of Layer C from Tabun, units 1-17 (22) and 18-26 (21), and Levels VI and VII from Kebara (17, 18), as well as the middle level, XXVII A/B, from Ksar Akil (24). All of these have been classified as Late Levantine Mousterian on technological criteria and all stratigraphically underlie even later Mousterian deposits. In two of the three cases, these higher units are in the upper sub-cluster, though no reliable data were available from Tabun B/Chimney to use here. Thus, the clustering shown here is not only consistent with the technologically based assemblage groupings, but also suggests a possible temporal trend during the Late Levantine Mousterian toward increasing Mousterian retouched tools at the expense of Upper Paleolithic type tools. This was previously suggested on the basis of fewer data (Marks and Volkman 1986:19).

If the upper cluster as a whole contained only those assemblages so far noted, the picture would be easily understood. Unfortunately, this is not the case; two other assemblages fall fully within it in the lower sub-cluster: Tabun, Unit IX (12) and Bezez B (20). On various grounds, Bezez B has been classified as Early Levantine Mousterian (Copeland 1983), and Tabun, Unit IX, is equivalent to Tabun, Layer D, the type assemblage for the Early Levantine Mousterian (Garrod and Bate 1937; Copeland 1975; Jelinek 1975).

How might these contradictions between clusterings based on technology and typology be resolved? It is not altogether clear. Both Tabun and Bezez are caves on the central Levantine coast. Only Ksar Akil is geographically comparable, while all of the other Early Levantine sites used here are open sites, located in the extreme southern Levant in the central Negev and southern Jordan. Therefore, an explanation might lie in differences in intensity of occupation, accounting for the higher percentages of the more heavily retouched Mousterian tools compared with more ephemerally occupied sites in the climatically marginal zones. Thus, the typological differences shown in Figure 10.2 may have to do with differential availability of raw materials or raw material acquisition behavior in and out of caves. On the other hand, the sample from Tabun comes from a situation where little primary flaking activity took place and finished tools were carried into the site in low numbers (Jelinek, pers. comm.). Therefore, these possible explanations do not work. The nature of the artifact accumulation at Tabun is not comparable to that of the other Early Levantine Mousterian assemblages used here. Yet, comparable or not, it resulted in an assemblage of retouched tools characteristic of the upper levels at Tabun, as well as of all Late Levantine Mousterian assemblages used here. However, since Bezez B is said to be Early Levantine Mousterian, Tabun, Unit IX, is not unique and this apparently aberrant typological pattern for the Early Levantine Mousterian must be considered further.

The lower assemblage cluster contains only assemblages classified on technological criteria as Early Levantine Mousterian. This cluster is rather attenuated and its curving aspect suggests a complex relationship among the three variables. At one end of the cluster are the temporally early Early Levantine Mousterian assemblages and at the other end is a more diffuse scatter of temporally late Early Levantine Mousterian assemblages. These later assemblages have small samples of tools, which probably accounts for some of the spread but, nonetheless, there is marked and clear variability in the percentage of retouched Middle Paleolithic tools for the whole of the Early Levantine Mousterian: from none to almost 38 percent. If only the temporally early Early Levantine Mousterian sites of Rosh Ein Mor (5–9), Nahal Aqev (10, 11) and Ksar Akil XXVIII A/B (23) are considered, almost all variability rests in shifts between retouched Mousterian tools and Upper Paleolithic tools; denticulates remain proportionately constant, except for slight deviation in Rosh Ein Mor, Level 9 (9). When the apparently temporally late Early Levantine Mousterian sites of Boker Tachtit, Levels 1 and 2 (2, 3), Tor Faraj A (4), and Ein Difla (1) are included, however, it is primarily the denticulates that become significant, while the influence of retouched Mousterian tools becomes almost non-existent. Thus, it appears that those assemblages technologically defined as Early Levantine Mousterian exhibit an overall greater typological diversity than do those of the Late Levantine Mousterian, particularly if Tabun, Unit IX, and Bezez B are included.

Since denticulates appear to account for very little of the typological variability in the Levantine Mousterian, except at those sites which have almost no typical Middle Paleolithic tools, a clearer picture of variability can be seen by looking only at the relationship between retouched Mousterian tools and Upper Paleolithic tools. These two variables alone tend to emphasize the extreme differences between the Early and Late Levantine Mousterian, with the exceptions of Tabun, Unit IX, and Bezez B (Fig. 10.3).

It is interesting to look more closely at variability within the Middle Paleolithic tools. First, there is no obvious division between the Early and Late Levantine Mousterian on these typological criteria. In fact,

both the Early and Late Levantine Mousterian have about the same spread. Second, if heavily retouched Mousterian sidescrapers and points are the result of more intensive resharpening, it might be expected that there should be proportionately few of these at sites in immediate proximity to raw material sources. A higher proportion of these complex scrapers should be expected in cave sites away from immediately available raw material and/or where high occupational intensity is postulated. The proportional distribution of simple versus complex scrapers forms, however, does not match these expectations (Table 10.1).

The two lowest levels (VII and VIII) from Kebara and both the Nahal Agev samples not only group together but also are very different from all the others. Here are examples where there is a very low occurrence of complex scraper forms and, therefore, where it might be expected that either raw material was immediately available and/or that occupation was ephemeral. Yet, it is unlikely that raw material availability at Kebara changed significantly between the occupations of Levels VIII–VII and VI–V. Moreover, Nahal Aqev was farther from raw material than Rosh Ein Mor, the latter of which has a higher incident of complex scrapers (Munday 1976). Therefore, a simple explanation based solely on raw material availability seems inappropriate.

Although intensity of occupation is difficult to judge, Boutié (1981:390) suggests that Kebara was continually occupied, indicating considerable occupational intensity; and the lower levels, at least, of Nahal Aqev have been viewed the same way (Munday 1979). The problem here is that all of Kebara has been judged to have similar occupational intensity (Boutié 1981), while a suggested change in occupational intensity at Nahal Aqev is not reflected in any change in the proportion of complex scrapers (13.0% vs. 12.0%). A similar situation occurs when Unit IX of Tabun is compared with Kebara VI. The unit clearly represents a highly ephemeral usage of the cave with little lithic production having taken place there, while Kebara VI has a high density of artifacts, indicating both intensive raw material flaking and retouched tool production. In spite of these marked differences, the percentage of complex scrapers in all scrapers is almost identical (30.4% vs. 29.6%). In the latter case, however, the paucity of blanks that were brought into the site may have resulted in more intensive resharpening of flakes, which is consistent with the Dibble/Rolland model.

At Kebara, there is a marked trend toward increasing proportions of complex scrapers upward through the deposits. Given the projected occupational consistency at Kebara, such an increase could reflect decreasing supplies of nearby raw material. This is reinforced by an overall decease in mean blank length for a number of major categories (Boutié 1981:354). Thus, Kebara might be considered consistent with Dibble's model. However, at Ksar Akil, which spans an even greater period, there is no such trend, although the percentage of sidescrapers increases overall, as at Kebara (Table 10.1). A similar situation exists at Rosh Ein Mor and Tabun, that is, a possibility of markedly different occupational modes with almost identical scraper patterns (Table 10.1). Thus, there are no consistent, positive correlations between site locality, raw material availability, intensity of occupation, and technological groupings with any tendency toward or away from complex and heavily

retouched Mousterian tools. In fact, there seems to be little consistency, at all.

An examination of the internal variability of the Upper Paleolithic tool group shows a certain consistency in patterning, although it is far from uniform (Fig. 10.4). For those assemblages traditionally defined as Late Levantine Mousterian, sample sizes pose massive problems; therefore, in some cases it has been necessary to combine adjacent level assemblages from the same sites to get a meaningful sample. This has been done for Kebara, where the largest single level sample for Upper Paleolithic tools was only 33 (Level VI). The total of combined Levels II through IV is 71; for Levels V and VI it is 63; and for Levels VII and VIII it is only 22. In each case, the separate level samples were consistent with each other, so that, for instance, there were no endscrapers in

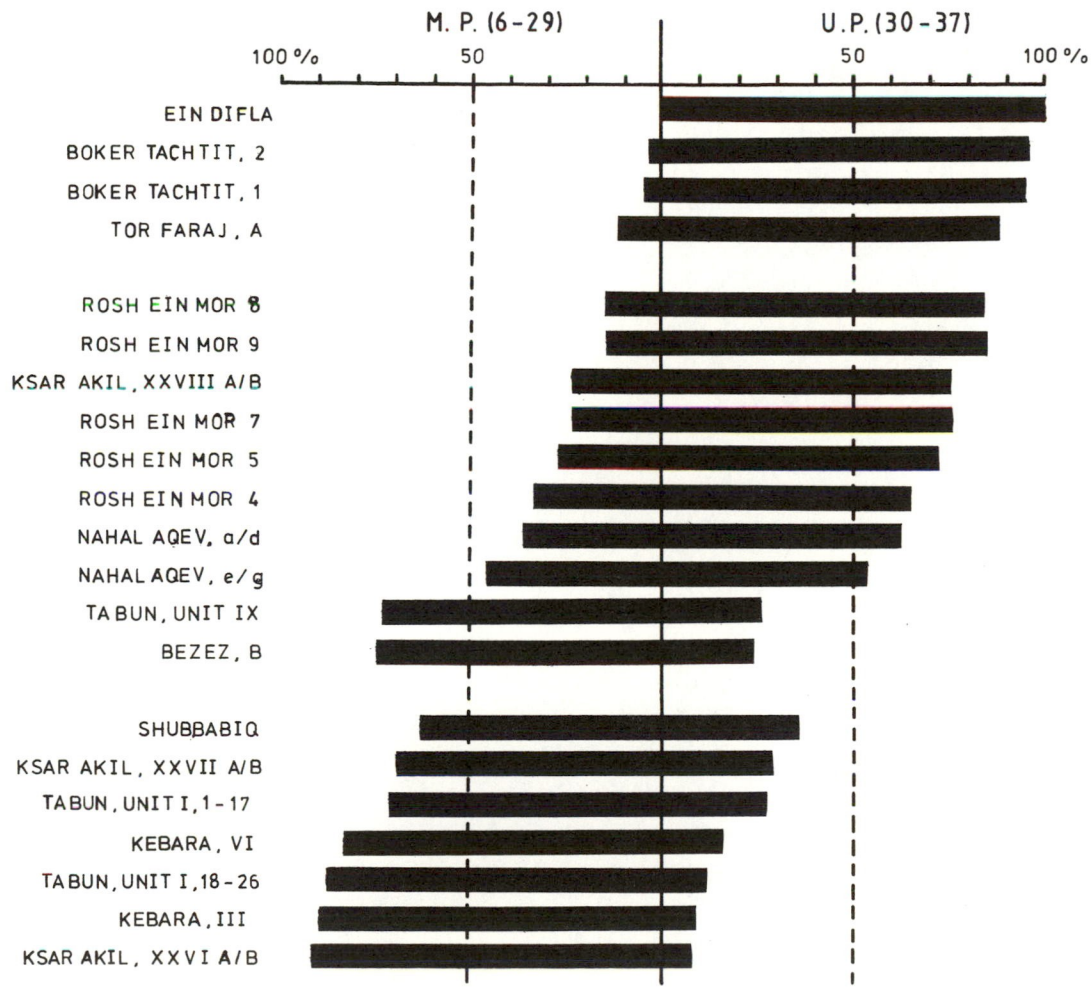

Figure 10.3   Proportions of Middle and Upper Paleolithic tools at various Levantine Mousterian sites.

either Levels VII or VIII, and burins dominated both levels (Boutié 1981:268, 270). Thus, while losing some detail, these groupings do not change the basic character of any individual level sample. For other Late Levantine Mousterian assemblages, only those assemblages were used where sample size reached over 20, which excluded the Tabun sample with only 12 Upper Paleolithic tools. For the Early Levantine Mousterian, sample problems also were present. The Jordanian sites have few retouched tools at all, even though most are of Upper Paleolithic type. The smallest sample used was that from Site 634, Ein Difla, where of 13 Upper Paleolithic tools, 11 were burins. As with the other observations, the Nahal Aqev levels were combined to form two samples: a through d, and e through g. Even then, each sample had only 36 and 30 Upper Paleolithic tools, respectively.

In spite of these sampling problems, there is some recognizable clustering. Nine of the twelve obvious Early Levantine Mousterian assemblages have less than 10% borers and backed knives among the Upper Paleolithic tools, while in the other three assemblages, this percentage increases to between 15% and 20% (Fig. 10.4). In every case, however, there is a lower percentage of borers and backed knives in these assemblages than exists in the Late Levantine Mousterian ones. Beyond this characteristic, little else can be noted. Level VII-VIII of Kebara (15) is highly aberrant, as is the Bezez B sample (20), which again falls within a Late Levantine Mousterian cluster. It is unfortunate that the Tabun, Unit IX Upper Paleolithic sample (12) consists of only 8 pieces, and this may explain why it also exhibits an aberrant pattern.

TABLE 10.1

THE RELATIONSHIP BETWEEN SIMPLE AND COMPLEX SIDESCRAPERS IN THE EARLY AND LATE LEVANTINE MOUSTERIAN.

	"Simple" Types 9, 10, 11, 25/26, 28	"Complex" Types 6, 7, 12/23, 27, 29	Sample (n =)
Late Levantine Mousterian			
Kebara II	53.7%	46.3%	149
Kebara III	54.1%	45.9%	283
Kebara IV	60.9%	39.1%	235
Kebara V	56.3%	43.7%	206
Ksar Akil XXVII A/B	61.1%	38.9%	113
Ksar Akil XXVI A/B	65.9%	34.1%	129
Shubbabiq	69.3%	30.7%	228
Kebara VI	70.4%	29.6%	169
Kebara VII	80.6%	19.4%	31
Kebara VIII	88.9%	11.1%	13
Tabun, Unit I	86.3%	13.7%	37
Early Levantine Mousterian			
Bezez B	52.3%	47.7%	130
Ksar Akil XXVIII A/B	64.7%	35.3%	18
Tabun, Unit IX	69.9%	30.4%	102
Rosh Ein Mor	68.8%	31.2%	154
Nahal Aqev, a/d	87.0%	13.0%	23
Nahal Aqev, e/g	88.0%	12.0%	25

DISCUSSION AND CONCLUSION

The purpose of this study was to see whether any significant inter-site patterning of Levantine Mousterian assemblages was present in terms of various typological categories and to compare it with patterning based upon traditionally used technological criteria. In addition, data were related to the new interpretations of Middle Paleolithic typology and assemblage variability derived from European data (Dibble and Rolland, this volume).

First, it does not appear that the fundamental variability documented for the European Mousterian pertains for either the Early or Late Levantine Mousterian. Not only do denticulates make an insignificant contribution to assemblage variability in both industries, but the patterning between the proportions of simple and complex sidescrapers does not correlate well with the kinds of data that would permit validating Dibble and Rolland's model. On the other hand,

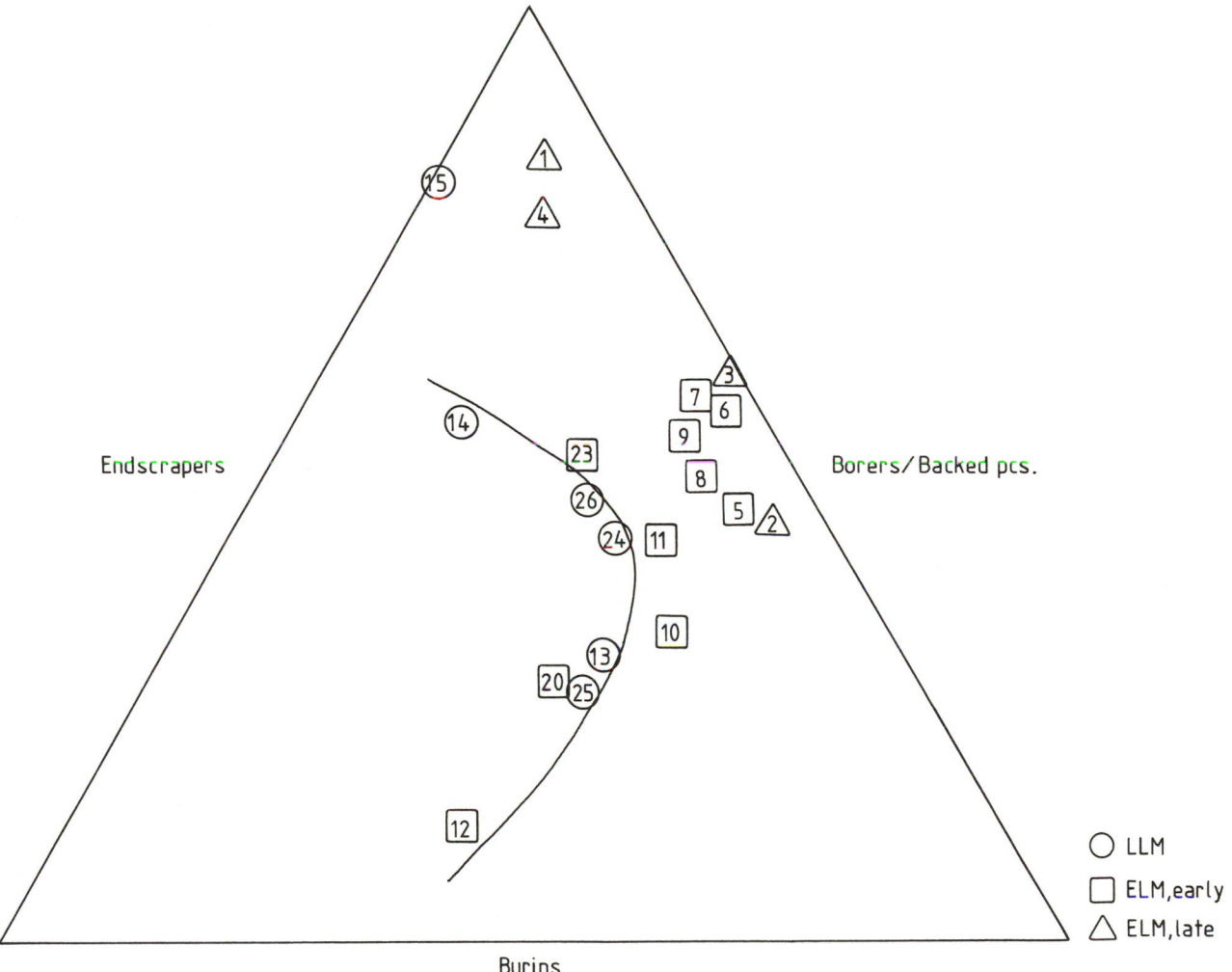

Figure 10.4   Tripole graph of burins, endscrapers, and borers/backed knives at Levantine Mousterian sites for Late Levantine Mousterian, temporally early Early Levantine Mousterian, and temporally late Early Levantine Mousterian. The site numbers are as follows: Ein Difla (1); Boker Tachtit, Level 1 (2) and Level 2 (3); Tor Faraj A (4); Rosh Ein Mor, Level 4 (5), Level 5 (6), Level 7 (7), Level 8 (8), and Level 9 (9); Nahal Aqev e-g (10) and a-d (11); Tabun, Unit IX (12); Kebara Levels II-IV (13), V-VI (14), and VII-VIII (15), Bezez B (20); Ksar Akil XXVIII A/B (23), XXVII A/B (24), XXVI A/B (25); Shubbabiq (26).

there is enough ambiguity that the model cannot be rejected outright for the Levant. Perhaps the patterns Dibble and Rolland see in Europe require either a certain level of occupational intensity or marked intra-regional variability in raw material resources to become clear. Among many Levantine sites the immediate abundance of raw material may not be exerting sufficient constraints to give rise to the typological variability observed in Europe.

Based on the proportional occurrences of the three major tool groups (Mousterian, Upper Paleolithic, and Denticulate), there is a clustering that maintains, and therefore reinforces, the dichotomy achieved through technological criteria, with only three out of 26 cases being obvious exceptions (Kebara VII-VIII, Tabun, Unit IX, and Bezez B), with one additional anomalous case (Shubbabiq). For the first three, it is significant that they also exhibit aberrant patterns in terms of the Upper Paleolithic tools alone. In two of these three cases, other data can be brought to bear. The assemblages from Kebara VII-VIII are technologically similar to those of its upper levels, all of which are classified as Late Levantine Mousterian. However, this assemblage exhibits another peculiarity, namely a tendency toward inverse retouch (Boutié 1981:189) which in Jordan, at least, is associated with the temporally late Early Levantine Mousterian (Henry 1986:15). If inverse retouch is a temporal marker, its presence in Kebara VII-VIII might suggest a connection between it and the Early Levantine Mousterian. On the other hand, the percentages of points in the Levallois group (Bordes types 1-4) for those levels (15.7% and 19%, respectively) are within the range for the upper Kebara levels (10.4% to 19.3%), and they fall well below the percentage occurrences at confirmed Early Levantine Mousterian assemblages (e.g., Rosh Ein Mor: 26.0%-33.3%; Nahal Aqev: 43.4%-49.7%; Ksar Akil XXVIII A/B: 42.7%). Thus, while the Kebara VII-VIII sample may be aberrant in terms of the relative proportions of the major tool groups and in the importance of inverse retouch, it is technologically consistent with the Late Levantine Mousterian.

The sample from Tabun, Unit IX comes from an unusual situation where occupation was, at best, highly ephemeral; and where finished tools were carried into the cave and there was little or no on-site production. Given the extensive technological studies of this assemblage (Jelinek 1975, 1981b, 1982) there is no question but that it is technologically Early Levantine Mousterian. The paucity of blanks, however, may

have resulted in more intensive resharpening of flakes than was usual during the Early Levantine Mousterian, providing a pattern of sidescraper dominance unusual in the Early Levantine Mousterian.

The aberrant pattern of Bezez B is not easily understood because it has not been subject to extensive technological studies. Typologically, it fits well with the Late Levantine Mousterian. It has been placed into the Early Levantine Mousterian based on a number of criteria, including Garrod's impression prior to the study of the material (Copeland 1983: 301); comparisons with Skinner's indices from Tabun (Copeland 1983:302-303), which were derived from a small selective sample; and more general impressions from looking at other materials, such as the selective collections from Abu Sif and Jerf Ajla (Copeland 1983:303-307). Given the high density of artifacts, however, the mode of artifact accumulation of Bezez B differed significantly from that at Tabun, Unit IX. Thus, if it is truly an Early Levantine Mousterian assemblage, it acquired a Late Levantine Mousterian typological "aspect" in some other way.[1]

When only the Upper Paleolithic tool group is considered, patterns are perhaps weaker but generally consistent with clustering based on the major typological groups and on technological criteria. As noted above, the assemblages that were aberrant for the major tool groups remain aberrant in relation to variability in the Upper Paleolithic group. Sample sizes are small, however, and the patterns can be taken only as minor reinforcement of the stronger patterns otherwise established.

In summary, it seems that the proportional occurrences of the major typological classes in Levantine Middle Paleolithic assemblages do pattern in ways that are parallel to those based upon technological criteria. Thus, the Early and Late Levantine Mousterian appear to be both technologically and typologically distinct, with the few exceptions noted. Moreover, each of these assemblage groups shows possible developmental vectors which proceed in different directions. For the Late Levantine Mousterian there are hints of an enhancement through time both of flake versus blade production and of Mousterian tools at the expense of Upper Paleolithic ones. For the Early Levantine Mousterian, on the other hand, the trend is the exact opposite—the loss of Mousterian retouched elements and the enhancement of elongated blank production. These different vectors of change raise serious questions as to the historic and cultural relationships between the two industries; certainly, Garrod's position that Tabun C and D were part of the same culture would no longer seem tenable. Now that there appears to be evidence for long and overlapping durations for both these industries, patterns of vectored change might be expected. While more dates certainly are needed, particularly for a range of Early Levantine Mousterian sites, it is already clear that this vectored change is yet another difference between the Middle Paleolithic of the Levant and that of western Europe.

NOTE

1. Recent examination of the Bezez B material by L. Meignen indicates that, even technologically, it is not Early Levantine Mousterian.

REFERENCES CITED

Akazawa, T.
1974   Paleolithic Assemblages from the Douara Cave Site. Pp. 1-167 in *The Palaeolithic Site at Doura Cave in Syria, Part II*, eds. H. Suzuki and F. Takai. Bulletin 6. Tokyo: University Museum, University of Tokyo.
1979   Middle Palaeolithic Assemblages from Douara Cave. Pp. 1-30 in *Paleolithic Site of Douara Cave and Paleogeography of Palmyra Basin in Syria, Part II*, eds. K. Hanihara and T. Akazawa. Bulletin 16. Tokyo: University Museum, University of Tokyo.

Arensburg, B.; Bar-Yosef, O.; Chech, M.; Goldberg, P.; Laville, H.; Meignen, L.; Rak, Y.; Tchernov, E.; Tillier, A. M.; and Vandermeersch, B.
1985   Une sépulture néandertalienne dans sa grotte de Kébara (Israël). *C. R. Scéances Acad. Sci.* (Paris ser. 2) 300:227-230.

Bar-Yosef, O.
1980   Prehistory of the Levant. *ARA* 9:101-133.

Bar-Yosef, O., and Goldberg, P.
1988   An Outline of the Chronology of the Middle Palaeolithic in the Levant. Pp. 13-21 in *L'homme de Néandertal*, ed. M. Otte. Vol. 2: *L'environnement*, ed. H. Laville. Liège: Université de Liège.

Bar-Yosef, O.; Vandermeersch, B.; Arensburg, B.; Goldberg, P.; Laville, H.; Meignen, L.; Rak, Y.; Tchernov, E.; and Tillier, A. M.
1986   New Data on the Origin of Modern Man in the Levant. *CA* 27:63-65.

Binford, L. R.
1973   Interassemblage Variability—The Mousterian and the Functional Argument. Pp. 227-254 in *The Explanation of Culture Change*, ed. C. Renfrew. London: Duckworth.

Binford, L. R., and Binford, S. R.
1966   A Preliminary Analysis of Functional Variability in the Mousterian of Levallois Facies. *AA* 68:238-295.

Boëda, E.
1988   Le concept levallois et valuation de son champ d'application. Pp. 13-26 in *L'homme de Néandertal*, ed. M. Otte. Vol. 4: *La technique*, eds. L. Binford and J.-P. Rigaud. ERAUL 31. Liège: Université de Liège.

Bordes, F.
1950   Principes d'une méthode d'étude des techniques de débitage et de la typologie du Paléolithique ancien et moyen. *L'Anthropologie* 54:19-34.
1955   Le Paléolithique inférieur et moyen de Jabrud (Syrie) et la question du pré-Aurignacien. *L'Anthropologie* 59:486-507.
1961   *Typologie du Paléolithique ancien et moyen*. 2 vols. MIPUB 1. Bordeaux: Delmas.
1973   On the Chronology and Contemporaneity of Different Paleolithic Cultures in France. Pp. 217-226 in *The Explanation of Culture Change*, ed. C. Renfrew. London: Duckworth.
1980   Le débitage levallois et ses variantes. *BSPF* 77:45-49.

Boutié, P.
1981   *L'industrie moustérienne de la grotte de kabara, Mount Carmel, Israël*. Museum National d'Histoire Naturelle, Musée de l'Homme Memoire 10. Paris: CNRS.

Caton-Thompson, G., and Gardner, E.
1932   The Prehistoric Geography of Kharga Oasis. *The Geographical Journal* 80:396-409.

Copeland, L.
1975   Middle and Upper Paleolithic of Lebanon and Syria in Light of Recent Research. Pp. 317-350 in *Problems in Prehistory: North Africa and the Levant*, eds. F. Wendorf and A. E. Marks. Dallas: Southern Methodist University Press.
1983   The Paleolithic Industries at Adlun. Pp. 89-366 in *Adlun in the Stone Age*, ed. D. Roe. BAR International Series 159. Oxford: BAR.

Copeland, L., and Hours, F.
1981   La fin de l'Acheuléen et l'avènement du Paléolithque moyen en Syrie. Pp. 225-238 in *Préhistoire du Levant*, eds. J. Cauvin and P. Sanlaville. Paris: CNRS.

Crew, H. L.
1975   An Evaluation of the Relationship between Mousterian Complexes of Eastern Mediterranean. Pp. 427-438 in *Problems in Prehistory: North Africa and the Levant*, eds. F. Wendorf and A. E. Marks. Dallas: Southern Methodist University Press.
1976   The Mousterian Site of Rosh Ein Mor. Pp. 75-112 in *Prehistory and Paleoenvironments in the Central Negev, Israel*, Vol. 1, ed. A. E. Marks. Dallas: Southern Methodist University Press.

Dibble, H.
1984   Interpreting Typological Variation of Middle Paleolithic Scrapers: Function, Style, or Sequence of Reduction? *JFA* 11:431-436.
1987   The Interpretation of Middle Paleolithic Scraper Morphology. *AmAnt* 52:109-117.
1988   Typological Aspects of Reduction and Intensity of Utilization of Lithic Resources in the French Mousterian. Pp. 181-197 in *Upper Pleistocene Prehistory of Western Eurasia*, eds. H. Dibble and A. Montet-White. Philadelphia: University Museum, University of Pennsylvania.
1989   The Implications of Stone Tool Types for the Presence of Language during the Middle Paleolithic. Pp. 415-432 in *The Human Revolution: Behavioural and Biological Perspectives on the Origins of Modern Humans*, eds. P. Mellars and C. Stringer. Edinburgh: Edinburgh University Press.

Ewing, S. J.
1947   Preliminary Note on the Excavations at the Paleolithic Site of Ksâr 'Akil, Republic of Lebanon. *Antiquity* 21:186-196.

Garrod, D.
1928   Excavation of a Palaeolithic Cave in Western Judea. *Palestine Exploration Fund*, Quarterly Statement 60:182-185.
1957   Notes sur le Paléolithic supérior du Moyen Orient. *BSPF* 54:439-446.

Garrod, D., and Bate, D. M. A.
1937   *The Stone Age of Mount Carmel*, Vol. I. Oxford: Clarendon Press.

Gilead, I., and Grigson, C.
1984   Far'ah II. A Middle Palaeolithic Open-Air Site in the Northern Negev, Israel. *PPS* 50:71-97.

Haller, J.
1946   Notes de préhistoire Phénicienne. *L'Abri de Abou-Halka (Tripoli). Bulletin Museum, Beyrouth* 6:1-19.

Henry, D.
1986   The Prehistory and Paleoenvironments of Jordan: An Overview. *Paléorient* 12(2):5-26.
1988   Summary of Prehistoric and Paleoenvironmental Research in the Northern Hisma. Pp. 7-37 in *The Prehistory of Jordan: The State of Research in 1986*, eds. A. Garrad and H. Gebel. BAR International Series 396(i). Oxford: BAR.

Henry, D., and Servello, F.
1974   Compendium of C-14 Determinations Derived from Near Eastern Prehistoric Sites. *Paléorient* 2:19-44.

Hours, F.; Copeland, L.; and Aurenche, O.
1973   Les industries paléolithiques du Proche-Orient, essai de correlation. *L'Anthropologie* 77:229-280, 437-496.

Jelinek, A.
1975   A Preliminary Report on Some Lower and Middle Paleolithic Industries from the Tabun Cave, Mount Carmel (Israel). Pp. 297-316 in *Problems in Prehistory: North Africa and the Levant*, eds. F. Wendorf and A. E. Marks. Dallas: Southern Methodist University Press.
1981a   The Middle Paleolithic of the Levant: Synthesis. Pp. 299-302 in *Préhistoire du Levant*, eds. J. Cauvin and P. Sanlaville. Paris: CNRS.
1981b   The Middle Paleolithic in the Southern Levant from the Perspective of the Tabun Cave. Pp. 265-280 in *Préhistoire du Levant*, eds. J. Cauvin and P. Sanlaville. Paris: CNRS.
1982   Tabun Cave and Paleolithic Man in the Levant. *Science* 216:1369-1375.

Jelinek, A.; Farrand, W.; Haas, G.; Horowitz, A.; and Goldberg, P.
1973   Excavations at the Tabun Cave, Mount Carmel, Israel, 1967-1972: A Preliminary Report. *Paléorient* 1(2):151-182.

Lindly, J., and Clark, G.
1987   A Preliminary Lithic Analysis of the Mousterian Site of 'Ain Difla (WHS Site 634) in the Wadi Ali, West-Central Jordan. *PPS* 53:279-292.

Marks, A. E.
1981   The Middle Paleolithic of the Negev. Pp. 278-298 in *Préhistoire du Levant*, eds. J. Cauvin and P. Sanlaville. Paris: CNRS.
1988   The Middle to Upper Paleolithic Transition in the Southern Levant: Technological Change as an Adaptation to Increasing Mobility. Pp. 109-123 in *L'homme de Néandertal*, ed. M. Otte. Vol. 8: *La mutation*, ed. J. Kozlowski. Liège: Université de Liège.
1990   The Middle and Upper Paleolithic of the Near East and the Nile Valley: The Problem of Cultural Transformations. Pp. 56-80 in *The Emergence of Modern Humans: An Archaeological Perspective*, ed. P. Mellars. Edinburgh: Edinburgh University Press.

Marks, A. E., and Freidel, D.
1977   Prehistoric Settlement Patterns in Avdat/Aqev. Pp. 131-158 in *Prehistory and Paleoenvironments in the Central Negev, Israel*, Vol. 2, ed. A. E. Marks. Dallas: Department of Anthropology, Southern Methodist University.

Marks, A. E., and Volkman, P.
1983   Changing Core Reduction Strategies: A Technological Shift from the Middle to the Upper Paleolithic in the Southern Levant. Pp. 13-34 in *The Mousterian Legacy: Human Biocultural Change in the Upper Pleistocene*, ed. E. Trinkaus. BAR International Series 164. Oxford: BAR.
1986   The Mousterian of Ksar Akil: Levels XXXVIA through XXVIIIB. *Paléorient* 12:5-20.

Meignen, L, and Bar-Yosef, O.
1988   Variabilité technologique au Proche-Orient: L'example de Kébara. Pp. 81-96 in *L'homme de Néandertal*, ed. M. Otte. Vol. 4: *La technique*, eds. L. Binford and J.-P. Rigaud. Liège: Université de Liège.

Munday, F.
1976   Intersite Variability in the Mousterian Occupation of the Avdat/Aqev Area. Pp. 113-140 in *Prehistory and Paleoenvironments in the Central Negev, Israel*, Vol. 1, ed. A. E. Marks. Dallas: Southern Methodist University Press.
1977   Nahal Aqev (D35): A Stratified, Open Air Mousterian Occupation in the Avdat/Aqev Area. Pp. 36-60 in *Prehistory and Paleoenvironments in the Central Negev, Israel*, Vol. 2, ed. A. E. Marks. Dallas: Department of Anthropology, Southern Methodist University.
1979   Levantine Technological Variability: A Perspective from the Negev. *Paléorient* 5:87-104.

Neuville, R.
1934   Le préhistorique de Palestine. *Revue Biblique* 443:237-259.
1951   Le Paleolithique et le Mesolithique du Desert de Judee. AIPH Mémoire 24.

Perrot, J.
1968   *La Préhistoire palestinienne. Supplement au Dictionnaire de la Bible VIII* 43:286-446.

Roe, D., ed.
1983 *Adlun in the Stone Age*. BAR International Series 159. Oxford: BAR.

Rolland, N.
1981 The Interpretation of Middle Paleolithic Variability. *Man* 16:15-42

Ronen, A.
1974 *Tirat-Carmel: A Mousterian Open-Air Site in Israel*. Publication 3. Tel Aviv: Institute of Archaeology, Tel Aviv University.
1984 *Sefunim Prehistoric Sites Mount Carmel, Israel*. BAR International Series 230(i and ii). Oxford: BAR.

Schwarcz, H.; Blackwell, P.; Goldberg, P.; and Marks, A.
1979 Uranium Series Dating of Travertine from Archaeological Sites, Nahal Zin, Israel. *Nature* 277:558-560.

Skinner, J.
1965 The Flake Industries of Southwest Asia: A Typological Study. Ph.D. dissertation, Columbia University. Ann Arbor: University Microfilms.

Stringer, C.; Grün, R.; Schwarcz, H.; and Goldberg, P.
1989 ESR Dates for the Hominid Burial Site of Es Skhul in Israel. *Nature* 338:756-758.

Valladas, H.; Joron, J; Valladas, G.; Arensburg, B.; Bar-Yosef, O.; Belfer-Cohen, A.; Goldberg, P.; Laville, H.; Meignen, L.; Rak, Y.; Tchernov, E.; Tillier, A.; and Vandermeersch, B.
1981 *Les hommes fossiles de Qafzeh (Israël)*. Paris: CNRS.
1987 TL Dates for the Neanderthal Burial Site at Kebara in Israel. *Nature* 330:159-160.

Weachter, J.
1952 The Excavation of Jabrud and its Relation to the Prehistory of Palestine and Syria. *Annual Report, Institute of Archaeology, University of London* 8:10-28.

Wrescher, E.
1967 The Geula Caves—Mount Carmel. *Quaternaria* 9:69-89.

XI

Transhumance During the Late Levantine Mousterian

Donald O. Henry

INTRODUCTION

After several decades of focusing on questions related to the origins of culture, Paleolithic archaeologists increasingly have become interested in defining the transition from the "protocultural" to the "cultural" behaviors that we associate with contemporary societies. In questioning the antiquity of our humanness, Lewis Binford (1985, 1987) has led the way in pointing to the late Pleistocene and specifically the appearance of fully modern *Homo sapiens sapiens* as marking the beginning of culture as we know it. Other scholars have similarly observed that the late Pleistocene was the time when hominids emerged into a "fully human ecological niche" (Sackett 1988:41) and have thus targeted the biological and macro-cultural transitions (i.e., Middle to Upper Paleolithic) that fall within this temporal sweep for detailed inquiry (Jelinek 1977, 1982a, 1988; Mellars 1973, 1989; Chase and Dibble 1987; White 1982; Marks 1988, 1989; Clark and Lindly 1989).

If answers to these questions were not difficult enough, in the Near East they are made even more problematic by the biological and cultural ambiguities in the archaeological record. Not only do we find the remains of *Homo sapiens sapiens* and *Homo sapiens neanderthalensis* within Middle Paleolithic horizons, but they are even associated with the same specific industry level taxa; e.g., Levantine Mousterian B and C types (Bar-Yosef and Meignen 1989). To further complicate the questions, the macro-cultural transition from the Middle Paleolithic to the Upper Paleolithic is weakly demarcated in the Levant (Marks 1988). Both typological (e.g., burins) and technological (blade production) elements normally taken as markers of the Upper Paleolithic occur consistently within Levantine Mousterian assemblages. Thus in the Levant, both biological and archaeological successions appear to be earlier than those of Europe. And if this is indeed the case, should we also expect the evolution of human adaptive strategies to have followed a similar pace?

MEASURES OF HUMANNESS

The archaeological expressions of anticipation and planning depth have been underscored by Binford (1979, 1985, 1987) as the principal means by which modern adaptive strategies might be detected in the prehistoric record. At an analytical level, archaeologists working on Middle Paleolithic materials have attempted to measure anticipation and planning depth through examination of: (a) procurement and transport of raw materials (Geneste 1988; Meignen 1988; Roebroeks et al. 1988); (b) curation strategies (Marks 1988); (c) lithic reduction streams (Munday 1976, 1979); (d) edge wear (Shea 1989); (e) intrasite artifact distributions (Heitala and Marks 1981); and (f) intersite patterns (Marks and Freidel 1977; Henry 1988; Marks 1989; Clark and Lindly 1989). Few settings or research programs have allowed for using these measures in combination, however.

THE ARCHAEOLOGICAL AND ENVIRONMENTAL BACKGROUND

The sheltered sites of Tor Sabiha and Tor Faraj (Henry 1982, 1988), situated on the southern flanks of the Jordanian Plateau, form the basis of the study (Fig. 11.1). Although both of the sites are positioned at high elevations and separated by only 17 km, their local settings and an elevational difference of 300 m

(Tor Sabiha at 1300 masl and Tor Faraj at 1000 masl) provide for some significant environmental contrasts. These contrasts are thought to have induced differences in the occupations of the two sites that were related both to the seasons in which they were used and the activities carried out by their inhabitants.

The region exhibits three distinct elevationally governed environmental zones (Al-Eisawi 1985): Mediterranean woodlands (1400–1700 masl), Asiatic steppe (1000–1400 masl), and African desert (below 1000 masl; Fig. 11.2). Tor Sabiha rests near the boundary dividing Mediterranean woodlands from

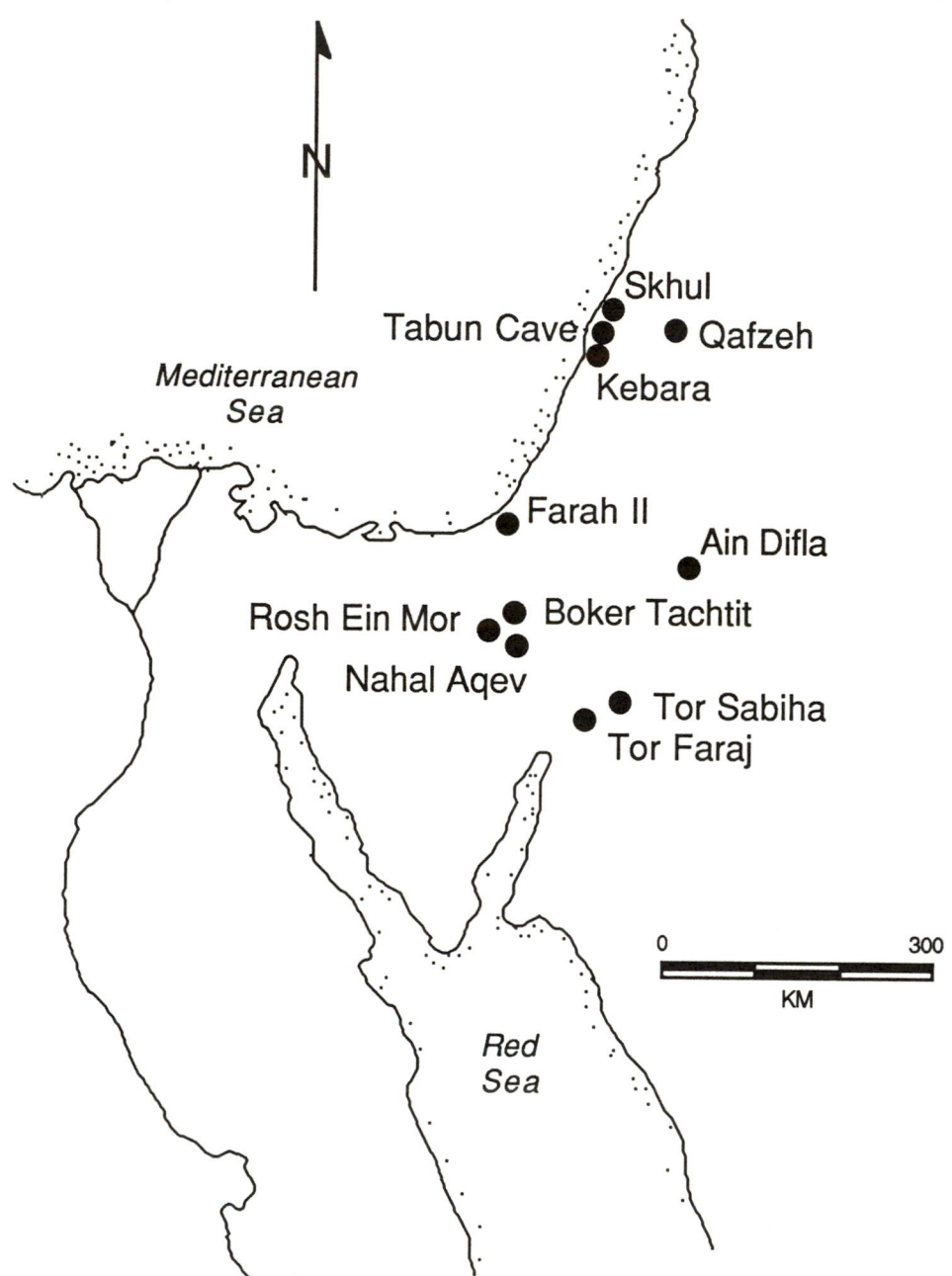

Figure 11.1   *Map of the southern Levant showing the locations of Levantine Mousterian sites mentioned in the text.*

steppe, while Tor Faraj is located at the lower edge of the steppe zone where it gives way to desert. In the main, this environmental zonation reflects the effects of elevation on temperature and precipitation patterns. The plateau and the higher elevations of its flanks experience much more precipitation (300–500 mm

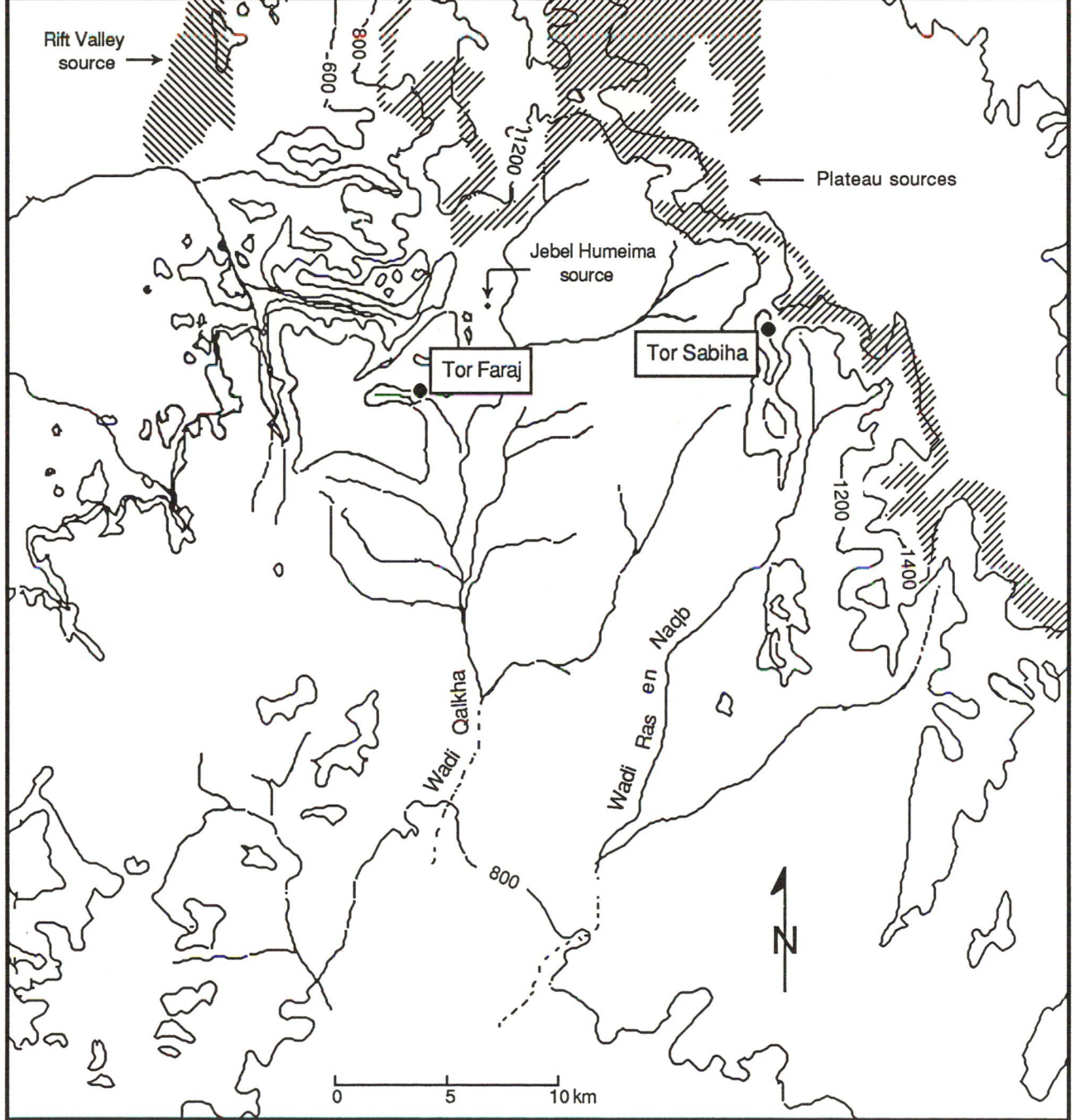

Figure 11.2   Map of the south Jordan study area showing the locations of Tor Faraj and Tor Sabiha relative to the local topography and chert sources (hatched).

annual average) and cooler temperatures than the adjacent steppe (100-200 mm annual average) and the desert lowlands (less than 100 mm annually).

Under modern conditions, the higher Tor Sabiha setting is uncomfortably cold during the winter (December through February) with nighttime temperatures averaging 0° C, whereas the lower setting of Tor Faraj rarely experiences frost. These differences in creature comfort, in fact, induce many villagers in the uplands to relocate to lower elevations over the winter months. It is also during the winter when almost 90% of the precipitation occurs, mainly confined to the uplands. The steppe and desert zones also receive their water at this time, but it is principally in the form of run-off. Although there were fluctuations in absolute temperature and precipitation levels during last glacial times, marked seasonality in rainfall seems to have been a characteristic of the climate, then as now.

Tor Sabiha, consisting of a small shallow cave and adjacent terrace, is set within a deep embayment high on the western wall of the Judayid Basin. Artifacts recovered from a thin (10-15 cm thick), shallowly buried (30-90 cm) horizon (Layer C) define a small occupation stretching over some 100-150 m^2. Its setting and eastern exposure limit sunlight to only the late morning. The paucity of sunlight coupled with the high elevation of the site suggests that it was unlikely to have been occupied during the cold season. However, no direct seasonal information could be obtained from the remains of gazelle and *Bos* and ostrich eggshell fragments. But regardless of the season of occupation, the small size of the site coupled with its thin cultural deposit and low artifact density indicate that it was used for relatively transitory camps by small groups who only rarely revisited the location (Table 11.1).

Tor Faraj consists of a large rockshelter and associated terrace situated on the wall of a deeply incised canyon that contains a major tributary—the Wadi Aghir. Its southern exposure provides for sunlight on the terrace and much of the shelter throughout the day. Given its lower elevation, its protection from the prevailing winter winds from the northwest, and its exposure to sunlight, the site would have provided an ideal winter camp. Tor Faraj displays a significantly larger and thicker cultural deposit than its upland counterpart in conjunction with richer artifact and tool densities. Artifacts were recovered from stratified horizons defined by hearths and ash lenses within a 140-cm-deep sounding of a plus 2.5-m-thick cultural deposit. The hearths and ash lenses, common within the Tor Faraj deposit, were not found at Tor Sabiha. Beyond suggesting winter occupations, these data point to more frequent, longer encampments—perhaps by larger groups—at Tor Faraj than at Tor Sabiha.

EVIDENCE OF CONTEMPORANEITY

If the behavioral residue recovered from the two sites resulted from occupations that formed segments of a common settlement-procurement system, then the associated chronological evidence should indicate contemporaneity—at least at an archaeological scale. And in fact, artifactual, paleoenvironmental, and chronometric data drawn from the two sites are consistent in pointing to their having been occupied synchronously.

TABLE 11.1

COMPARISON OF SEVERAL NATURAL AND ARTIFACTUAL CHARACTERISTICS
OF THE TOR FARAJ AND TOR SABIHA ROCKSHELTERS.

	Tor Faraj (J430)	Tor Sabiha (J8)
Elevation (masl)	1000	1300
Exposure	South	East
Area (m^2)	200-250	100-150
Thickness of cultural deposit (cm)	+250	15-20
All artifacts	114-118/.1m^3	85/.1m^3
Tools	10.1/.1m^3	4.5/.1m^3
Hearths	present	absent

INDUSTRIAL AFFILIATION

The techno-typological characteristics of the assemblages from the two sites place them within the same industrial level taxon—Levantine Mousterian D type. Elongated Levallois points and relatively high blade indices characterize the assemblages of the industry. Given the traditional three-phase sequence based upon stratigraphic successions recognized from sites in the Mediterranean zone, such as at Tabun Cave (Jelinek 1981) and others in Lebanon (Copeland 1981), an "early" or "Phase 1" position within the Levantine Mousterian is suggested. But, as will be discussed later, recent radiometric dates from the sites of Qafzeh and Skhul challenge this traditionally held succession. And perhaps more relevant to the temporal placement of the south Jordan sites, evidence recovered from sites in the arid zone indicates a persistence of the D type industry from early last Glacial times (ca. 90,000 B.P.) until it was replaced by Upper Paleolithic industries some 45-50,000 years ago (Marks 1989; Henry 1982). The highland Negev sites of Nahal Aqev (early) and Boker Tachtit (transitional) bracket the D type industry within the arid zone to between 85,200 ± 10,000 B.P. and 45,300 ± 9050 B.P. (Schwartz et al. 1979; Marks 1983). The apparent absence of C and B type (phases 2 and 3) industries within the arid zone, coupled with the persistence of D type assemblages into Middle/Upper Paleolithic transitional times, suggests dichotomous regional developments were present within the Levantine Mousterian and that these were broken along environmental lines.

ANALYSIS OF AMINO ACID RACEMIZATION

Ostrich eggshell samples from Tor Faraj and Tor Sabiha were submitted to Gifford Miller, Institute for Arctic and Alpine Research, for analysis of their amino acid racemization. The samples included five specimens from Layer C (80-90 cm level) of Tor Faraj and five specimens from Layer C (95-100, 105-110 cm levels) of Tor Sabiha. One of the Tor Sabiha specimens was found to have very low levels of amino acids, probably as a result of having been burnt, and was deleted from analysis.

The analysis yielded mean D/L ratios of .496 ± .014 for the Tor Faraj sample and .345 ± .031 for the Tor Sabiha sample. A comparison of the D/L ratios of the samples from the two sites requires some thermal modeling given their differences in elevation, the influence of elevation on temperature, and the effect of temperature on rates of racemization. Based upon the universal lapse rate of 0.6° C per 100 m, Tor Sabiha is about 2° C cooler on the average than Tor Faraj. The Tor Sabiha sample thus would have experienced a slower rate of racemization than the sample from Tor Faraj. Based upon kinetic equations for ostrich eggshell and a 2-2.5° C temperature offset, Miller (pers. comm. 1989) reports that the two sites are of the same age; i.e., D/L ratios of 0.50 and 0.35 are equivalent if the lower ratio is associated with a 2-2.5° C cooler temperature.

In order to convert the D/L ratios of the samples to absolute ages their thermal histories must be determined by estimating the glacial age temperature reduction. If the integrated thermal histories are assumed to be 4° C lower than present, Miller (pers. comm. 1989) calculates the ages of both sites to be ca. 65,000 B.P.; but he cautions that the ages are highly dependent upon how their thermal histories are modeled. Ground temperature measurements at both sites coupled with comparisons to D/L ratios that have been calibrated to other radiometric dates need to be undertaken.

ATTRIBUTE STUDIES

In an effort to redefine the chronologic positioning of Levantine Mousterian assemblages within this long 40-50,000 year temporal sweep several attribute studies have been employed.

JELINEK'S METRIC STUDIES

In his research at Tabun Cave, Jelinek (1982b) observed stratigraphic trends in two data sets: the width/thickness ratios of complete flakes and the length/width ratios of Levallois points. He observed that flakes became progressively thinner with respect to their width through time and that this was paralleled by gradual increments in the variances of the samples. He also noted a time-trend in the progressive fattening of Levallois points as reflected in the stratigraphic trends of their length/width ratios. The application of Jelinek's seriation scheme to other Levantine Mousterian assemblages in the Levant has been criticized on the basis of conflicting radiometric dates, stratigraphic sequences (Bar-Yosef and Meignen 1989), and ambiguities in attribute patterns (Gilead and Grigson 1984; Clark and Lindly 1989).

When the variances of the width/thickness ratios of flakes from Levantine Mousterian assemblages are plotted against reported radiometric dates, only the Boker Tachtit (Marks 1983) and Skhul (AAR) (Masters 1982) dates fit the curve developed from the Tabun data (Fig. 11.3). Beyond the conflicting dates developed from different techniques for Skhul and Qafzeh, dates from Nahal Aqev, Tor Sabiha, Tor Faraj, and Kebara (Valladas et al. 1987) parallel the Tabun curve, but they show higher variances than recorded at Tabun. And the recent controversial TL (Valladas et al. 1988) and ESR (Schwarcz et al. 1988; Stringer et al. 1989) dates from Qafzeh and Skhul contrast sharply with the ages predicted by the seriation curve, as does the U-series date for Skhul (Schwarcz 1980).

If only D type assemblages from the arid zone are considered, however, a strong linear correlation (r = –.998) emerges between the variances of length/width

ratios and the ages of the assemblages (Fig. 11.3). Such a clear time-trend is consistent with the proposed persistence and continuity of the D type industry in the arid zone. The technological breaks associated with the industrial partitions (e.g., D, C, and B types) seen within the assemblages of the Mediterranean zone perhaps act to mask such a trend.

In turning to the other time-trend noted at Tabun, that of the progressive widening of Levallois points, significant correlations between point dimensions and their ages are not indicated for Levantine Mousterian assemblages as a whole or for D type assemblages restricted to the arid zone. This is true regardless of whether the controversial TL and ESR dates for Skhul

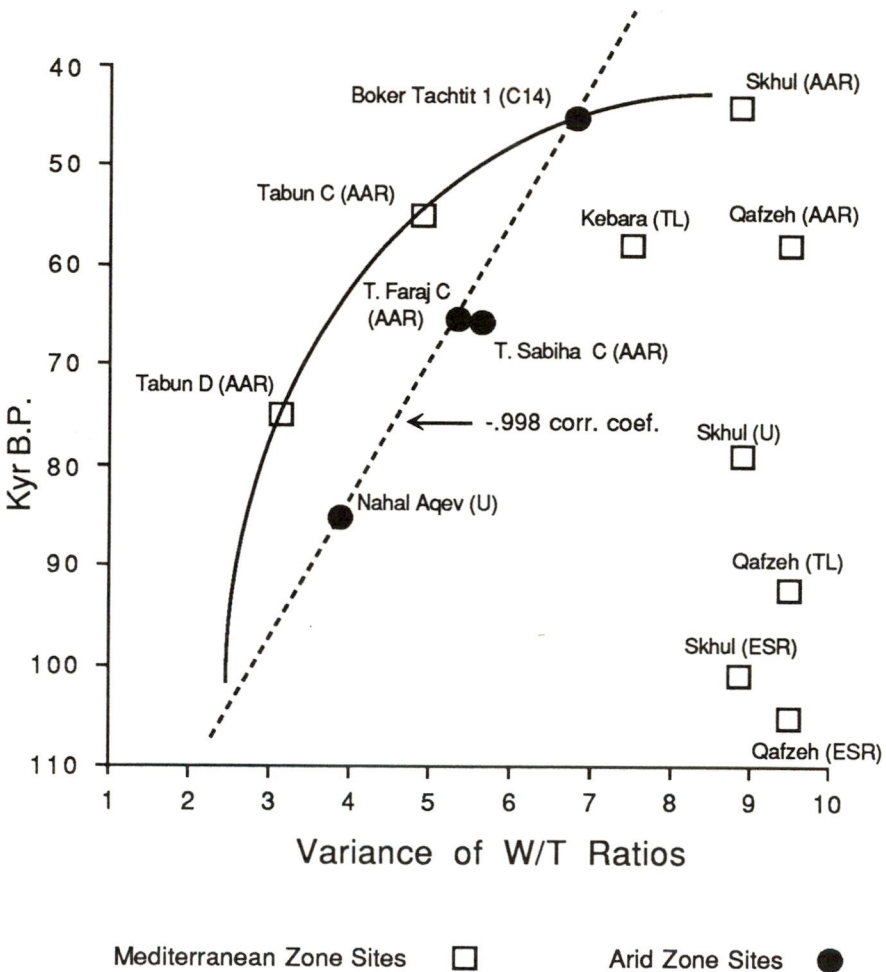

Figure 11.3   The variance of width/thickness ratios of complete flakes for Levantine Mousterian assemblages plotted against radiometric dates. C14 = radiocarbon, AAR = amino acid racemization, TL = thermoluminescence, ESR = electron spin resonance, U = uranium series.

and Qafzeh are used in the plot or whether the AAR dates from these sites are employed. The failure of point dimensions to show widespread time-trends within the Levantine Mousterian may be linked to differences between sites in respect to their proximity to sources of large flint nodules (Jelinek, pers. comm. in Lindly and Clark 1987).

MARKS' SCAR PATTERN ANALYSIS

In discussion of temporally related attributes within the Levantine Mousterian of the highland Negev, Marks (1983) noted a major change in Levallois point preparation between the "early" assemblage of Rosh Ein Mor and the "transitional" assemblage of Boker Tachtit, Level 1. The assemblage from Rosh Ein Mor shows little (2.7%) bidirectional preparation of points, whereas 95.2% of the points from Boker Tachtit, Level 1 were struck from opposed platform cores. Although specific data on scar patterns for points from the nearby dated site of Nahal Aqev are not available, Crew (1976), Munday (1977), and Marks (1989) have noted its techno-typological similarities to Rosh Ein Mor. Additionally, all of the points illustrated from Nahal Aqev (Munday 1977) show unidirectional preparation. A comparison of the patterns of point preparation seen at Tor Faraj and Tor Sabiha (ranging from 25-53%) with those of the Negev assemblages indicates an intermediate placement, a position consistent with the 65,000 B.P. AAR dates for the sites (Table 11.2). Lindly and Clark (1987)

report that 67.7% of the points from Ain Difla display bi-directional preparation.

INVERSE RETOUCH, A STYLISTIC ATTRIBUTE

Although the Tor Sabiha and Tor Faraj assemblages share a great number of techno-typological characteristics with other Levantine Mousterian D type assemblages, the south Jordan assemblages differ markedly from all other Levantine Mousterian assemblages relative to proportions of inverse retouch. The assemblages from Tor Sabiha and Tor Faraj display from 43-51% inverse retouch across various tool classes (e.g., points, scrapers, notches/denticulates, and retouched pieces; Fig. 11.4), whereas figures of 0-4% are reported for the rest of the Levantine Mousterian. Even assemblages recovered from sites only some 70-80 km away (central Negev and the Wadi Hasa) fail to show such high proportions of inverse retouch. In that this pattern is unique and spatially limited, it suggests that the occupants of the two sites shared an unusual and rather precise form of behavior. The behavior appears not to have been functionally driven, given that the inverse retouch is present on a wide range of tools—the same tools that are formed almost exclusively by obverse retouch in the rest of the Levantine Mousterian. In my mind, these data point to the occupants of the two sites as having been contemporary in the sense that they were members of a system of social interaction at relatively refined spatial and temporal scales.

TABLE 11.2

COMPARISON OF THE TECHNO-TYPOLOGICAL ATTRIBUTES OF TOR FARAJ AND TOR SAHIBA WITH THOSE OF EARLY (ROSH EIN MOR) AND MP/UP TRANSITIONAL (BOKER TACHTIT, LEVEL 1) ASSEMBLAGES (MODIFIED AFTER HENRY 1985).

	Rosh Ein Mor	Tor Faraj A	Tor Faraj up C	Tor Faraj mid C	Tor Sahiba	Boker Tachtit
Percent of Levallois points within tool assemblage	38.4	40.9	57.5	65.8	39.3	46.6
Percent of Levallois flakes within debitage	52.2	8.6	4.1	4.3	1.2	0.0
Percent of Levallois points struck from opposed platform cores within Levallois points	2.7	25.5	53.6	25.0	46.0	95.2

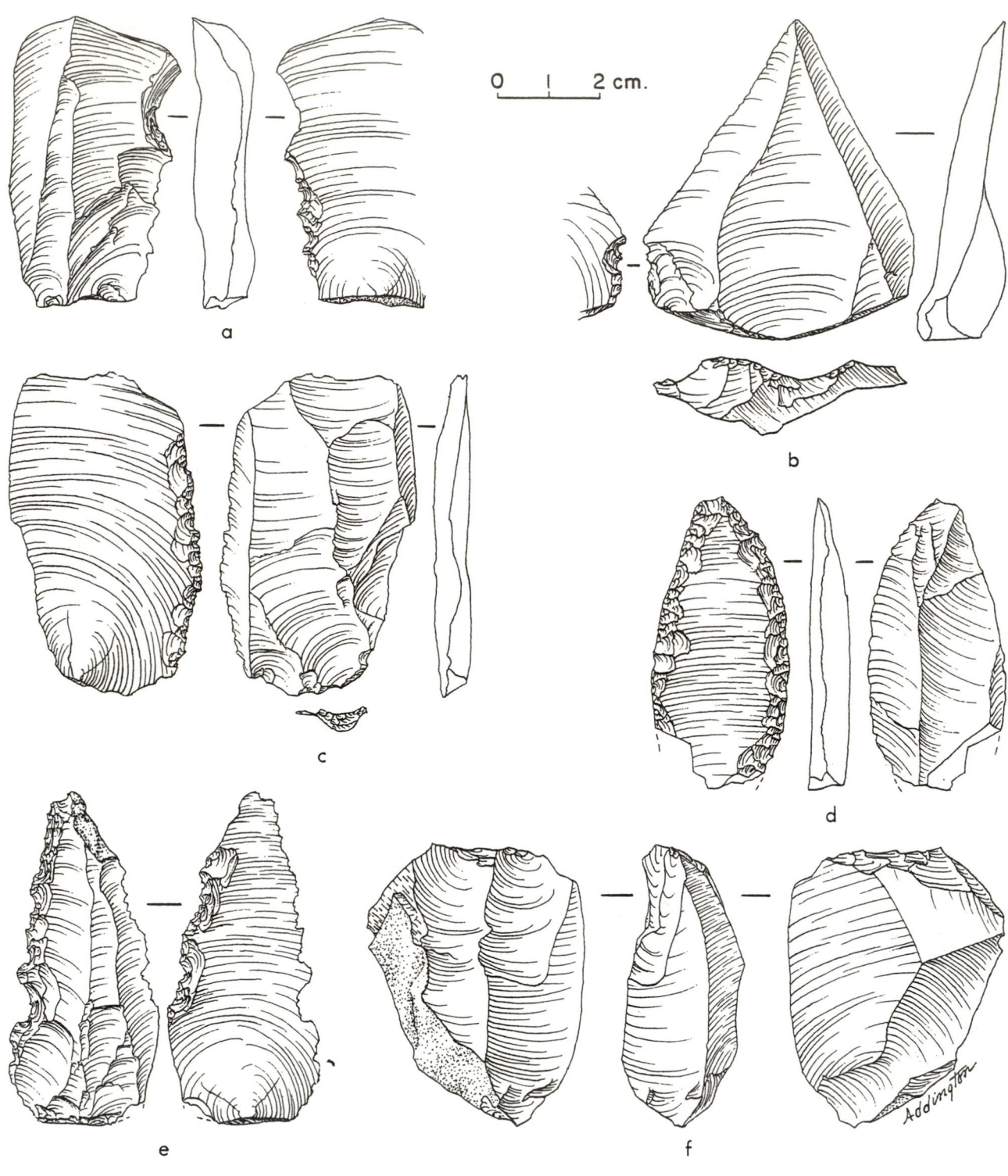

Figure 11.4   *Illustrations of artifacts from Layer C of Tor Sabiha. Note the inverse retouch on specimens a-e.*

PALEOENVIRONMENTAL EVIDENCE

There is general consensus that the early part of the Levantine Mousterian was associated with pluvial conditions, whereas the later part experienced drier and most likely colder conditions (Jelinek 1982b; Marks 1989; Bar-Yosef and Vandermeersch 1981; Henry 1986). Although the overall chronology of the period is poorly understood, the best estimates place the climatic reversal as having commenced about 70,000 B.P.

At Tor Sabiha, a deposit of weakly weathered sand containing the remains of gazelle and ostrich eggshell fragments suggests a dry setting. A study of the pollen from Layer C, only 15 cm thick, denotes a progressive decline in arboreal pollen (ca. 13 to 3%) accompanied by a decline in pollen from the warmth loving, halophytic shrubs, *Chenopodiaceae* type Noaea (Emery-Barbier 1988). These data suggest that Layer C was deposited under predominantly dry conditions during an interval of increasing aridity and progressively lower temperatures. Other than for the remains of gazelle and ostrich eggshell, paleoenvironmental data from Tor Faraj are unavailable. Although scanty, the environmental evidence we have for Tor Sabiha is consistent with the artifactual and radiometric data that point to a late Levantine Mousterian age of about 65,000 B.P.

RAW MATERIAL DISTRIBUTIONS, REDUCTION STREAMS, AND PLANNING DEPTH

In addition to representing two distinct segments of a Levantine Mousterian settlement cycle, the occupations at Tor Faraj and Tor Sabiha would have commanded catchments with quite different distributions of raw materials suitable for stone tool production (Fig. 11.2). While the catchment of Tor Faraj is virtually empty of chert (with sources for easily procured, high quality material situated some 16-20 km away), Tor Sabiha's catchment contains an abundance of high quality cherts that are within 2 km of the site.

The nature of the sites and their settings then seem to provide an ideal opportunity for investigating the strategies that their Levantine Mousterian occupants followed in the procurement of chert resources. The research at the two sites has centered on how different levels of mobility and availability of resources influenced decisions on procurement and conservation of cherts and their products. With this in mind, the operational components of the study included: (a) a classification of the chert varieties found within the assemblages and the identification of their sources within the study area; and (b) a tracking of the different raw material varieties within the reduction streams of the assemblages.

RAW MATERIAL STUDY

Within the study area in situ cherts are mainly confined to Late Cretaceous limestones and chalks that form the plateau and its flanks (Fig. 11.2). The foothills and lowlands fronting the plateau lack cherts as they are composed mainly of Lower Cretaceous, Cambrian, and Precambrian sandstones and granites. Derived or gravel chert sources are found in the wadi beds that drain the plateau, but large, knappable-sized cobbles are present only 2-3 km from their sources at the edge of the plateau. An exception to this general distribution was discovered on a small hill in the lowlands about 1 km northeast of Jebel Humeima. Here a good quality chert was found to occur in nodules within limestone parent rock. The fact that the nodules are relatively small and difficult to extract may account for why the source was not intensively exploited by the occupants of nearby Tor Faraj. In 1985 a field study was undertaken to understand the distribution of raw material sources within the area. The initial plan of the study called for spatially sampling specific Late Cretaceous stratigraphic units (i.e., Santonian-Turonian-Cenomanian; Senonian or Dan-Maestrian-Campanian) for cherts aided by geologic maps developed by Bender (1974) and others. These samples were then to be classified as to chert varieties and then ultimately compared to the varieties identified within the assemblages of Tor Faraj and Tor Sabiha. What this plan failed to take into account, however, was the abundance and great diversity of cherts exposed on the plateau. For example, along the escarpment near Ras en Naqb dozens of chert veins occur stratified within a 400-m thick section. They display marked variation across a range of attributes (e.g., color, pattern, inclusions, shape, luster) and occur in veins from a few centimeters to over a meter in thickness. Confronted with this overwhelming mass of information the plan of study was modified to first classifying the chert varieties contained within the archaeological assemblages and then searching for the sources of these varieties in the field.

CLASSIFICATION OF CHERTS

In an effort to standardize the classification and to define more objectively the variations in the cherts, an attribute study was conducted for each assemblage. The study focused on seven major attributes (Table 11.3) with four analysts crosschecking results until a high degree of standardization was achieved. Ultimately the study resulted in the identification of seven varieties and an additional category that included "all other varieties."

Chert varieties 1 through 6 were found to come from sources on the plateau, while varieties 7 and 8 were found in the lowlands near Jebel Humeima and the eastern edge of the Rift Valley, respectively (see Fig. 11.2 and Table 11.5). The great majority of the plateau cherts identified within the assemblages exhibited limestone or chalk cortex, in contrast to gravel cortex, thus indicating that in situ as opposed to derived sources provided the bulk of the material. Gravel cortex was not recorded on artifacts from the Jebel Humeima and Rift Valley sources.

REDUCTION STREAMS

Comparisons of the artifact assemblages recovered from the Tor Sabiha excavation and the Tor Faraj sounding reinforce the proposal that the sites experienced different kinds of occupations and activities. In the main, these data point to an emphasis upon tool manufacture and maintenance at Tor Sabiha. At Tor Faraj, on the other hand, a full range of lithic processing activities (involving core preparation, blank production, tool manufacture, and maintenance) was undertaken. This is expressed in the higher percentages of cores and primary elements (specimens with greater than 1/3 of their surface covered in cortex) within the Tor Faraj assemblages (Table 11.4). Tool:core and tool:primary element ratios also underscore the emphasis that was placed upon the initial phases of lithic reduction by the occupants of Tor Faraj.

What is so surprising about the intensity of the initial processing at Tor Faraj is that the great majority of raw material (i.e., 71-95%) was imported from the plateau and the Rift Valley sources some 16-20 km away (see Table 11.5). And the relative abundance of primary elements in the Tor Faraj assemblages indicates that the chert was introduced to the site having undergone little decortification. In contrast to this pat-

tern, the limited initial processing at Tor Sabiha is primarily (89%) linked to the cherts found within the site's catchment on the plateau some 1-2 km away.

The data from Tor Faraj and Tor Sabiha thus fail to fit our conventional wisdom regarding lithic procurement strategies. This is generally associated with a "gravity model" in which initial processing activities (e.g., decortification, core shaping) would be expected to decline with distance from the source of raw material. For example, Munday's (1976) study of Levantine Mousterian assemblages from the highland Negev defined the distance to raw material as the principal factor accounting for debitage size and core weight. The failure of the assemblages from Tor Faraj and Tor Sabiha to fit this model suggests that factors other than proximity to raw material may have influenced decisions related to procurement. One such factor may have been that of residential mobility. Johnson (1989) has recently provided an extensive discussion on the interplay of mobility and resource availability within biface technologies, and his observations seem equally pertinent to prepared core technologies.

Occupants of ephemeral encampments with catchments containing numerous chert sources are likely to have acquired most of their raw materials in an opportunistic manner as they went about other tasks. In such a setting most tools would have been expediently manufactured, used, and often abandoned away from camp. For those tasks that were undertaken in camp, tools, blanks, and mature cores that had been produced at or near raw material sources were probably imported and used. For such transitory encampments in close proximity to raw material sources, there would have been little incentive to import raw material in bulk. This essentially is what Binford (1980) has described as a "foraging" strategy.

Occupants of long-term camps distant from raw material sources are likely to have adopted a procurement strategy in which materials were imported in bulk. These bulk imports may have taken the form of only slightly modified raw material, cores, or even blanks. The specific form of import would have depended on a group balancing its anticipated tool needs with the breadth of tool options allowed for at certain points (e.g., raw material, core, blank) in a reduction stream (Henry 1989). This approach in acquiring materials is what Binford (1980) has termed a "logistical" strategy. Linking the occupation of Tor Sabiha with an opportunistic foraging strategy and the occupations of Tor Faraj with a logistical procurement strategy is not based solely upon the relative abun-

TABLE 11.3

LIST OF ATTRIBUTES USED FOR THE ANALYSIS OF CHERT VARIETIES.

I.   COLOR/PATTERN/INCLUSIONS
     (Example) Reddish brown/Uniform/Pepper-size white specks

          Color: From Munsell chart
          Pattern: Uniform, banded, wavy, swirl, mottled, etc.
          Inclusions: Fossils, others, shape, size

II. CORTEX
     (Example) Limestone with well-defined boundary

          Options: Limestone or gravel with well-defined or diffuse boundary

III. PATINA
     (Example) Weakly patinated light gray (color from Munsell chart)

          Degree of patination:
               Weak (1-33% of surface)
               Moderate (34-66% of surface)
               Heavy (67-100% of surface)

IV. SHAPE AND SIZE OF RAW MATERIAL
     (Example) Nodular (50-70mm L by 20-30mm Th)

          Shape:
               Bedded/Vein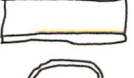

               Nodular

               Plate

               Stream Cobble/Gravel

               Other

V.   LUSTER
     (Example) Low luster

          Degree of luster: Non-lustrous, low luster, high luster

VI. GRAIN SIZE
     (Example) Coarse grained

          Options: Fine grained, coarse grained

VII. DEGREE OF TRANSLUCENCE
     (Example) Low

          Assessed by checking 1-2mm edge against a 100-watt bulb
          Options: Opaque (non-translucent), low (slightly translucent), high (fully translucent)

TABLE 11.4

THE DISTRIBUTION OF TOOLS AND DEBITAGE AT TOR FARAJ (J430) AND TOR SAHIBA (J8).

	A	Tor Faraj up C	mid C	Tor Sahiba C
CLASS				
Tool				
Levallois points, retouched	11.8	16.6	7.3	17.8
Levallois points, unretouched	29.1	40.9	58.5	21.5
Side scrapers	3.1	0.0	0.0	3.7
End scrapers	2.4	1.5	0.0	0.9
Burins	16.5	7.5	0.0	1.9
Perforators	1.6	0.0	0.0	0.9
Backed pieces	0.8	1.5	0.0	1.9
Truncations	1.6	0.0	0.0	3.7
Notches	3.9	4.5	7.3	5.6
Denticulates	0.8	0.0	2.4	7.5
Retouched pieces	28.4	27.3	24.4	34.6
		99.8	99.9	
	N = 127	N = 66	N = 41	N = 107
Debitage				
Cores	5.8	0.7	1.0	0.6
Blades	16.2	9.7	5.2	32.7
Flakes	40.4	57.1	54.6	55.4
Levallois blades	3.0	6.3	3.6	1.6
Levallois flakes	8.6	4.1	4.3	0.7
Core trim elements	5.3	–	–	1.0
Primary elements	20.5	19.9	29.9	8.0
		2.1	1.3	
		99.9	99.9	
	N = 396	N = 413	N = 304	N = 689
Ratios				
Tool:Core	5.5	22.0	13.7	26.7
Tool:Primary element	1.6	0.8	0.5	1.9

dances of primary elements, cores, and tools within the assemblages. In comparing the chert varieties identified for primary elements within the assemblages of the two sites, there is less diversity in the Tor Faraj assemblages (Table 11.5). At Tor Faraj, from 88-94% of the chert within an assemblage is accounted for by only four varieties. It is important to note, however, that these are not the same four varieties for each

TABLE 11.5

THE DISTRIBUTION OF CHERT VARIETIES FOR PRIMARY ELEMENTS
AND LEVALLOIS POINTS IN THE TOR FARAJ AND TOR SAHIBA ASSEMBLAGES.

| | Tor Faraj (J430) | | | | | | Tor Sahiba (J8) | |
| | A | | up C | | mid C | | C | |
RAW MATERIAL	Prim. El.	Points	Prim. El.	Points	Prim. El.	Points	Prim. El.	Points
1 Plateau	49.02%	51.35%	35.00%	37.50%	60.53%	64.10%	5.34%	4.48%
2 Plateau	13.07	18.02	10.00	18.75	18.42	10.26	2.29	2.99
3 Plateau	10.46	10.81	3.75	31.25	5.26	15.38	35.11	31.34
4 Plateau	0.00	4.50	0.00	6.25	0.00	0.00	9.16	17.91
5 Plateau	1.31	2.70	2.50	0.00	0.00	5.13	22.90	22.39
6 Plateau (all other)	1.31	1.80	0.00	0.00	2.63	0.00	13.74	7.46
7 Jebel Humeima	9.15	5.41	28.75	6.25	5.26	0.00	7.63	13.43
8 Rift Valley	15.69	5.41	20.00	0.00	7.89	5.13	3.82	0.00
TOTAL	100.00%	100.00%	100.00%	100.00%	100.00%	100.00%	100.00%	100.00%

assemblage. In contrast, at Tor Sabiha all seven specific chert varieties account for only 86% of the assemblage with the remaining 14% falling in the "all other variety" category. At Tor Faraj this catchall category accounts for only 0-2.6% of the cherts.

I interpret these data to denote a procurement strategy at Tor Faraj that entailed the targetting of specific chert sources for direct, bulk procurement. While the primary source (chert variety number 1) remained the same from occupation to occupation, lower ranked sources varied. For example, secondary sources included chert variety number 8 (Rift Valley) for the Layer A occupation, variety number 7 (Jebel Humeima) for the Upper Layer C occupation, and variety number 2 (plateau) for the Middle Layer C occupation (Table 11.5). On the other hand, the data from Tor Sabiha are more consistent with an opportunistic foraging strategy in which a greater diversity of cherts were acquired from various sources within the catchment (i.e, plateau sources).

In an effort to check for curation as a strategy for procuring and conserving chert, the distributions of chert varieties were compared for the beginning (primary elements) and end (Levallois points) of a reduction stream. The underlying assumption of this analysis is that the proportionate distribution of chert varieties should be similar at the beginning and end of the

manufacturing process unless chert sources enter (e.g., curated blanks or tools) or leave (e.g., off-site tool losses) the stream in proportions that differ from those at the initial stage of manufacture.

While primary elements unambiguously denote an initial step in a reduction stream, Levallois points are equally diagnostic of an end stage as they are produced from specially shaped cores. Within the Levantine Mousterian—especially the D type industry—Levallois points are particularly good candidates for curation given that:

a. they regularly form from 25-50% of the tool assemblages;

b. they functioned as multi-purpose tools as defined by edge-wear studies (Lee 1987; Shea 1989);

c. their production was labor intensive relative to other tool blanks; and

d. their production consumed relatively large amounts of chert relative to other tools.

When the assemblages from Tor Sabiha and Tor Faraj are compared according to the distributions of chert varieties (collapsed into the three sources: Rift Valley, Plateau, Jebel Humeima) for primary elements and Levallois points some clear patterns emerge (Fig. 11.5). Each of the occupation layers at Tor Faraj shows plateau cherts to be over-represented for Levallois points when compared to primary elements. This would suggest that in addition to targeting certain plateau sources for direct, bulk procurement, the occupants of Tor Faraj also augmented their chert acquisition with curated points manufactured from plateau cherts. The assemblage from Tor Sabiha, on the other hand, shows plateau cherts to be about equally represented for primary elements and Levallois points. Given the paucity of evidence (primary elements and cores) for initial processing at the site, as discussed earlier, few of the points were likely to have been produced on the site. In this case, the balance seen in the use of plateau cherts for primary elements and Levallois points does not indicate continuity in the reduction stream, but merely the emphasis upon

acquiring raw material and curated points from within the site's catchment.

Examination of the distributions of the Jebel Humeima chert reveals a curious reversal of the pattern seen for the plateau cherts (Fig. 11.5). That is, at Tor Faraj the Jebel Humeima source is under-represented for Levallois points, but at Tor Sabiha it is over-represented for the points. The Rift Valley chert, although generally poorly represented in the assemblages, shows a consistent pattern in which the variety is over-represented for primary elements. The study of how different chert varieties are distributed within the reduction streams of the two sites shows that the closest sources, those located within the catchments of the

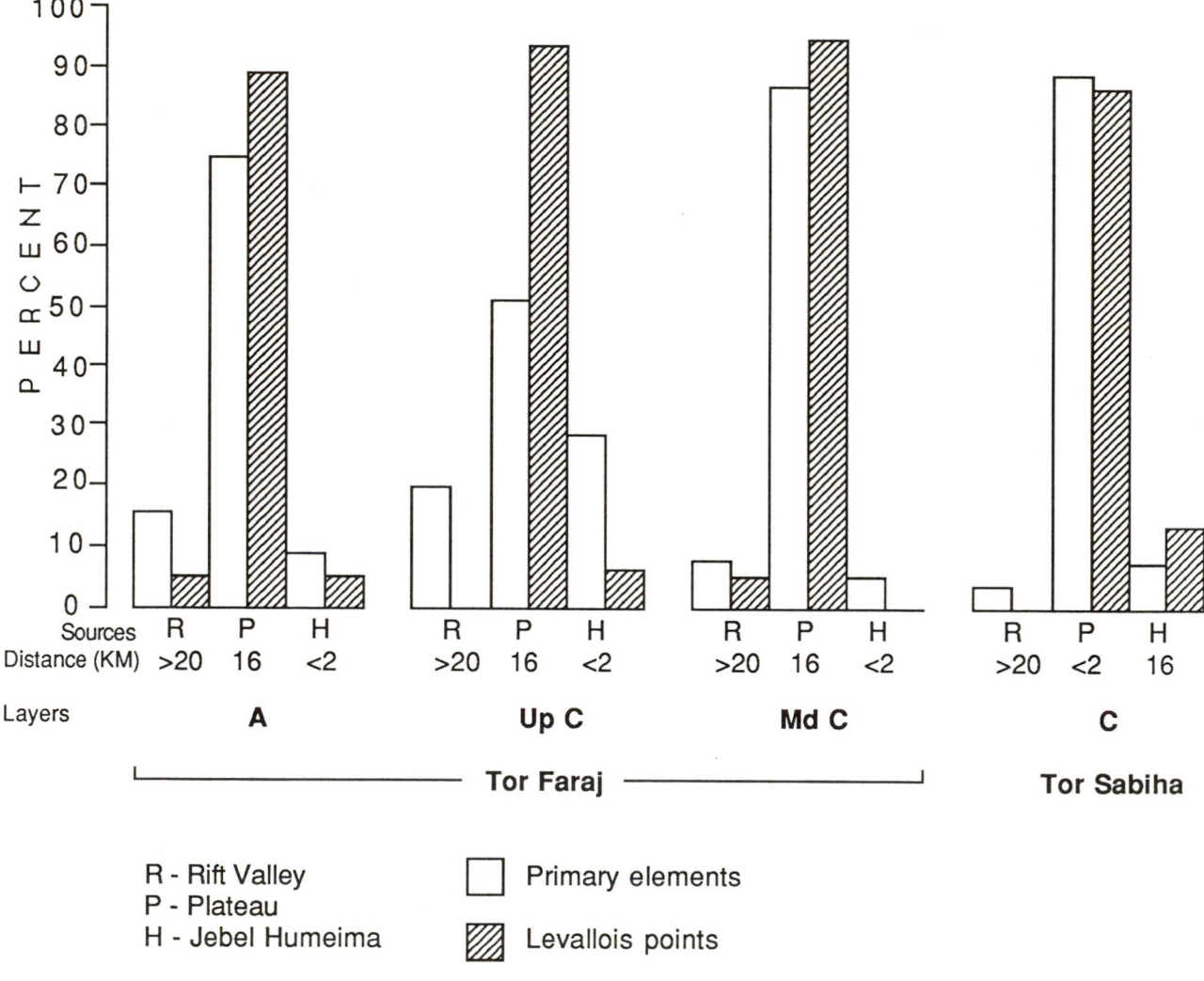

Figure 11.5   Proportionate distributions of chert varieties in the Tor Faraj and Tor Sabiha assemblages according to beginning (primary elements) and end points (Levallois points) on a reduction stream.

sites, are over-represented within the primary elements and under-represented in the points. This would indicate that regardless of whether a logistical or opportunistic strategy was followed, the curation of points was emphasized to a lesser extent when they were manufactured from sources within the catchment. As might be expected, we see a reversal of the above pattern for sources beyond the catchments of the sites. With exception to the Rift Valley chert, distant sources are under-represented for primary elements, but over-represented for points. The Rift Valley chert fails to follow the general pattern perhaps because it is generally not well represented in the assemblages or because it was used to a greater extent in the fabrication of tools other than points.

PLANNING DEPTH AND MEMORY

In acquiring specific chert varieties in bulk from sources 16-20 km away, the occupants of Tor Faraj appear to have had the capacity to plan ahead. And given that a quite different, opportunistic strategy was employed at Tor Sabiha, these logistical behaviors apparently were not routinized but were employed only under certain conditions mainly governed by mobility levels and raw material availability. The knowledge of where certain sources were situated for exploitation beyond the limits of a site's catchment and the procurement of chert for future use both imply a certain degree of anticipation.

From another perspective, such anticipation seems to be grounded in memory. That is to say, a cognitive map of chert sources and a knowledge that chert would be needed for future use would have been dependent upon memory of past experiences. An examination of memory and related cognitive changes in the ontogeny of modern humans may shed some light on evolutionary developments of the late Pleistocene. This is not to imply that the cognitive ontogeny of modern humans necessarily mirrors our hominid phylogenic development. But a general understanding of cognitive changes in modern humans may provide inspiration for model building in much the same way that an understanding of contemporary social systems gives rise to ethnographic analogies.

THE PIAGET MODEL

Much of the thinking in developmental psychology is based upon the theories of Jean Piaget in which he argued that cognition develops in a series of dis-

crete stages: sensorimotor, preoperations, concrete operations, and formal operations (Bjorklund 1989; Table 11.6). Piaget's stages have been questioned as to whether they represent distinct steps in a cognitive succession or merely segments along a continuum of change (Carey 1985; Flavell 1978) and as to whether they necessarily occur naturally in the lock-step way he decribed (Case 1985; Fisher 1980). Although there have also been questions about the cross-cultural applicability of Piaget's findings, these appear to stem more from the use of inappropriate measures than true differences (Ember 1977; Price-Williams 1961). Thus there seems to be general consensus among developmental psychologists and anthropologists that within the cognitive ontogeny of the species, levels of cognition undergo fundamental changes in a rather uniform way.

In returning to the question of cognitive evolution during the Late Pleistocene, what concerns us here are the differences in thinking that are related to opportunistic and logistical behaviors. Perhaps not by coincidence, these behaviors are based upon cognitive patterns that distinguish Piaget's preoperational and operational stages. And, even more pertinent to the nature of procurement strategies, the ability to comprehend conservation is diagnostic of the operational stage and was viewed by Piaget as the basis for all rational thinking (Bjorklund 1989:24).

Piaget's classic conservation problem involved showing children two glasses of equal volume that were filled with water; pouring the water from one of the original glasses to a taller, thinner glass; and then asking "Is there the same amount of water in the two glasses now, or does one have more? Why?" He and others found the concept of conservation (involving the dimensions of length, number, mass, weight, area, and volume) to be the principal factor distinguishing the cognitive levels of preschoolers from school-age children.

ARCHAEOLOGICAL CORRELATES OF THE PIAGET MODEL

Logistical behaviors that were tied to provisioning through direct bulk procurement of chert from distant sources would have required a conservation logic that involved an understanding of relationships in and between measures of length, volume, weight, and even number. On the other hand, opportunistic behaviors associated with expedient procurement and curation would not have required such logic. In fact, the intuitive and egocentric aspects of Piaget's preoperational stage are consistent with those behaviors in which raw

TABLE 11.6

PIAGET'S STAGES OF DEVELOPMENT AND THEIR PRINCIPAL CHARACTERISTICS
(BJORKLUND 1989).

Period and Approximate Age Range	Major Characteristics
Sensorimotor: birth to 2 years	Intelligence is limited to the infant's own actions on the environment. Cognition progresses from the exercise of reflexes (for example, sucking, visual orienting) to the beginning of symbolic functioning.
Preoperations: 2 to 7 years	Intelligence is symbolic, expressed via language, imagery, and other modes, permitting children to mentally represent and compare objects out of immediate perception. Thought is intuitive rather than logical and is egocentric, in that children have a difficult time taking the perspective of another.
Concrete operations: 7 to 11 years	Intelligence is symbolic and logical. (For example, if A is greater than B and B is greater than C, then A must be greater than C.) Thought is less egocentric. Children's thinking is limited to concrete phenomena and their own past experiences; that is, thinking is not abstract.
Formal operations: 11 to 16 years	Children are able to make and test hypotheses; possibility dominates reality. Children are able to introspect about their own thought processes and, generally, can think abstractly.

materials would have been acquired expediently by individuals during the course of other activities.

Memory would also have played an important role in a logistical procurement strategy. A knowledge of where high quality chert sources were located in relation to the base camp, topographic features, and other resources (e.g., water, fuel, etc.) would have been required. The heavy relief of the study area in south Jordan would have made a rather precise cognitive map a necessity for efficient movement to and from chert sources. Deep, vertically walled canyons and sheer-faced escarpments create numerous barriers to straight-line travel. Furthermore, during most of the year water and fuel sources are hard to find.

The kind of memory and recall related to cognitive maps is termed "constructive" by developmental psychologists. Such memory is based upon our experiences as a function of what we already know about the world and our recall of events as shaped by previous knowledge (Bjorklund 1989:158). As with general cognitive development, Piaget and his colleagues also conducted research on reconstructive memory (Piaget and Inhelder 1973). They found improved constructive memory to be strongly correlated with the transition from the preoperational to the operational stage of development.

Recent research has shown, however, that constructive memory may be directly linked to how well the information is initially encoded (Liben 1981). And from a developmental perspective, encoding at the operational stage is more reflective of reality than at earlier stages. Liben (1981), for example, found that children's concepts of verticality improved with maturity (Fig. 11.6). When they were asked to reconstruct pictures, incorporating these different concepts of verticality, from memory at immediate, 1-week, and 5-month delays, the more mature children consistently reconstructed the "mature" picture more accurately than younger children across all three memory delays. The most important finding in the study, however, is that there was virtually no difference in how the immature children reconstructed the "mature" picture

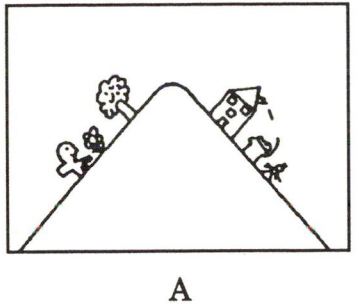
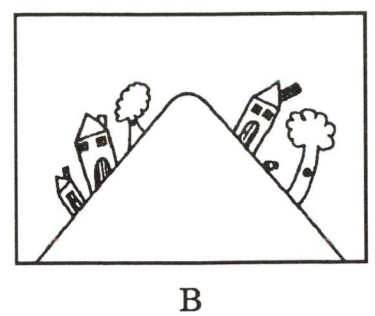
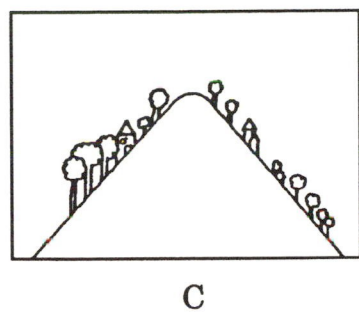

A B C

Figure 11.6 Children's drawings representing (a) immature, (b) transitional, and (c) mature concepts of verticality (Liben 1981).

across all three memory delays. Their immediate copies and their reconstructions from memory after a 5-month delay showed an immature version of the picture. In short, Liben's findings indicate that the memories of the immature children were accurate, but that their initial perceptions of the pictures were inaccurate and not representational of the real world.

A comparison of the thought processes involved in alternative procurement strategies and the cognitive ontogeny of modern humans indicates that a logistical strategy would have required mature or operational level cognitive skills. In contrast, an opportunitic foraging strategy could have likely been sustained at lower levels of development.

SUMMARY AND CONCLUSIONS

The differences in settings, contexts, and artifactual patterns of Tor Sabiha and Tor Faraj indicate that the sites experienced different kinds of occupations, most likely over different seasons. Tor Sabiha is thought to represent a transitory warm season camp while Tor Faraj is viewed as a long-term cold season encampment. Chronological information drawn from artifact comparisons, analysis of amino acid racemization, and paleoenvironmental studies are consistent in suggesting that the sites were synchronously occupied around 65,000 B.P.

A comparison of the assemblages on the basis of their reduction streams and distributions of chert varieties points to fundamental differences in the ways in which the occupants of the two sites provisioned themselves. A logistical procurement strategy involving direct acquisition of cherts in bulk from distance sources is indicated for Tor Faraj, whereas an opportunistic foraging strategy tied to the expedient collection of cherts from within the catchment characterized the occupation of Tor Sabiha.

In comparing the thought processes that would have been associated with these alternative procurement strategies to the stages recognized in the cognitive ontogeny of modern humans, a logistical strategy would have demanded a mature "operational" (Piaget) cognitive level. The presence of such a strategy at Tor Faraj thus implies that by at least 65,000 years ago, modern cultural behaviors were most likely present in the southern Levant. Unfortunately, without fossil evidence we are uncertain as to whether this behavior should be attributed to archaic (Neandertal) or morphologically modern humans. Interestingly, in the Levantine Mousterian similar behaviors have been inferred only in relation to those occupations belonging to the D type industry (Marks 1989) and this is the only industry to lack a fossil association.

REFERENCES CITED

Al-Eisawi, D. M.
1985   Vegetation in Jordan. Pp. 45–58 in *Studies in the History and Archaeology of Jordan*, Vol. II, ed. A. Hadidi. Amman: Department of Antiquities.

Bar-Yosef, O., and Meignen, L.
1989   Levantine Mousterian Variability in the light of New Dates from Qafzeh and Kebara Caves, Israel. Paper presented at the 54th Annual Meeting of the SAA (New Orleans, Atlanta).

Bar-Yosef, O. and Vandermeersch, B.
1981   Notes concerning the Possible Age of the Mousterian Layers in Qafzeh Cave. Pp. 281–285 in *Prehistoire du Levant*, eds. J. Cauvin and P. Sanlaville. Paris: CNRS.

Bender, F.
1974   *Geology of Jordan*. Berlin: Gerbruden Borntaeger.

Binford, L.
1979   Organization and Formation Processes: Looking at Curated Technologies. *JAR* 35:255–273.
1980   Willow Smoke and Dog's Tails: Hunter-Gatherer Settlement Systems and Archaeological Site Formation *AmAnt* 45:4–20.
1985   Human Ancestors: Changing Views of Their Behavior. *JAA* 4:292–327.
1987   Searching for Camps and Missing the Evidence? Another Look at the Lower Paleolithic. Pp. 17–32 in *The Pleistocene Old World*. New York: Plenum.

Bjorklund, D. F.
1989   *Children's Thinking: Developmental Functions and Individual Differences*. Pacific Grove, CA: Brooks/Cole.

Carey, S.
1985   *Conceptual Changes in Childhood*. Cambridge, MA: MIT Press.

Case, P.
1985   *Intellectual Development: Birth to Adulthood*. New York: Academic Press.

Chase, P., and Dibble, H.
1987   Middle Pleistocene Symbolism: A Review of Current Evidence and Interpretations. *JAA* 6:263–293.

Clark, G., and Lindly, J.
1989   Modern Human Origins and the Levant and Western Asia. *AA* 91:962–985.

Copeland, L.
1981   Chronology and Distribution of the Middle Paleolithic, as Known in 1980, in Lebanon and Syria. Pp. 299–302 in *Prehistoire du Levant* eds. J. Cauvin and P. Sanlaville. Paris: CNRS.

Crew, H. L.
1976   The Mousterian Site of Rosh Ein More. Pp. 113–140 in *Prehistory and Paleoenvironments in the Central Negev, Israel*, Vol. 1, ed. A. Marks. Dallas: Southern Methodist University Press.

Ember, Carol R.
1977   Cross-Cultural Cognitive Studies. *ARA* 6:33–56.

Emery-Barbier, A.
1988   Analyses polliniques du Quaternaire Supérieur en Jordanie Méridionale. *Paléorient* 14:111–117.

Fisher, K. W.
1980   A Theory of Cognitive Development: The Control and Construction of Hierarchies of Skills. *Psychological Review* 87:477–531.

Flavell, J. H.
1978   Developmental stage: Explanans or Explanandum? *The Behavioral and Brain Sciences* 2:187.

Geneste, J.-M.
1988   Economie des ressources dans le Moustérien du Sud-Ouest de la France. Pp. 75–79 in *L'homme de Néandertal,* ed. M. Otte. Vol. 6: *La subsistance*. ERAUL 33. Liège: Université de Liège.

Gilead, I., and Grigson, C.
1984   Far'ah II: A Middle Paleolithic Open Air Site in the Northern Negev. *PPS* 50:71–98.

Henry, D.
1982   The Prehistory of Southern Jordan and Relationships with the Levant. *JFA* 9:417–444.
1985   Late Pleistocene Environment and Paleolithic Adaptations in Southern Jordan. Pp. 67–78 in *Studies in the History and Archaeology of Jordan*, Vol. 2, ed. A. Hadidi. Amman: Department of Antiquities.
1986   The Prehistory and Paleoenvironments of Jordan: An Overview. *Paléorient* 12:5–26.
1988   Summary of Prehistoric and Paleoenvironmental Research in the Northern

Hisma. Pp. 7-37 in *The Prehistory of Jordan*, eds. A. N. Garrad and H. G. Gebel. BAR International Series 396 (i). Oxford: BAR.

1989   Correlations Between Reduction Patterns and Settlement Patterns. Pp. 139-156 in *Alternative Approaches to Lithic Analysis*, eds. D. Henry and G. Odell. Archaeological Papers of the American Anthropological Association 1. Washington.

Hietala, H., and Marks, A.

1981   Changes in Spatial Organization at the Middle to Upper Paleolithic Transitional Site of Boker Tachtit, Central Negev, Israel. Pp. 305-318 in *Prehistoire du Levant*, eds. J. Cauvin and P. Sanlaville. Paris: CNRS.

Jelinek, A.

1977   The Lower Paleolithic: Current Evidence and Interpretation. *ARA* 6:11-32.

1981   The Middle Paleolithic of the Levant: Synthesis. Pp. 299-302 in *Prehistoire du Levant*, eds. J. Cauvin and P. Sanlaville. Paris: CNRS.

1982a   The Middle Paleolithic in the Southern Levant with Comments on the Appearance of Modern Homo Sapiens. Pp. 57-101 in *The Transition from the Lower to the Middle Paleolithic and the Origin of Modern Man*, ed. A. Ronen. BAR International Series 151. Oxford: BAR.

1982b   The Tabun Cave and Paleolithic Man in the Levant. *Science* 216: 1369-1375.

1988   Technology, Typology, and Culture in the Middle Paleolithic. Pp. 199-212 in *Upper Pleistocene Prehistory of Western Asia*, eds. H. L. Dibble and A. Montet-White. Philadelphia: University Museum, University of Pennsylvania.

Johnson, J. K.

1989   The Utility of Production Trajectory Modeling as a Framework for Regional Analysis. Pp. 119-138 in *Alternative Approaches to Lithic Analysis*, eds. D. Henry and G. Odell. Archaeological Papers of the American Anthropological Association 1. Washington.

Lee, C. M.

1987   A Functional Analysis of Levallois Points from Two Middle Paleolithic Sites in South Jordan: Results and Interpretations. M.A. thesis, University of Tulsa, Oklahoma.

Liben, L. S.

1981   Copying and Reproducing Pictures in Relation to Subjects' Operative Levels. *Developmental Psychology* 17:357-365.

Lindly, J, and Clark, G.

1987   A Preliminary Lithic Analysis of the Mousterian Site of Ain Difla (WHS site 634) in the Wadi Ali, West-Central Jordan. *PPS* 53:279-292.

Marks, A.

1983   The Sites of Boker Tachtit and Boker: A Brief Introduction. Pp. 15-38 in *Prehistory and Paleoenvironments in the Central Negev, Israel*, Vol. 3, ed. A. Marks. Dallas: Department of Anthropology, Southern Methodist University.

1988   The Curation of Stone Tools During the Upper Pleistocene. Pp. 275-285 in *Upper Pleistocene Prehistory of Western Asia*, ed. H. L. Dibble and A. Montet-White. Philadelphia: University Museum, University of Pennsylvania.

1989   Early Mousterian Settlement Patterns in the Avdat/Aquev Area. Pp. 115-126 in *L'homme de Néandertal*, ed. M. Otte. Vol. 6: *La subsistance*. ERAUL 33. Liège: Université de Liège.

Marks, A., and Freidel, D.

1977   Prehistoric Settlement Patterns in the Avdat/Aqev area. Pp. 131-159 in *Prehistory and Paleoenvironments in the Central Negev, Israel*, Vol. 1, ed. A. Marks. Dallas: Southern Methodist University Press.

Masters, P. M.

1982   An Amino Acid Racemization Chronology for Tabun. Pp. 433-56 in *The Transition from the Lower to the Middle Paleolithic and the Origin of Modern Man*, ed. A. Ronen. BAR International Series 151. Oxford: BAR.

Mellars, P.

1973   The Character of the Middle-Upper Paleolithic Transition in Southwest France. Pp. 255-276 in *The Explanation of Culture Change*, ed. A. C. Renfrew. London: Duckworth.

1989 Major Issues in the Emergence of Modern Humans. *CA* 30:349-384.

Meignen, L.

1988 Un exemple de comportement technologique différentiel selon les matières premières: Marillac, couches 9 et 10. Pp. 71-79 in *L'homme de Néandertal*, ed. M. Otte. Vol. 4: *La technique*, ed. L. Binford and J.-P. Rigaud. ERAUL 31. Liège: Université de Liège.

Munday, F.

1976 Intersite Variability in the Mousterian Occupation of the Avdat/Aqev area. Pp. 113-140 in *Prehistory and Paleoenvironments in the Central Negev, Israel*, Vol. 1, ed. A. Marks. Dallas: Southern Methodist University Press.

1977 Nahal Aqev (D35): A Stratified, Open-Air Mousterian Occupation in the Avdat/Aqev Area. Pp. 35-60 in *Prehistory and Paleoenvironments in the Central Negev, Israel*, Vol. 2, ed. A. Marks. Dallas: Department of Anthropology, Southern Methodist University.

1979 Levantine Mousterian Technological Variability: A Perspective from the Negev. *Paléorient* 5:87-104.

Piaget, J., and Inhelder, B.

1973 *Memory and Intelligence*. New York: Basic Books.

Price-Williams, D.

1961 A Study Concerning Concepts of Conservation of Quantities among Primitive Children. *Acta Psychologica* 18:297-305.

Roebroeks, W.; Kolen, J.; and Rensink, E.

1988 Planning Depth, Anticipation and the Organization of Middle Paleolithic Technology: The "Archaic Natives" Meet Eve's Descendants. *Helinium* 28(1):17-34.

Sackett, J.

1988 The Mousterian and its Aftermath: A

View from the Upper Paleolithic. Pp. 413-426 in *Upper Pleistocene Prehistory of Western Asia*, eds. H. L. Dibble and A. Montet-White. Philadelphia: University Museum, University of Pennsylvania.

Schwarcz, H.

1980 Absolute Age Determinatin of Archaeological Sites by Uranium Series Dating of Travertines. *Archaeometry* 22(1):3-24.

Schwarcz, H. P.; Blackwell, B.; Goldberg, P.; and Marks, A. E.

1979 Uranium Series Dating of Travertine from Archaeological Sites, Nahal Zin, Israel. *Nature* 277:558-560.

Schwarcz, H. P.; Grün, R.; Vandermeersch, B.; Bar-Yosef, O.; Valladas, H.; and Tchernov, E.

1988 ESR Dates for the Hominid Burial Site of Qafzeh in Israel. *JHE* 17:733-737.

Shea, J.

1989 A New Evolutionary Perspective on Neanderthals from the Levantine Mousterian. A report to the L. S. B. Leakey Foundation: 1-26.

Stringer, C. B.; Grün, R.; Schwarz, H. P.; and Goldberg, P.

1989 ESR Dates for the Hominid Burial Site of Es Skhul in Israel. *Nature* 338:756-758.

Valladas, H.; Joron, J. L.; Valladas, G.; Arensburg, B.; Bar-Yosef, O.; Belfer-Cohen, A.; Goldberg, P.; Laville, H.; Meignen, L.; Rak, Y.; Tchernov, E.; Tillier, A. M.; and Vandermeersch, B.

1978 Thermoluminescence Dates for the Neanderthal Burial Site at Kebara in Israel. *Nature* 330:159-160

Valladas, H.; Reyss, J. L.; Joron, J. L.; Valladas, G.; Bar-Yosef, O.; and Vandermeersch, B.

1988 Thermoluminescence Dating of Mousterian "Proto-Cro-Magnon" Remains from Israel and the Origin of Modern Man. *Nature* 331:614-616.

White, R.

1982 Rethinking the Middle/Upper Paleolithic Transition. *CA* 23:169-192.

XII

Insights into Levantine Middle Paleolithic Cultural Variability

O. Bar-Yosef

L. Meignen

INTRODUCTORY REMARKS

The aim of this paper is to discuss the behavioral attributes which can be inferred from the study of Levantine lithic variability.

The currently published TL and ESR dates from several Levantine Mousterian sites (Fig. 12.1) where hominid remains have been found support earlier suggestions concerning the chronology of the Middle Paleolithic of this region (Bar-Yosef and Vandermeersch 1981; Bar-Yosef 1989; Valladas et al. 1987, 1988; Schwarcz et al. 1988, 1989; Stringer et al. 1989). The new chronology establishes the sequence of Tabun cave as a basic one for the southern Levant and indicates that an additional sequence should be established for the northern Levant. In both sub-regions it appears that the Acheulo-Yabrudian precedes the Mousterian. It is superfluous to mention today that the new TL and ESR dates have re-opened an old debate concerning the emergence of modern humans and the transition to the Upper Paleolithic. In a seminal paper Howells (1976) put forward the two alternative models to explain the presence of two hominid morphotypes during the Middle Paleolithic. One was named the "Neanderthal Phase" hypothesis and was represented by Hrdlička, Weidenreich, Brace and more recently by Wolpoff (1989), Trinkaus (1984), and Clark and Lindly (1989). The second hypothesis—the "Noah's Ark"—was represented by Boule, Leakey, Vallois, Vandermeersch (1982, 1985, 1989), and Stringer (1989). Recent discoveries in the field of mtDNA seem to support the latter interpretation but are still open to criticism.

Phylogenetic interpretations of the available fossils have not resolved the question of whether Neandertals were part of the local Near Eastern population or only late comers. Without direct dating of the fossils or the layers in which they were embedded only speculation can be offered. Relative chronologies based on biostratigraphy or paleoclimatic interpretations (Bar-Yosef and Vandermeersch 1981; Tchernov 1981) were considered insufficient indicators and were open to various criticisms (Jelinek 1982a). The new TL and ESR dates from Qafzeh, Kebara, Skhul, and Tabun caves, as well as ESR and Th/U dates from Acheulo-Yabrudian sites in Syria and Israel, demonstrate the great antiquity of the modern looking hominids (Fig. 12.1). Therefore, it seems that the search for understanding of the nature of Middle Paleolithic cultural variability has become even more important than in the past decade.

It is a commonplace assumption in archaeology and anthropology that archaeological remains should directly and/or indirectly reflect the behavior of humans. This assumption is made explicit when archaeological residues of Upper Paleolithic sites are analyzed. Analogies of organizational properties in the distribution of bones and artifacts between prehistoric sites and recent camp-sites of hunter-gatherers are commonly employed as explanatory devices. However, extension of this method into the Middle Paleolithic deserves constant re-examination. To assume that the hominids responsible for the formation of Middle Paleolithic sites behaved like modern humans, even if physically some of them were very similar to us, is to assume what we have to demonstrate. In addition, it is well-known by now that Neandertals were uncovered in Chatelperronian (Early Upper Paleolithic) contexts, such as at St. Césaire (Vandermeersch 1984) and Arcy-sur-Cure in western Europe. On the other hand, no hominid remains are available as yet from the very early Aurignacian deposits in Europe and no human fossils have been recorded from the earliest Upper Paleolithic assemblages in the Near East. For example, none were found in Boker Tachtit, where bones were not preserved, nor in the various layers which contain the transitional industries in Ksar Akil, Abri Antelias, Abu Halka, El-Wad, and Emireh. The only early Ahmarian fragmentary skulls were found by R. Neuville in Qafzeh cave (Ronen and Vandermeersch 1972; Bar-Yosef and Belfer-Cohen 1988), but these are as yet unpublished.

The current state of research leads us to conclude that there are no obvious direct correlations between the archaeological remains and the two different human morphotypes often defined as Near Eastern Neandertals and "Proto-Cro-Magnons" (Valladas et al. 1988; Meignen and Bar-Yosef 1989; Bar-Yosef, in press). We therefore need to examine the archaeological assemblages without reference to the available fossils and readdress several issues, such as the cultural sequence, the classification of industries, and the identification of human intentional or intuitive behavior as reflected in artifact manufacture, utilization, curation, recycling, and repair.

This paper is based primarily on the current results of our ongoing work in Kebara and Qafzeh caves, but briefly refers to other sites as well. We begin by briefly presenting previous methods employed in Middle Paleolithic lithic studies, followed by a description of the operational chain (*chaîne opératoire*) currently employed for uncovering lithic variability as reflecting the technical behavior of humans, and end with a brief discussion concerning the presence/absence of selected cultural attributes such as hearths and burials. We

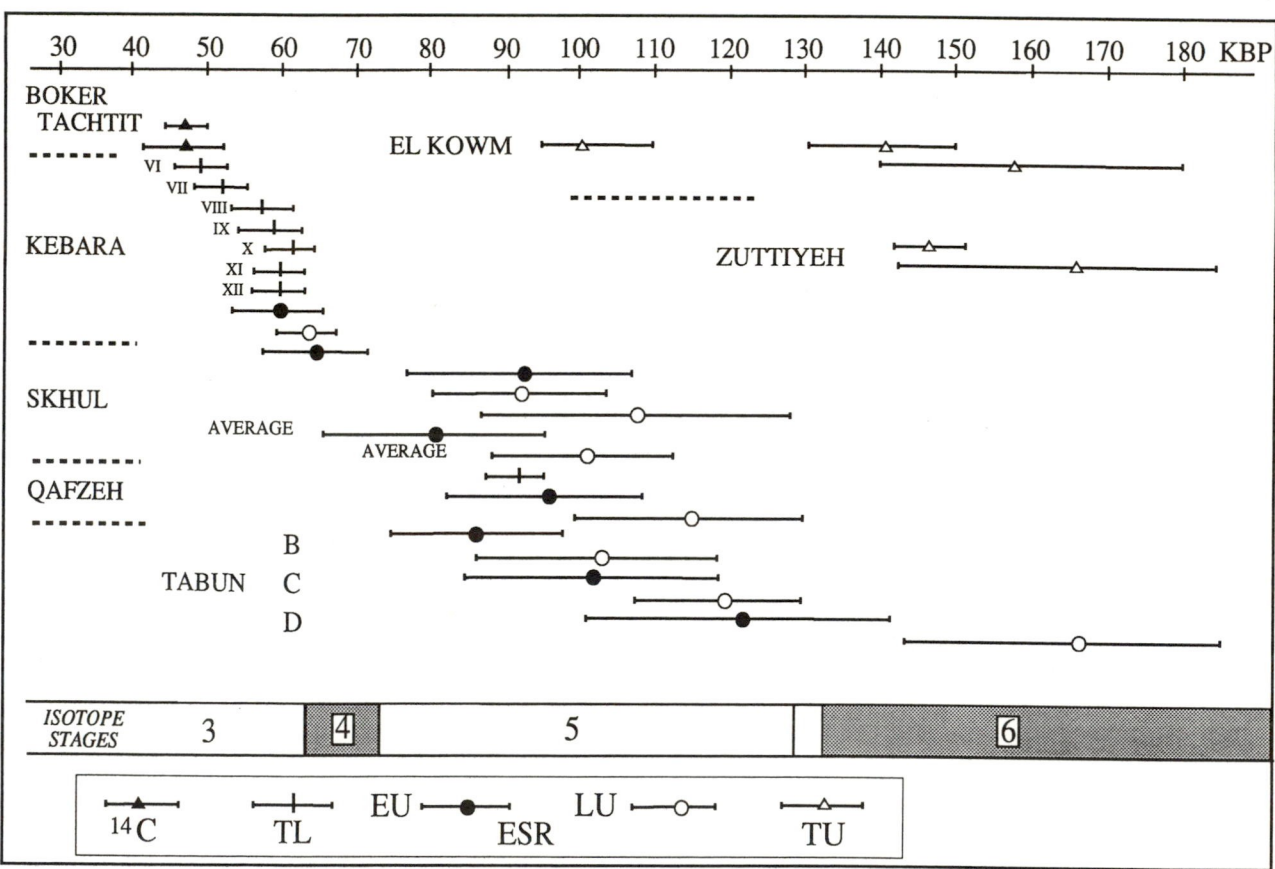

Fig. 12.1 *^{14}C, Th/U, TL and ESR dates from Boker Tachtit, Kebara, Skhul, Qafzeh, Tabun and Zuttiyeh caves, and the El-Kowm sites (after Marks 1983; Henning and Hours 1982; Valladas et al. 1987, 1988; Schwarcz et al. 1988, 1989; Stringer et al. 1989; Grün et al., in press). Note that the Skhul dates are given as both the two extreme readings and the averages. The Acheulo-Yabrudian Th/U dates partially overlap the ESR dates from Tabun D.*

do not intend to treat several important issues, such as site formation processes, the contribution made by the excavation of open air sites, or discuss in depth the potential meanings of the non-lithic cultural attributes. All these deserve special attention which is beyond the scope of this paper.

THE SEARCH FOR LITHIC VARIABILITY
AMONG MIDDLE PALEOLITHIC INDUSTRIES

During the last 40 years the systematic study of the Middle Paleolithic lithic variability resulted in the development of several methods of research. The first one was established by F. Bordes (1950, 1961) who suggested studying each assemblage along two lines:

1. The frequencies of morphological tool types recorded in a list of 63 types which can be essentially subdivided into three categories: Levallois products, retouched tool-types, and accidental tools. This procedure is also known as "typological analysis."

2. Quantitative recording of all the blanks by types (flakes, blades, and points). This includes all the retouched items recorded in the type-list as well as the non-retouched pieces, which fall under two general categories: Levallois and non-Levallois. Debris (pieces smaller than 1 cm) are counted but not classified.

While Bordes' interpretations concerning the presence and contemporaneity of several Mousterian groups during the Middle Paleolithic have been heavily criticized, fewer researchers think that the entire classificatory system should be abandoned. Whether tools were shaped intentionally or were instead the results of successive resharpening, their formal classification is needed as a basis for re-interpretations such as those suggested by Binford and Binford (1966) and by Dibble (1987, 1988, 1989). It is worth stressing that currently artifacts are often classified in clusters such as convergent tools, scrapers, Upper Paleolithic tools, and the group of *becs*, notches, and denticulates. Thus a short version of the type-list serves for inventorying and reporting the recovered assemblages. However, the main drawback of *la methode Bordes* is its static approach which only focuses on the end-products including retouched pieces and blanks and ignores the methods by which the artifacts were made (as examplified below).

The second methodological approach, offered by Jelinek (1977, 1981, 1982a, b) in the course of his work on Tabun cave, introduces metrical attributes. By measuring complete flakes Jelinek was able to demonstrate two important observations:

1. Old collections from excavations carried out in the 1930s, despite being selective, still reflect the original metrical trends.

2. The most useful index is the ratio of Width/Thickness. In the sequence of Tabun cave, this ratio exhibits a constant increase in value over time which means that the flakes become relatively thinner.

Based on the chronology of Tabun cave, as reconstructed at the time by Farrand, Jelinek suggested plotting the values of the Width/Thickness ratio of other Mousterian sites on the curve which he obtained for the Tabun sequence in order to place them in chronological order. The high ratio for the Qafzeh assemblages, in comparison with other assemblages, was taken to indicate its late Mousterian age. Moreover, given the relatively short time span suggested for the entire Mousterian sequence (Jelinek 1981; Farrand 1979) the accelerated shift in this ratio, or the rapid increase in frequencies of thin flakes and blades, was seen as being caused by the emergence of modern humans from the local stock of Neandertals. This proposal supported the classification of the Qafzeh-Skhul hominids as "Proto-Cro-Magnons," which meant that they had emerged during the latest phase of the Mousterian. It is not surprising that the results obtained by Jelinek were embraced by those physical anthropologists who saw a direct local evolution from the Near Eastern Neandertals to modern humans. Unfortunately, the new dates do not support a simple interpretation of the human fossils as reflecting a local Near Eastern linear evolution.

The third approach to Middle Paleolithic lithic variability is based on understanding the different stages in tool production from the acquisition of raw material to the final abandonment of the desired and/or used objects. This process is known in the French literature on lithic studies as *chaîne opératoire* and is translated here as "operational sequence." This kind of analysis aims to reconstruct the technical decisions made by prehistoric humans in the process of tool making. Sequences of technical gestures are considered to have been the expressions of technical traditions. We assume that these technical gestures, in the form of learned behavior, were passed from one generation to the next.

An operational sequence is commonly subdivided into three stages: (a) raw material procurement; (b) core reduction; and (c) tool manufacture/tool use. A brief explanation of each of these operational stages, illustrated with a few examples, is given below.

RAW MATERIAL PROCUREMENT

The analysis begins with the identification of the exploited raw materials and their geographic sourcing in relation to the site. The recognition of specific transport strategies, which reduced the efforts needed to transport the flint to the site, demonstrates the nature of selective technical behaviors in lithic resource procurement. This analysis is crucial when the various phases of the *chaîne opératoire* were executed in different localities and in different times and thus reflect the cost of energy expenditure involved in the procurement of raw material and/or the transport of the finished tools (Geneste 1988). Local raw material was often imported as unmodified nodules and processing was carried out on site resulting in a proliferation of blanks and particularly cortical elements. In contrast, distant raw material was brought in as already technically elaborated items such as Levallois products and/or retouched pieces. Numerous examples for this combination can be found across Europe (Geneste 1985, 1988, 1990; Meignen 1988; Roebroeks et al. 1988). The low frequency of good quality raw material from distant sources implies accidental transport by either natural agencies (as river gravels, for example), infrequent monitoring of remote environments, or the presence of extensive exchange systems.

The relationship between the size and quality of raw material and the chosen method of debitage is not as simple as some authors would lead us to believe. Obviously, there is no way to obtain large flakes from small pebbles. But there are many assemblages in which the artifacts were manufactured from a variety of sizes and qualities of nodules, demonstrating that the chosen knapping method was not dictated by the raw material. This is especially evident when we examine the final products. For example, from the same type and size of flint nodules, prehistoric artisans produced thin flakes by using the Levallois *chaîne opératoire* or alternatively obtained thick flakes by the "Quina-type" core reduction. Such are the cases of the Acheulo-Yabrudian and the Mousterian in the El-Kowm basin (northern Syria) or Tabun cave on Mt. Carmel.

CORE REDUCTION STRATEGIES

The variability of flaking methods can be identified by a variety of means including refitting of cores, recognition of specific technical products such as *éclat débordant* (Beyries and Boëda 1983) or the first and second removals which follow the shaping or reshaping of a core (Boëda 1986, 1988a, b, c), detailed investigation of the cores themselves, and finally by experimental replication of core reduction sequences. Examination of discarded cores cannot provide the same information concerning the entire reduction strategy as can refitted cores. Exhausted cores reflect only the final stages of the reduction sequences which could be very different from the original strategies (Marks and Volkman 1986:11). However, study of the scar patterns on the entire suite of Levallois blanks enables us to identify the initial reduction phases. In our current research we have followed the example put forth by the studies of Boëda (1986, 1988a, b, c) on Levallois assemblages in northern France.

The variability among core reduction strategies can be identified on different levels as follows.

VARIABILITY AMONG THE DESIRED END-PRODUCTS

A core reduction strategy may have aimed to produce Levallois flakes, Levallois points, or Levallois blades. However, even though the main intention may have been to produce just one of those (for example, Levallois points), it often happened that Levallois blades and flakes were by-products of the same reduction process (e.g., Jelinek 1977, 1981). Both the main and by-products often were used and retouched.

VARIABILITY AMONG THE PROCESSES OF REDUCTION

Two levels of analysis are included under this category: productivity and the dynamic pattern of removals:
1. The prehistoric productivity of lithic techniques refers to the ratio of desired end-products to by-products to be obtained from each core. Variability in the degree of productivity results from the method chosen for core reduction. For example, there appears to have been two Levallois methods, lineal and recurrent (definition after Boëda 1986, 1988a):
Lineal—When only one preferential Levallois blank was removed from each prepared surface, this required that core preparation was repeated before each desired

flake, blade, or point was removed. This is the classical Levallois technique of core reduction which, when used for the production of flakes, sometimes resulted in so-called 'tortoise cores'.

Recurrent—In this strategy the basic core preparation enabled a series of sequential flake, blade, and/or point removals from each prepared surface (Fig. 12.2).

The repetitive preparation of Levallois cores before each sequence of blank removals caused the subsequent blanks to become smaller than the previous series. If practiced systematically, this results in cores which are considerably smaller than the first series of blanks. The recurrent core reduction method is the most frequent one among Levallois-dominated industries.

2. Variability in the dynamic pattern of removals means that each of these methods (lineal or recurrent) can be achieved by centripetal (radial), or by uni/bi-directional core preparation and exploitation. In the cores worked by the recurrent method the scar pattern changes over the course of the reduction sequence. We have examples from Kebara cave which demonstrate that the uni-directional strategy, practiced in the first phase of the core reduction, became radial by the final phase. The resulting cores are often small and known as "discoidal cores" or "discoids."

TOOL PRODUCTION/TOOL USE

This phase of the *chaîne opératoire* encompasses the study of blank selection, the process of retouch or resharpening, and tool use.

On the basis of systematic observations of retouched and used pieces, we conclude that blank selection for further retouch or use was rarely done at random, especially in Levallois-dominated industries.

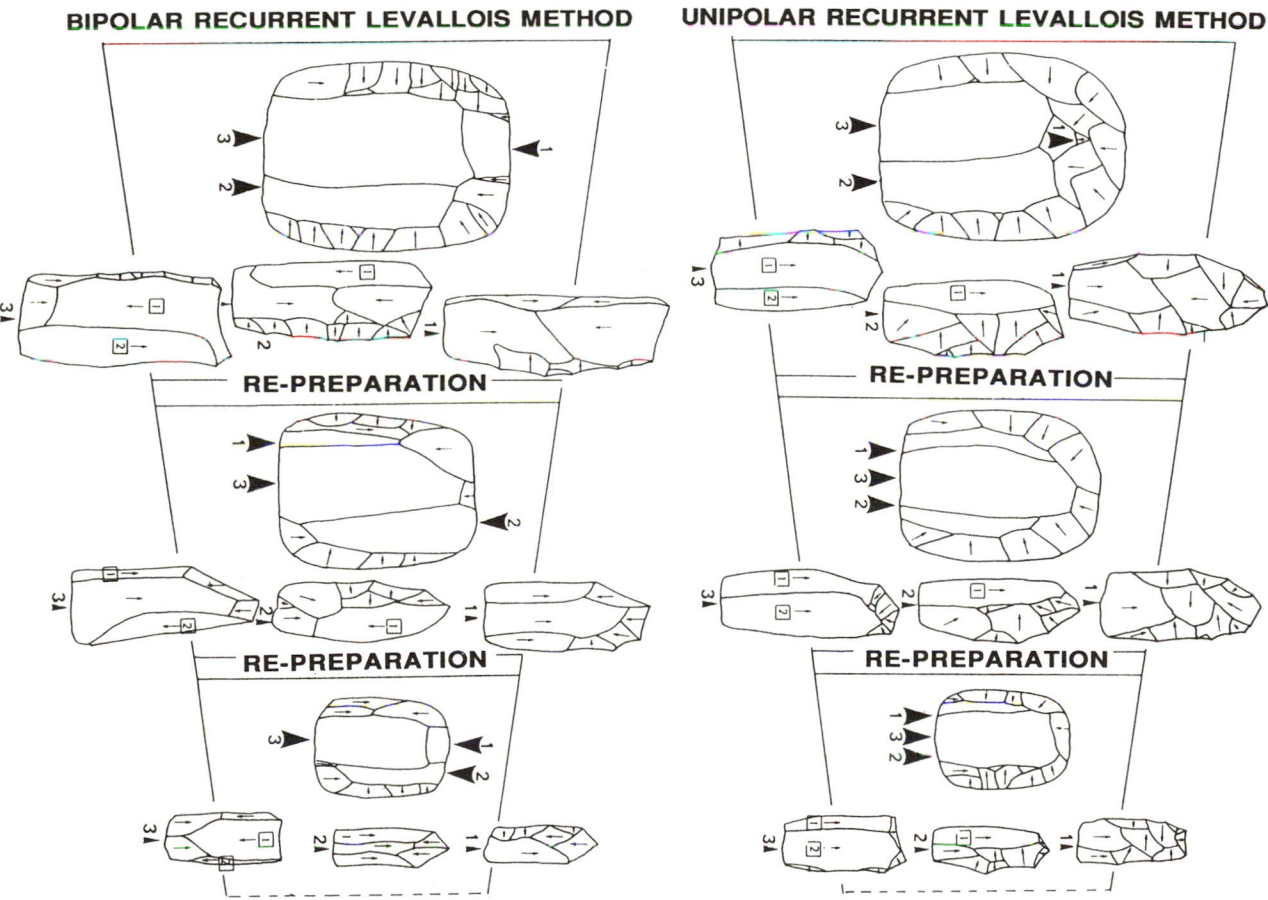

Fig. 12.2   Schematic representation of the bi-polar and uni-polar recurrent Levallois method as reconstructed by E. Boëda (from Boëda 1988c, with the permission of the author).

The final form of the used artifact could have been obtained by adjusting the removal method to achieve the desired shape or by modifying the form of the detached blank to the desired shape by retouch. This is not to say that forms of retouched pieces which were resharpened or recycled do not grade morphologically into one another. For example, convex sidescrapers grade into transverse scrapers or sometimes into convergent scrapers (Dibble 1987, 1988) a phenomenon also known as the "Frison effect" (Jelinek 1976). Various examples demonstrate, however, that not all retouched pieces in an assemblage grade morphologically into one another. For example, large transverse Quina scrapers do not seem to have passed through a previous phase of convex sidescrapers. These scapers are large, wide, and often symetrical in form. They differ from the *racloir oblique* which has been produced by the successive resharpening which began with a simple sidescraper and ended in a transverse shape, as described by Dibble (1987, 1988). Apparently, large transverse flakes were intended as blanks for this scraper type. Another example are the retouched elongated Levallois points, such as at Biache (Tuffreau 1988; Boëda 1988b), in which the retouch improves the blank and gives it the desired pointed form. Moreover, symetrical convergent retouched pieces in this site were hafted while other types of scrapers were not (Beyries 1988). This corresponds to observations made by use-wear analysis which concluded that pointed forms such as Levallois points were often hafted (Shea 1989a). Thus, it will be difficult to deny on the part of Middle Paleolithic humans some intentional correlation between several planned forms and their potential use, even if the level of such correlation is lower by comparison to late Upper Paleolithic tool types.

When the issue of recycling, often achieved by resharpening or additional modification (such as burin blows) is considered, it is probably worthwhile mentioning a few Upper Paleolithic and Epi-Paleolithic examples. Refitting in Meer II demonstrated that recycled *becs* (perforators) became burins (Cahen et al. 1979). Burins reshaped into endscrapers are well known and are sometime defined as *outils transformés* (Tixier 1963). The potential of many Upper Paleolithic tool types to become, during their "life histories," a different sub-type (e.g., various types of scrapers or burins), or an entirely different tool-type, can be exemplified from the archaeological records. This would not deprive modern humans from having mental templates as has been suggested for similar reasons for their immediate ancestors by some sweeping generalizations. It is our contention that the level of planning is most clearly reflected in the basic steps of the *chaîne opératoire* as presented above.

THE STUDY OF THE KEBARA LITHIC ASSEMBLAGES

The stratigraphy of Kebara cave has been described in details in other publications (Bar-Yosef et al. 1986; Goldberg and Laville 1988; Laville and Goldberg 1989). In brief, the lowermost units are an accumulation of sterile sandy-silty deposits (Units XV-XIV) above an uneven bedrock. Subsidence into a swallow-hole and subsequent erosion were followed by sedimentation of a depositional admixture created by alternating activities of biogenic and natural agencies (Units XIII-VII). This part of the sequence contains ashy deposits, hearths, bone accumulations, isolated human bones, a human burial (Bar-Yosef et al. 1988), and rich Mousterian lithic assemblages (Meignen and Bar-Yosef 1988a, b). Most of the in-situ Mousterian sequence (Units XII-VII), which geologically forms one major entity, continuously deposited, was dated by TL to 60-48 kyr (Valladas et al. 1987; Valladas and Joron 1989). ESR dates for Unit XI were 60 ± 6 for Early Uptake and 64 ± 4 for Linear Uptake (Schwarcz et al. 1989).

An additional major event of subsidence in the swallow-hole led to slumping and micro-faulting of the Mousterian layers at the rear part of the cave and was followed by erosion and burrowing activities. Thus, the cave floor during Early Upper Paleolithic times formed a basin slanting steeply towards the rear cave wall. Continuous erosion and burrowing led to the mixed accumulation of Upper Paleolithic and Mousterian artifacts in the lower part of this basin. Some Upper Paleolithic artifacts penetrated into Units V and VI (which are primarily Mousterian) and some earlier elements found their way into Unit III, which is primarily Upper Paleolithic. Unit IV is a thin lens and its cultural affinities are as yet not established. Radiocarbon dates for the remaining Upper Paleolithic sequence, after the removal of the major portion of the sequence by F. Turville-Petre in 1930, demonstrates a range from 42/38 to 28 kyr (Bar-Yosef et al., in preparation).

Preliminary field work around Kebara cave indicates that sources of good quality flint are located within 15 km. These are situated in Nahal Kebara, Nahal HaTaninim, Nahal HeMe'arot (Wadi el Mugharah), and Nahal Oren (Wadi Fallah), in Middle Cenomanian and Lower Eocene formations (J. Shea, pers. comm.).

Although analysis of the raw material economy is still in its preliminary stage, the presence of numerous cores and large cortical flakes and the abundance of blanks indicates that the primary phase of core preparation and most phases of core reduction were done inside the cave. Raw material was imported as blocks, cobbles, and pebbles and the primary elements, often large in size, are concentrated near the northern wall.

The studied sample (over 11,000 items) includes Units VII-XII covering a stratigraphic thickness of about 4 m. In the first stage of detailed analysis, we concentrated on the lithic assemblages of Units IX-X which we feel are representative of the entire sequence (see Tables 12.1 and 12.2 and Figs. 12.3-5) but brief comments on the other units are given as well.

Blank production in Kebara was frequently done by the Levallois method (see Figs. 12.6-7; Levallois Index in Unit IX = 11.8; in Unit X = 20). Short, broad-based Levallois points and the triangular flakes are the desired end-products (see Fig. 12.7). They were frequently obtained by uni-directional convergent removals. The production system is that of the "recurrent" method described above (Boëda 1988a, b) and its use is demonstrated by characteristic triangular

TABLE 12.1

TECHNOLOGICAL INDICES AND FREQUENCIES OF LEVALLOIS PRODUCTS IN KEBARA CAVE.

Units	Ilam	IL	% Lev. Flakes	% Lev. Blades	% Lev. Points
VII	12.0	18.1	73.8	19.4	6.8
VIII	10.9	19.4	78.4	17.1	4.5
IX	9.6	11.8	63.2	22.4	14.4
X	13.3	20.0	59.3	22.6	18.1
XI	20.2	22.6	61.1	30.5	8.4
XII	22.9	30.5	59.0	29.9	11.1

TABLE 12.2

TECHNOLOGICAL ATTRIBUTES OF THE LEVALLOIS PRODUCTS FROM KEBARA CAVE.
IFS = RESTRICTED INDEX OF PLATFORM FACETAGE; IF = TOTAL FACETED PLATFORMS;
ITL = INDEX OF PLAIN PLATFORM.

Unit	Types of Striking Platforms				Dorsal Scar Pattern					
	IFs	IF	Chapeau de Gendarme	ITl	total uni-directional	uni-directional convergent	radial	bi-directional	no. of scars	N =
VII	53.1	58.2	6.7	20.9	44.5	35.0	25.6	19.3	4	254
VIII	54.1	59.1	9.2	19.4	51.0	41.8	28.6	11.2	4	98
IX	78.1	79.3	40.2	11.5	68.9	67.8	10.3	9.2	3	87
X	71.9	75.4	26.0	10.4	52.9	48.5	17.4	14.5	4	338
XI	64.1	70.2	10.0	18.1	56.0	43.6	17.4	20.1	4	259
XII	83.3	87.5	19.0	8.3	62.5	51.4	6.9	25.0	4	72

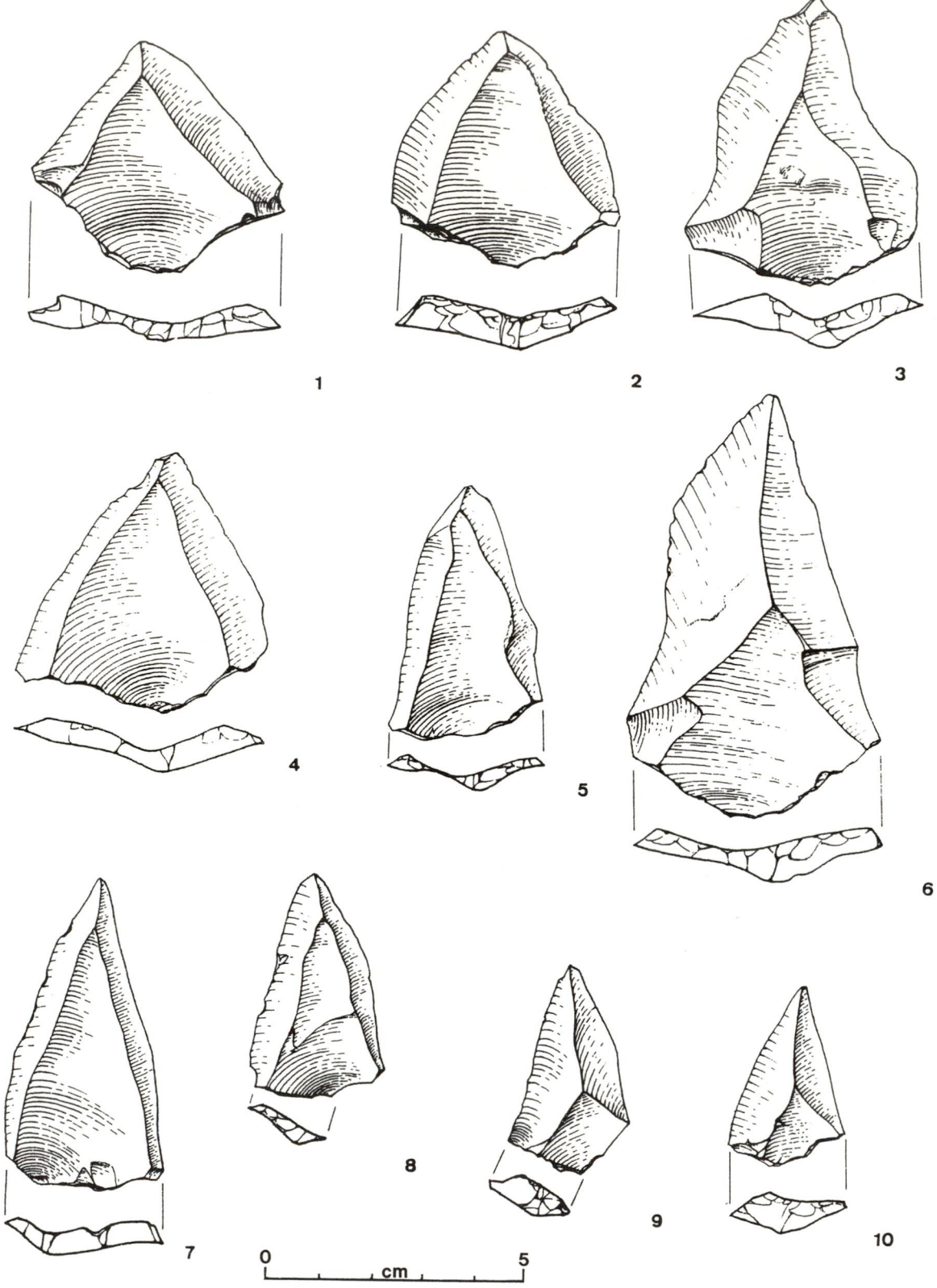

Fig. 12.3   Selected artifacts from Kebara Units X-IX. 1-7: Levallois points; 8-10: triangular flakes.

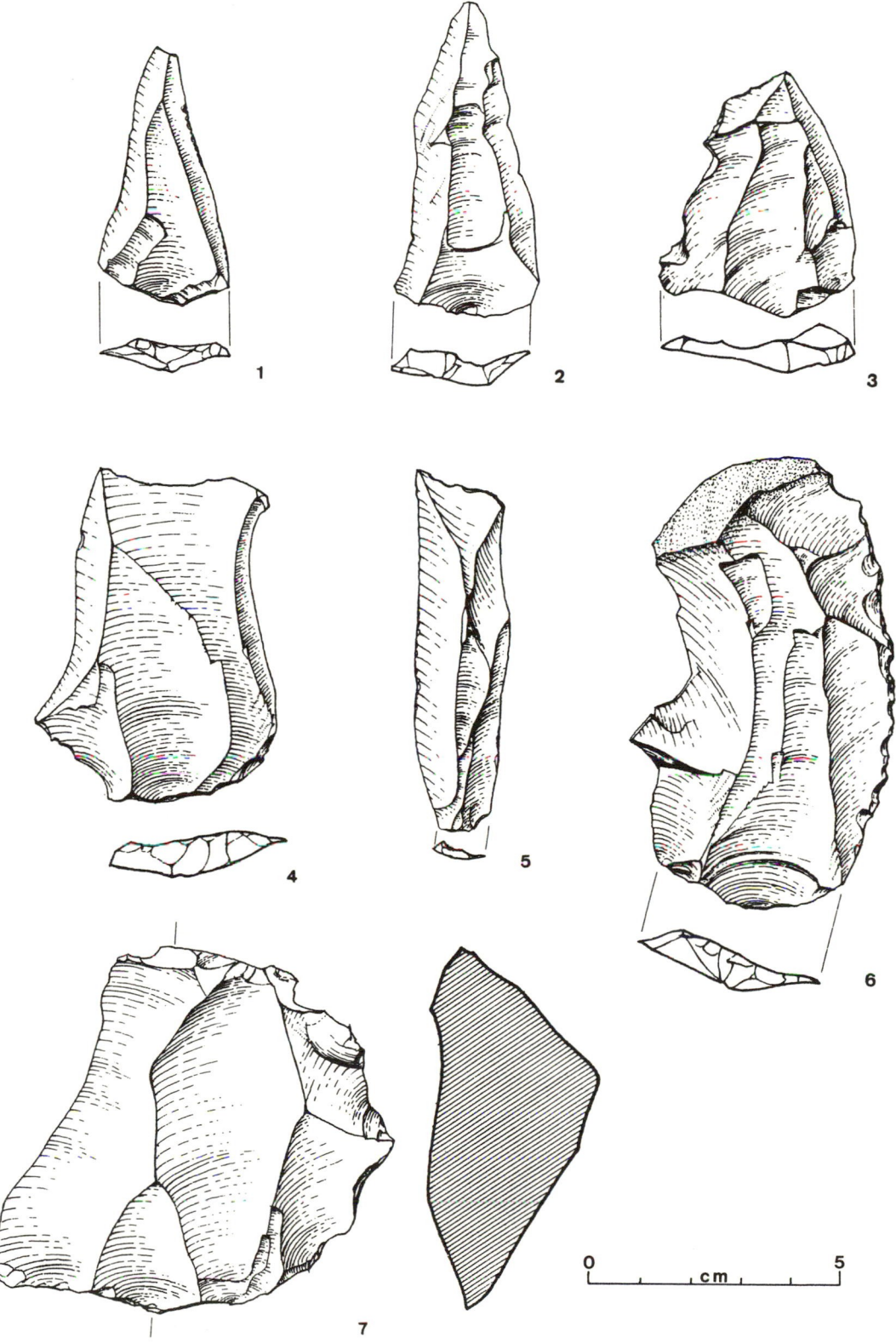

Fig. 12.4   Selected artifacts from Kebara Units X-IX. 1-3: Triangular flakes; 4: Levallois flake; 5: Levallois blade; 6: uni-directional cortical flake; 7: Levallois core.

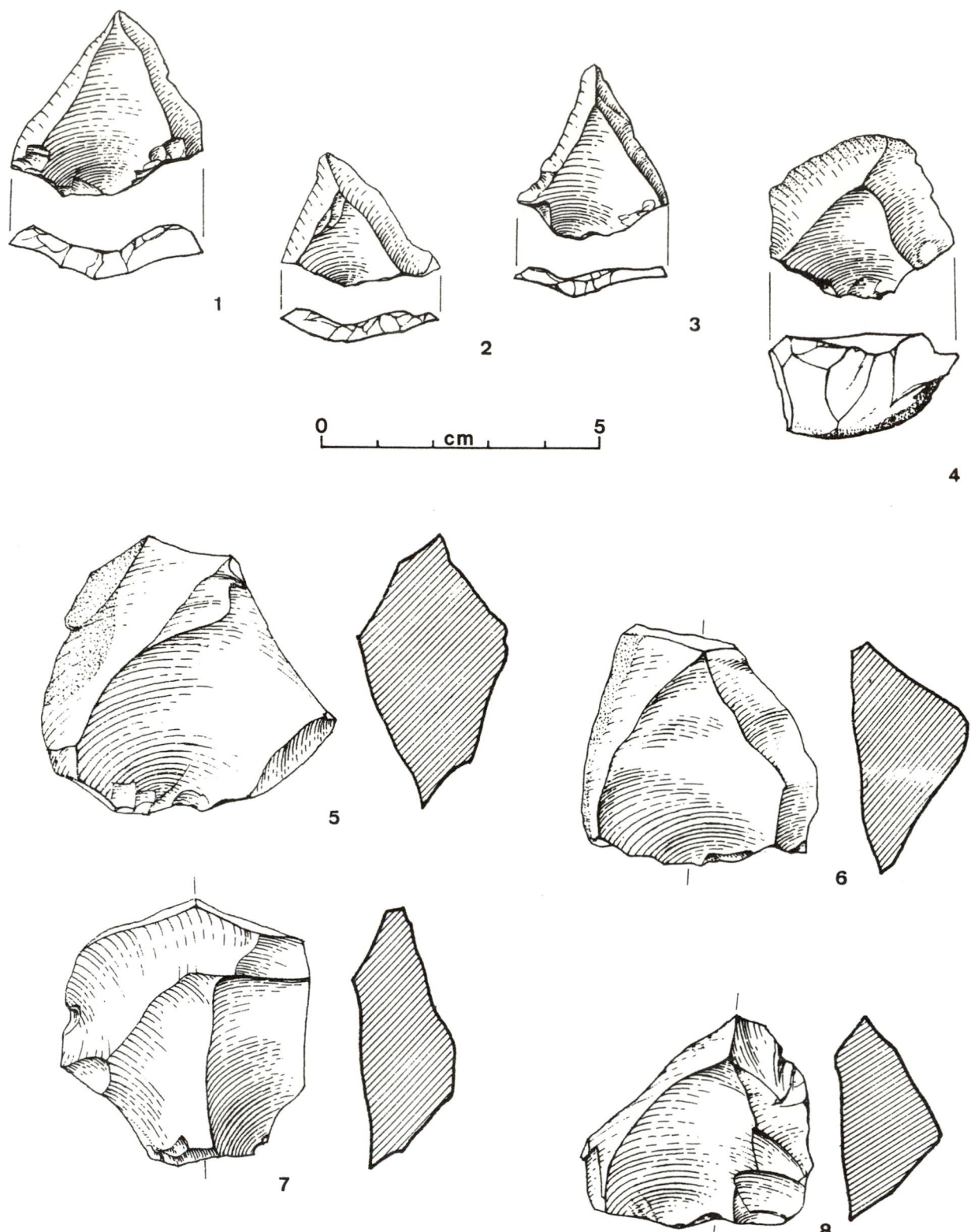

Fig. 12.5   Selected artifacts from Kebara Units X-IX. 1-3: Small Levallois points; 4-8: cores.

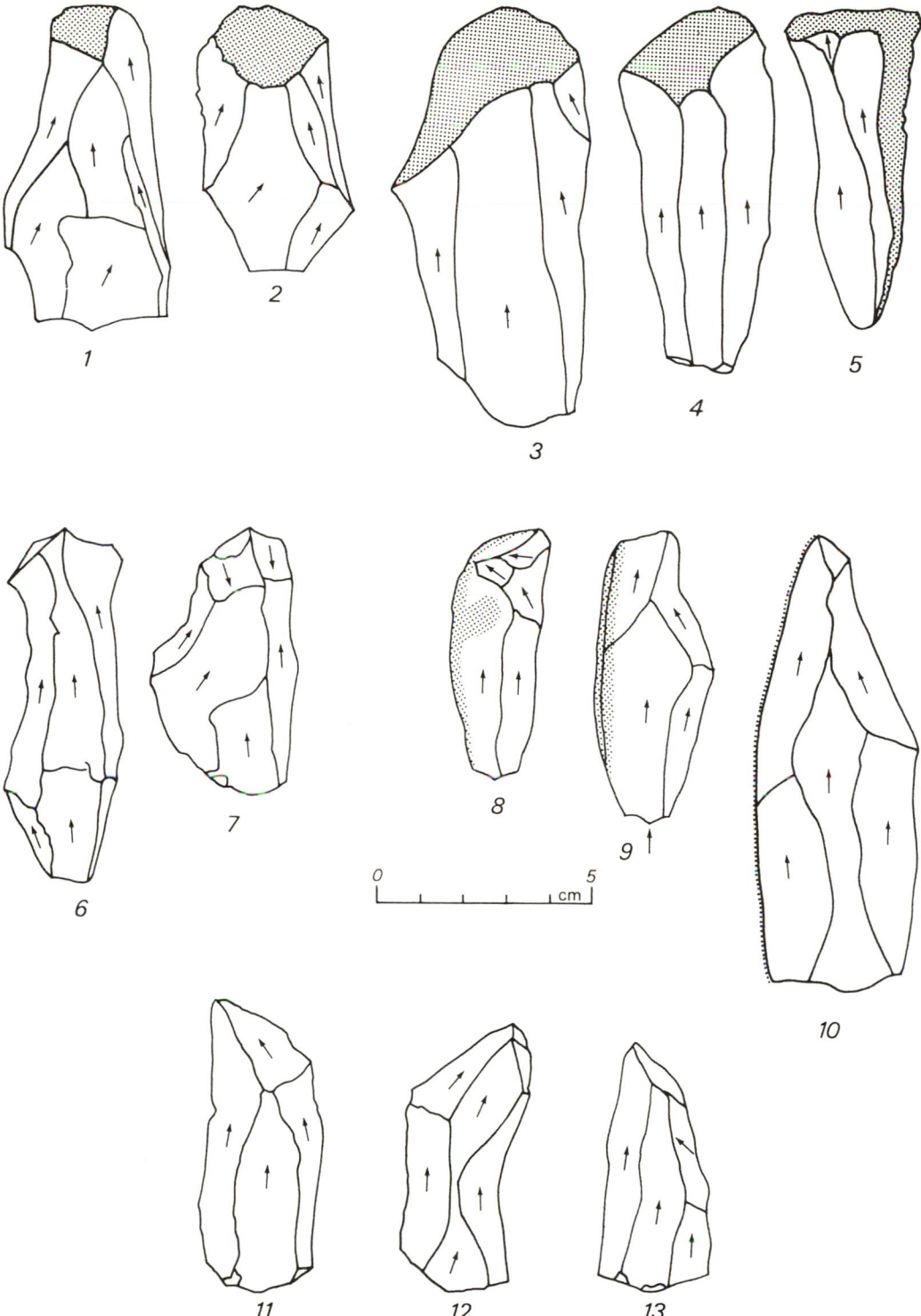

Fig. 12.6   Schematic drawing of artifacts from Kebara. 1-5: Cortical elements obtained during the initial core preparation; 6-7: core re-sharpening elements; 8-10: backed cortical elements (lames debordantes) corresponding to the re-shaping of the core for the additional removal of desired products; 11-13: elongated asymmetrical Levallois products.

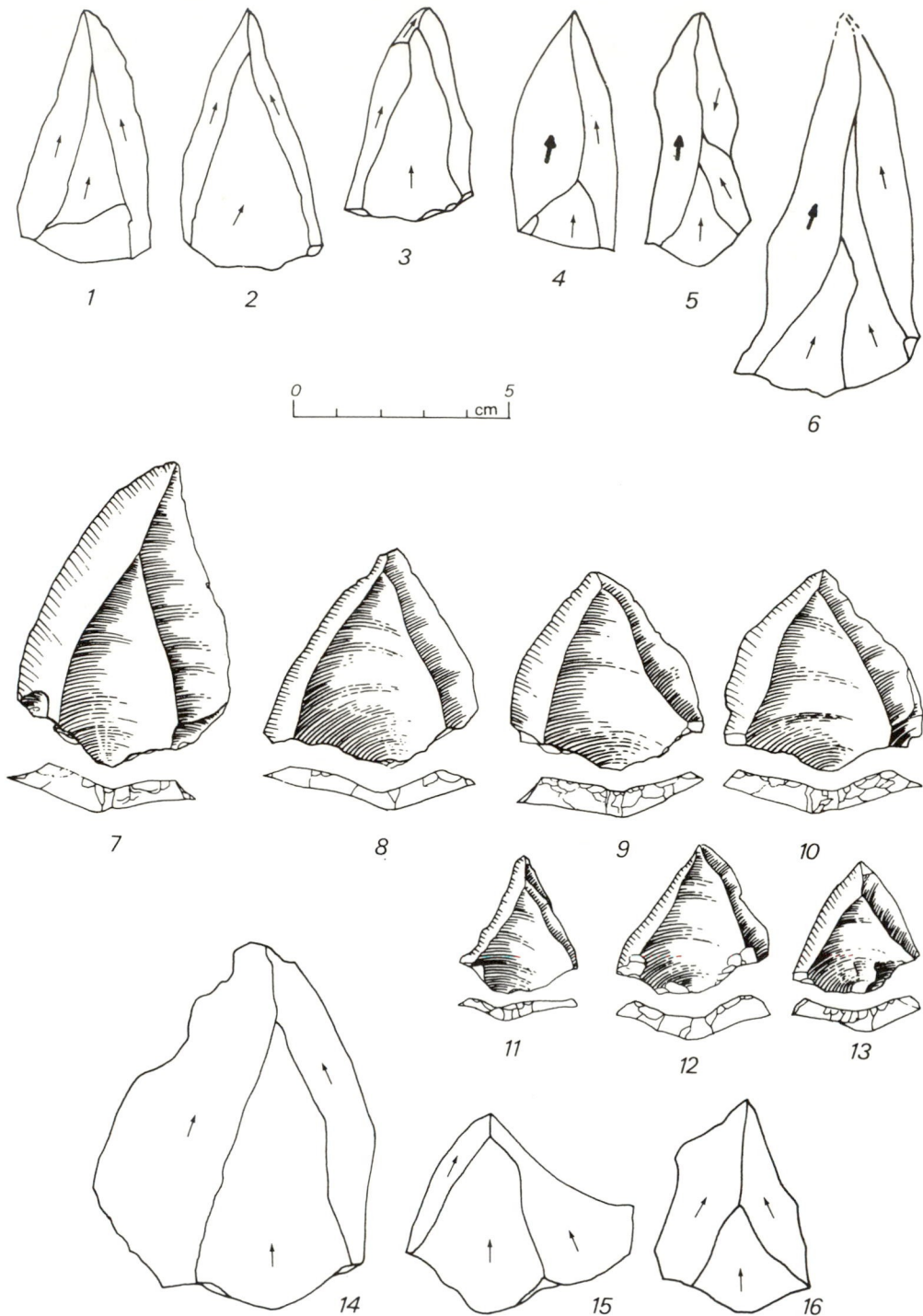

Fig. 12.7   *Schematic drawing of artifacts from Kebara: 1-3: triangular Levallois flakes; 4-6: enlevements II of a triangular shape; the heaviest arrow marks the scar of the last removal before the flake/blade itself was struck from the core; 7-13: a series of Levallois points demonstrating the size variability; note the facetted striking platform known as* chapeau de gendarme *which indicates the systematic prepaartion even for small points; 14-16: missed asymmetric Levallois points.*

flakes called *enlevements* II (Fig. 12.7:4-6). Morphometric study of the points and cores indicates that the sequence of removals was repeated several times until the cores were exhausted (Fig. 12.5:4, 6, 8). This stage of core exploitation was reached despite the proximity of the site to raw material sources.

Following the removal of the cortex by uni-directional flakes and/or blades, the sequence of manufacturing began with the initial shaping of the core by large *débordant* and *outrepassant* flakes. These are uni-directional convergent flakes which remove the edges of the core or its distal end, respectively. It should be stressed that in order to secure the detachment of Levallois blanks the core had to have both longitudinally and transversally convex profiles. This was achieved in Kebara Units X-XI by the *éclats débordants* and *outrepassants* (Fig. 12.6:1-5, 8).

In the following phase of reduction mainly triangular flakes and classical Levallois points were removed. It seems that at least in the Kebara assemblages typical Levallois points are associated with the type of striking platform known as *chapeau de gendarme*. This striking platform has the advantage that its central protrusion (when aligned with the overturned 'Y' form of the main ridge of the existing scar pattern on the core) guides the blow in order to precisely obtain the desired symmetrical point (Fig. 12.3:1-6; Fig. 12.5:1-3). It should be noted here that we have adopted a very strict definition for the Levallois point. In this study the term "Levallois point" refers to items with symmetrical morphology, a clearly pointed distal end with the overturned 'Y' dorsal scar pattern obtained by three or at most four removals regardless of their direction. Other triangular products were classified as "triangular flakes." This restricted definition is held by us because in our view the careful preparation of the striking platforms and the symmetry of the end-products seem to reflect the intentions of the prehistoric artisans.

A series of blanks including Levallois points and sub-triangular Levallois flakes (Fig. 12.3:1-10; Fig. 12.4:1-3; Fig. 12.5:1-3; Fig. 12.7:1-6) were removed from every surface of the Levallois core before the entire sequence was repeated. Between each sequence of removals the convexity of the core had to be restored and this was done by the backed cortical *éclat débordant* (Fig. 12.6:8-10). It should be stressed that the convexity of the dorsal face of the cores is one of the most important elements in this method. It is therefore understandable why the prehistoric knappers have additionally exploited flakes as cores by taking advantage of the natural convexity of their bulbar (ventral) face. These are known in the literature as flake cores.

Retouched pieces in Kebara are quite rare (Units IX-X: 2.5% of the total); these include a few sidescrapers as well as Upper Paleolithic tool types, mainly burins. The Levallois points are rarely retouched but both low power and high power use-wear analyses indicate that they have often been used. This means that the final form was the desired product. On the whole, the Levallois products were used five times more commonly than were the other blanks (Shea 1989a). Levallois points and triangular flakes bear traces of hafting and signs of wood working, butchery, and some impact fractures (Shea 1989b, c).

The differences between the lithic assemblages of the various units are relatively minor. All were made by the Levallois method (Table 12.1). The recurrent method was frequently used and often with uni-directional removals (Table 12.2). The morphological variability of the blanks seems to be better reflected in the desired end-products. In the lower units (XI-XII) there is a slight tendency toward laminar products either Levallois or not (Table 12.1). The upper units (VII and VIII) exhibit a proliferation of Levallois flakes (Table 12.1) obtained by either uni-directional or radial removals. The Levallois blanks of the lower units are on the average larger than those of the upper units. This phenomenon probably resulted from the use of the uni-directional method and a higher degree of platform faceting.

BRIEF COMPARISONS
WITH THE TABUN AND QAFZEH ASSEMBLAGES

The sequence of Tabun cave is not only the deepest and longest in the Near East, but also the one which has been studied by more scholars than any other Levantine Mousterian site. It is probably superfluous to summarize again the main traits of this sequence but given the amount of confusion concerning operational sequences and their end-products we offer a few comments based on general comparisons with the Kebara assemblages (see Table 12.3).

Tabun cave is located 13 km north of Kebara on the western escarpment of Mt. Carmel and in a similar ecological environment. D. Garrod defined three

Mousterian layers, labelled from bottom to top layers D, C (where the burial of Tabun I was uncovered), and B. The latter was overlain by the filling of the chimney which also contained Mousterian products. Jelinek, whose main excavation concentrated in layers D and C (Units IX, VIII-I) did not sample Tabun B due to its limited preserved surface. The chimney deposits had been entirely removed by Garrod (Garrod and Bate 1937).

The uni-directional convergent method of core preparation in Kebara is reminiscent of that reported from Tabun D. However, two major elements separate these assemblages: (1) the frequencies of the different Levallois products; and (2) the type of Levallois points.

First, Levallois flakes in Kebara are always the dominant group while in Tabun D blades and points are the most frequent products (Jelinek 1981). Secondly, the Levallois points at Kebara are short with a broad base and a striking platform often shaped in the form of *chapeau de gendarme*. In Tabun the points are elongated and the majority fall within the ratio of L/W > 2.45. Thus it seems that the two industries differ considerably from one another. On the other hand, the upper layers in Kebara (Units VII and VIII) represent a composition of Levallois products, dominated by flake production, which resembles Unit I (18-26) in Tabun (the upper part of Tabun C). As the sample from Jelinek's excavations from Tabun B is too small, the best available description of this assemblage

is that of Copeland (1975). According to her observations this industry is characterized by the production of short Levallois points (more or less abundant), obtained from cores with uni-directional or radial preparation; and the presence of thin flakes among which the narrow laminar forms are dominant (Copeland 1975:335). It seems that the Kebara assemblages and in particular those of Units IX and X would fall under the category of "Tabun B" industry.

Observations on the other assemblages from the Wadi Mughara sites are as yet too scanty to allow an affirmative technological comparison. A small collection from Skhul cave, stored at the Peabody Museum (Harvard), resembles the Tabun C material and the assemblages from Qafzeh. The technological attributes of this site were studied, on the basis of the series excavated by B. Vandermeersch, by P. Boutié (1989). The Qafzeh collection was found to be characterized by the production of Levallois flakes mainly through radial removals and is thus comparable to Units II-VIII in Tabun ("Tabun C"). The Qafzeh lithic assemblages differ from those of Kebara even when compared with the material from layer XV (= 12 inside the cave) where the frequency of Levallois points is the highest within the sequence. Tentatively, therefore, we conclude that, as previously noted by Hours et al. (1973), there are at least three distinct industrial facies within the Levantine Mousterian which correspond to the main stratigraphic units in Tabun cave (D, C, and B).

NON-LITHIC ATTRIBUTES OF LEVANTINE MOUSTERIAN SITES

The presence of two different morpho-types of hominids during the Levantine Mousterian sequence seems to be established. Their temporal relationship,

however, is unclear and they could have been contemporary for only a relatively short time (Fig. 12.1). This situation does not differ from the overall contempo-

TABLE 12.3

COMPARISON BETWEEN THE FREQUENCIES OF LEVALLOIS PRODUCTS IN KEBARA AND TABUN (THE TABUN DATA AFTER JELINEK 1982A). THE KEBARA UNITS RESEMBLE TABUN B (GARROD AND BATE 1937). TABUN I, 1-17 AND 18-26 CORRESPOND TO TABUN C AND TABUN IX TO TABUN D OF GARROD'S EXCAVATIONS.

Levallois products	Kebara VII	Kebara VIII	Kebara IX	Kebara X	Kebara XI	Tabun I 1-17	Tabun I 18-26	Tabun IX
% Flakes	73.8	78.4	63.2	59.3	61.1	53.3	73.8	23.5
% Points	6.8	4.5	14.4	18.1	8.4	28.0	7.9	34.4
% Blades	19.4	17.1	22.4	22.6	30.5	18.5	18.3	42.1

raneity between Neandertals and Cro-Magnons at the beginning of the European Upper Paleolithic. Their presence in the same region raises the question of their specific adaptation, or to what extent the non-lithic archaeological remains reflect the presence of two hominid types. It is of course possible that the archaeological remains do not closely monitor the behavioral differences between the various hominids. The following is therefore just a brief survey which further indicates that separation on the basis of the available knowledge between two "cultural entities" is rather tenuous.

RED OCHRE AND MARINE SHELLS

There is clear evidence for the use of red ochre in Levantine Mousterian sites. The best evidence is a scraped lump found in Qafzeh in the hominid-bearing layers (Vandermeersch 1969). Red ochre is present in the archaeological contexts of Kebara.

Marine shells, all *Glycemeris,* were found in Qafzeh and in Skhul (B. Vandermeersch, pers. comm.; Garrod and Bate 1937). Their small number in each site precludes the possibility that they are food refuse.

HEARTHS

During the excavation of Kebara cave, we were able to expose a series of features including various hearths which do not differ from those found in Upper Paleolithic sites in their rounded and oval shapes (Meignen et al. 1989). Replicatory study and charcoal identification indicate that most often local firewood had been used. The firewood was collected in the immediate environment of the site and was mainly Tabor oak (U. Baruch and E. Werker, pers. comm.). There is no evidence for the use of stones for warmth banking.

Similar small hearths were found in Qafzeh and we suspect that the same is true in other Mousterian sites where the deposits are well preserved.

BONE ACCUMULATIONS

An additional specific feature recovered in Kebara are the "bone accumulations" located in the central area of the cave. They are sometimes oval in shape and contain numerous bones and artifacts. Diagenic processes could have been responsible for the destruction of bones outside these patches. A preliminary analysis by J. D. Speth (Museum of Anthropology, University of Michigan, Ann Arbor, pers. comm.) indicates that the

bones represent a wide array of species and many of the bones bear cut marks while gnawed pieces are extremely rare. Mineralogical analyses indicate that most of these patches are well preserved prehistoric accumulations (S. Weiner, Isotope Department, Weizmann Institute of Science, pers. comm.). These assemblages, in the central area of the cave, differ slightly from the bone deposits near the northern cave wall which resulted from the intermittent activities of humans and carnivores. However, diagenic processes have been responsible for the destruction of bones outside the central and northern area, largely in the zone below the chimney and towards the southern portion of the cave.

BURIALS

The issue of Middle Paleolithic burials has recently come under re-examination and with a proliferation of cautionary notes (e.g., Chase and Dibble 1987; Bar-Yosef 1988; Tillier et al. 1988; Lindly and Clark 1990). While the reporting from early excavations can be criticized for not following the standards of the 1980s, it will be difficult to dismiss all Middle Paleolithic skeletons found in anatomical connection as simple accidents. For a skeleton to remain in anatomical connection in the dynamic environment of a Near Eastern cave-site, where the rate of sedimentation is very slow and alternate occupations of scavengers, birds of prey, and humans are well evidenced, it certainly was buried. As an illustration we can refer to the Mousterian sequence in Kebara which is about 4 m deep and dated to 60-48,000 years. This implies an accumulation of 4 m over 12,000 years, about 33 cm per thousand years or 0.33 mm a year. Even if a double or triple rate of sedimentation is assumed, it will take quite a long time to cover up an adult burial such as the one recently discovered. Moreover, the excavation of a narrow pit into which the corpse was introduced kept the thoracic cavity intact, occupying a depth of about 20 cm.

In conclusion, we see the burials from Kebara, Tabun, Qafzeh, Skhul, and Amud as a repetitive pattern which can not be explained by natural site formation processes and thus reflects the intentional actions taken by Middle Paleolithic hominids. A large, half-complete fallow deer antler such as the one exposed across the chest of the child burial in Qafzeh, is unique in the Levantine caves. It is unlikely due to sampling bias, given the volume excavated in all these sites since the 1930s. If one doubts the symbolic nature of the burials, we should remind ourselves that the same is attributed to modern burials and by analogy to Neolithic burials where no grave goods are found. The excavated pit is not always well preserved and some of the bones are sometimes missing. But it is the anatomical connection of the main skeletal parts which indicates the presence of intentional burial. Within the framework of the new chronology for the Levantine sites, the burials of early modern humans seem to precede those of Neandertals (Vandermeersch 1988). However, the cumulative archaeological evidence in the Mediterranean Levant indicates that only a few of the cultural expressions attributed to Upper Paleolithic Cro-Magnons are already found among Middle Paleolithic contexts in the Levant. Finding the causes for these early manifestations, tracing the evidence which indicates that Middle Paleolithic humans were adapted (or not) to the variable environments of the Near East, and understanding the nature of the transition to the Upper Paleolithic may help to resolve some of the intriguing questions concerning the origins of modern humans.

CONCLUDING REMARKS

Every additional set of dates will improve our knowledge of Levantine Mousterian chronology. This is the unavoidable consequence of scientific progress which challenges old models and opens the field to new kinds of analyses. But whatever the final chronology, we are still faced with the need to document and explain the lithic variability of the Mousterian assemblages. In order to understand these Middle Paleolithic humans (for whom we have no living analogues) and to decipher their behavioral patterns, we have to try to tie the archaeological observations to other aspects of human behavior. In this search we believe that understanding the phases in the *chaîne opératoire* in each assemblage and site will provide us a means to "read" the minds of the prehistoric artisans, and gain an insight into the ways in which they handled their environment. This undoubtedly is just one aspect among others which together constituted the changing lifeways of Middle Paleolithic humans.

ACKNOWLEDGMENTS

We would like to express our gratitude to our colleagues in the project on "The Origin of Modern Humans in Southwest Asia" with whom we shared the ideas expressed in this paper, to the L. S. B. Leakey Foundation, the French Ministry of Foreign Affairs, the CNRS, the CARE Archaeological Foundation, and the Israel Exploration Society for enabling all of us to carry out the excavations at Kebara, the research in Qafzeh cave, and the study of Levantine lithic collections. We are grateful to J. Shea, D. Lieberman (Department of Anthropology, Harvard University), J. D. Speth (Museum of Anthropology, University of Michigan) and J. Phillips (University of Illinois at Chicago Circle) who made numerous comments on earlier drafts of this paper. Needless to stress, only we, the authors, are responsible for the interpretations incorporated in the above pages.

REFERENCES CITED

Bar-Yosef, O.
1988   The Date of the South-West Asian Neandertals. Pp. 31-38 in *L'homme de Néandertal*, ed. M. Otte. Vol. 3: *L'anatomie*, ed. E. Trinkaus. ERAUL 30. Liège: Université de Liège.
1989   Geochronology of the Levantine Middle Paleolithic. Pp. 589-610 in *The Human Revolution: Behavioural and Biological Perspectives on the Origins of Modern Humans*, eds. P. Mellars and C. Stringer. Edinburgh: Edinburgh University Press.

in press   Middle Paleolithic Chronology and the Transition to the Upper Paleolithic in Southwest Asia. In *Continuity or Complete Replacement: Controversies in* Homo sapiens *Evolution*, eds. F. H. Smith and G. Bräuer. Rotterdam: Balkema Press.

Bar-Yosef, O., and Belfer-Cohen, A.
1988   The Early Upper Paleolithic in Levantine Caves. Pp. 23-41 in *The Early Upper Paleolithic*, eds. J. F. Hoffecker and C. A. Wolf. BAR International Series 437. Oxford: BAR.

Bar-Yosef, O.; Laville, H.; Meignen, L.; Tillier, A. M.; Vandermeersch, B.; Arensburg, B.; Belfer-Cohen, A.; Goldberg, P.; Rak, Y.; and Tchernov, E.
1988 La sepulture neanderthalienne de Kebara, Unité XII. Pp. 17-24 in *L'homme de Néandertal*, ed. M. Otte. Vol. 6: *La penseé*. ERAUL 33. Liège: Université de Liège.

Bar-Yosef, O., and Vandermeersch, B.
1981 Notes Concerning the Possible Age of the Mousterian Layers in Qafzeh Cave. Pp. 281-286 in *Prehistoire du Levant*, eds. J. Cauvin and P. Sanlaville. Paris: CNRS.

Bar-Yosef, O.; Vandermeersch, B.; Arensburg, B.; Belfer-Cohen, A.; Goldberg, P.; Laville, H.; Meignen, L.; Rak, Y.; Speth, J. D.; Tchernov, E.; Tillier, A. M.; and Weiner, S.
in preparation *The Excavations in Kebara Cave, Mt. Carmel.*

Bar-Yosef, O.; Vandermeersch, B.; Arensburg, B.; Goldberg, P.; Laville, H.; Meignen, L.; Rak, Y.; Tchernov, E.; and Tillier, A. M.
1986 New Data Concerning the Origins of Modern Man in the Levant. *CA* 27:63-64.

Beyries, S.
1988 Etude tracéologique des racloirs du niveau IIA. Pp. 215-230 in *Le gisement paléolithique moyen de Biache-Saint-Vaast (Pas-de-Calais)*, Vol. 1, eds. A. Tuffreau and J. Sommé. MSPF 21. Paris.

Beyries, S., and Boëda, E.
1983 Etude technologique et traces d'utilisation des "éclats débordants" de Corbehem (Pas-de-Calais). *BSPF* 80:275-279.

Binford, L. R., and Binford, S. R.
1966 A Preliminary Analysis of Functional Variability in the Mousterian of Levallois Facies. *AA* 68:238-295.

Boëda, E.
1986 Approche technologique du concept Levallois et évaluation de son champ d'application: étude de trois gisements saaliens et weichséliens de la France septentionale. Ph.D. thesis, Université de Paris.

1988a Le concept Levallois et évaluation de son champ d'application. Pp. 13-26 in *L'homme de Néandertal*, ed. M. Otte. Vol. 4: *La technique*, eds. L. Binford and J.-P. Rigaud. ERAUL 31. Liège: Université de Liège.

1988b Analyse technologique du débitage du niveau IIA. Pp. 185-214 in *Le gisement paléolithique moyen de Biache-Saint-Vaast (Pas-de-Calais)*, Vol. 1, eds. A. Tuffreau and J. Sommé. MSPF 21. Paris.

1988c Le debitage Levallois de Biache St-Vaast (Pas-de-Calais): premiere étude technologique. Pp. 209-218 in *Chronostratigraphie et faciès culturels du Paléolithique inférieur et moyen dans l'Europe du nord-ouest*, eds. A. Tuffreau and J. Sommé. *BAFEQ* Supplément 26. Paris: AFEQ.

Bordes, F.
1950 Principes d'une méthode d'étude des techniques de débitage et de la typologie du Paléolithique ancien et moyen. *L'Anthropologie* 54:19-34.

1961 *Typologie du Paléolithique ancien et moyen.* 2 vols. MIPUB 1. Bordeaux: Delmas.

Boutié, P.
1989 Etude technologique de l'industrie moustérienne de la Grotte de Qafzeh (pres de Nazareth, Israel). Pp. 213-230 in *Investigations in South Levantine Prehistory*, eds. O. Bar-Yosef and B. Vandermeersch. BAR International Series 497. Oxford: BAR.

Cahen, D.; Keeley, L. H.; and Van Noten, F. L.
1979 Stone Tools, Toolkits, and Human Behavior in Prehistory. *CA* 20(4):661-684.

Chase, P., and Dibble, H.
1987 Middle Paleolithic Symbolism: A Review of Current Evidence and Interpretations. *JAA* 6:263-296.

Clark, G., and Lindly, J. M.
1989 The Case for Continuity: Observations on the Bio-Cultural Transition in Europe and Western Asia. Pp. 626-676 in *The Human Revolution: Behavioural and Biological Perspectives on the Origins of Modern Humans*, eds. P. Mellars and C. Stringer. Edinburgh: Edinburgh University Press.

Copeland, L.
1975   The Middle and Upper Paleolithic of Lebanon and Syria, in the Light of Recent Research. Pp. 317-350 in *Problems in Prehistory: North Africa and the Levant*, eds. F. Wendorf and A. E. Marks. Dallas: Southern Methodist University Press.

Dibble, H.
1987   The Interpretation of Middle Paleolithic Scraper Morphology. *AmAnt* 52:109-117.
1988   Typological Aspects of Reduction and Intensity of Utilization of Lithic Resources in the French Mousterian. Pp. 181-198 in *Upper Pleistocene Prehistory of Western Eurasia,* eds. H. Dibble and A. Montet-White. Philadelphia: University Museum, University of Pennsylvania.
1989   The Implications of Stone Tool Types for the Presence of Language during the Lower and Middle Paleolithic. Pp. 415-432 in *The Human Revolution: Behavioural and Biological Perspectives on the Origins of Modern Humans*, eds. P. Mellars and C. Stringer. Edinburgh: Edinburgh University Press.

Farrand, W. R.
1979   Chronology and Palaeoenvironment of Levantine Prehistoric Sites as Seen from Sediment Studies. *JAS* 6:369-392.

Garrod, D. A. E., and Bate, D. M. A.
1937   *The Stone Age of Mount Carmel.* Oxford: Clarendon Press.

Geneste, J.-M.
1985   Analyse lithique des industries moustériennes du Périgord: une approche technologique du comportement des groupes humains au Paléolithique moyen. Thesis, University of Bordeaux.
1988   Systemes d'approvisionnement en matieres premieres au Paléolithique moyen et au Paléolithique superieur en Aquitaine. Pp. 61-70 in *L'homme de Néandertal*, ed. M. Otte. Vol. 8: *La mutation*, ed. J. K. Kozlowski. ERAUL 35. Liège: Université de Liège.
1990   Développement des systèmes de production lithique au cours de Paléolithique moyen en Aquitaine septentri-

onale. Pp. 203-214 in *Paléolithique moyen recent et Paléolithique supérieur ancien en Europe*, ed. C. Farizy. Mémoires de Musée d'Ile de France 3. Nemours.

Goldberg, P., and Laville, H.
1988   Le contexte stratigraphique des occupations paléolithiques de Kebara. *Paléorient* 14(2):117-122.

Grün, R.; Stringer, C. B.; and Schwarcz, H. P.
in press   ESR Dating of Teeth from Garrod's Tabun Cave Collection. *JHE.*

Henning, G., and Hours, F.
1982   Dates pour le passage entre l'Acheulian et le Paléolithique moyen à El-Kowm, Syrie. *Paléorient* 8:81-83.

Hours, F.; Copeland, L.; and Aurenche, O.
1973   Les industries paléolithiques du Proche Orient, essai de corrélation. *L'Anthropologie* 77:229-280, 437-496.

Howells, W. W.
1976   Explaining Modern Man: Evolutionists Versus Migrationists. *JHE* 5:477-495.

Jelinek, A. J.
1976   Form, Function, and Style in Lithic Analysis. Pp. 19-33 in *Cultural Change and Continuity: Essays in Honor of James Bennett Griffin*, ed. C. E. Cleland. New York: Academic Press.
1977   A Preliminary Study of Flakes from the Tabun Cave (Mount Carmel). *Eretz Israel* 13:87-96.
1981   The Middle Paleolithic in the Southern Levant from the Perspective of the Tabun Cave. Pp. 265-280 in *Préhistoire du Levant*, eds. J. Cauvin and P. Sanlaville. Paris: CNRS.
1982a   The Middle Paleolithic in the Southern Levant. Pp. 57-104 in *The Transition from Lower to Middle Paleolithic and the Origins of Modern Man*, ed. A. Ronen. BAR International Series 151. Oxford: BAR.
1982b   The Tabun Cave and Paleolithic Man in the Levant. *Science* 216:1369-1375.

Laville, H., and Goldberg, P.
1989   The Collapse of the Mousterian Sedimentary Regime and the Beginning of the Upper Paleolithic at Kebara. Pp.

75-96 in *Investigations in South Levantine Prehistory*, eds. O. Bar-Yosef and B. Vandermeersch, BAR International Series 497. Oxford: BAR.

Lindly, J. M., and Clark, G. A.
1990   Symbolism and Modern Human Origins. *CA* 31(3):233-262.

Marks, A. E.
1983   *Prehistory and Paleoenvironments in the Central Negev, Israel*. Vol. 3: *The Avdat/Aqev Area*. Part 3. Dallas: Southern Methodist University Press.

Marks, A. E., and Volkman, P.
1986   The Mousterian of Ksar Akil: Levels XXVIA through XXVIIIB. *Paléorient* 12:5-20

Meignen, L.
1988   Un exemple de comportement technologique differentiel selon les matieres premieres: Marillac, couches 9 et 10. Pp. 71-80 in *L'homme de Néandertal*, ed. M. Otte. Vol. 4: *La technique*, eds. L. Binford and J.-P. Rigaud. ERAUL 31. Liège: Université de Liège.

Meignen, L., and Bar-Yosef, O.
1988a   Variabilite technologique au Proche Orient: l'exemple de Kebara. Pp. 87-95 in *L'homme de Nèandertal*, ed. M. Otte. Vol. 4: *La technique*, eds. L. Binford and J.-P. Rigaud. ERAUL 31. Liège: Université de Liège.
1988b   Kebara et le Paléolithique moyen du Mont Carmel (Israel). *Paléorient* 14(2):123-130.
1989   Nouvelles recherches sur le Paléolithique moyen d'Israel: la Grotte de Kebara, Unités VII à XII. Pp. 169-184 in *Investigations in South Levantine Prehistory*, eds. O. Bar-Yosef and B. Vandermeersch. BAR International Series 497. Oxford: BAR.

Meignen, L.; Bar-Yosef, O.; and Goldberg, P.
1989   Les structures de combustion moustériennes de la Grotte de Kebara (Mont Carmel, Israel). Pp. 141-146 in *Mémoires du Musée de Prehistoire d'Ile de France*, Vol. 2, eds. M. Olive and Y. Taborin.

Roebroeks, W.; Kolen, J.; and Rensink, E.
1988   Planning Depth, Anticipation and the Organization of Middle Palaeolithic Technology: The "Archaic Natives" Meet Eve's Descendants. *Helinium* 28:17-34.

Ronen, A., and Vandermeersch, B.
1972   The Upper Paleolithic Sequence in the Cave of Qafza (Israel). *Quaternaria* 16:189-202.

Schwarcz, H. P.; Buhay, W. M.; Grün, R.; Valladas, H.; Tchernov, E.; Bar-Yosef, O.; and Vandermeersch, B.
1989   ESR Dating of the Neandertal Site, Kebara Cave, Israel. *JAS* 16:653-659.

Schwarcz, H. P.; Grün, R.; Vandermeersch, B.; Bar-Yosef, O.; Valladas, H.; and Tchernov, E.
1988   ESR Dates for the Hominid Burial Site of Qafzeh, Israel. *JHE* 17:733-737.

Shea, J. J.
1989a   Tool Use and Human Evolution in the Upper Pleistocene of Israel. Pp. 611-625 in *The Human Revolution: Behavioural and Biological Perspectives on the Origins of Modern Humans*, eds. P. Mellars and C. Stringer. Edinburgh: Edinburgh University Press.
1989b   Spear Points from the Middle Paleolithic of the Levant. *JFA* 15(4):441-450.
1989c   Tool Use in the Levantine Mousterian of Kebara Cave, Mt. Carmel. *Mitequfat Ha'even* 22:15-30.

Stringer, C. B.
1989   The Origin of Early Modern Humans: A Comparison of the European and Non-European Evidence. Pp. 232-244 in *The Human Revolution: Behavioural and Biological Perspectives on the Origins of Modern Humans*, eds. P. Mellars and C. Stringer. Edinburgh: Edinburgh University Press.

Stringer, C. B.; Grün, R.; Schwarcz, H. P.; and Goldberg, P.
1989   ESR Dates for the Hominid Burial Site of Es Skhul in Israel. *Nature* 338:756-758.

Tchernov, E.
1981   The Biostratigraphy of the Middle East.

Pp. 67-98 in *Préhistoire du Levant*, eds. J. Cauvin and P. Sanlaville. Paris: CNRS.

Tillier, A. M.; Arensburg, B.; Rak, Y.; and Vandermeersch, B.
1988   Les sépultures néanderthaliennes du Proche Orient: l'état de la question. *Paléorient* 14(2):130-134.

Tixier, J.
1963   *Typologie de l'Epipaleolithique du Maghreb.* Mémoires du Centre de Recherches Anthropologiques, Préhistoriques et Ethnographiques 2. Paris.

Trinkaus, E.
1984   Western Asia. Pp. 251-293 in *The Origins of Modern Humans: A World Survey of the Fossil Evidence*, eds. F. H. Smith and F. Spencer. New York: Alan R. Liss.

Tuffreau, A.
1988   L'industrie lithique du niveau IIA. Pp. 171-186 in *Le gisement paléolithique moyen de Biache-Saint-Vaast (Pas-de-Calais)*, Vol. 1, eds. A. Tuffreau and J. Sommé. MSPF 21. Paris.

Valladas, H., and Joron, J. L.
1989   Application de la thermoluminescence a la datation des niveaux moustériens de la grotte de Kebara (Israel): age preliminaires de Unites XII, XI et VI. Pp. 97-100 in *Investigations in South Levantine Prehistory*, eds. O. Bar-Yosef and B. Vandermeersch. BAR International Series 497. Oxford: BAR.

Valladas, H.; Joron, J. L.; Valladas, G.; Arensburg, B.; Bar-Yosef, O.; Belfer-Cohen, A.; Goldberg, P.; Laville, H.; Meignen, L.; Rak, Y.; Tchernov, E.; Tillier, A. M.; and Vandermeersch, B.
1987   Thermoluminescences Dates for the Neandertal Burial Site at Kebara, Mount Carmel, Israel. *Nature* 330:159-160.

Valladas, H.; Reyss, J. L.; Joron, J. L.; Valladas, G.; Bar-Yosef, O.; and Vandermeersch, B.
1988   Thermoluminescence Dating of Mous-

terian Proto-Cro-Magnon Remains from Israel and the Origin of Modern Man. *Nature* 331:614-616.

Vandermeersch, B.
1969   Les nouveaux squelettes moustériens decouvérts à Qafzeh (Israël) et leur signification. *Comptes rendus Hebdomadaires des Seances de l'Academie des Sciences* 268:2562-2565.

1982   The First *Homo sapiens sapiens* in the Near East. Pp. 297-299 in *The Transition from Lower to Middle Paleolithic and the Origin of Modern Man*, ed. A. Ronen. BAR International Series 151. Oxford: BAR.

1984   A propos de la découverte du squelette néandertalien de Saint Césaire. *Bulletin et Mémoires de la Société d'Anthropologie de Paris* 19:191-196.

1985   Neanderthal Man and the Origins of Modern Man. Pp. 95-102 in *Homo: Journey to the Origins of Man's History*. Venice: Cataloghi Marsilio.

1989   The Evolution of Modern Humans: Recent Evidence from Southwest Asia. Pp. 155-164 in *The Human Revolution: Behavioural and Biological Perspectives on the Origins of Modern Humans*, eds. P. Mellars and C. Stringer. Edinburgh: Edinburgh University Press.

Vandermeersch, B., and Bar-Yosef, O.
1988   Evolution biologique et culturelle des populations du Levant au Paléolithique moyen. Les données récentes de Kebara et Qafzeh. *Paléorient* 11(2):115-116.

Wolpoff, M. H.
1989   Multiregional Evolution: The Fossil Alternative to Eden. Pp. 62-108 in *The Human Revolution: Behavioural and Biological Perspectives on the Origins of Modern Humans*, eds. P. Mellars and C. Stringer. Edinburgh: Edinburgh University Press.

XIII

Continuity or Replacement?
Putting Modern Human Origins
in an Evolutionary Context

G. A. Clark

"Human beings are trapped inside the dead faces of their
remote ancestors, repeated from generation to generation"
(from the novel *Mascara*, by Ariel Dorfman)

INTRODUCTION

This essay is concerned with the origins of modern humans, and what three different branches of research—archaeology, human paleontology and molecular biology—can tell us about this question, both in general and in regard to the situation in the Levant. Although modern human origins research goes back a century or more (see Spencer [1984] for a brief history), the tempo of scholarly exchanges has increased markedly in recent years, and the debate has taken on a global dimension both within and outside the scientific community. These differences of opinion have to do, in part, with very different conceptions of what science "is" or "does." In consequence, it is not always easy to convey the nature of these discussions accurately either to the general public or to an audience of fellow academics.

Within the anthropological community, differences are largely owed to differences in paradigmatic biases that affect choices of alternative biological and cultural evolutionary models—choices that ultimately determine the variables considered significant to measure and the methods deemed appropriate to measure them. In respect of the public, there is the widespread but erroneous perception that the field advances almost exclusively on the basis of discoveries, the significance of which are supposed to be readily appar-

ent to the prepared mind. This view has its origins in a long-discredited empiricist conception of science, but one that nevertheless exhibits a remarkable tenacity. A 1979 Sigma Xi survey showed that only about 9% of the American public thinks of science as a method of inquiry, as opposed to any other definition they might care to give it (the most common one was "an accumulation of facts"). More recent polls are even more discouraging, with only about 5% of American adults qualifying as "scientifically literate" in 1988—a drop that indicates a substantial decline in the public understanding of science over the past decade (Hively 1988; Green 1989). However, in neither the public nor the academic forum are the inferential bases for knowledge claims usually made explicit, nor do the social and natural sciences enjoy the consensus at the metaphysical level that is characteristic of some experimental disciplines like physics and chemistry.

Much of my recent work, and that of my students John Lindly and Nancy Coinman, constitutes a reaction to the idea, heavily promoted in the media, that morphologically modern humans (MMHs) evolved only in Africa, and replaced either archaic *Homo sapiens* (AHS) or 'Neandertals' throughout their ranges with little or no admixture. This notion of replacement without admixture is the major implication of the mitochondrial DNA (mtDNA) scenario for a recent African origin for moderns promulgated by Rebecca Cann and her colleagues (Cann et al. 1987a, b; Cann 1988) and, in my opinion, too readily accepted by archaeological 'replacement' advocates.

The idea that Neandertals were abruptly replaced, at least in Europe, by humans of modern form has, of course, a respectable antiquity (Spencer 1984). Since the early 1960s, however, and until about 1987, what was probably the majority view in the anglo-american research traditions favored relatively gradual, largely in situ change, and a degree of evolutionary continuity over the biological transition from AHS to MMHs (e.g., Brace 1962, 1964, 1965, 1968). That viewpoint is changing rapidly. Punctuated equilibrium models (e.g., Gould and Eldredge 1977) combined with currently popular cladistic approaches (e.g., Stringer et al. 1984; Stringer and

Andrews 1988; cf. Brace 1988a, b) have shifted much scientific (and practically all public) opinion back to the pre-1960s idea that MMHs evolved only in a single locus and spread relatively rapidly from that locus into Eurasia, outcompeting, displacing, extirpating, extinguishing or, most generally, replacing widespread AHS populations, themselves the products of earlier and similar 'adaptive radiations' (e.g., Foley 1987, 1989).

The distribution of archaic *Homo sapiens* and morphologically modern human fossil remains in the Mediterranean Basin and adjacent parts of Europe, North Africa, and the Levant is given in Figure 13.1. AHS is used here to include 'Neandertals', and MMH remains are taken to be those of *Homo sapiens sapiens*. The extreme geographical bias in favor of Europe is obvious, and is especially problematical because of the poor temporal resolution of the combined AHS/MMH sample elsewhere (see Clark and Lindly 1989a for a discussion of the effects of sampling bias).

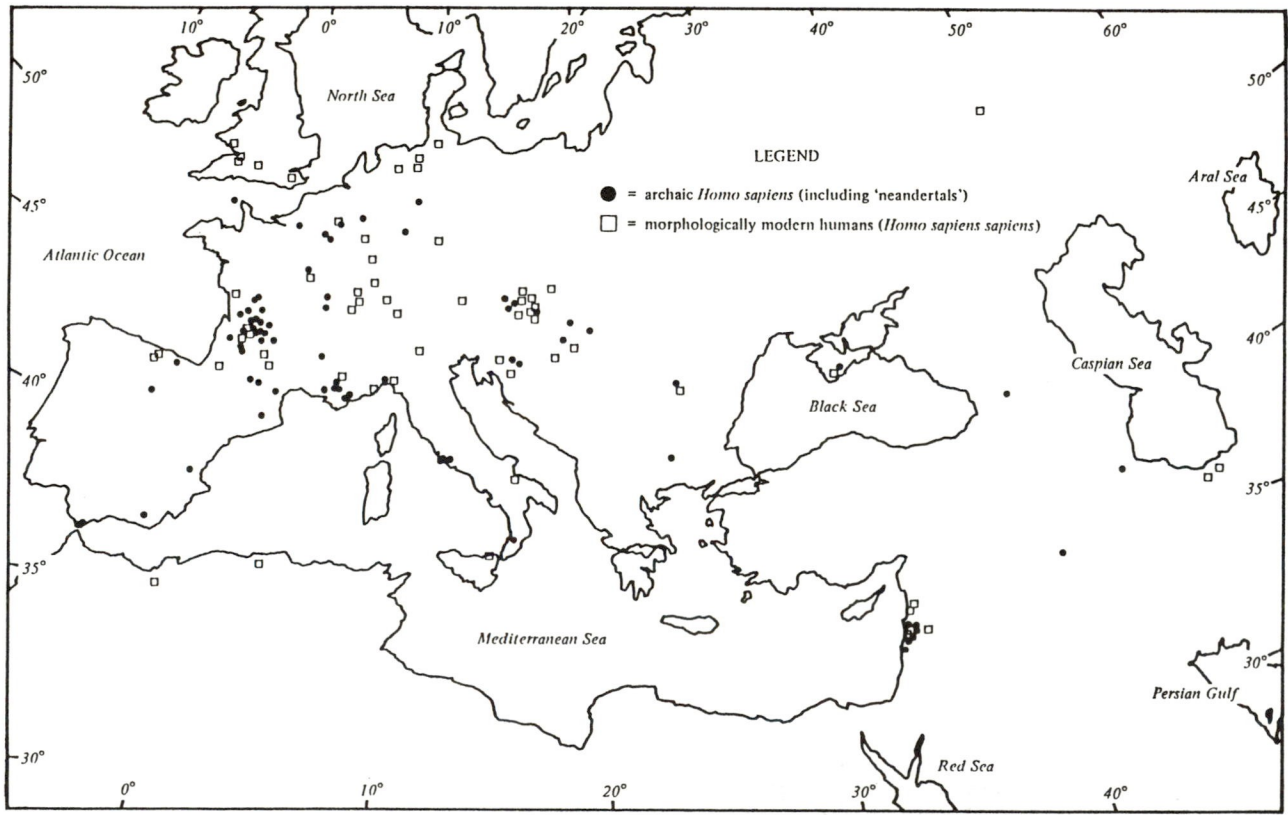

Figure 13.1   *Upper Pleistocene fossil hominid localities in western and east-central Europe, the Levant, and western Asia (Clark and Lindly 1989b:fig. 1, used with the permission of the American Anthropological Association).*

ALTERNATIVE VIEWS OF THE BIOLOGICAL TRANSITION

A major geographical area of debate is, of course, the Levant and western Asia, and here, two opposing hypotheses have been offered to describe (and supposedly explain) the transition between archaic and modern humans (Fig. 13.2). Hypothesis No. 1 states that moderns appeared early there, and coexisted with archaic *Homo sapiens*, who arrived at a later date (e.g., Bar-Yosef et al. 1986; Vandermeersch 1989; Bar-Yosef and Meignen 1989). Hypothesis No. 2 states that moderns evolved there, as elsewhere, from the local archaic *Homo sapiens* stock (e.g., Wolpoff 1980, 1989; Trinkaus 1983, 1986). The recently published dates for 'robust' moderns at Qafzeh (TL/92 $\pm$ 5 kyr, ESR/115 $\pm$ 15 kyr) (Valladas et al. 1988; Schwarcz et al. 1988) and Skhul in Israel (ESR/98 $\pm$ 6 kyr) (Stringer et al. 1989), and the later determinations for alleged 'Neandertals' at nearby Kebara (TL/60 $\pm$ 4 kyr, ESR/62 $\pm$ 6 kyr) (Valladas et al. 1987; Schwarcz et al. 1989) have led to claims that Levantine Neandertals are later immigrants from Europe, and are unrelated to modern human origins in the Levant.[1] While the Qafzeh, Skhul, and Kebara dates are provocative, what they mean is open to question.

Supporters of Hypothesis No. 1 might be called 'replacement advocates' (Fig. 13.3). They make a distinction between AHS and 'Neandertals', and postulate a series of adaptive radiations out of Africa, rather than a single prolonged one. They typically ignore grade/clade distinctions, emphasize cladogenic over anagenic speciation, invoke 'splitter' taxonomies, and

dendritic phylogenies (see below). They seek support for a particular construal of the fossil evidence by invoking a chronology implied by a particular construal of the mtDNA evidence (Cann et al. 1987a, b). They suggest that archaic *Homo sapiens* was displaced or extirpated by moderns in the Levant (and elsewhere, except in Africa), and that there was no admixture between them. This is the replacement without gene flow position advocated by many Continental and Israeli archaeologists.

Supporters of Hypothesis No. 2 might be called 'continuity advocates' (Fig. 13.4). They consider Neandertals to be the European and west Asian clades of AHS and postulate a single, prolonged hominid radiation out of Africa corresponding to the *Homo erectus* grade in human evolution.[2] They emphasize grade/clade distinctions, anagenic over cladogenic speciation, 'lumper' taxonomies, and reticulate phylogenies (see below). They claim that MMHs evolved from AHS throughout the range originally colonized by *Homo erectus*. They see many indications of morphological (hence genetic) continuity in the fossil evidence and invoke a chronology implied by another construal of the mtDNA evidence, that of Masatoshi Nei (1985, 1987). They suggest that admixture was not only likely but inevitable (assuming, for the sake of argument, the presence of 'immigrants') and that local continuity and gene flow, rather than replacement without admixture, characterized the evolution of modern humans in the Levant and elsewhere. This

---

HYPOTHESIS NO. 1

Morphologically modern humans (MMHs) appear early (ca. 90-100 kyr B.P.) in the Levant and co-exist with archaic *Homo sapiens* (AHS) who arrives at a later date (ca. 60 kyr B.P.). AHS eventually 'dies out' and plays no part in modern human origins. Moderns did not evolve from 'Neandertals'.

HYPOTHESIS NO. 2

Moderns evolve in the Levant, as elsewhere, from the local AHS stock. An influx of 'Neandertals' from Europe at ca. 60 kyr B.P. cannot be documented. Local continuity and gene flow across the AHS/MMH transition lead to moderns in the Levant and elsewhere.

Figure 13.2   Alternative hypotheses about modern human origins in the Levant (from Valladas et al. 1987, 1988; Bar-Yosef and Meignen 1989).

is the multiregional continuity position first advocated by Schwalbe (1906a, b), Hrdlička (1927), and Weidenreich (1943, 1947) more than 50 years ago. While the replacement advocates have garnered most of the publicity so far (cover articles in *Newsweek*, *Discover*, etc.), a coordinated response to the replacement position is mounting on the archaeological, human paleontological, and molecular biological fronts.

ARCHAEOLOGICAL ISSUES

The continuity position in archaeology refers to evidence for continuity in pattern over the Middle-to-Upper Paleolithic transition. It is probably true to say that the consensus in the New World has always been in favor of clinal (although not necessarily regular) change over the archaeological transition (e.g., Freeman 1964, 1973, 1981; Straus, in press; Straus and Heller 1988), but there is a growing Old World literature that also supports this position and that represents a departure from previously established views (e.g., Geneste 1988; Svoboda 1988; Kozlowski 1988). The argument is simply that if one looks at anything more comprehensive than the retouched stone tools emphasized by traditional European typological systematics, *there is continuity over the Middle-Upper Paleolithic transition on every single archaeological monitor of human adaptation.* By continuity, I mean vectored, clinal change in (1) the major technological characteristics of lithic industries, (2) raw material procurement and use, (3) patterns in faunal exploitation (although one cannot say much about plant use), (4) evidence for symbolic behavior and ritual, and (5) settlement patterns (site numbers, types, settings, and distributions)—in short, all of the criteria archaeologists use to monitor adaptation. I do not claim that all regions exhibit continuity on all variables, nor that the *rate* of change is everywhere the same. It is clear and definite, though, that there are few if any instances of marked disjunction across a suite of variables that coincides with locally-defined Middle/Upper Paleolithic transition boundaries.[3]

ADAPTATIONIST BIASES

Implicit in this position is what might be called an 'adaptationist' view of human social behavior, which is also conceptualized, after Binford (1962, 1964, 1965), as systemic in nature. I define adaptation as evolutionary biology does: any structure, physiological process, or behavioral pattern that makes an organism more fit to survive and to reproduce (Wilson 1975:577). Behavior can be viewed as "the dynamics of adaptation"—a strategy for survival and reproduction (Binford 1972:133). It could be argued that an important goal for archaeologists involved in modern human origins research is to develop a perspective for the study of the paleolithic that emphasizes changing adaptive systems. While scarcely a novel idea from an Americanist point of view (see, e.g., Binford 1962, 1964,

---

REPLACEMENT ADVOCATES

- make a distinction between archaic *Homo sapiens* (AHS) and 'Neandertals'
- postulate a series of adaptive radiations out of Africa, rather than a single, prolonged one
- invoke Cann's rapid mtDNA base substitution rate (2-4%/Mya) to argue for morphologically modern humans (MMHs) evolving in Africa (ca. 300 kyr B.P.)
- ignore grade/clade distinctions
- emphasize cladogenic speciation over anagenic speciation
- invoke 'splitter' taxonomies and dendritic phylogenies
- claim that archaic *Homo sapiens* and *Homo erectus* are replaced throughout their ranges by MMHs between 200-400 kyr B.P.
- claim that there was no admixture between AHS and MMHs (except in Africa, where MMHs evolve from AHS through anagenic speciation)

Figure 13.3   Major tenets of the 'replacement' position.

1965; Flannery 1967, 1968, 1973), most Old World archaeological research traditions either (1) concentrate almost exclusively on the characteristics of the retouched stone tool components of lithic assemblages, as if these were somehow 'meaningful' in their own right (see Clark 1989a), and/or (2) treat subsistence, paleoenvironmental and site distributional information as if these were categories of data independent of the lithics. Integrated systems perspectives are not common outside the anglophone research traditions, and the tendency to compartmentalize aspects of the research gets in the way of a more unified approach.

ADAPTATION: A REGIONAL PROBLEM

For all hunter-gatherers, adaptation is a regional problem. It can be defined either biologically (in terms of inclusive fitness) or, in the present context, culturally, by identifying particular behavioral solutions from a range of possible solutions that would allow human groups to persist over time. Put another way, human adaptation is "the possession of a valid set of solutions to a variety of problems" (Jochim 1981:19). These solutions are developed in different contexts to meet various objectives (some specific, others general), only one of which need be reproductive success.[4] Studies cast in a broadly ecological, systems framework seek to understand the adaptive significance of different kinds of human behavior without making the assumption that all such behavior is necessarily maximally adaptive

(i.e., some behaviors might be adaptively neutral, maladaptive, etc. over the long run). More important, adaptation has *specific empirical referents* that can be monitored using archaeological data and that can potentially inform us about the nature of change or process (i.e., whether change is directional, continuous or not; whether change is occurring at similar or different rates; whether patterns of change are correlated with one another across different variables, etc.). Analyses guided by these biases should be able to identify modal site and artifact functional categories and simultaneously monitor changes in function over time. Paleoclimatic fluctuations are controlled by the palynological, sedimentological, and geomorphological studies that are so fundamental to the European natural science research traditions. Time, however, is regarded as a 'reference variable' against which to measure change attributed to other causes. Whenever possible, time is controlled by absolute dating methods and, in default of samples suited to such techniques, by paleoclimatic information—*never* by the supposedly time-sensitive characteristics of the retouched tool components themselves.

BIASES ABOUT THE NATURE OF THE UPPER PLEISTOCENE ARCHAEOLOGICAL RECORD

The near-total collapse of European typlogical systematics in recent years is due both to empirical and theoretical factors (e.g., Straus 1987; Clark, in

---

CONTINUITY ADVOCATES

- do not make a distinction between archaic *Homo sapiens* and 'Neandertals'
- postulate a single, prolonged hominid radiation out of Africa corresponding to the *Homo erectus* grade in human evolution
- invoke Nei's slower mtDNA base substitution rate (0.71%/Mya) to argue for MMHs evolving in Africa ca. 850 kyr B.P.
- emphasize grade/clade distinctions
- emphasize anagenic speciation over cladogenic speciation
- invoke 'lumper' taxonomies and reticulate phylogenies
- claim that MMHs evolved from AHS throughout the range originally colonized by *Homo erectus*
- claim that there was substantial genetic admixture between AHS and MMHs, and that local continuity, rather than replacement, marked the biological transition

Figure 13.4   Major tenets of the 'continuity' position.

press). Among the more important of the latter is the realization that the local microtraditions posited by many European workers require the existence of identity-conscious social units that have no known (or imaginable) ethnographic counterparts. Whether it is reasonable to suppose that Middle and Upper Paleolithic humans exhibited the kinds of stylistic behavior that would have resulted in the existence of microtraditions is hotly debated, with some workers arguing that a separate axis of stylistic variation cannot be detected prior to the Upper Paleolithic (e.g., Binford 1973) and/or that what had been perceived to be stylistic variation in the Middle Paleolithic is in fact explicable by reference to a generalizable sequence of reduction and resharpening stages (Dibble 1987, 1988).

For what it is worth, it is my opinion that local microtraditions (*sensu* Sackett [1982]; Close [1978]) probably existed in the fabrication of stone artifacts, and that they might also have exhibited some directional change within regions during the Upper Pleistocene. However, I think that the Upper Pleistocene archaeological record is so coarse-grained that the probability of identifying them 'on the ground' is virtually nil (see Dibble and Rolland, this volume). Reasons for my skepticism about our ability to do this (an ability taken for granted by many European prehistorians) include the observation that (1) the basic retouched tool types defined by conventional European and Levantine systematics are practically universal (I, at least, cannot distinguish a Spanish backed bladelet, endscraper, or burin from one found in Turkey, Jordan, or Israel); (2) no known Upper Paleolithic site sequence, or series of sites, is anywhere near fine-grained enough to allow us to identify the residues of identity-conscious social units that would have been the bearers of microtraditions (i.e., assemblage resolution and integrity are far too low); (3) the generally acknowledged fluidity of hunter-gatherer group territorial boundaries would have impossibly confounded patterns of ethnicity in the archaeological context; and (4) a kind of 'Pompeii Premise' (Binford 1981) is invoked in arguments to the contrary, which basically hold that Upper Pleistocene sites have high resolution and integrity so far as formation processes are concerned. I do not think that is the case at all, and, in any event, it must be demonstrated (rather than assumed) that intervening cultural and natural formation processes have not perturbed the archaeological record to the extent that a 'Pompeii Premise' is warranted.

IMPLICATIONS OF CONTINUITY

The case for archaeological continuity is obviously crucial to an understanding of the biological transition, since evidence for continuity in various aspects of the archaeological record would tend to undermine the notion of replacement without admixture assumed by the Garden of Eden hypothesis (Brace 1986; Wolpoff 1989). The nature of the archaeological evidence for the Middle/Upper Paleolithic transition was much debated at the recent 'Origin of Modern Humans' symposium, held at Cambridge in March, 1987 (Mellars and Stringer 1989). The contributions included a long comparative paper on the European and west Asian evidence by Clark and Lindly (1989a). In that essay, we first tried to identify the paradigmatic biases that are characteristic of the research traditions of the two areas, which are rather different in terms of basic assumptions, and which also contrast in several significant ways with the Americanist research traditions, and then went on to consider the evidence bearing on the transition itself. We looked at (1) the systematics that underlie lithic typology and technology on both sides of the transition, (2) the nature of the Mousterian facies, (3) the role of raw material variability in the determination of lithic reduction strategies, (4) the specific character of the retouched tool and debitage components of EUP industries, (5) bone technology, (6) art and symbolic behavior, (7) taphonomic and demographic aspects of the archaeofaunal record, (8) hunting strategies, (9) site numbers, location and use, and (10) settlement patterns. While perceptions of differences and similarities in 'normative' characterizations of lithic assemblage types tend to be heavily influenced by biases expressed through the typological 'filters' used to describe them, we came to the conclusion that the biological transition was to a large extent (perhaps completely) independent of the archaeological transition between the Middle and the Upper Paleolithic. As was the case with the biological transition, we detected only vectored, clinal change in the cultural variables that we examined, and recognized few differences between Europe and the Near East in regard to those variables. No correlations were found between archaeological industries and 'types' of early man, nor did important changes in monitors of adaptation—technology, subsistence, and settlement patterns—coincide with the biological transition interval in either area. Finally, a 'change in the rate of change' (Smith et al. 1989a, b; Smith and Trinkaus, in press; Simek and Price, in press) and archaeological evidence for the appearance of fully modern behavioral patterns (Straus and Clark 1986) seemed to postdate both the Middle-Upper Paleolithic transition and the appearance of morphologically modern humans by at least 15-20 kyr.

ADAPTATION AGAIN

If no differences in adaptation are discernible over the Middle-Upper Paleolithic transition, or if the only differences discernible are differences in the *rate* of change from one area to another, arguments for replacement are reduced to nothing more than assertions of biological superiority—MMHs replaced AHS because they were allegedly 'more advanced' (whatever that means). In default of convincing paleoanthropological demonstrations that archaic and modern humans were not only 'different' from one another, but very different (i.e., different at or near the species level), the archaeological replacement position becomes nothing more than a 'just so' story that assumes what it claims to demonstrate. Even in the hopelessly inadequate (although time-honored) typological systematics of European paleolithic archaeology, there is evidence for continuity. Supposedly 'diagnostic' Middle and Upper Paleolithic tools often do not assort themselves in time the way they are supposed to according to normative characterizations (e.g., Straus 1987; Straus and Heller 1988) and, further, are often produced on similar kinds of blanks, indicating technological continuity cross-cutting, or operating independently of typological discontinuity (e.g., Smith 1982; Clark and Lindly 1989a, b).[5] Although research is more preliminary in western Asia, anomalies with normative characterizations based on Middle and Upper Paleolithic type sequences underscore similar problems with Levantine systematics (e.g., Lindly and Clark 1987).

HUMAN PALEONTOLOGY

So far as human paleontology is concerned, the chief modern advocates of continuity are Milford Wolpoff (e.g., 1980, 1989; Wolpoff et al. 1984) and, of course the intellectual 'father' of the multiregional continuity position, C. Loring Brace (e.g., 1964, 1965, 1988a). The adversaries are British scholars (e.g., Stringer and Andrews 1988; Stringer et al. 1984) or Continentals (e.g., Brauer 1984; Vandermeersch 1989). Some Americans also subscribe to one or another form of the replacement paradigm (e.g., Klein 1989; Howell 1984—see discussion in Smith et al. 1989a).

REPLACEMENT MODELS

The major tenets of the replacement position are summarized in Figure 13.3. As noted, replacement advocates tend to ignore grade/clade distinctions, invoke cladogenesis and 'splitter' taxonomies (i.e., they make a distinction between AHS and 'Neandertals'), and appeal for support to the Cann construal (Cann et al. 1987a, b) of the mtDNA evidence. They argue that *Homo erectus* and archaic *Homo sapiens* were replaced throughout their ranges by humans of modern form sometime between 200 and 400 kyr B.P. Replacement advocates appear to subscribe to what I would call a 'dendritic' view of human evolution (Fig. 13.5). The illustration depicts a typical dendritic phylogeny of the kind endorsed by the Leakeys, Walker, Stringer, and Vandermeersch. Notice that a series of relatively brief 'adaptive radiations' are postulated (rather than a single prolonged one), and a corresponding series of replacements. All but one of the 'branches' ends in extinction. It is not clear what the adaptive mechanisms were, nor what biological or behavioral characteristics supposedly conferred an 'advantage' (however defined) on one form over another.

Dendritic phylogenies originate in a 'Leakey-type' perspective on human biological evolution that has implications for the modern human origins debate, as well as for the more ancient hominid fossil record. The Leakeys, *père et fils*, have consistently produced interpretations of the human fossil record that support the notion of an early divergence and separate evolutionary trajectory of genus *Homo*, and that result in bifurcate or trifurcate phylogenies. With the discovery in 1986 of the 2.5-Mya-old 'Black Skull' (WT-17000), the latest of these phylogenies has been modified to a trifurcate model, which proposes a separate evolutionary trajectory for an East African hyperrobust australopithecine lineage (Walker et al. 1986; Lewin 1986). There are problems with this—some specific to the interpretation of the fossil itself, others to general issues in paleontological systematics (Clark 1988). It is interesting to note that the Leakeys themselves have seldom published phylogenies, leaving it to other workers to construct them on the basis of their own investigations, guided by the Leakeys' numerous, detailed descriptive publications. As Brace (1988a) has pointed out recently, dendritic models like Figure 13.5 tend to be favored by cladists.[6]

In the provocative essay from which Figure 13.5 is taken, Robert Foley (1987) invokes a particular cladogram to support the idea of an association between particular kinds of hominids and particular stone tool assemblages, arguing that a capacity to make stone tools is unique to genus *Homo* (and is, therefore, an apomophy within that lineage). The idea that some hominids were stone tool makers and others not is a convention bound up in the history of the 'Leakey line', first formulated at Olduvai Gorge. There is very little evidence in support of it, since

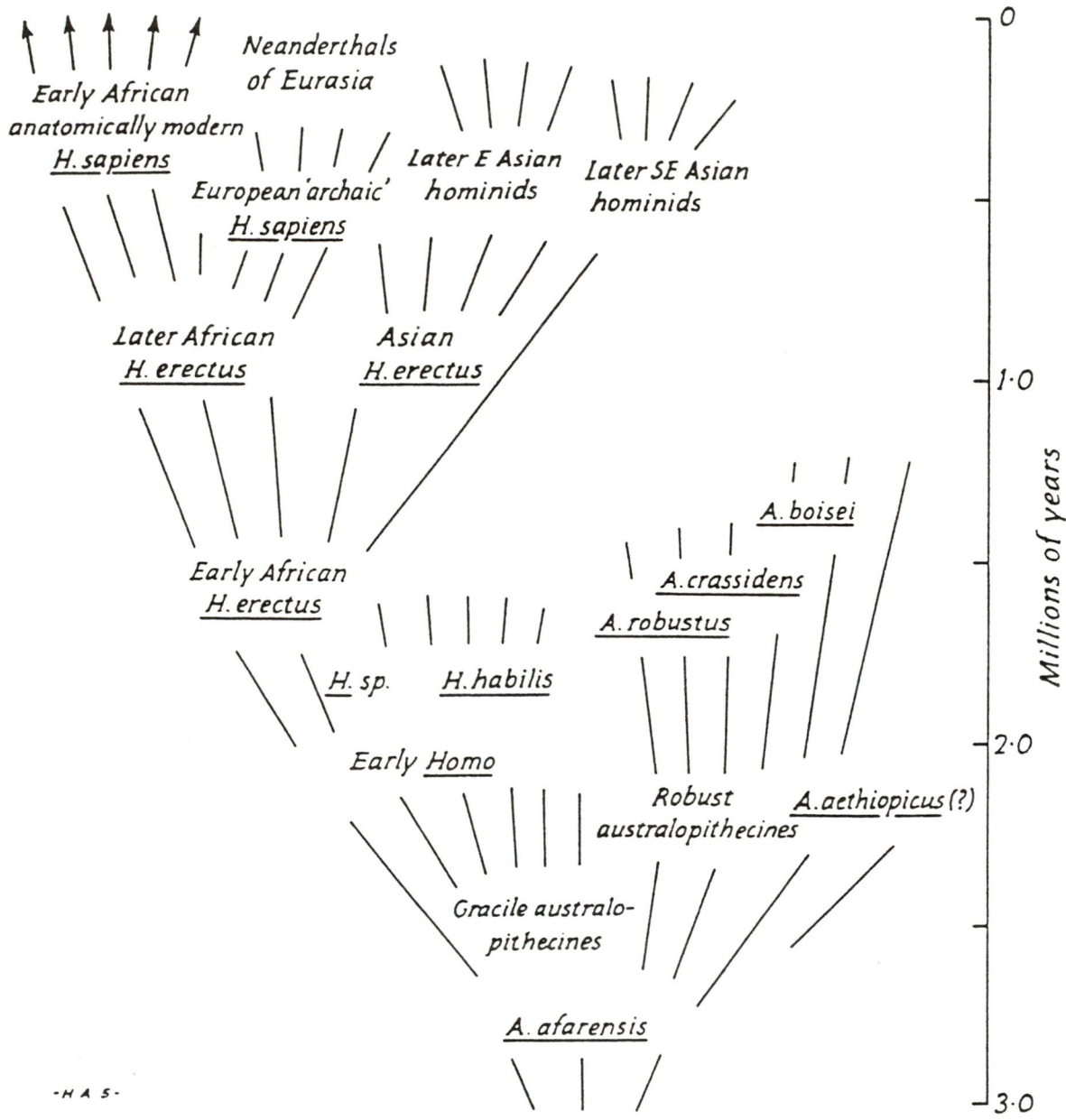

Figure 13.5   *A dendritic phylogeny: hominid evolution portrayed as a series of adaptive radiations, rather than as a single, unilineal process. Note that all lines but one end in extinction (Foley 1987:fig. 1, used with the permission of the author and of Antiquity).*

stone tools have been found associated with robust australopithecines not only at Olduvai (at FLK-1, the *Zinjanthropus* 'living floor'), but also at Swartkrans (Brain 1978; Howell 1982) and Chesowanja (Bishop et al. 1975). A similar claim has been made for gracile australopithecines at Sterkfontein and at the Sterkfontein Extension Site (Brain 1958, 1976). In addition to these matters of 'fact', there are also the theoretical objections embodied in the competitive exclusion principle which essentially argues that the primary human adaptation is culture (i.e., structured, learned behavior) and that because of cultural adaptation all hominid species occupy the same extremely broad, adaptive niche (Mayr 1950). For this reason, allopatric species would tend to become sympatic, and the most likely outcome would be the continued survival of only a single hominid lineage (Wolpoff 1971). While clearly controversial when applied to australopithecines, whose cultural repertoire probably was minimal, the competitive exclusion principle can also be invoked in regard to later hominids. Mary Leakey's notion (e.g., 1975) of the Acheulian as an allochthonous 'intrusion' at the Gorge, borne by *Homo erectus*, is a good example. It is seldom taken seriously since there is much evidence for gradual, in situ development out of an Oldowan base, not only at Olduvai but elsewhere (e.g., coastal north Africa [Biberson 1957, 1961, 1967; Biberson et al. 1960]). In light of these empirical and theoretical considerations, it is at least as credible (more credible, in my opinion) to infer that these hominids made the artifacts found with them than to invoke the presence of a hypothetically 'more advanced' member of the genus *Homo*.[7]

The dendritic view of evolution has an explicit theoretical justification with respect to modern humans in Howells' (1976) Noah's Ark model, which held that all living populations had a single (and recent) origin from a source that was already essentially modern. Howells did not indicate whether he believed that the 'essentially modern' source was different at the species level from preexisting hominids in any geographical region, nor did he suggest a point of origin for the spread of morphological moderns. He thought that modern *Homo sapiens* colonized the globe, displacing or intermixing with other, more primitive hominids who were already occupying the subtropical latitudes of Eurasia. Racial differences developed relatively recently. The fact that he did not take a position on whether differences were at the species or

subspecies level turns out to be crucial to understanding the evolutionary implications of subsequent versions of the model (e.g., Stringer and Andrews 1988; Foley 1987, 1989). Obviously, if differences were subspecific, admixture between indigenous and colonizing populations would have been possible. The problem is that we have no way of assessing the magnitude of difference empirically.

CONTINUITY MODELS

Continuity advocates tend to invoke grade/clade distinctions, anagenesis and 'lumper' taxonomies (i.e., they consider 'Neandertals' to be the European and west Asian clades of AHS), and argue that there was only a single hominid radiation out of Africa between about 1.7 and 0.7 Mya, corresponding to the *Homo erectus* grade in human evolution. They also contend that there was substantial gene flow between the colonizing *Homo erectus* population and subsequent populations of archaic *Homo sapiens* (and gene flow between AHS and MMHs), resulting in a pattern of local continuity between archaic and modern populations throughout the geographical range originally colonized by *Homo erectus*.

The continuity position is based upon what I would call a 'reticulate grade model' for the later phases of human evolution (Fig. 13.6). The diagram is my rendition of Wolpoff's multiregional continuity model (Wolpoff 1980, 1989; Wolpoff et al. 1984, 1988) combined with aspects of Brace's unilineal stage model (Brace 1965, 1988a, b).[8] The reticulate grade model is based on the idea that the human evolutionary record is characterized by broad and very roughly contemporaneous similarities in organizational level (i.e., grades—*sensu* Le Gros Clark [1967]), and by characteristics indicating common descent within a region that are superimposed upon grade features (i.e., clades, or geographical clades—*sensu* Wolpoff [1980]). It should be emphasized that grade features are only meaningful in relation to features characteristic of bracketing taxa. An African origin for the Hominidae is assumed, and a *Homo erectus* radiation out of Africa ca. 1.7-0.7 Mya that colonized much of the subtropical and temperate latitudes of Eurasia. Like Figure 13.5, the diagram is schematic because the sample of fossil remains is so sparse and so widely scattered in space and time that grade boundaries are rather arbitrary (i.e., the hatched lines are probably too narrow, and do not 'dip' enough in the Africa column). Only some of the more significant fossils are included. Also, as Africanists will note, the African fossils are only correctly placed in time relative to their grade designations. In most cases, they cannot be very precisely dated. The rest of the chronological placements are approximately accurate in relation to the scale on the left, and within the limits of the various absolute dating techniques. At present, there are no African 'Neandertals' (i.e., everything not MMH is AHS), a 'fact' that has implications for systematics and for the effects of biases inherent in regional research traditions, since they allegedly show up in the nearby Levant. Although the five geographical regions could be considered clades, it should be emphasized that they vary enormously in area—a fact often forgotten by eurocentric scholars. Some dozen or so 'Europes' would fit within the continental landmass of Africa,

which could also contain all of the other geographical regions combined. Within regions, however, the fossil find spots are often fairly tightly concentrated in space (reflecting the uneven distribution of depositional contexts suitable for the preservation of fossils and therefore areas of concentrated research), thus lending credibility to an approach that emphasizes grade/clade distinctions. Europe and west Asia, which are small in area and with relatively numerous, localized fossil samples, might be expected to best reflect clade features.

The reticulate view of human evolution is a modified version of another of Howells' (1976) evolutionary paradigms, the modified 'candelabra' model (cf. Coon 1962). It postulates an archaic *Homo sapiens* grade interposed between that of *Homo erectus* and that comprising 'modern' populations. It

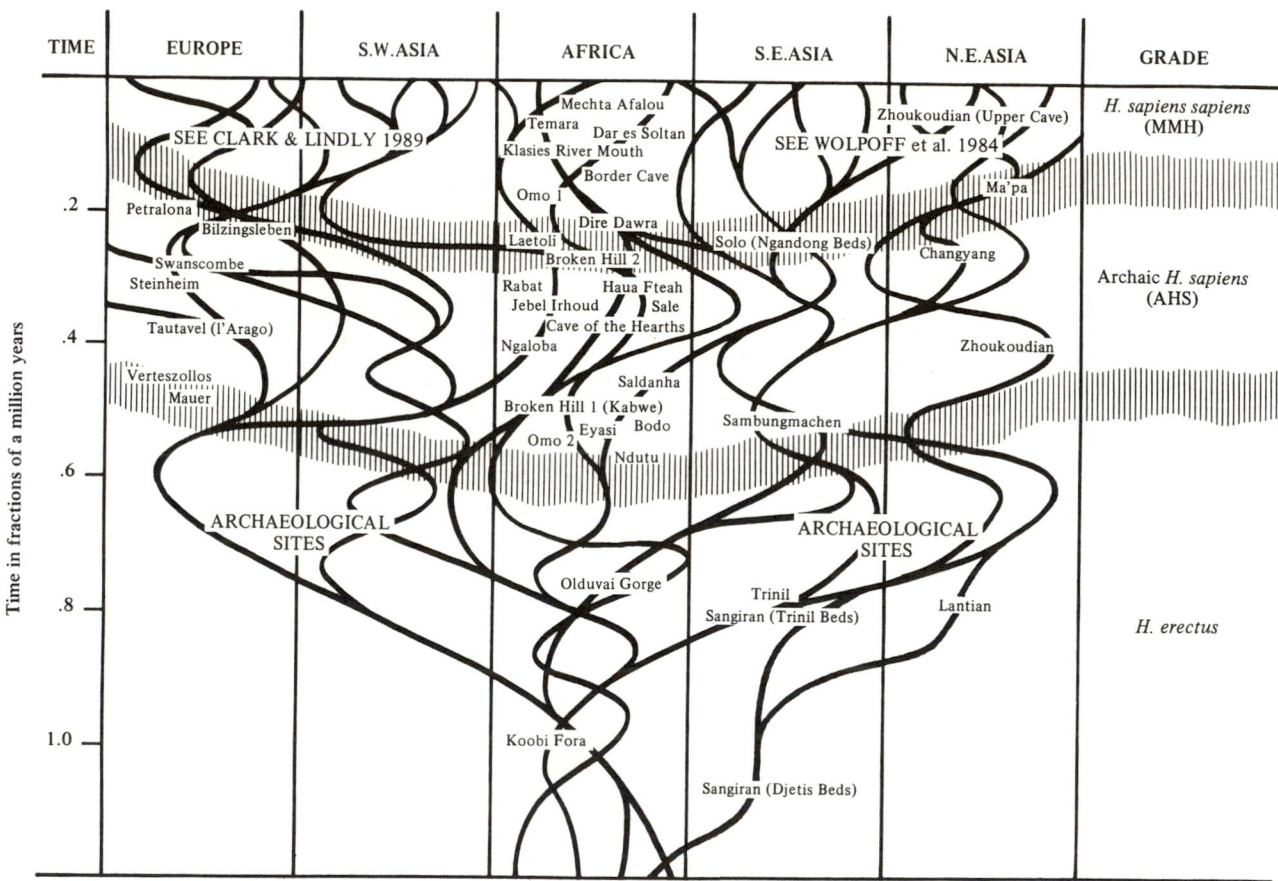

Figure 13.6   A reticulate phylogeny: hominid evolution characterized by broad and roughly contemporaneous similarities in organizational level (grades) and by characteristics indicating common descent within regions (clades). My rendition of Wolpoff's multiregional continuity model (Wolpoff 1989) combined with Brace's unilineal stage model (Brace 1988b).

differs from the Noah's Ark model in that it assumes a single adaptive radiation out of Africa corresponding to the *H. erectus* grade, with subsequent colonization of most of the uninhabited areas of the Old World during the Middle and Upper Pleistocene. A trellis-like configuration is envisioned, with penecontemporaneous development of parallel lineages through a succession of grades, but connected with one another across space by greater or lesser amounts of gene flow. Whereas the Noah's Ark model is grounded in rather narrow characterizations of hominid taxa, and what might be called a 'splitter' mentality, the reticulate view reflects an appreciation that (1) both *H. erectus* and AHS samples are temporally and spatially variable; (2) that the nature and *rate* of change varied geographically and temporally; and (3) that biological changes did not take place in a behavioral vacuum, and must have reflected adaptation in ways that are, at present, only partly understood. The reticulate view (4) emphasizes grade/clade distinctions, which are analytically essential if the elements of continuity that characterize the various regional samples (clades) are to be separated from those that reflect the general organizational level (grade). Finally, (5) it presupposes that hominids of a given grade were capable of interbreeding throughout their ranges (i.e., that, at any given time interval within a grade and within a region, they were members of a single species).

A logical entailment of a multiregional/unilineal perspective is that AHS grade characteristics would be globally intermediate between those of *H. erectus* and those of *H. sapiens sapiens*. Since any division between *H. erectus* and AHS must be an arbitrary one, AHS grade characteristics should exhibit a continuation of morphological trends seen first in *H. erectus*. Those characteristics have been widely summarized (e.g., Brace 1965, 1988b; Wolpoff 1980; Trinkaus 1986) and, so far as I can determine, are not much debated. They include (1) an expansion in brain size (braincase breadth approaches cranial breadth as the brain expands), (2) changes in cranial proportions (expansion of the upper part of the occiput, expansion of the frontal areas as the braincase becomes more 'inflated' relative to *H. erectus*), (3) decreases in the surface areas of the posterior dentition, (4) increases in anterior tooth size and in the size and robusticity of their support structures (perhaps indicating increasing use of the anterior dentition as an adjunct to technology), (5) possible decreases in the area of nuchal muscle attachment

and in the volume of spongy bone in the basicranium, and (6) decreases in the skeletal indicators of cranial and post-cranial muscular robusticity. It is essential to keep in mind that these morphological trends are expressed to varying degrees in regional geographical samples of AHS, that they are only very broadly contemporaneous (see Fig. 13.6), that they are not irreversible and that they are only meaningful in relation to grade characteristics of bracketing taxa. Superimposed on these grade features are clade features that reflect continuity in descent within relatively circumscribed geographical areas.

Any convincing fossil evidence for morphological continuity outside of Africa would conclusively refute all replacement models, and would also call into question the credibility of the Cann construal of the mtDNA evidence (Cann et al. 1987a, b; Cann 1988). Along with other continuity advocates, I submit that there is overwhelming evidence for morphological continuity in the two areas that have produced the largest samples of fossil evidence bearing on the evolution of modern humans: Europe and western Asia. Moreover, the same general kinds of processes and morphoclinal trends appear to be documented over the AHS/MMH transition in both areas. Specifically, there seems to be widespread agreement that (1) the lower face reduces substantially, almost certainly because of a decrease in the habitual paramasticatory use of the anterior dentition, (2) incisors and canines themselves reduce, and for the same reasons, (3) the occlusal surface areas of the molar dentition decrease somewhat, (4) browridges shrink and change shape in response to reduction in anterior tooth loading,[9] (5) overall midfacial prognathism decreases, (6) the anteroposterior length of the jaws decreases because of decreases in the size of the anterior teeth, causing retromolar spaces to disappear and chins to develop, (7) nuchal muscle attachment areas continue to decrease and 'migrate' to a lower position on the occiput, (8) the neurocranium becomes more spherical as a result of changes in the physics of muscle attachment and in the rate of development of different parts of the brain, (9) the proportions of the appendicular skeleton approach the modern condition, and, finally, (10) there is a decrease in the skeletal indicators of muscular robusticity (Trinkaus 1984, 1986). These *are* the changes that mark the appearance of MMHs throughout their range.

Although the samples are poor because they are so discontinuous in space and time, these changes are temporally vectored and, taken as a group, seem to have a universal character. They also correspond reasonably well to projections of morphoclinal change in the AHS grade characters just summarized. Many workers explain them by invoking behavioral changes and linked technological dependencies which, over the long run, required less reliance upon the maintenance of energetically expensive physical strength and endurance (e.g., and esp. Trinkaus 1982, 1983, 1984, 1986). *It cannot be emphasized enough that the reticulate view of evolution is a polythetic model.* If the overall pattern of morphological change is in the indicated direction, and if a Trinkaus-like functional morphological explanation for directional change is regarded as credible,[10] then it matters not at all that individual characteristics on particular specimens are at variance with the expected pattern. Such anomalies could be dismissed on the basis of sampling error alone.

A LEVANTINE EXAMPLE OF THE ARCHAEOPALEONTOLOGICAL DEBATE

To illustrate the contrasting positions with a Levantine example, it is alleged that the founding population of anatomically modern people from Africa had already reached Qafzeh Cave in Israel by about 90-100 kyr B.P. (Bar-Yosef et al. 1986; Valladas et al. 1988; Vandermeersch 1989). The apparent 'fact' that Neandertal remains at nearby Kebara date to a more recent time interval suggests either (1) that MMHs and Neandertals lived side by side for more than 30 kyr without interbreeding, or (2) that Neandertals moved southward into the Levant from Europe about 60 kyr B.P., where they coexisted with modern people until the latter began to colonize Europe about 25,000 years later (Bar-Yosef, in press; Bar-Yosef and Meignen 1989). Replacement advocates tend to argue that the contemporaneity of AHS and MMHs in the Levant is an indication of no direct relationship between them and their cultural attributes. I think instead that it is much more likely that the validity of the biological taxonomic units themselves is suspect. However they are interpreted, the Israeli dates have helped to sharpen conceptual issues relating to modern human origins, and have often and vociferously been invoked by replacement advocates in support of their position.

I suggest, however, that the dates are only 'problematical' if (1) it is accepted that paleoanthropologists can unambiguously distinguish a 'Neandertal' from a morphological modern, (2) that such alleged distinctions are 'significant' or 'important' ones in functional morphological terms (i.e., that the two forms are really different from one another), and (3) that replacement advocates can come up with a plausible explanation as to how on earth two allegedly different hominids (i.e., Neandertals, moderns) could have coexisted for nearly 30 kyr in an area about the size of Rhode Island without interbreeding (thereby implying that they are indeed different species) and without showing any archaeologically detectable differences in adaptation. To anyone well grounded in evolutionary ecology, the idea is preposterous on the face of it. Yet this is exactly what some Continental and Israeli scholars are arguing. Although my objections to this point of view are not based just on characteristics of lithic assemblages (see Clark and Lindly 1989a, b), most Levantine prehistorians (including, ironically, some of the replacement advocates) would acknowledge that the industries associated with Neandertals at Kebara and moderns at Qafzeh are in general and in most details alike (Bar-Yosef 1989; Shea 1989). This directly contradicts expectations under all replacement scenarios published so far.

ADAPTATION AGAIN: THE COMPETITIVE EXCLUSION PRINCIPLE

To suggest that two species with the same adaptation could have occupied the same niche within a small area at the same time over a long period of time flies in the face of the competitive exclusion principle and, in fact, everything we know about basic evolutionary ecology (e.g., Hardesty 1980). The replacement advocates have tried to explain away this contradiction by suggesting that Neandertals and moderns either lived in different microenvironmental zones (Bar-Yosef, in press) or participated in a kind of climatically induced 'time sharing', with moderns living at a site for a time, then dying out locally or emigrating, and Neandertals moving in, etc. (Mellars 1989:361). Neither scenario explains why the two populations appear to have had identical stone technologies, lived in virtually the same locations (e.g., Tabun and Skhul on Mt. Carmel), and procured exactly the same range of animals in exactly the same ways over long periods of time (Edwards 1989; Clark and Lindly 1988, 1989a, b). Nor does it explain why these populations evidently used the stone tools they made in exactly the same ways (Shea 1989). Invoking alleged differences in 'grave goods' associated with MMH remains at Qafzeh and Skhul, and dismissing identical 'offerings' from west Asian Neandertal contexts as 'utilitarian' (Mellars 1989:362, quoting Chase and Dibble [1987]) simply does not make sense (Lindly and Clark 1990a, b). Even allowing, for the sake of argument, the unlikely possibility of long range migration, to claim that an originally cold-adapted Neandertal population arrived in the Levant from Europe with the same adaptation as an indigenous modern population stretches credulity to the breaking point.

BIASES AGAINST 'MIGRATION'

Finally, and along with Jelinek (1982) and Trinkaus (1982), I wish to express a profound dislike for the concept of 'migration,' at least as it is used in the archaeopaleontological sense of a relatively short-term, long-range event or process. Migration is a *deus ex machina* notion that is nonetheless central to all of the replacement scenarios but is especially important to those of Europe and the Levant. Like Trinkaus (1982), I consider migration to be a density-dependent phenomenon that is essentially confined to the latest prehistoric, protohistoric, and historic periods (i.e., those periods when human population densities were locally high in some areas). *I simply do not believe that the physical migration of peoples played a significant role in human macro-evolution, and am hard-pressed to come up with a single instance where a more compelling alternative explanation is not possible.*[11] Documenting migration is by no means an easy task and to do so would, at a minimum, call for the identification of a source area and donor population which could be shown to be both antecedent to and distinct from the indigenous population in the recipient area. In my opinion, no one connected with the modern human origins debate has been able to do this at all convincingly. However, most workers have implicit biases in respect of migrations and consequently either dismiss them out of hand as improbable (e.g., Trinkaus, Jelinek, Straus, me) or regard them as possible 'causes' for observed patterns (e.g., Harrold, Bar-Yosef, White—any benighted soul who thinks that the Aurignacian represents an 'invasion from the East'). Biological and cultural information of the kind required to document migration is transmitted by gene flow and stimulus diffusion respectively, and locally will exhibit either stability or change over time and space. However, I submit that, although we can conceptualize these transmission mechanisms in the abstract, we are not usually in a position to use that information effectively to determine whether or not a migration has in fact occurred. Because of the coarse 'grain' of the Upper Pleistocene archaeological and paleontological records, there is no way to 'test' for them empirically, so people either regard them as plausible or not, depending on their biases.

MOLECULAR BIOLOGY

In respect of molecular biology, the sticking point with the Cann mtDNA scenario has always been that no admixture could be accommodated (Cann et al. 1987a, b; Cann 1988). If true, this would imply that differences between moderns and other earlier hominids *had to be at the species level.* Replacement advocates picked up on the rapid base substitution rate published by Cann (2-4%/Mya), which indicated a modern human origin somewhere in Africa at about 300 kyr B.P. Initially, at least, there was little realization by archaeologists and paleoanthropologists that (1) other base substitution rates were published and defended—especially that of Nei (0.71%/Mya), which implied a hominid radiation out of Africa ca. 850 kyr B.P. corresponding to the *Homo erectus* grade. These other rates can be recon-ciled much more easily with the fossil and archaeological records than can that of Cann (Wolpoff 1989). (2) Most workers did not seem to realize that the Cann rate implied an absurdly late hominid/pongid split, at about 3.5 million years ago, for which there is no fossil evidence whatsoever. (3) Finally, there seemed to be little appreciation of the fact that, just like any other field, molecular biology has an internal dynamic characterized by the same kinds of controversy and debate found in other disciplines (Lewin 1988a, b). In short, replacement advocates jumped on the Cann bandwagon because it supported their biases about the course of human evolution. They did not appreciate how incompatible her arguments were with the fossil and archaeological records.

THE LATEST FROM REBECCA CANN AND HER COLLEAGUES

In the most recent of a series of essays, Stoneking and Cann (1989) take up the question of what might have happened when the dispersing African population encountered earlier resident hominids in Asia and Europe. Accepting their rate of base pair substitution as approximately accurate, they note that there appear to be no divergent non-African mtDNA types in modern human populations. Ancient, non-African mtDNA types with an estimated divergence date of ca. 1 Mya would be expected if resident non-Africans had contributed mtDNA to modern populations. Three possible explanations for the lack of ancient, non-African mtDNA types are offered: (1) sampling error is responsible for their absence (i.e., such types actually exist in modern populations but have not been detected so far in the more than 1000 non-African individuals sampled to date), (2) resident non-Africans did in fact contribute mtDNA types to the dispersing African population but these were subsequently lost either through natural selection or by stochastic processes, and (3) divergent non-African DNA types are not found in modern human populations because they were never there in the first place (i.e., the dispersing African population replaced non-African resident populations without admixture).

The first possibility can only be evaluated with the accumulation of more data—either divergent non-African types will eventually be found, or they will be shown to have a true frequency of zero. The second alternative is difficult to assess mainly because it is generally believed that most mtDNA mutations now present in human populations are effectively neutral. If this was also true in the past (and there is no reason to think that it was not true), then it would be hard to suggest a selective advantage that mtDNA types in the dispersing population might have had over those present in the resident populations. However, theoretically, if such an advantage did in fact exist, then the resident types would eventually be lost. At present there is no way to evaluate such a possibility empirically. Stoneking and Cann (1989) conclude that, if the first two alternatives can be ruled out, the third alternative—replacement without admixture—is the only viable possibility.

SPUHLER'S COUNTERARGUMENTS

As might be expected, this interpretation of pattern in the molecular evidence, and what it might mean, has been questioned by continuity advocates both within (e.g., Saitou and Omoto 1987; Darlu and Tassy 1987; Spuhler 1988) and outside (e.g., Wolpoff et al. 1988; Wolpoff 1989; Clark 1989b; Clark and Lindly 1989a, b) the field of molecular biology. Of these critiques, the most devastating (because it is the most thorough) probably has been that of James Spuhler (1988). Spuhler has observed that the significant regional variation and great time depth of human mtDNA differences combine to make a single, relatively recent origin for all modern humans unlikely. He suggests instead that *H. sapiens* arose by regional phyletic transition from *H. erectus*, starting in Africa in the Middle Pleistocene. Spuhler points out that mtDNA types vary greatly not only between but *within* regional African, Asian, Near Eastern, European, and Australian populations and that there are many types that are not only unique to a region but that are also very old in that region. Also, divergence times for regional populations are characterized by enormous error terms, regardless of rate and, therefore, are of limited utility for determining ages for much more recent, smaller scale divergences like the appearance of MMHs. The implication is that polymorphism in the mtDNA genome existed prior to racial divergence and that the appearance of the geographically somewhat circumscribed present racial stocks cannot be correlated with particular divergence events.

Spuhler also notes that there are serious sampling problems with current mtDNA investigations in that only 1,500 base pairs are used for comparisons (out of the 16,500 bases that make up the complete human mtDNA genome). Moreover, he points out that Cann et al.'s (1987a, b) crucial African sample is limited to 20 individuals, 18 of whom were American-born blacks. Observing that most mtDNA gene variation is shared and invariant in all living human races, he comes to the conclusion that, given its procedural drawbacks and problematic assumptions, the mtDNA evidence produced so far lends more support to the multiregional continuity position than to an hypothesis of relatively rapid, worldwide replacement by migration from a single geographical origin point (Spuhler 1988:42, 43). The point is well taken that this research (compared with that using nuclear DNA) is in its infancy, and that we must wait for molecular biology to resolve the nettlesome conceptual and procedural issues alluded to above (see also Lewin 1988a, b).[12]

CONCLUSIONS

In summary, the principal points being made here are, first, that preconceptions about human biological evolution have real consequences for interpretations of the archaeological record (*contra* Bar-Yosef and Meignen 1989). Things that are 'reasonable to conclude' under one set of paradigmatic biases are 'not reasonable to conclude' under another. The tendency to draw and defend subdisciplinary boundaries is a legacy of the long-discredited empiricist conception of science which is, unfortunately, still alive and well in paleoanthropology. It is a legacy in which we can no longer afford to indulge. A second point is that biological replacement without admixture runs counter to *any* construal of the archaeological evidence. Third, cladistic analyses of the kind upon which replacement advocates tend to rely have major practical and conceptual problems. I have outlined some of these in a recent paper (Clark 1988). Fourth, we contend that the archaeological record over *both* the biological transition from archaic to modern humans, *and* the cultural transition from the Middle to the Upper Paleolithic, shows strong evidence for continuity on any and all archaeological monitors of adaptation. Discontinuity would clearly be expected under all of the replacement scenarios published so far. Fifth, we argue that the two transitions did not coincide in time and were, therefore, probably not directly related to one another. Sixth, we think that the archaeological time/space grid, because it is more complete than that of the fossil evidence, can sometimes be used to generate test implications about biological evolution. Seventh, we recognize no correlation whatsoever between archaeological industries and particular hominid taxa, as has recently been claimed by some British workers (e.g., Foley 1987; cf. Clark 1989b) and which is clearly implied by those replacement scenarios involving the Aurignacian. Finally, some of us, at least, think that archaeological evidence for fully modern behavioral patterns post-dates the Middle-Upper Paleolithic transition by at least 15-20,000 years. In other words, the advent of the Upper Paleolithic at ca. 40,000 years ago in the Levant and in Europe does not also mark the appearance of biological moderns equipped with a fully modern behavioral repertoire (cf. Chase and Dibble 1987; Lindly and Clark 1990a, b). In terms of cultural evolution, the boundary between the early Upper Paleolithic and the late Upper Paleolithic at about 20,000 years ago is beginning to look like a more significant behavioral 'rubicon' than the traditional boundary between the Middle and the Upper Paleolithic at about 40,000 years ago.

EPILOGUE

In light of its long and dismal history as a 'significant' anthropological debate, it is not unreasonable to ask why anthropology cannot solve the modern human origins question. The current version of the debate, provoked by St. Césaire, the Israeli TL dates, and the mtDNA evidence, is only the latest in a long series of episodes of accelerated discussion that go back almost a century and that show up with a periodicity of about a generation. I suggest that the reason we have made relatively little progress is because anthropology stubbornly clings to a discredited empiricist conception of science. In this conception, 'facts' have a certain autonomy and observations are considered to be more reliable sources of knowledge than theories. Thus, the latter remain in a rudimentary state of development. It is not that the relevant theory does not exist; it is more a question of a failure to use it to generate expectations that can be tested against archaeological and paleontological data.

All this essay really tries to do is to show that there are major contradictions in the expectations generated by the research paradigms that govern the different aspects of the debate. In the classic positivist view of science articulated by Karl Popper (1959, 1972, 1983), those expectations, embodied in the concept of prediction, are the main function of scientific theories, and corroboration of a prediction (either before or after the fact) is strong evidence of the tenability of a theory, as is a willingness to put a theory 'at risk' by making falsifiable predictions (Brush 1989). But, are there any theories in anthropology that are truly falsifiable? Are there any guidelines at all that will allow us to determine the credibility of a 'fact'? Is a theory that successfully predicts a new 'fact' better than one that does not? Does a 'fact' provide better evidence for a theory if it was not known before being deduced from the theory? Given the present lack of discussion of the epistemological status of theory in most aspects of paleoanthropology, these questions essentially have no meaning.[13] It is not even clear to me what a theory *is* in paleoanthropology.

One might imagine that this last, great hominid transition would be the best understood of all of those in the human career, but, as the present controversy shows, there is as much diversity of opinion as ever (possibly more, with the addition of the mtDNA evidence). If we are ever going to understand the transition to modern humans, it must be studied *as a transition*. We can no longer afford to deal with it as if it were neatly compartmentalized into archaeology, paleoanthropology, and molecular biology components. Preconceptions about biological evolution have important consequences for interpretations of the archaeological record (and vice versa), and archaeologists can only ignore the findings of the other disciplines at their peril. The archaic ancestors of modern humans represent a long-lasting adaptive phase immediately preceding us. To claim that they were extinguished without issue over most of their range without coming up with a plausible explanation of *why* and *how* such an event or process could have taken place does little to engender much confidence in the explanatory potential of anthropological research designs.

NOTES

1.   This point of view assumes that there were in fact 'immigrants' and that 'migration' had occurred. I suggest that large scale population movements are density-dependent phenomena and, given the consensus view that early Upper Pleistocene population densities were *extremely low*, were unlikely to have occurred in these remote time ranges. Population densities clearly varied in a mosaic pattern from one region to the next; they also varied over time within regions. If changes in population densities occurred, they were clearly long-term changes.

2.   It is worth remarking that the 'out of Africa' model for human origins assumed by both replacement and continuity advocates alike might be subject to serious revision. Evidence is accumulating for a *very early* human presence in various parts of Eurasia (e.g., in Pakistan's Soan Valley, where undisputed bifacially flaked quartzite artifacts have been recovered from the Riwat section of the Upper Siwalik formation, dated at 2.0 ± 0.2 Mya—Rendell et al. 1987; Dennell et al. 1988). The implications of these discoveries are considerable, since they are older than any African bifacial industry and nearly as old as the oldest stone artifacts known (ca. 2.8 Mya). If the dates and context are good, they indicate the presence of hominids outside of Africa prior to anyone's construal of the earliest colonization of Eurasia, and call into question the credibility of the African origin of the Hominidae.

3.   If, in any given region, one group was 'replacing' another over a relatively short time interval, such a replacement 'event' or 'process' should be evident in the archaeological monitors of adaptation just mentioned.

4.   Biological definitions of adaptation are practically impossible to test empirically since, in the absence of representative samples of biological populations, there is no way to measure reproductive success. Since it is more complete, the archaeological record can sometimes be used, as here, to generate test implications about aspects of biological evolution. This assumes that the creators of an archaeological record can be identified (which, in light of the deplorable state of paleonotological systematics, is an enormous assumption to make!).

5.   In most Old World research traditions, typology has been emphasized at the expense of technology, so that it is more difficult to get a clear picture of technological patterns than it is to get a picture of typological patterns. The real issue, though, is what do these patterns 'mean' in behavioral terms?

6.   Richard Leakey is not a cladist in a formal sense, however, nor is his archrival, Donald Johanson.

7.   Especially one whose taxonomic status is hotly debated.

8.   Despite alleged differences between the creators of these models, I can detect little to distinguish them. Brace (1988a) and Wolpoff (1989) appear to be operating on basically the same sets of assumptions and principles. Brace's model is more of a stage (grade) model, but he certainly recognizes and endorses efforts to trace geographical clades, whereas Wolpoff's emphasizes geographical clades which are, nonetheless, superimposed on grades. Wolpoff has perhaps done more to put empirical 'teeth' into multiregional continuity.

9.   It has been suggested that higher, rounder foreheads were apparently equally or better able to counteract such stress (Endo 1966).

10. Because biomechanical reasons for morphological changes are given by Trinkaus, Oxnard, Marzke, Tuttle, and other functional morphologists, I consider their explanations of change to be more credible than those of cladists (and, in fact, those of *any* comparative study based exclusively on morphology). This is not to imply that functional morphological interpretations are not debated, or even sometimes completely wrong, but cladistics is not the answer. Despite their current popularity, there are major conceptual and methodological problems with cladistic approaches (Clark 1988, 1989c). Apart from very sticky problems with deciding what is in fact a derived character, one must demonstrate that derived characters not present in an ancestral group are shared by all members of a clade. However, paradigms in paleoanthropology emphasize different suites of variables differentially. What actually happens is that practical considerations take over in the context of any problem domain, influenced by *a priori* identification of taxonomic units (i.e., the groups to be compared, which differ from one worker to the next) and by biases that assign weights to particular suites of variables, even if the variables themselves are equally weighted. Ways to make these decisions are essentially subjective and, in consequence, mechanical applications of cladistic analyses can sometimes produce absurd results (Stringer et al.'s [1989] conclusion that European Neandertals are more like modern Europeans than they are like Upper Paleolithic Europeans is a splendid example). A partial solution is to try to use outgroup comparisons of

distantly related taxa to identify primitive characters, although this doesn't always work either. Very occasionally, quantified parameter estimates are generated for variables determined to be relevant to a particular problem.

11. It might be claimed that the appearance of the Aurignacian in western Europe from a presumed source in eastern Europe is a good candidate for a physical migration (actual movement of people). However, very early Aurignacian dates at ca. 40 kyr B.P. have recently been reported from l'Arbreda and El Castillo caves in northern Spain (Bischoff et al. 1989; Cabrera and Bischoff 1989). These dates, *at the far western end* of the Aurignacian geographical distribution, are as old, or older than alleged early Aurignacian dates from eastern Europe, strongly suggesting that the Aurignacian does not represent an actual migration of people, but rather a simultaneous technological development manifest over wide areas of Europe (Straus 1989).

12. To judge from a number of recent exchanges in the journal *Science*, the whole field of DNA clock models is becoming increasingly problematical (Lewin 1988a, b). Because they are relatively new, mtDNA clock models suffer from these conceptual and methodological drawbacks to an even greater extent than do nuclear DNA clock models, which have a much longer history. Although DNA clock models appear to have been relatively successful in respect of dating landmark divergence events like the initial appearance of the Hominidae (i.e., the hominid/pongid split), it is reasonable to question whether they are equally effective in determining ages for much more recent, smaller-scale, divergences like the appearance of MMHs. Specifically, is the assumption of a constant rate of mtDNA mutation valid over relatively 'short' time spans, or could there be problems with the resolution of these techniques the closer one gets to the present? Nobody knows.

13. There is some history of a concern with these epistemological issues in anglo-american archaeology, and with efforts to identify paradigmatic biases at the level of the metaphysic and to distinguish paradigms (statements about the way the world is, or appears to be) from theories (statements about *why* the world, or some portion of it, appears to be the way it seems) (e.g., Binford and Sabloff 1982; Watson et al. 1971, 1984). An explicit concern with epistemology is not particularly common outside the anglophone research traditions, with occasional exceptions (e.g., Gallay 1989).

REFERENCES CITED

Bar-Yosef, O.
1989   Geochronology of the Levantine Middle Paleolithic. Pp. 598–610 in *The Human Revolution: Behavioural and Biological Perspectives on the Origins of Modern Humans*, eds. P. Mellars and C. Stringer. Edinburgh: Edinburgh University Press.
in press   Upper Pleistocene Human Adaptations in South-West Asia. In *Corridors, Cul-de-Sacs and Coalescence: The Biocultural Foundations of Modern People*, ed. E. Trinkaus. Cambridge: Cambridge University Press.

Bar-Yosef, O., and Meignen, L.
1989   Levantine Mousterian Variability in the Light of New Dates from Qafzeh and Kebara. Paper presented at the 54th Annual Meeting of the SAA (Atlanta, April).

Bar-Yosef, O.; Vandermeersch, B.; Arensberg, B.; Goldberg, P.; Laville, H.; Meignen, L.; Tchernov, E.; and Tillier, A.-M.
1986   New Dates on the Origin of Modern Man in the Levant. *CA* 27:63–64.

Biberson, P.
1957   Nouveaux élements sur la 'Pebble Culture' du Maroc Atlantique. Pp. 153–158 in *Actas del V° Congreso INQUA*. Madrid: INQUA.
1961   *Le Paléolithique inférieur du Maroc Atlantique*. Rabat: Publications de la Service des Antiquités du Maroc 17.
1967   Some Aspects of the Lower Paleolithic of Northwest Africa. Pp. 447–476 in *Background to Evolution in Africa*, eds. W. Bishop and J. D. Clark. Chicago: Aldine.

Biberson, P.; Choubert, G.; Faure-Mauret, M.; and Lecointre, G.
1960   Contribution à l'étude de la 'Pebble Culture' du Maroc Atlantique. *Bulletin Archéologique Marocaine* 3:27–33.

Binford, L.
1962   Archaeology as Anthropology. *AmAnt* 28:217–225.
1964   A Consideration of Archaeological Research Design. *AmAnt* 29:425–441.
1965   Archaeological Systematics and the Study of Culture Process. *AmAnt* 31:203–210.
1972   Contemporary Model Building: Paradigms and the Current State of Paleolithic Research. Pp. 109–166 in *Models in Archaeology*, ed. D. Clarke. London: Methuen.

1973 Interassemblage Variability—the Mousterian and the 'Functional' Argument. Pp. 227-254 in *The Explanation of Culture Change*, ed. C. Renfrew. Pittsburgh: University of Pittsburgh Press.

1981 Behavioral Archaeology and the 'Pompeii Premise'. *JAR* 37:195-208.

Binford, L., and Sabloff, J.
1982 Paradigms, Systematics and Archaeology. *JAR* 38:137-153.

Bischoff, J.; Soler, N.; Maroto, J.; and Julia, R.
1989 Abrupt Mousterian/Aurignacian Boundary at *c*. 40 ka bp: Accelerator ^{14}C Dates from l'Arbreda Cave (Catalunya, Spain). *JAS* 16:553-576.

Bishop, W.; Pickford, M.; and Hill, A.
1975 New Evidence Regarding the Quaternary Geology, Archaeology and Hominids of Chesowanja, Kenya. *Nature* 258:204-208.

Brace, C. L.
1962 Refocusing on the Neanderthal Problem. *AA* 64:729-741.

1964 The Fate of the 'Classic' Neanderthals: A Consideration of Hominid Catastrophism. *CA* 5:3-43.

1965 *The Stages of Human Evolution*. Englewood Cliffs, NJ: Prentice-Hall.

1968 Neanderthal. *Natural History* 77:38-45.

1986 Modern Human Origins: Narrow Focus or Broad Spectrum? *American Journal of Physical Anthropology* 69:180.

1988a Punctuationism, Cladistics and the Legacy of Medieval Neoplatonism. *Human Evolution* 3:121-138.

1988b *The Stages of Human Evolution: Human and Cultural Origins*. 3rd ed. Englewood Cliffs, NJ: Prentice-Hall.

1989 Medieval Thinking and the Paradigms of Paleoanthropology. *AA* 91:442-446.

Brain, C. K.
1958 *The Transvaal Ape-Man Bearing Cave Deposits*. Transvaal Museum Memoirs 11. Pretoria: Transvaal Museum.

1976 A Reinterpretation of the Swarkrans Site and its Remains. *South African Journal of Science* 72:141-146.

1978 Some Aspects of the South African Australopithecine Sites and their Bone Accumulations. Pp. 131-164 in *Early Hominids of Africa*, ed. C. Jolly. London: Duckworth.

Brauer, G.
1984 A Craniological Approach to the Origin of Anatomically Modern *Homo sapiens* in Africa and Implications for the Appearance of Modern Europeans. Pp. 327-410 in *The Origins of Modern Humans: A World Survey of the Fossil Evidence*, eds. F. H. Smith and F. Spencer. New York: Alan R. Liss.

Brush, S.
1989 Prediction and Theory Evaluation: The Case of Light Bending. *Science* 246:1124-1129.

Cabrera Valdés, V., and Bischoff, J.
1989 Accelerator ^{14}C Dates for Early Upper Paleolithic (Basal Aurignacian) at El Castillo Cave (Spain). *JAS* 16:577-584.

Cann, R.
1988. DNA and Human Origins. *ARA* 17:127-143.

Cann, R.; Stoneking, M.; and Wilson, A.
1987a Mitochondrial DNA and Human Evolution. *Nature* 325:31-36.

1987b Disputed African Origin of Human Populations. *Nature* 327:111-112.

Chase, P., and Dibble, H. L.
1987 Middle Paleolithic Symbolism: A Review of Current Evidence and Interpretations. *JAA* 6:263-296.

Clark, G. A.
1988 Some Thoughts on the Black Skull: An Archeologist's Assessment of WT-17000 (*A. boisei*) and Systematics in Human Paleontology. *AA* 90:357-371.

1989a Romancing the Stones: Biases, Style and Lithics at La Riera. Pp. 27-50 in *Alternative Approaches to Lithic Analysis*, eds. D. Henry and G. Odell. Archeological Papers of the American Anthropological Association 1. Washington, DC: American Anthropological Association.

1989b   Alternative Models of Pleistocene Bio-cultural Evolution: A Response to Foley. *Antiquity* 63:153-162.

1989c   Paradigms and Paradoxes in Paleoanthropology: A Response to C. Loring Brace. *AA* 91:446-450.

in press   Reflexiones sobre epistemología: una respuesta a Utrilla. *Trabajos de Prehistoria* 46.

Clark, G. A., and Lindly, G.

1988   The Biocultural Transition and the Origin of Modern Humans in the Levant and Western Asia. *Paléorient* 14:159-167.

1989a   The Case for Continuity: Observations on the Biocultural Transition in Europe and Western Asia. Pp. 626-676 in *The Human Revolution: Behavioural and Biological Perspectives on the Origins of Modern Humans*, eds. P. Mellars and C. Stringer. Edinburgh: Edinburgh University Press.

1989b   Modern Human Origins in the Levant and Western Asia: The Fossil and Archeological Evidence. *AA* 91:962-985.

Close, A.

1978   The Identification of Style in Lithic Artifacts. *WA* 10:223-237.

Coon, C.

1962.   *The Origin of Races*. New York: Alfred Knopf.

Darlu, P., and Tassy, P.

1987   Disputed African Origin of Human Populations. *Nature* 329:111.

Dennell, R.; Rendell, H.; and Hailwood, E.

1988   Early Tool-Making in Asia: Two Million-Year-Old Artefacts in Pakistan. *Antiquity* 62:98-106.

Dennell, R.; Rendell, H.; and Halim, M.

1985   New Perspectives on the Palaeolithic of Northern Pakistan. Pp. 9-20 in *South Asian Archaeology 1983*, eds. J. Schotsmans and M. Taddei. Istituto Universitario Orientale 23. Naples: Instituto Universitario Orientale.

Dibble, H.

1987   The Interpretation of Middle Paleolithic Scraper Morphology. *AmAnt* 52:109-117.

1988   Typological Aspects of Reduction and Intensity of Utilization of Lithic Resources in the French Mousterian. Pp. 181-198 in *The Upper Pleistocene Prehistory of Western Eurasia*, eds. H. Dibble and A. Montet-White. Philadelphia: University Museum, University of Pennsylvania.

Dorfman, A.

1988   *Mascara*. New York: Viking.

Edwards, P.

1989   Revising the Broad Spectrum Revolution. *Antiquity* 63:225-246.

Endo, B.

1966   Experimental Studies on the Mechanical Significance of the Form of the Human Facial Skeleton. *Journal of the Faculty of Sciences of the University of Tokyo*, Section 5 (Anthropology) 3:1-106.

Flannery, K.

1967   Culture History versus Culture Process: A Debate in American Archaeology. *SciAm* 217:119-122.

1968   Archaeological Systems Theory and Early Mesoamerica. Pp. 67-87 in *Anthropological Archaeology in the Americas*, ed. B. Meggers. Washington, DC: Anthropological Society of Washington.

1973   Archaeology with a capital 'S'. Pp. 47-53 in *Research and Theory in Current Archaeology*, ed. C. Redman. New York: Wiley.

Foley, R.

1987   Hominid Species and Stone-Tool Assemblages: How are They Related? *Antiquity* 61:380-392.

1989   The Search for Early Man. *Archaeology* 42:26-32.

Freeman, L. G.

1964   Mousterian Developments in Cantabrian Spain. Ph.D dissertation, Department of Anthropology, University of Chicago.

1973   The Significance of Mammalian Faunas from Paleolithic Occupations in Cantabrian Spain. *AmAnt* 38:3-44.

1981   The Fat of the Land: Notes on Paleolithic Diet in Iberia. Pp. 104-165 in *Omnivorous Primates*, eds. R. Harding and G. Teleki. New York: Columbia University Press.

1989 Logicism: A French View of Archaeological Theory Founded in Computational Perspective. *Antiquity* 63:27-39.

Geneste, J.-M.
1988 Systèmes d'approvisionnement en matières premiéres au Paléolithique moyen et au Paléolithique supérieur en Aquitaine. Pp. 61-70 in *L'homme de Néandertal*, ed. M. Otte. Vol 8: *La mutation*, ed. J. K. Kozlowski. ERAUL 35. Liège: Université de Liège.

Gould, S., and Eldredge, N.
1977 Punctuated Equilibria: The Tempo and Mode of Evolution Reconsidered. *Paleobiology* 3:115-151.

Green, K.
1989 A Profile of Undergraduates in the Sciences. *American Scientist* 77:475-480.

Hardesty, D.
1980 The Use of General Ecological Principles in Archaeology. Pp. 157-187 in *Advances in Archaeological Method and Theory*, ed. M. B. Schiffer. New York: Academic Press.

Hively, W.
1988 How Much Science Does the Public Understand? *American Scientist* 76:439-444.

Howell, F. C.
1982 Origins and Evolution of the African Hominidae. Pp. 70-156 in *The Cambridge History of Africa*. Vol. 1: *From the Earliest Times to c. 500 BC*, ed. J. D. Clark. Cambridge: Cambridge University Press.
1984 Introduction. Pp. xiii-xxii in *The Origins of Modern Humans: A World Survey of the Fossil Evidence*, eds. F. H. Smith and F. Spencer. New York: Alan R. Liss.

Howells, W.
1976 Explaining Modern Man: Evolutionists versus Migrationists. *JHE* 5:477-496.

Hrdlička, A.
1927 The Neanderthal Phase of Man. *Journal of the Royal Anthropological Institute* 67:249-269.

Jelinek, A.
1982 Discussion. Pg. 318 in *The Transition from Lower to Middle Paleolithic and the Origin of Modern Man*, ed. A. Ronen. BAR International Series 151. Oxford: BAR.

Jochim, M.
1981 *Strategies for Survival*. New York: Academic Press.

Klein, R.
1989 *The Human Career*. Chicago: University of Chicago Press.

Kozlowski, J.
1988 L'apparition du Paléolithique supérieur. Pp. 11-22 in *L'homme de Néandertal*, ed. M. Otte. Vol. 8: *La mutation*, ed. J. K. Kozlowski. ERAUL 35. Liège: Université de Liège.

Leakey, M.
1975 Cultural Patterns in the Olduvai Sequence. Pp. 476-498 in *After the Australopithecines*, eds. K. Butzer and G. Isaac. The Hague: Mouton.

Le Gros Clark, W.
1967 *Man Apes or Ape Men?* New York: Holt, Rinehart and Winston.

Lewin, R.
1986 New Fossil Upsets Human Family. *Science* 233:720-722.
1988a Conflict Over DNA Clock Results. *Science* 241:1598-1600.
1988b DNA Clock Conflict Continues. *Science* 241:1756-1759.

Lindly, J., and Clark, G. A.
1987 A Preliminary Lithic Analysis of the Mousterian Site of 'Ain Difla (WHS Site 634) in the Wadi Ali, West-Central Jordan. *PPS* 53:279-292.
1990a Symbolism and Modern Human Origins. *CA* 31:233-240.
1990b On the Emergence of Modern Humans. *CA* 31:59-66.

Mayr, E.
1950 Taxonomic Categories in Fossil Hominids. *Cold Spring Harbor Symposia on Quantitative Biology* 15:109-118.

Mellars, P.
1989   Major Issues in the Emergence of Modern Humans. *CA* 30:349-385.

Mellars, P., and Stringer, C., eds.
1989   *The Human Revolution: Behavioural and Biological Perspectives on the Origins of Modern Humans.* Edinburgh: Edinburgh University Press.

Nei, M.
1985   Human Evolution at the Molecular Level. Pp. 41-64 in *Population Genetics and Molecular Evolution*, eds. T. Ohta and K. Aoki. Tokyo: Japan Science Press.
1987   *Molecular Evolutionary Genetics.* New York: Columbia University Press.

Popper, K.
1959   *The Logic of Scientific Discovery.* London: Hutchinson.
1972   *Objective Knowledge.* New York: Oxford University Press.
1983   *Realism and the Aim of Science.* Totowa, NJ: Rowman and Littlefield.

Rendell, H.; Hailwood, E.; and Dennell, R.
1987   Magnetic Polarity Stratigraphy of Upper Siwalik Sub-Group, Soan Valley, Pakistan: Implications for Early Human Occupance of Asia. *Earth and Planetary Science Letters* 85:488-496.

Sackett, J.
1982   Approaches to Style in Lithic Archaeology. *JAA* 1:59-112.

Saitou, N., and Omoto, K.
1987   Time and Place of Human Origins from mtDNA Data. *Nature* 327:288.

Schwalbe, G.
1906a   *Studien zur Vorgeschichte des Menschen I: zur Frage der Abstammung des Menschen.* Stuttgart: E. Scheizerbart.
1906b   *Studien zur Vorgeschichte des Menschen II: das Schadelfragment von Brux und Verwandte Schadelform.* Stuttgart: E. Scheizerbart.

Schwarcz, H. P; Buhay, W. M.; Grün, R.; Valladas, H.; Tchernov, E.; Bar-Yosef, O.; and Vandermeersch, B.
1989   ESR Dating of the Neanderthal Site, Kebara Cave, Israel. *JAS* 16:653-660.

Schwarcz, H. P.; Grün, R; Vamdermeersch, B.; Bar-Yosef, O.; Valladas, H.; and Tchernov, E.
1988   ESR Dates for the Hominid Burial Site of Qafzeh in Israel. *JHE* 17:733-737.

Shea, J.
1989   A Functional Study of the Lithic Industries Associated with Hominid Fossils in the Kebara and Qafzeh Caves, Israel. Pp. 611-625 in *The Human Revolution: Behavioural and Biological Perspectives on the Origins of Modern Humans*, eds. P. Mellars and C. Stringer. Edinburgh: Edinburgh University Press.

Simek, J., and Price, H.
in press   Chronological Change in Perigord Lithic Assemblage Variability. In *The Emergence of Modern Humans: An Archaeological Perspective*, ed. P. Mellars. Edinburgh: Edinburgh University Press.

Simons, E.
1989   Human Origins. *Science* 245:1343-1350.

Smith, F.
1982   Upper Pleistocene Hominid Evolution in South-Central Europe: A Review of the Evidence and an Analysis of Trends. *CA* 23:667-703.

Smith, F.
1984   Fossil Hominids from the Upper Pleistocene of Central Europe and the Origins of Modern Europeans. Pp. 137-209 in *The Origins of Modern Humans: A World Survey of the Fossil Evidence*, eds. F. H. Smith and F. Spencer. New York: Alan R. Liss.

Smith, F.; Falsetti, A.; and Donnelly, S.
1989a   Modern Human Origins. *Yearbook of Physical Anthropology* 32:35-68.

Smith, F.; Simek, J.; and Harrill, M.
1989b   Geographic Variation in Supraorbital Torus Reduction during the Later Pleistocene (*c.* 80,000-15,000 BP). Pp. 172-193 in *The Human Revolution: Behavioural and Biological Perspectives on the Origins of Modern Humans*, eds. P. Mellars and C. Stringer. Edinburgh: Edinburgh University Press.

Smith, F., and Trinkaus, E.
in press Modern Human Origins in Central Europe: A Case for Continuity. In *Aux Origines de la Diversité Humaine*, eds. J. Hublin and A.-M. Tillier. Paris: Presses Universitaires de France.

Spencer, F.
1984 The Neanderthals and their Evolutionary Significance: A Brief Historical Survey. Pp. 1-50 in *The Origins of Modern Humans: A World Survey of the Fossil Evidence*, eds. F. H. Smith and F. Spencer. New York: Alan R. Liss.

Spuhler, J.
1988 Evolution of Mitochondrial DNA in Monkeys, Apes and Humans. *Yearbook of Physical Anthropology* 31:15-48.

Stoneking, M., and Cann, R.
1989 African Origin of Human Mitochondrial DNA. Pp. 17-30 in *The Human Revolution: Behavioural and Biological Perspectives on the Origins of Modern Humans*, eds. P. Mellars and C. Stringer. Edinburgh: Edinburgh University Press.

Straus, L.
1987 Paradigm Lost: A Personal View of the Current State of Upper Paleolithic Research. *Helinium* 27:157-171.
1989 Age of the Modern Europeans. *Nature* 342:476-477.
in press The Early Upper Paleolithic of Southwestern Europe. In *The Emergence of Modern Humans: An Archaeological Perspective*, ed. P. Mellars. Edinburgh: Edinburgh University Press.

Straus, L., and Clark, G. A., eds.
1986 *La Riera Cave: Stone Age Hunter-Gatherer Adaptations in Northern Spain*. Arizona State University Anthropological Research Papers 36. Tempe: Arizona State University.

Straus, L., and Heller, C.
1988 Explorations in the Twilight Zone: The Early Upper Paleolithic of Vasco-Cantabrian Spain and Gascony. Pp. 97-133 in *The Early Upper Paleolithic: Evidence from Europe and the Near East*, eds.

J. Hoffecker and C. Wolf. BAR International Series 437. Oxford: BAR.

Stringer, C., and Andrews, P.
1988 Genetic and Fossil Evidence for the Origins of Modern Humans. *Science* 289:1263-1268.

Stringer, C.; Grün, H.; Schwarcz, H.; and Goldberg, P.
1989 ESR Dates for the Hominid Burial Site of es-Skhul in Israel. *Nature* 338:756-758.

Stringer, C.; Hublin, J.; and Vandermeersch, B.
1984 The Origin of Anatomically Modern Humans in Western Europe. Pp. 51-135 in *The Origins of Modern Humans: A World Survey of the Fossil Evidence*, eds. F. H. Smith and F. Spencer. New York: Alan R. Liss.

Svoboda, J.
1988 Early Upper Paleolithic Industries in Moravia: A Review of the Recent Evidence. Pp. 169-192 in *L'homme de Néandertal*, ed. M. Otte. Vol. 8: *La mutation*, ed. J. K. Kozlowski. ERAUL 35. Liège: Université de Liège.

Trinkaus, E.
1982 Evolutionary Continuity among Archaic *Homo sapiens*. Pp. 301-320 in *The Transition from Lower to Middle Paleolithic and the Origin of Modern Man*, ed. A. Ronen. BAR International Series 151. Oxford: BAR.
1983 Neanderthal Postcrania and the Adaptive Shift to Modern Humans. Pp. 165-200 in *The Mousterian Legacy: Human Biocultural Change in the Upper Pleistocene*, ed. E. Trinkaus. BAR International Series 164. Oxford: BAR.
1984 Western Asia. Pp. 251-293 in *The Origins of Modern Humans: A World Survey of the Fossil Evidence*, eds. F. H. Smith and F. Spencer. New York: Alan R. Liss.

Valladas, H.; Joron, J. L.; Valladas, G.; Arensberg, B.; Bar-Yosef, O.; Belfer-Cohen, A.; Goldberg, P.; Laville, H.; Meignen, L.; Rak, Y.; Tchernov, E.; Tillier, A. M.; and Vandermeersch, B.
1987 Thermoluminescence Dates for the Neanderthal Burial Site at Kebara in Israel. *Nature* 330:159-160.

Valladas, H.; Reyss, J. L.; Joron, J. L.; Valladas, G.; Bar-Yosef, O.; and Vandermeersch, B.
1988   Thermoluminescence Dating of Mousterian 'Proto-Cro-Magnon' Remains from Israel and the Origin of Modern Man. *Nature* 331:614-616.

Vandermeersch, B.
1989   The Evolution of Modern Humans: Recent Evidence from Southwest Asia. Pp. 155-164 in *The Human Revolution: Behavioural and Biological Perspectives on the Origins of Modern Humans*, eds. P. Mellars and C. Stringer. Edinburgh: Edinburgh University Press.

Walker, A., et al.
1986   2.5 Myr *Australopithecus boisei* from West of Lake Turkana, Kenya. *Nature* 322:517-522.

Watson, P.; LeBlanc, S.; and Redman, C.
1971   *Explanation in Archeology*. New York: Columbia University Press.
1984   *Archeological Explanation*. New York: Columbia University Press.

Weidenreich, R.
1943   The 'Neanderthal Man' and the Ancestors of *Homo sapiens*. *AA* 45:39-45.

1947   Facts and Speculations Concerning the Origin of *Homo sapiens*. *AA* 49:187-203.

Wilson, E. O.
1975   *Sociobiology: The New Synthesis*. Cambridge, MA: Harvard University Press.

Wolpoff, M.
1971   Competitive Exclusion among Lower Pleistocene Hominids: The Single Species Hypothesis. *Man* 6:601-614.
1980   *Paleoanthropology*. New York: Alfred Knopf.
1989   Multiregional Evolution: The Fossil Alternative to Eden. Pp. 62-108 in *The Human Revolution: Behavioural and Biological Perspectives on the Origins of Modern Humans*, eds. P. Mellars and C. Stringer. Edinburgh: Edinburgh University Press.

Wolpoff, M.; Wu, X.; and Thorne, A.
1984   Modern *Homo sapiens* Origins: A General Theory of Hominid Evolution Involving the Fossil Evidence from East Asia. Pp. 411-483 in *The Origins of Modern Humans: A World Survey of the Fossil Evidence*, eds. F. H. Smith and F. Spencer. New York: Alan R. Liss.

Wolpoff, M., et al.
1988   Modern Human Origins. *Science* 241:772-773.

XIV

The Significance of Middle Paleolithic Water Holes Found at Bir Sahara in the Western Desert of Egypt

Amy L. Campbell

This is a discussion of a series of unique features found in a Middle Paleolithic site in Egypt's Western Desert. Today, this region is hyper-arid, receiving on average less than 1 mm of precipitation per year; in reality this translates to about one rainstorm every century. Bir Sahara, or "Well of the Sahara" in Arabic, is one of three deflational basins which lie some 350 km west of the Nile, in the eastern reaches of the Sahara Desert (Fig. 14.1). The basin supports sparse vegetation in the immediate area where underground water rises to within 1.5 m of the surface.

These basins have been the subject of intensive research by the Combined Prehistoric Expedition under the direction of Dr. Fred Wendorf of Southern Methodist University. The basins were first investigated in 1973, shortly after a geologist with the Geological Survey of Egypt recognized exposures of lacustrine sediments which rose above the sand plain, associated with stone artifacts made of indigenous quartzitic sandstone. Investigations revealed that there had been repeated occupation of the basins by Acheulian, Middle Paleolithic, and Neolithic groups during times of increased humidity in the region. Not only were some stretches of these basins literally carpeted with aeolized artifacts which lay on deflational surfaces, but many locales with in-situ remnants of human occupation were discovered, associated with ancient lake sediments and fossil spring vents. In point of fact, the region presently has an "inverted topography": the portions of the basins which had once been low-lying wet areas are now protrusions of resistant lacustrine sediments, while the areas away from the fossil lake basins (in all probability including some of the most

intensively-occupied sites) had less resistant sediments and have been heavily deflated by tens of millennia of aeolian action. The initial seasons of archaeological, geological, and paleoenvironmental research in the region were reported by Wendorf and Schild (1980).

Six to nine separate cycles of lacustrine episodes associated with the Middle Paleolithic occupations have been determined for the Bir Tarfawi-Bir Sahara basins. Wendorf et al. (in press) have suggested that lacustrine cycles correlated with the northward shift of rainfall patterns for periods of centuries to millennia during interglacials or interstadials. Recent dating of these sediments, by thermoluminescence and uranium-series techniques, although problematical, indicates a span for the Middle Paleolithic environmental cycles of ca. 200,000-70,000 years ago (Wendorf et al. 1987). The successive lacustrine sediments are sometimes superimposed, but often are offset, because the accumulation of dense sediments such as limestone and marl effectively "plugged" former spring vents, causing the next cycle of lake formation to occur in a slightly different location. This poses a problem for exact correlation of the archaeological sequence, one not yet fully resolved by tool typology or absolute dating. No Middle Paleolithic hominid skeletal material has yet been recovered from Egypt, and due to startling new dates for hominids from the Levant (Valladas et al. 1988), it is not possible to state with any certainty which hominid type (or types) produced the Middle Paleolithic artifacts in the Western Desert.

Further investigations of the archaeology of the Western Desert were initiated in 1986, with concentration on the Middle Paleolithic lacustrine erosional

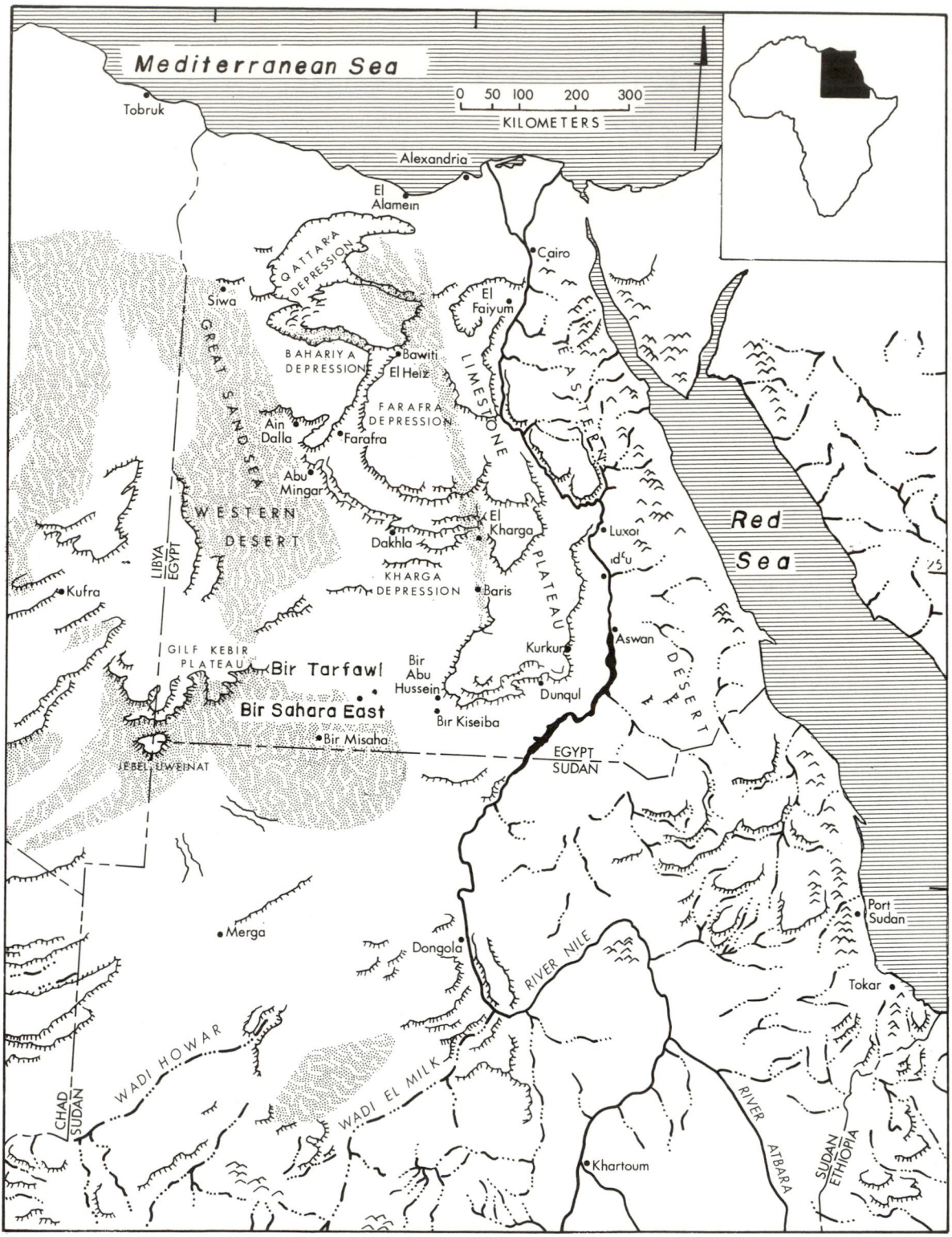

Figure 14.1   Egypt showing the location of Bir Sahara.

remnants in the deflational basins. (A full report of the 1986 through 1988 research will be published in a volume currently in preparation.) Bir Sahara, a basin about 8 km in length, has several lacustrine remnants of this age. One of these remnants preserves a stratigraphic record of a full sequence of one environmental cycle of transition from desert to full lake conditions in the area. From lowest to highest its sedimentary units include: dune sands, dark organic sands (designated as the "black sand" unit), green silt, and white marls and limestones. It was in this erosional remnant that Bir Sahara-12, as well as many other locales with in-situ Middle Paleolithic artifacts, was located.

The BS-12 locale was first investigated in 1973 (Wendorf and Schild 1980:40-43). The presence of numerous Middle Paleolithic artifacts on the surface of the erosional remnant slope indicated potential for in-situ cultural material. Several trenches were dug in that season to clarify the stratigraphy of the remnant in relationship to the archaeology. A horizontally and vertically diffuse distribution of Denticulate Mousterian tools, the most common Middle Paleolithic facies in the region, was revealed. In addition one of the trenches revealed an artificial feature in the sedimentary record: a small pit with steep, sharply defined edges which had been dug through several contrasting layers of sediment and into the black sands (thus indicating that it was dug down from a later stratum). There were no artifacts associated, but it was interpreted as most probably a water hole dug during a dry season, as the layer from which it was dug did not appear to represent one of the full lake phases (Wendorf and Schild 1980:28).

In the 1988 season, I was designated to re-investigate the BS-12 locale. An area southeast of the original trenches was chosen (Fig. 14.2), because its location at the southernmost tip of the erosional plateau was felt to have possibly protected in-situ artifact-bearing sediments from the erosional forces of the prevailing winds. The possible discovery of additional "water holes" was considered, but was not a major determinant in the decision to excavate. Following the techniques developed by the Combined Prehistoric Expedition, excavation was done in 1-m squares. The Bedouin workmen each had a wooden board representing their square, on which all materials (stone, bone, etc.) found in situ would be placed, so that each item could be accurately mapped. All sediment was screened through 1-cm mesh. Vertical mapping was not done, but the workmen know to dig in small vertical intervals and the squares were closely

monitored for the possible presence of distinct sedimentary or cultural layers. Extensive photographic documentation was done, as a supplement to maps, notes, and sketches. All analysis, mapping, artifact illustration, and preliminary write-up is done in camp during the season, since all artifacts are turned in to the Egyptian Museum in Cairo at the end of the season and a report is made to the Egyptian Antiquities organization before the team leaves the country.

As anticipated from the stratigraphy observed in other portions of this erosional remnant, the 1988 excavations at BS-12 exposed a portion of the earlier phases of a humid cycle, probably prior to the onset of full-lake conditions of that cycle. These excavations caught the very edge of the fossil basin represented by this remnant. As the excavations proceeded northward into the remnant, it became clear that we were moving from the very edge of the fossil basin into the deeper portion of the basin. Artifacts found in situ were sparse and diffused throughout the culture-bearing deposits; nowhere was it possible to identify an actual "occupation floor." Most of the artifacts were fresh, but a few were abraded by aeolian action. Bone was scarce; a few preserved scraps tentatively have been identified as those of small antelopids. As were the artifacts recovered on the nearby surface and in the 1973 trenches, those from the 1988 excavations constituted a Denticulate Mousterian facies (Figs. 14.3-4), with a significant presence of the Levallois technique. All lithic artifacts recovered were made on quartizitic sandstone, a locally available resource. The artifacts became more scarce as the excavations proceeded into the deeper part of the fossil basin, a distribution which corresponded nicely to human activity bounded by the edge of a moist, and later, watery area.

In the course of excavations, several basin or pit-shaped features with clearly defined margins were discovered. In contrast to the surrounding consolidated sands of light to medium grey, these features were dark grey to black. The dark coloration of the sediments in these features was felt by geo-archaeologists on the expedition's team to be the result of intense organic activity within the features. The sediments were the darkest at the very edges of the features. The possibility that they could have been infilled natural sand "blowout" features was considered, but was discounted for several reasons: (a) in many cases the profiles were too steep and the depth/width ratio too great to imply a sand blowout; (b) stratigraphic indications: the features were dug at the edge of a deepening basin which probably held contemporary moisture, and from a soil-forming layer into a loose white sand (probably an active water-percolation layer); and the dark organic zones along the inner pit edges were coeval with the existence of the open pits, which is consonant with organic activity encouraged by the conditions within the pits; (c) the contact of the "black sand" unit, in which the features occurred, with the green silt layer above showed no disconformity, indicating that there were no significant episodes of arid conditions/aeolian erosion during this part of the humid cycle. The possibility that animals could have been solely responsible for the features was also

ruled out because the edges of these features were too smooth and clearly defined to have been created by animal digging.

Additionally, the two largest features intersected, indicating that they were dug and infilled successively (see Fig. 14.5). In the creation of these features, a pedogenic or soil-forming process had been interrupted. The overlapping margins indicate that the easternmost feature was dug into the infilled (earlier) western feature. Soil formation resumed once both features were filled in. Above, and clearly later in time than these features, is a layer of olive-green silt which rep-

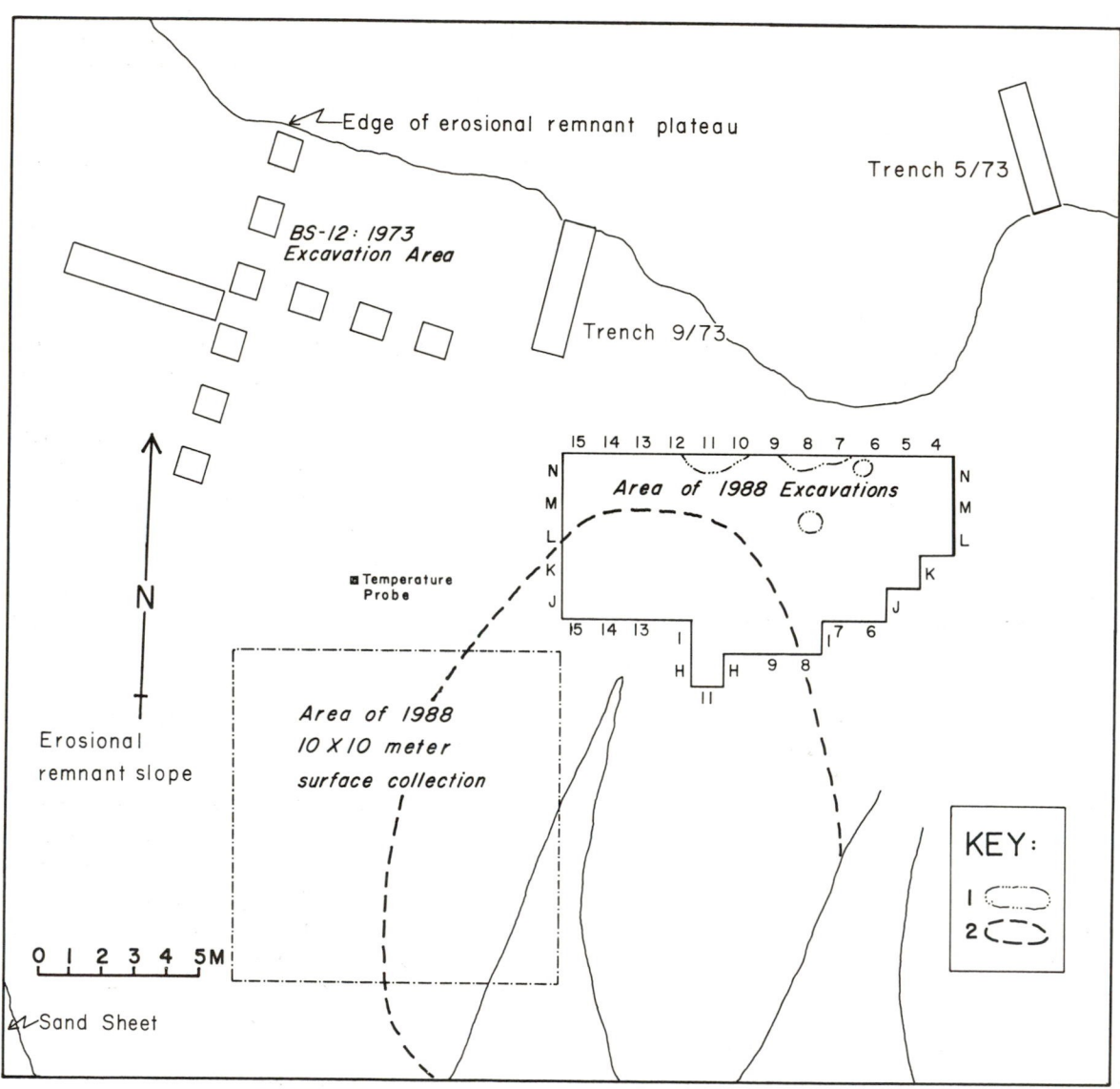

Figure 14.2   Plan map of the BS-12 locale.
Key: 1 = possible water holes; 2 = heavy concentration of surface artifacts.

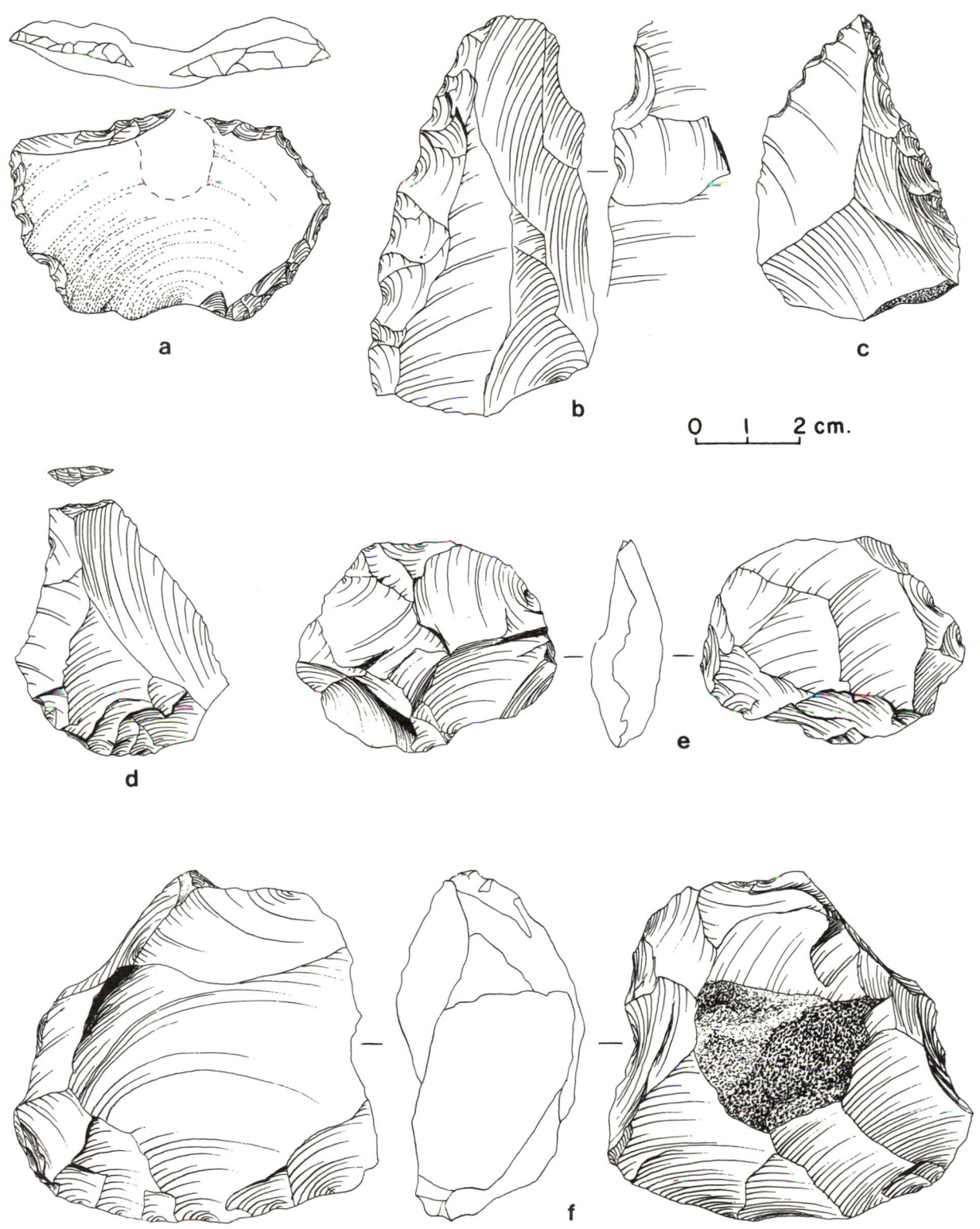

Figure 14.3   Artifacts from the BS-12 locale: a) double straight convex sidescraper (atypical); b, c) Tayac points; d) truncation on a pointed Levallois flake; e) discoidal core; f) Levallois core.

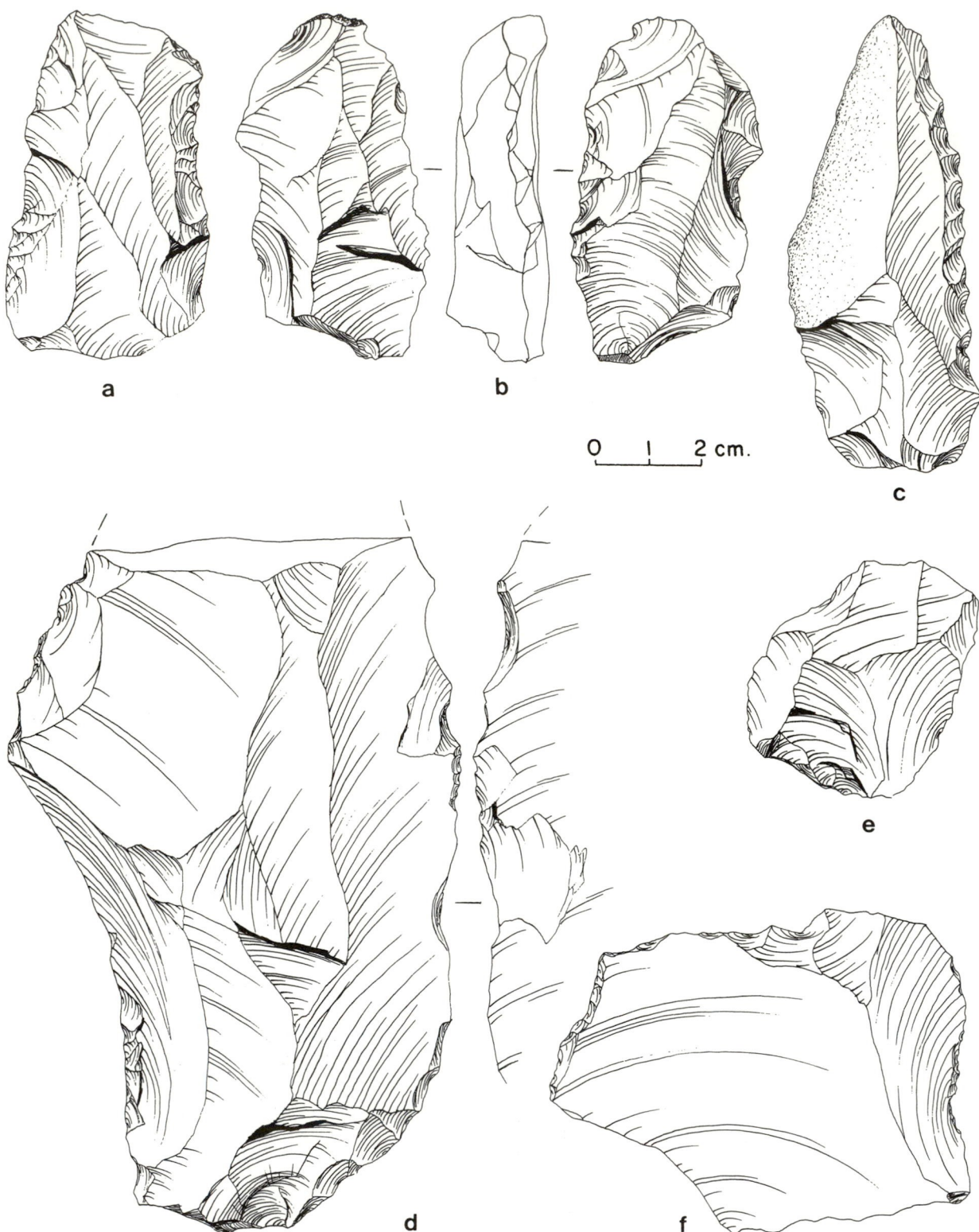

Figure 14.4   Artifacts from the BS-12 locale: a-c) denticulates; d) Levallois flake with alternate retouch; e) Levallois flake; f) marginally denticulated piece.

resents the onset of more substantial local moisture in this humid cycle.[1]

The close placement of these two features indicates a closeness in time in terms of the formation of this phase of the Bir Sahara basin, and supports their similar function as (perhaps seasonal) water holes in such a context. Again, the dark organic fill of the earlier well and the surrounding pedogenic sediments tend to argue against these having been natural blowouts of dry, unconsolidated sands; in times of true aridity in this region (as exemplified by the late Holocene conditions), soil formation even in the vicinity of sparse vegetation is so poor that any disturbance of the growth will cause erosion and deflation of the sand sheet on a much greater scale than seen in features such as these.

In contrast to the surrounding "black sand" sedimentary unit, most of the features lacked cultural debris. This could be attributed both to their placement at the edge of a deepening (probably somewhat soggy) basin, indicating that the features were placed at the very edges of a habitable area; and perhaps also to a careful maintenance/cleaning of the these pits. If these were natural erosional features, one might expect random inclusion of lithic artifacts in the fill, as the pits filled in with surrounding sediments; or alternatively artifacts occurring on the bases of the features as lag deposits from sediment blowout. No artifacts

were found in direct association with the two largest artificial features discussed above. However, a smaller, more steeply-sided feature (inset, Fig. 14.5) did yield associated artifacts. This feature sharply interrupted the stratigraphy of the surrounding sediments, which were gently sloping upwards to the east. In this feature, at about 95-105 cm below the erosional slope surface, was a cluster of over 30 pieces of debitage, many of which were Levallois preparation flakes. This debitage was quartizitic sandstone of a homogenous color and texture, quite possibly representing a single original blank of this material, which is normally quite variable in color and texture. In fact, the cluster of debitage in this pit looked suspiciously like a single episode of core-trimming in which the waste was deposited in an infilling pit. Such a secondary use—that of an infilling feature (well, storage pit, hearth, etc.) being used as a repository for waste material—would not be unusual. Perhaps in this case the secondary use as a refuse pit for debitage came after fluctuation of the water table made this waterhole unusable: it is unfortunate that the black sands and the strata above are now so truncated in many portions of the site that relative sequencing of the individual feature depths was impossible.

In all, four identifiable features were discovered in the 1988 excavations of the BS-12 site (Fig. 14.2). One small dark circle at the eastern edge of the exca-

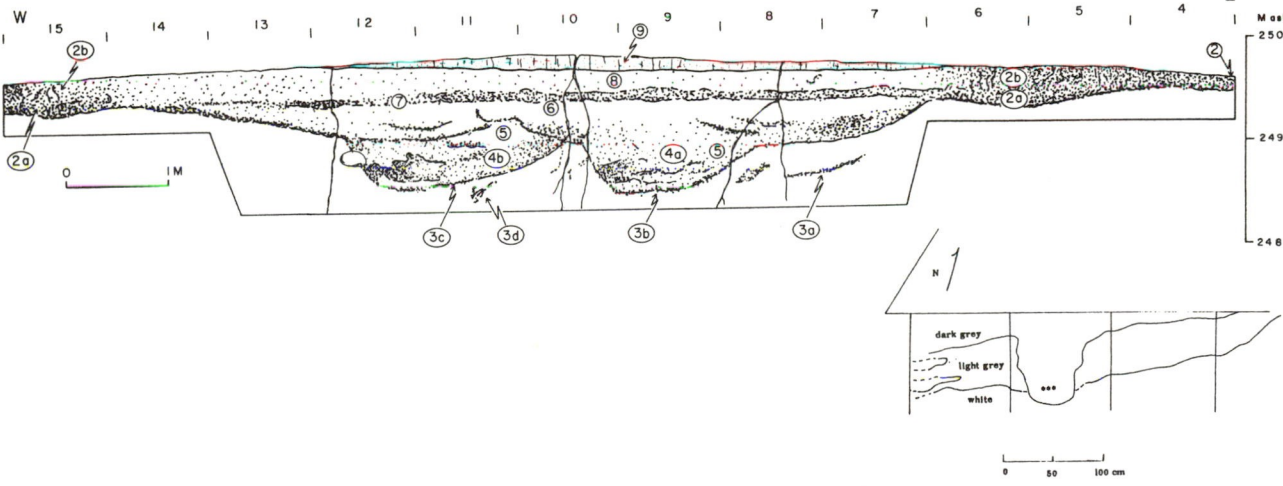

Figure 14.5   *Water well profiles. Stratigraphic summary: zone 1) white basal dune sands; zone 2) pedogenic (soil-forming) zone, interrupted by excavation of wells; zone 3) margins of wells, black color produced by intense organic activity; zones 4 and 5) fill of wells, with variable medium-dark grey staining; zone 6) light grey upper portion of eastern well fill; zone 7) resumption of pedogenesis upon completion of well infilling; zone 8) light grey indurated sands; zone 9) light olive-green silts [culturally sterile].*
Inset: profile of smaller, narrow-sided well centered in square L8. All sediments are sands.
"★★★" indicates where a cluster of Levallois core preparation flakes were found in situ.

vation (not depicted on the plan) may also have been a water hole severely truncated by erosion. All of the features were oval or circular in plan, all of them were clearly defined in profile, and all were distinguished from surrounding sediments by much darker sediments outlining and filling the features. As noted before, the stratigraphy of the sediments indicated that the features were positioned at the edge of a deepening fossil basin, which represented a low-lying area that gradually became a full-fledged lake bottom. At the time that the features were originally created, paleoenviromental reconstructions indicate a marshy low area which may have had some rainy-season surface water (R. Schild, pers. comm.). It is central to their interpretation that these features, which underlay the full-lake silts and marls, were situated at the edge of this fossil basin. Eventually, the basin became water-filled, and there would no longer have been a need to dig artificial wells.

Further argument for the function of these features as water holes or "wells" can be made on the basis of archaeological and ethnographic comparisons. Water wells are present in the much later Neolithic occupations of the Western Desert, such as at site E-79-8 at Bir Kiseiba (Connor 1984:220), nearly identical in morphology to the BS-12 feature depicted in the Figure 14.5 inset. In fact, there is abundant evidence that early Neolithic pastoralists who occupied the Western Desert of Egypt relied almost entirely upon wells for both their water and the watering of cattle (Wendorf and Schild 1984). In these later times, wells were obviously a way of adapting to a semi-arid climate in which standing water was at least seasonally unavailable (the Holocene humid cycle apparently never progressed into a full "lake phase" for the Western Desert). Wells very similar morphologically to those at Bir Sahara have also been found recently in the high plains of northwest Texas, in the context of the Altithermal dry phase of the early to mid-Holocene (Meltzer and Collins 1987). Few artifacts were found in or around the foregoing examples, an important similarity with the BS-12 wells which will be discussed below. The Kalahari bushmen of southern Africa routinely maintain water holes in the sandy scrub plain, to utilize during the dry season (Silberbauer 1981:44). Similar activity has also been witnessed to the south of the Sahara in the Sahel, where desertification has led to the digging of wells in drying river beds (Ellis 1987:159). The black or "organic" coloration of these Sahelian river bed sediments is very similar to the coloration of the Bir Sahara features.

A possible correlation between the location of water holes and general sparsity of cultural remains found in and around them is found in the Kalahari example, where it was noted that camps and primary activity areas were placed fairly distant to the wells so that the water would not be contaminated; and so that game would be attracted to the wells (Silberbauer 1981:221). A correlation with the Middle Paleolithic features may also be found at Bir Sahara itself. The Bedouin workmen dug a water hole at the lowest point of the basin, where ground water currently comes closest to the surface. The profile of their well (unfortunately no photographs were taken of it) had a marked "stepped" appearance, as they had pulled the 30 to 40-cm-thick layer of loose, dry surface sand away from the edges of the well to prevent its infilling (personal observation, 1988). One of the large features at BS-12 also had a "stepped" or "shelved" profile (Fig. 14.5), perhaps similarly to keep loose sediment and debris from falling into it. The Kalahari peoples use their water holes secondarily to attract game; something which the Bedouin workmen attempted to do by placing small-animal traps around the well they had dug at Bir Sahara in the 1988 season.

There is one additional explanation for the sparsity of cultural material around the features, if indeed their function has been interpreted correctly. Even with no surface water available today at Bir Sahara (except when a well is dug), the vegetation is sufficient to produce swarms of flies which can be very annoying; thus the expedition's camp is not erected in close proximity to the vegetation. Glynn Isaac (1977:84) hypothesized that Acheulian sites in the Olorgesailie (Kenya) area were placed some distance from moist areas and lakes, because of their propensity to breed insects, especially mosquitoes. This hypothesized site location preference was supported by comparison with modern Maasai occupation preferences in that vicinity, who camp well away from areas of insect proliferation. All of the above explanations support the proposal that the features at BS-12 were water holes and that the relative sparsity of cultural remains around them is to be expected. The above discussion might also explain why the densest artifact concentrations are found in deflated positions in the Bir Sahara basin, that is, some distance from the fossil lake sediments: for primary occupation, more open and dry areas were probably preferable.

A search of the literature has not revealed any other examples of water procurement features of such great antiquity. Isaac, reporting on the Acheulian occurrences at the Olorgesailie locale, hypothesized such activity (Isaac 1977:83). His reconstruction of occupations near ephemeral stream beds raised for him the possibility that the Acheulian hominids might have obtained drinking water by digging pits in the seasonally dry watercourses. However, he did not actually discover traces of any such features. One of the future research goals in the Bir Tarfawi-Bir Sahara region will be to determine whether the Acheulian hominids occupied the basins only after full-lake conditions had been reached. Of the several Acheulian locales investigated thus far, none have yielded anthropogenic features analogous to those at BS-12.

The water hole features at BS-12 are significant in terms of understanding Middle Paleolithic adaptations, in relation to the cycles of changing environment in the eastern Sahara. Paleoenvironmental studies of different sorts have been carried out on the lacustrine sediments. No pollen has been recovered from the sediments. However, freshwater snail shells are abundant in the full-lake sediments, and microfaunal remains including species of birds and rodent have been identified (Wendorf and Schild 1980; Wendorf et al., in press). The microfauna and megafauna are all of the tropical types, extant species of which exist today in areas of Africa with at least 500 mm of precipitation per year. Although just slightly above the range of a semi-arid climate (defined by Webster's Third International Dictionary as 220-440 mm rainfall per annum), such rainfall, when combined with the gradual recharge of underground aquifers, would support a scrub-savannah environment rich in game. Hominids could easily move in to occupy these areas, having adapted to nearly identical conditions previously in the sub-Saharan regions to the south.

However, the discovery of the water holes in the Middle Paleolithic context in Egypt's Western Desert indicates that humans were capable of occupying the region before optimum, or full-lake conditions were reached, because one of their adaptive behaviors was the digging and maintenance of water holes when surface water was unavailable. The implications that creating water holes would have for the ability of Middle Paleolithic humans in the region to survive in at least seasonally dessicated conditions have been hypothesized previously, in relation to Middle Paleolithic adaptations in the nearby Bir Tarfawi basin (Wendorf et al. 1987:55, 62). There a stratum of gley

development associated with artifacts indicated that human occupation had continued in the area even though, in that phase, water was to be found only in a subsurface situation. Although the hypothesized wells have not yet been found in the Bir Tarfawi basin, their presence at nearby Bir Sahara supports the proposal that the Middle Paleolithic inhabitants of the region were accustomed to adapting to a periodic lack of surface water.

The presence of water wells in a Middle Paleolithic locale would make them the earliest examples of an adaptive strategy oriented toward water scarcity to date. If the definition of a "marginal" environment is one in which the basic necessities of life (that is, warmth, food, and water) are at least seasonally not within easy access, then the Middle Paleolithic occupants of Bir Sahara seem to have had the adaptability to occupy successfully a marginal environment.

However, while the context and appearance of these features clearly suggest that they were water-procurement holes to whose origin hominids contributed, the behavioral implications are less clear. A review of major primate studies did not yield any examples in which non-human primates detected or utilized subterranean water sources. However, elephants (and probably other mammals) have been known to dig or enlarge water holes (e.g., Johnson 1928). Thus, the features at Bir Sahara could have been created by hominids who possessed the foresight to anticipate how water might be obtained during dry periods; alternatively, the animals in the area might have initiated the digging for moisture in low-lying areas during dry spells, and the hominids may merely have imitated this behavior (or even maintained water holes begun by animals) and thus fortuitously gained a way in which to survive less than optimal conditions.

Regardless of whether the presence of water procurement features in a Middle Paleolithic context suggests the cognitive capacity of foresight or merely imitative behavior, if the practice of obtaining subsurface water became habitual, it would have resulted in considerably less restriction in the movement of hominids during this period than if they were restricted to regions with constant surface water. It has been suggested that the Nile Valley may have been a "continental bridge" through which anatomically modern humans diffused to Eurasia during the later Lower Paleolithic and after (Bar-Yosef 1987:29). By extension, that corridor would have included the adjacent deserts when humid cycles made them habitable. Additionally, contact between sub-Saharan and northwest Africa, virtually impossible during cycles of Pleistocene aridity, would have been re-established during the periodic blooming of the Saharan belt. If humans were able to diffuse across these regions only after optimal conditions were reached, there would have been only very narrow temporal windows in which such movement could have been accomplished. If, however, Middle Paleolithic hominids had the prescience to dig simple water holes, both the temporal windows available for interregional dispersals and the range of habitable environments during this time period would have been broadened considerably.

ACKNOWLEDGMENTS

The research of the Combined Prehistoric Expedition is funded by the National Science Foundation; and is sponsored by a cooperative effort of Southern Methodist University, the Polish Academy of Sciences, and the Geological Survey of Egypt.

NOTE

1. The stratigraphic explanation for the wells and surrounding sediments was provided by Dr. Romuald Schild, co-director of the Combined Prehistoric Expedition, and the director of the Institute for the History of Material Culture, Polish Academy of Sciences, Warsaw.

REFERENCES CITED

Bar-Yosef, O.
   1987   Pleistocene Connexions Between Africa and Southwest Asia: An Archaeological Perspective. *The African Archaeological Review* 5:29-38.

Connor, D.
   1984   Report on Site E-79-8. Pp. 217-250 in *Cattle Keepers of the Eastern Sahara: The Neolithic of Bir Kiseiba*, assembled by F. Wendorf and R. Schild. New Delhi: Pauls Press.

Ellis, W.
   1987   Africa's Stricken Sahel. *National Geographic* 172(2):140-179.

Isaac, G. L.
   1977   *Ologesailie: Archaeological Studies of a Middle Pleistocene Lake Basin in Kenya.* Chicago: University of Chicago Press.

Johnson, M.
   1928   *Safari: A Saga of the African Blue.* New York: G. P. Putnam's Sons.

Meltzer, D., and Collins, M.
   1987   Prehistoric Water Wells on the Southern High Plains: Clues to Altithermal Climate. *JFA* 14:9-27.

Silberbauer, G.
   1981   *Hunter and Habitat in the Central Kalahari Desert.* New York: Cambridge University Press.

Valladas, H.; Reyss, J. L.; Joron, J. L.; Valladas, G.; Bar-Yosef, O.; and Vandermeersch, B.
   1988   Thermoluminescence Dating of Mousterian 'Proto-Cro-Magnon' Remains from Israel and the Origin of Modern Man. *Nature* 331:614-616.

Wendorf, F.; Close, A.; and Schild, R.
   1987   Recent Work on the Middle Paleolithic of the Eastern Sahara. *The African Archaeological Review* 5:49-63.

Wendorf, F.; Close, A.; Schild, R.; Gautier, A.; Schwarcz, H.; Miller, G.; Kowalski, K.; Krolik, H.; Bluszcz, A.; Robins, D.; Grün, R.; and McKinney, C.
   in press *Chronology and Stratigraphy of the Middle Paleolithic at Bir Tarfawi, Egypt*, ed. J. D. Clark. Mainz: Proceedings of the 9th UISPP Congress.

Wendorf, F., and Schild, R.
   1980   *Prehistory of the Eastern Sahara.* New York: Academic Press.

Wendorf, F., and Schild, R. (assemblers).
   1984   *Cattle Keepers of the Eastern Sahara: The Neolithic of Bir Kiseiba.* New Delhi: Pauls Press.

CONTRIBUTORS TO THIS VOLUME

Ofer Bar-Yosef
Department of Anthropology
Peabody Museum
Harvard University
Cambridge, MA 02138
USA

Federico Bernaldo de Quirós
Departamento de Estudios Clasicos
Facultad de Filosofia y Letras
Universidad de León
24071 León
SPAIN

Victoria Cabrera Valdes
Departamento de Prehistoria e
  Historia Antigua
Facultad de Geografia e Historia
Universidad Nacional de Educa-
  cion a Distancia
28040 Madrid
SPAIN

Amy L. Campbell
Department of Anthropology
Southern Methodist University
Dallas, TX 75275
USA

Geoffrey A. Clark
Department of Anthropology
Arizona State University
Tempe, AZ 85287
USA

Francine David
Laboratoire d'Ethnologie Préhistorique
UA no. 040275 du CNRS
44, rue de l'Amiral Mouchez
75014 Paris
FRANCE

André Debénath
Institut du Quaternaire
UA 133 CNRS
Université de Bordeaux I
33405 Talence
FRANCE

Harold L. Dibble
Department of Anthropology
University of Pennsylvania
Philadelphia, PA 19104
USA

Catherine Farizy
Laboratoire d'Ethnologie Préhistorique
UA no. 040275 du CNRS
44, rue de l'Amiral Mouchez
75014 Paris
FRANCE

Leslie G. Freeman
Department of Anthropology
University of Chicago
1126 E. 59th Street
Chicago, IL 60637
USA

Donald O. Henry
Anthropology Department
University of Tulsa
600 S. College Avenue
Tulsa, OK 74104-3189
USA

Anthony E. Marks
Department of Anthropology
Southern Methodist University
Dallas, TX 75275
USA

Lilliane Meignen
Centres de Recherches
  Archéologiques
ERA 28 du CNRS
Sophia Antipolis
06565 Valbonne
FRANCE

Paul Mellars
Department of Archaeology
University of Cambridge
Downing Street
Cambridge CB2 3DZ
GREAT BRITAIN

Marcel Otte
Département de Préhistoire
Université de Liège
Place du XX Août 7
B-4000 Liège
BELGIUM

Nicholas Rolland
Department of Anthropology
University of Victoria
P.O. Box 1700
Victoria, BC V8W 2Y2
CANADA

Alain Tuffreau
Centre d'Etudes et de Recherches
  Préhistoriques
Université de Lille
59655 Villeneuve D'Ascq
FRANCE

Alain Turq
Direction des Antiquités Préhistoriques d'Aquitaine
6 bis, Cours de Gourgue
33074 Bordeaux
FRANCE

WITHDRAWN

GETTYSBURG COLLEGE

63 0020205 2

DATE DUE

1998